Natural Right and Political Philosophy

Natural Right and Political Philosophy

Essays in Honor of
Catherine Zuckert and Michael Zuckert

Edited by
Ann Ward and Lee Ward

University of Notre Dame Press
Notre Dame, Indiana

Notre Dame, Indiana 46556
www.undpress.nd.edu

Manufactured in the United States of America

Library of Congress Cataloging-in-Publication Data

Natural right and political philosophy : essays in honor of Catherine Zuckert and Michael Zuckert / edited by Ann Ward and Lee Ward.
pages cm
Includes bibliographical references and index.
ISBN 978-0-268-04427-5 (pbk. : alk. paper) — ISBN 0-268-04427-9 (pbk. : alk. paper)
1. Political science—Philosophy. 2. Natural law. I. Zuckert, Catherine H., 1942– honoree. II. Zuckert, Michael P., 1942– honoree. III. Ward, Ann, 1970– editor of compilation. IV. Ward, Lee, 1970– editor of compilation.
JA71.N327 2013
320.01—dc23

2012050651

∞ *The paper in this book meets the guidelines for permanence and durability of the Committee on Production Guidelines for Book Longevity of the Council on Library Resources.*

Contents

Part II. Modern Natural Rights

Part III. American Political Thought and Practice

Acknowledgments

We would like to thank the contributors to this volume for their scholarly insights and professionalism and the enthusiasm they brought to this project. Their efforts made our task much more manageable than it might otherwise have been. The editorial and production team at the University of Notre Dame Press have been a joy to work with, and we are grateful for their unstinting support for this project from its inception.

We also would like to thank Campion College at the University of Regina for its continued support of our research, in particular, a grant from the Campion College President's Fund, which helped toward the completion of this volume. And of course we thank Catherine Zuckert and Michael Zuckert for their friendship over many years. It goes without saying that without their inspiration this volume would not have been possible.

Introduction

Practically every student of political philosophy is familiar with Aristotle's remark that philosophy begins in wonder. Rare, perhaps, is the great fortune of experiencing the principle of wonder embodied in the life and work of individuals. Catherine Zuckert and Michael Zuckert are two such individuals. This volume aspires to be a fitting tribute to these political philosophers who in deed and speech have inspired their many students, colleagues, friends, and admirers across a broad range of the American academy and beyond.

Catherine Zuckert and Michael Zuckert were undergraduates at Cornell University and graduate students at the University of Chicago. They bear the impress of legendary teachers and carry these examples into their own teaching careers at Carleton College, Fordham University, and the University of Notre Dame, where they have taught for the past decade and a half. In addition, the Zuckerts have been visiting professors and scholars at the University of Michigan, the University of Delaware, Bowling Green University, and the Liberty Fund. They have also been invited lecturers throughout North America, Europe, and Asia, bringing their wit and wisdom from Toledo to Tokyo.

To the Zuckerts' record of inspirational teaching and speaking must be added their research achievements. Between them they have authored, coauthored, and edited more than a dozen books and an astonishing one hundred articles and book chapters. It is scarcely imaginable how with such a record of scholarly accomplishments the Zuckerts have also managed to remain active citizens of the profession, whether in a number of official capacities in the American Political Science Association and its various sections or serving on editorial boards, including Catherine Zuckert's role as editor of the journal *Review of Politics*.

The Zuckerts have always tended to disdain the beaten path. Whether it is in their studies of politics and literature, American political thought and postmodern philosophy, or their introduction of political philosophy to wider audiences through adaptations for radio and television, the Zuckerts have always been the founders of new ways of thinking about old, still vital questions. However, what is important about the Zuckerts is not solely what they are doing and what they have done but also crucially who they are. Catherine Zuckert and Michael Zuckert are among the pioneering American academic couples. Among their teachers very few if any had spouses who were also academics. Today, as this volume attests, many of the Zuckerts' students, friends, and colleagues are academic couples who have always seen in their example not only the fruitful blending of professional, personal, and philosophical commitments but also collaboration as a model of philosophic friendship—a way of life noble and good.

One of the animating principles of this volume is the notion that in order to honor the Zuckerts properly, we must also explore an idea. The idea of natural right or natural justice that exists independently of human convention is arguably the unifying thread that binds the diverse elements of the Zuckerts' vast oeuvre. We do not presume here in this introduction to propose an authoritative definition of natural right. In this respect, the Zuckerts' work speaks for itself, as does that of the contributors to this volume, each of whom in his or her chosen way addresses an aspect of natural right and natural rights. Investigating the complications and challenges to the concept of that which is right by nature, the chapters in the present volume bring to light themes such as the tension between natural right and divine command and the many controversies and debates surrounding natural right and the history of philosophy. For instance, is natural right and what is best moral action, or is it philosophy? Is it natural law or natural rights, ancient or modern utopianism, democracy or something better, enlightened liberalism or non-Enlightenment liberation? As the contributions to this volume suggest, the Zuckerts' body of innovative and diverse research, whether on Plato, Locke, Jefferson, or Strauss, has never been about following the intellectual fads and trends one sees so often in academic circles. Rather the Zuckerts' career has been marked by the challenge to orthodoxy offered through respectful and engaging but also deeply penetrating scholarship of the highest order.

Catherine Zuckert has sought to rediscover natural right through a rediscovery of the classical political philosophy of Plato. She does so first through an examination of the rejection of natural right in her book *Postmodern Platos: Nietzsche, Heidegger, Gadamer, Strauss, Derrida* (1996). Zuckert calls these thinkers "Platos" because all return to Plato to recover the original character of philosophy, making their understanding of Plato central to their thought as a whole. These thinkers are "postmodern" because they all return to Plato in the conviction that modern rationalism, its promise and possibilities, has collapsed. Considering the meaning and significance of the claim made by Nietzsche and Heidegger that Platonic philosophy is no longer possible, Zuckert examines the responses of Gadamer, Strauss, and Derrida to this challenge in the different ways of reading texts that each develops: hermeneutics, secret teaching, and deconstruction.

Zuckert turns to the Platonic dialogues themselves to experience the rediscovery of classical natural right. In *Plato's Philosophers: The Coherence of the Dialogues* (2009), Zuckert argues against reading the dialogues according to the now standard but highly problematic theory of "chronology of composition"—"early," "middle," and "late" dialogues based on the time Plato wrote them—in favor of the "dramatic" dating of the dialogues—using internal indications by Plato himself to discover when the conversations recorded actually took place. When read in the sequence Plato suggests by means of their dramatic dates, Zuckert, taking a comprehensive view of the dialogues as a whole, argues that the dialogues manifest an overarching narrative. The dialogues, in which Socrates is Plato's most important philosopher, depict the problems that gave rise to Socratic philosophy. The most important problem of pre-Socratic philosophy is its failure to give a "teleological" account of human nature, or to explain what the naturally best way of life for the human being is. The other philosophers Plato depicts—the Athenian Stranger, Parmenides, Timaeus, and the Eleatic Stranger—pose challenges to Socratic philosophy and, according to Zuckert, reveal its limits. One of its key limits is that Socrates, focusing on the human being in abstraction from its context within nonhuman nature, is unable to present a cosmology or an account of the intelligibility of nature as a whole. Socrates thus leaves an apparently unbridgeable gap between our understanding of human life and the nonhuman world. Despite dramatizing its limitations, Zuckert argues that Plato shows his own understanding to be that in the end there is no alternative preferable to Socratic philosophy.

Literature, for Zuckert, has also been an important source of reflection on natural right. In *Natural Right and the American Imagination: Political Philosophy in Novel Form* (1990), Zuckert argues that the major motif of the American novel—the hero's withdrawal from civil society to live in nature and subsequent return to society—is a reflection on the "state of nature" and "social contract" philosophy on which America was explicitly founded. Presenting not only a fictional rebellion against established laws and customs, this motif also considers new grounds on which a just community may be established. Thus Zuckert argues that in mythologizing the rational principles of the American founding, American novelists also self-consciously reinterpret them.

In John Locke, Michael Zuckert finds perhaps the most seminal thinker of the modern period; the intellectual figure most responsible for shaping the way citizens of modern liberal democracies understand rights and constitutional government. In *Natural Rights and the New Republicanism* (1994), Zuckert locates Locke in the broader sweep of seventeenth-century English political thought. However, he presents a vision of Locke as a philosopher of the first order, who eludes the conventional interpretive categories established many years ago by the followers of C. B. MacPherson, Leo Strauss, or the Cambridge school led by Quentin Skinner. For Zuckert, reexamining Locke is not an exercise in ideological self-affirmation or a mere antiquarian curiosity but rather a reconsideration of what he calls "the phenomenology . . . of human rights claiming" (Zuckert 1994, 277). Zuckert's Locke is a bold and original thinker who anticipates much of later philosophy by positing the individual as a being capable of self-creation and of moral ownership of the rights he or she possesses. It is little wonder that Zuckert's *Launching Liberalism* (2002) is at its core an extensive treatment of Locke and his enormous influence on modernity.

The second main element of Michael Zuckert's intellectual project is his interpretation of the political thought of the American founding. As we see from Zuckert's analysis in *The Natural Rights Republic* (1996), Lockean philosophy is the bedrock of the American natural rights republic. That is to say, for Zuckert the United States is a regime distinct from all that came before precisely because it is the first polity to self-consciously derive its fundamental principles from Locke. Whether it is the affirmation of human equality in the *Declaration of Independence,* Thomas Jefferson's democratization of Lockean liberalism in a uniquely American political naturalism, or the "completion" of the Constitution of 1787 by the Civil War Amendments, Zuckert constantly seeks rich intellectual streams to explore the philosophical foundations of American democracy. As such, Zuckert's work is simply required reading for all those who Alexander Hamilton identified in *Federalist #9* as "enlightened friends to liberty" (Hamilton 1961, 72); that is to say, all those supporters of liberal democracy who seek to better understand who we are, who we think we are, and who we wish to become.

Catherine Zuckert and Michael Zuckert have collaborated to show how students and admirers of Leo Strauss can be those enlightened supporters of liberty that Hamilton wished for. In *The Truth about Leo Strauss: Political Philosophy and American Democracy* (2006), Catherine and Michael seek to make sense of Strauss's complex and often tension-ridden approach to America and liberal democracy. Exploring Strauss's political thought, the Zuckerts explain how he held together his philosophic advocacy of a "return to the ancients" with his qualified political endorsement of modern liberal democracy.

The chapters in this volume are organized according to the four main themes of the Zuckerts' scholarly writings: ancient political philosophy, early modern political theory, American political thought, and politics and literature. In the first part, "Classical Natural Right," there are five chapters. In chapter 1 Lorraine Smith Pangle addresses Socrates' famous claim that knowledge is virtue by exploring the relationship between moderation and self-control in Xenophon's *Memorabilia.* For Xenophon's Socrates, mastery of the body is deeper and more fundamental than moderation, and thus it is self-control that is the basis of virtue and wisdom. Pangle, for this reason, argues that Xenophon's account is superior to Aristotle's in the *Nicomachean Ethics.* While self-control may be less important for more ordinary and less philosophic natures like Xenophon, it is the grounding of Socrates' life. Ann Ward, in chapter 2, explores Socrates' mediation of the claims of moral absolutism and moral skepticism in Plato's *Euthyphro.* Through the action of the dialogue, Ward argues, Plato suggests that both certainty of moral knowledge and the embrace of moral ignorance can be damaging to human life. Socrates is seen pushing Euthyphro toward a middle position between these two conditions by pointing to the way in which divine things, such as the "idea" of the pious, reveal themselves to human beings. Socrates' unique engagement with these moral positions reaffirms the value of the family in human life. Yet Socrates also suggests that pious love of the gods can be transcended by the philosophic quest for the ideas or nature of things.

In chapter 3 Kevin M. Cherry investigates Aristotle's critique of Plato's *Laws,* most notably for the understanding of philosophy and its place in political life that is revealed. Cherry argues that from Aristotle's perspective the Athenian Stranger's proposal for philosophic rule provides a cosmology that is an improper basis for political order. In contrast to the cosmology in the *Laws* that shows a disorderly universe precarious to human flourishing, Aristotle grounds his concept of the universe in an unmoved mover and his understanding of political philosophy in questions of what is just and equal in the *polis.* In chapter 4 Mary P. Nichols focuses on how the *Nicomachean Ethics* supports both Aristotle's criticism of Plato and his own alternative approach to political life in the *Politics.* Nichols argues that Aristotle's critique of Plato's idea of the good in book 1 of the *Ethics* is in fact demanded by friendship, and by his understanding of the good life for human beings, including happiness and virtue. Turning to Aristotle's *Politics,* Nichols shows how the *Ethics* is consistent with Aristotle's political critique of the *Republic* as well as his own political thought. In reducing individuals to the class of which they are members, Plato denies human beings the diversity of goods for which they strive. Without the distinct contributions made by members of a community, there is no politics in Aristotle's sense, where differences justify participation.

Mary Keys, in chapter 5, explores Augustine's defense of the virtue of humility in books 1 through 5 of the *City of God.* Keys argues that Augustine's defense of humility is not only a defense of Christianity and divine grace, but also of a new concept of natural right. Humility gladly acknowledges familial bonds, thus showing that humility has a foothold in human nature despite its fallen state. Augustine also critiques the natural wrongness of victory by aggression against peaceful neighbors in favor of the greater natural goodness of moderate political self-rule. Countering false divinization of self and society and so strengthening commitment to moderation and justice among human beings, humility, Keys concludes, is for Augustine what is right according to nature.

Part II, "Modern Natural Rights," illustrates the development of modern political theory from the early modern period to the end of the twentieth century. In chapter 6 David Lewis Schaefer tackles the debate surrounding the moral theory in the apparently unsystematic work of the sixteenth-century French essayist Michel de Montaigne. For Schaefer, Montaigne represents a distinct break from the classical tradition and a lowering of the standards of moral responsibility in a manner much more akin to Machiavelli's *Prince* than Aristotle's morally serious individual. In Montaigne's permissive approach to dealing with presumed vice Schaefer sees a version of humane and moderate government that would become a model for later Enlightenment philosophers.

In chapter 7 Lee Ward examines the classical question about the best regime as it is reworked in Spinoza's famous treatment of the Hebrew Commonwealth in the Old Testament. Ward argues that Spinoza used his treatment of the Hebrew Commonwealth to illustrate the important differences between theocracy and democracy. Democracy, for Spinoza, is the most natural and hence best regime because it reflects a true understanding of humanity's status in nature, whereas theocracy is the most narcissistic regime because it encourages a false idea about the moral significance of what is distinctly human in nature. In particular Ward identifies the tension between the claims about divine and human origins of divine law as a permanent source of instability in the Hebrew polity and a cautionary tale for moderns about the perennial problem of theocracy.

In chapter 8 Vickie Sullivan argues that the revulsion from cruelty and arrogance, which we saw in Montaigne in chapter 6, assumes even greater significance in the later work of his compatriot Montesquieu. In particular Sullivan examines the importance Montesquieu places on the role of due process and rights of the accused. For Sullivan, not only does the treatment of criminal procedure in the *Spirit of the Laws* signify a crucial element in providing for the subjective feeling of security enjoyed by individuals in moderate regimes; it also represents an important aspect of Montesquieu's project to secularize political society. In chapter 9 Jeffrey Church offers an opportunity to reexamine the well-known Hegelian critique of Lockean natural rights theory. Contrary to the many critics of the Lockean "atomistic individual" inspired by Hegel, Church argues that in crucial respects Hegel was actually indebted to Locke, especially in terms of Hegel's reliance on the Lockean idea of moral "personhood" and the central role of property in determining the features of civil society. However, where Locke and Hegel differ seriously, according to Church, is in their disagreement about the human good. For Hegel, the human good is not the contentless Lockean concept of happiness but rather the inescapably ethical and political nature of the self and civil society. As such, Hegelian political society includes but cannot be reduced to the protection of individual natural rights.

In the final chapter in Part II Walter Nicgorski returns to the question of the theologico-political problem. Nicgorski examines perhaps the most famous contemporary expounder of this problem, Leo Strauss. He concludes that Strauss saw openness to the challenge posed by theology as one of the preconditions of philosophy. In this respect, Nicgorski argues, Pope John Paul II was a good counterpart to Strauss. In the 1998 encyclical *Fides et Ratio* Nicgorski sees an argument for the fruitful relation between reason and faith establishing philosophy and theology as mutually supporting endeavors. Insofar as Strauss and John Paul II balanced the benefits of revelation's purifying critique of reason with reason's capacity to exalt the human person, then both figures, Nicgorski suggests, can be seen as instrumental in renewing a form of Socratic rationalism in the wake of modernity's demise into a postmodern future.

Part III examines various aspects of American political thought and practice. The contributors look at the first natural rights republic from a number of perspectives, including theoretical, historical, biographical, and institutional. In chapter 11 Peter Lawler looks back to the intellectual and theological roots of America by examining the relation between the Lockean and Christian features of American republicanism. He challenges the assumption that New England's Puritan founders were in any sense hostile to liberty. However, he takes issue with Lockean liberalism in arguing that Michael Zuckert's post-Christian Lockean individual represents an ultimately incoherent ground for personal identity. Lawler finds in the work of the novelist Marilynne Robinson an alternative to self-interested utility lying in Christian inspired love and meaningful service to others.

In chapter 12 Jean Yarbrough asks, Was Thomas Jefferson the first American Progressive? By locating Jefferson in the orbit of French enlightenment figures such as Turgot and Condorcet, Yarbrough highlights Jefferson's great confidence in progress, especially in the redemptive power of education and his endorsement of the salutary effects of periodic, major political change and renewal. Yarbrough concludes by tracing the complex legacy of Jefferson for twentieth-century Progressives such as Herbert Croly and John Dewey, who sought to harness Jefferson's democratic spirit while largely jettisoning his, in their view outdated, theory of natural rights. As such, Yarbrough doubts whether later Progressives can claim to be authentic heirs of Jefferson.

David Nichols turns our gaze away from the founding era luminary Jefferson toward the lesser known but highly influential Gouverneur Morris. In chapter 13 Nichols argues that this talented New Yorker has every claim to be called the "Father of the Constitution." He identifies in Morris a robust defense of liberalism and the key role he played in shaping the language of the final draft of the Constitution of 1787. In particular, Nichols credits Morris with presenting the most sophisticated defense of an independent executive and with being the most committed nationalist at the Convention. With his emphasis on a strong national government, modern economy, the abolition of slavery, the rise of political parties, and the central role of the presidency, Morris, Nichols finds, is not only a lost jewel among founding-era figures but also a foreshadowing of modern American life.

In chapter 14 David Alvis examines one of the institutions close to Morris's heart, namely, the U.S. presidency. Alvis argues that contrary to first impressions, the adoption of the electoral college was not intended to be a check on democratic or majoritarian impulses. Rather, Alvis claims that careful analysis of the debate about the presidency at the 1787 Convention reveals that the framers viewed the electoral college as a way to protect the interests of smaller states while allowing for the benefits of popular election of the chief executive. Thus, rather than dilute democracy in the way Hamilton suggests in the *Federalist Papers,* Alvis argues, the Convention debates emphasized the role the electoral college would play in securing some kind of popular preference for successful presidential candidates.

The final two chapters in Part III continue the theme of statesmanship in American history by examining two different kinds of leaders. In chapter 15 Diana Schaub considers the African American civil rights leader Booker T. Washington's reflections on the "Great Emancipator" Abraham Lincoln. In her detailed and careful treatment of the text and structure of several of Washington's speeches, Schaub finds the use of Lincoln as a model of self-emancipation for African Americans and an inspiration for future reconciliation and even racial harmony in America. In chapter 16 Kirk Emmert examines Theodore Roosevelt's political biographies of Oliver Cromwell, Thomas Hart Benton, and Gouverneur Morris. Emmert argues that Roosevelt conceived of his biographical writings as a form of political education, according to which Americans could learn to identify what kind of leaders they should seek and what qualities should be encouraged among a democratic citizenry in a natural rights republic.

Part IV is an exploration of topics in politics and literature. Arlene W. Saxonhouse, in chapter 17, examines the relationship between Aristophanes' portrait of Euripides and the performance of Euripides' tragedies. Saxonhouse shows the Aristophanic Euripides putting ordinary, common people onstage, thereby democratizing tragedy and turning the noble into the ignoble to undermine the hierarchies of ancient myth.

When we turn to Euripides' plays themselves, we see that Euripides critiques democracy; democracy must articulate a difference between high and low to confront the passionate drive for power of the unworthy. Saxonhouse concludes that while Euripides endorses the democratic principle of equality, he also brings to light its complications.

In chapter 18 Timothy Spiekerman considers why Shakespeare in *Julius Caesar* wants to draw us into a conspiracy to save a republic that was supposedly doomed to fail. Spiekerman explores the possibility that Shakespeare did not in fact believe that the monarchy established by the Caesars was inevitable but was rather the result of crucial errors made by the conspirators against Julius Caesar, Brutus and Cassius. Their most important failure from Shakespeare's perspective, Spiekerman contends, was a superstition arising from their guilty consciences. Shakespeare also implies that their fatalism resulted from their propensity to think too much, leading Spiekerman to conclude that Shakespeare saw a connection between philosophy and political weakness. In chapter 19 Thomas L. Pangle explores the mystery of the authorial voice and perspective of *Don Quixote.* According to Pangle, Cervantes suggests that he is an Averroist philosopher who proceeds without the light of faith, guided as he is by the natural light. As an Averroist he is interested in debunking the books of chivalry because they represent a Christian imperialism specifically and the militancy of "modern" religion more generally. The figure of Don Quixote himself, Pangle argues, embodies how the great monotheistic religions appear to a natural philosopher. Although not leading us to hate Quixote, Cervantes suggests two alternatives to his religious lunacy: romantic love or a synthesis of Quixote as courageous warrior with Sancho Panza as representative of legislative and judicial common sense.

Christine Dunn Henderson, in chapter 20, examines the place of what Alexis de Tocqueville would call mores and social convention in Edith Wharton's *The Age of Innocence.* Convention, Henderson argues, is only one of three forces operating in the novel. Convention must be understood with two other themes—change and character—for it is the intersection of these three forces that drives the novel along. In chapter 21 Michael Davis suggests how we might begin to understand Tom Stoppard's dramatic trilogy, *The Coast of Utopia.* Assuming that the trilogy is a powerfully antiutopian project, Davis asks why Stoppard shows great affection for his utopian characters. Stoppard, Davis argues, believes that political utopians are noble spirits who long to usher in a settled world but a world in which ironically there is not a place for them. Nonetheless utopians cannot resist the attempt to establish an impossible world because we are most alive in the moment we anticipate a noble future. Stoppard's affection, therefore, is affection for humanity the core of which is to dream or idealize. Davis concludes that Stoppard's critique of utopianism rests on his belief that both politics and the eroticism of private life are grounded in what limits us owing to our nature as temporal creatures.

This volume represents our best efforts to provide a fitting tribute to Catherine Zuckert and Michael Zuckert. As editors, this volume is both a professional and a personal experience for us. We had the great fortune to be students of the Zuckerts, as well as students of other contributors to this volume, most significantly Mary Nichols, David Nichols, Michael Davis, and Thomas Pangle. The deep outpouring of respect and affection for the Zuckerts that we have witnessed since this project began has been truly moving. Several more volumes could have been filled with contributions from other students, colleagues, friends, and admirers of the Zuckerts, who wished to add their voices to this tribute. Sadly, it was impossible to include everyone. However, we hope that this offering exudes the generous spirit of the Zuckerts and their abiding confidence that we can know some important things about the most important questions.

REFERENCES

Hamilton, Alexander, James Madison, and John Jay. [1788] 1961. *The Federalist Papers.* Ed. Clinton Rossiter. New York: Bantam Books.

Zuckert, Michael. 1994. *Natural Rights and the New Republicanism.* Princeton: Princeton University Press.

PART I

Classical Natural Right

Chapter One

Virtue and Self-Control in Xenophon's Socratic Thought

LORRAINE SMITH PANGLE

Socrates is famous for his radical claim that knowledge is the necessary and sufficient cause of virtue. Anyone who truly understands what is good will do it, he often argues, and anyone who does wrong should be educated and not punished. Aristotle devotes much of the *Nicomachean Ethics* to examining this audacious claim and developing a moderate, nuanced version of it as the basis of his teaching on moral virtue. He argues, along Socratic lines, that the virtuous life is not only the most noble but the most beneficial and pleasant, since the greatest natural pleasures for human beings are those that virtue gives us the capacity to appreciate. The character of Aristotelian virtue is beautifully illustrated in his account of moderation (*sophrosunē*). Moderation is not painful self-denial but the enjoyment of all life's pleasures in the way that is most dignified and most conducive to happiness. One who has not yet acquired moderation must fight with himself to abstain from overindulgence, but the moderate person "takes no pleasure in what he should not," and rates each pleasure at its true worth (*NE* 1119a11–20; cf. 1113a29–33). In him, knowledge and desire converge perfectly on what is in every way best. Or so Aristotle suggests. I myself have never met such a person.

But part of the strength of Aristotle's account is that he also shows why this harmonious life of virtue is so rare and difficult to attain, and why most of us manage at best to reach a much lower form of goodness, the self-control (*enkrateia*) of the struggling soul that is forever hacking away at a hydra's head of disorderly impulses. True virtue requires correct education of the tastes and passions and long habituation to noble action, so that one comes to love what at first seemed onerous. Virtue also requires complete self-understanding, so that one sees to the bottom of one's confusions and works through all one's ambivalences. Above all, complete virtue turns out to require an unusually good nature (*NE* 1144b1–14). When we consider these requirements, and especially when we consider the sacrifices that virtue so often calls upon us to make, we must wonder whether the life of harmony and balance that Aristotle depicts at the outset is not extremely, even vanishingly rare. And this doubt is reinforced from a different direction at the end of the book, for in the case of the very best natures what Aristotle recommends is not moderation in all things but an unceasing effort to develop what is highest in us, our capacity for contemplation. What is the character of this highest and most completely virtuous life, which Aristotle sketches so briefly in the closing pages of the *Ethics*? Even if it is overwhelmingly devoted to one activity, philosophy, does it still have the serene harmony that Aristotle has led us to expect from perfect virtue? Or does his new account of the best life signal that the glowing promises he at first made for virtue involved a certain noble exaggeration, and that strenuous efforts at self-overcoming will always be needed to prevent one's energies from dissipating into myriad unworthy channels? Aristotle does not say.

To understand the teaching of classical Socratic philosophy on the virtuous life at its peak, it is helpful to turn to Xenophon's *Memorabilia,* which takes as its explicit theme the character of Socrates himself as the epitome of human excellence. And what is surprising about this account is that here, where we see Socrates making the case for the efficacy of knowledge as radically and insistently as he ever does anywhere, we also find Xenophon giving central place to self-control as the foundation of Socratic virtue, as if even the best soul never ceases to be rife with contrary impulses that must be vigilantly opposed.

Socrates applies his classic argument for the sovereignty of wisdom to the virtues of moderation and self-control at *Memorabilia* 3.9. There Xenophon says that Socrates did not distinguish between wisdom and moderation but "decided that one is both wise and moderate who, knowing the noble and good things, uses them, and knowing the shameful ones, avoids them." And when he was asked in addition whether he held those to be wise and self-controlled who understand what they should do but do the opposite, he said, "No more than unwise and self-indulgent, for I think that all, choosing from among the possibilities the things they think are most to their advantage, do those things; I hold, then, that those who do not act correctly are neither wise nor moderate" (3.9.4). What does it mean to equate wisdom with moderation? Apparently it is not the same as to argue that all knowledge is efficacious in action, for Socrates is conceding that one may somehow know what one should do and fail to do it. The context of this passage, coming immediately after a discussion of courage, might suggest that knowledge must be supplemented by courage or a strength of self-overcoming to produce the wisdom that guarantees its own implementation, as if wisdom has a component that is not intellectual. Yet Socrates indicates here that the fundamental failing that causes knowledge to be disregarded in action is the incompleteness of knowledge itself, for he says that all choose "the things that they think are most to their advantage." One may know that a virtuous act is noble but fail to understand that what is genuinely noble is also beneficial, and it is the latter insight that makes the difference for action and that constitutes wisdom. Socrates goes on to argue that justice is wisdom, since the just things are noble and good, or gentlemanly (*kala te kai agatha*), and that hence those who know the noble and good things would neither choose anything else nor be incapable of doing what is best.[1] But if, as this passage implies, a thorough understanding of good and bad is sufficient for virtue according to Socrates, the dependence of that understanding in turn upon self-control is a major and perplexing theme of the *Memorabilia*.

Nor is the relationship between self-control or *enkrateia* and moderation or *sophrosunē* as clear and straightforward here as in Aristotle's *Ethics.* Whereas Aristotle has narrowed the traditional scope of *sophrosunē* to treat it as fundamentally the correct attitude towards bodily pleasures, Xenophon retains more of the original richness and ambiguity of the word. He opposes moderation not only to immoderation but to hubris and to madness as well. Moderation, which in some way encompasses the whole of Socratic virtue, is the sobriety born of a deep self-understanding that shows itself in a frank acknowledgment of one's ignorance, one's needs, and one's limits; in the avoidance of boastfulness; in the acceptance of the inevitability of death; and in the respectful treatment of legal authority and traditional piety. Moderation includes both the ability to marshal all one's resources in pursuit of the solid good that one needs and the habit of eschewing what is nonessential. It is equally opposed to the madly erotic quest for eternal glory and to the reckless disparaging of law and traditional piety seen in thoughtless students of philosophy like Aristodemus, who are drunk with their own sense of liberation from conventional beliefs, or lashing out in anger over their own disappointed hopes, or both. Xenophon contrasts Socratic moderation with the spirit of pre-Socratic philosophy, which Socrates charges gave insufficient reflection to things human and in particular to the problems of grounding human knowledge and examining why knowledge is good for us (1.1.11–15). Socrates likens ignorance of oneself and of what one knows and does not know to madness, showing that what others consider to be a small mistake is for him the fundamental mistake that makes true sanity impossible (3.9.6–7). Sometimes Socrates uses the terms *self-control* and *moderation* almost synonymously, as in the passage at 3.9.4 cited above, but in general self-control in the *Memorabilia* has a narrower scope than moderation and denotes the proper response to pleasures and pains. Yet this self-control is presented as in some ways deeper and more fundamental than moderation and as the indispensable basis rather than the consequence of wisdom. Xenophon says that Socrates was the most self-controlled of all human beings in matters of sex and appetite; that he had the greatest endurance of cold, heat, and labor; and that he schooled himself to have extremely limited needs so that his meager possessions would suffice for him (1.2.1). Why is such austerity necessary?

MODERATION AND SELF-CONTROL IN SOCRATIC EDUCATION

Xenophon begins to show the reasons for the importance of self-control in his description of the defective virtue of Socrates' most ambitious students. He attributes a limited form of moderation, the outward behavior that wisdom dictates, to the young Critias and Alcibiades but never calls them self-controlled. While these two are under Socrates' spell they imitate his actions and heed his admonitory speeches, and for a time they think his is indeed the right way to live (1.2.18). But theirs is only a borrowed strength. They lack the vigorous habits of self-control that they would need to keep confronting Socrates' painful admonitions and to absorb them into the innermost parts of their souls, and so they never acquire the wisdom that is the only self-sustaining root of moderation. Instead, they remain, even while they are with him, profoundly ambivalent as to whether his way of life is the most admirable or whether death would not in fact be preferable to a whole life of such austerity (cf. 1.2.16 and 46 with 1.2.18 and 39).

Xenophon is on the defensive as he tries to clear Socrates of the charge that he ought to have taught moderation before he taught political and rhetorical skills to would-be tyrants such as Critias and Alcibiades (1.2.17). Perhaps Socrates did teach moderation in the only way that it can be taught, by example and by refutations that force others to acknowledge—for as long as they are paying attention—the superiority of his way of life (see Strauss 1972, 12–13). But these two spectacular failures of Socratic education suggest another side to the story—that it is precisely the most ambitious souls in which Socrates is most interested and that he can perhaps attract them to philosophy only by arousing their most audacious hopes and stirring them to question traditional piety and human authority in ways that can be dangerous if their conversion to philosophy proves abortive.[2] Perhaps only time can tell whether these unusually strong souls, which have the greatest potential for evil as well as good and which are most in need of education (4.1.3–4), have the extraordinary strength needed to follow reason to its end and to grasp and put into practice what it demands of them.

In contrast, in the discussion of Socrates' education of Euthydemus in book 4, Xenophon suggests that Socrates did successfully teach him moderation before anything else (4.3.1). But Euthydemus is unusually lacking in spiritedness. One consequence of this lack is a willingness to accept arguments on Socrates' authority without challenging him. But Xenophon indicates that Socrates reserves his most thorough investigations for the students who do challenge him, and that with others he succeeds in generating agreement but not necessarily truth (4.6.13–15; cf. 4.2.40). The education of Euthydemus to a simulacra of moderation, or to a fairly conventional piety and justice, shows what Socrates attempted to accomplish with his less promising and reflective students. And it may be only such people who can be made moderate before learning anything about taking action and speaking in politics, for only this type would be sufficiently docile. But this moderation is not the moderation of Socrates.

In discussing the defective moderation of Alcibiades and Critias, Xenophon makes a remarkable observation.

> Now perhaps many of those who claim to philosophize would say that one who is just would never become unjust, nor would the moderate one become insolent, nor would anyone who has learned anything else that can be learned ever lose that knowledge. But I, for my part, do not reach the same judgment about these matters. For I see that, just as those who do not train the body are unable to do bodily work, so also those who do not train the soul are unable to do the work of the soul. For they are able neither to do what they should nor to refrain from what they should.
>
> . . . And when someone forgets the speeches that admonish, he has forgotten also the things that the soul experienced when it desired moderation. As he has forgotten these, it is no wonder that he forgets moderation as well. (1.2.19, 21)

As Leo Strauss observes (1972, 13), this is the only philosophic discussion Xenophon ever enters into in his own name in his Socratic writings, and the position he attributes to "many who claim to philosophize" is of course Socrates' own position. How deep a disagreement does this discussion reveal between Xenophon and Socrates on the power of knowledge? Does Xenophon mean that even perfect understanding can be lost? But why would one who understands the full importance of remembering "the speeches that admonish" let himself forget them? Xenophon never says that he would; hence he likely has no disagreement with Socrates about the most perfect understanding. Does he simply wish, then, to emphasize the instability of the defective virtue that the vast majority of us are able to attain? The immediate examples of Critias and Alcibiades suggest that he does have in mind the lesser form of virtue that rests on opinion rather than on complete and fully digested knowledge. But perhaps Xenophon means to go further and to bring out a deep paradox in the Socratic thesis that virtue is knowledge. The knowledge that undergirds virtue is as much experiential as conceptual and much more active than static. One possesses it not as one possesses a statue but as one possesses physical fitness: it is developed through long practice and sustained by intimate daily experience of the goodness of virtue and the deep but at first strange satisfactions of living life fully awake.

The experience of the beginner's soul when it desires moderation, as for a time Alcibiades and Critias do, would be rather different from the experience of the mature philosopher who cherishes the moderation he already has. In both cases there would be a pleasure in one's own clarity and progress in clarity, a satisfying recognition of one's own strength in facing one's former confusions, and an initially strange sense of disdain for even the most renowned men who still inhabit the moral fog that one has left behind. Alcibiades experiences for at least a moment a profound reorientation of his judgments in his cross-examination of the great Pericles, as it becomes clear that Pericles has not thought through any of the fundamental issues that lie at the foundation of his life's work. When Pericles finally concedes defeat in the argument, saying, "We too were quite clever indeed at things of this sort when we were your age," Alcibiades replies, "Would that I could have been your companion at that time, Pericles, when you were at your cleverest" (1.2.46). At that moment, at least, the life of the simple but profound Socrates seems to him superior to the life of the great but wooly-headed Pericles. Yet even here we see the flaw in Alcibiades' desire for Socratic understanding. Alcibiades' cross-examination is a clever imitation but only an imitation of a Socratic cross-examination. For where Alcibiades merely touches on the deepest question about law, the question of its relation to what is truly and naturally good (1.2.42), Socrates would have pursued this question doggedly; where Alcibiades is motivated primarily by the love of victory, Socrates chiefly seeks progress in understanding. The love of victory may fascinate Socrates' followers with philosophy for a time, but to devote one's life to acquiring wisdom one must love it for itself.[3]

In Plato's *Symposium* we see Alcibiades pointing to another side of what the soul may experience when it desires moderation. Alcibiades speaks there of the repeated experience of being humbled by Socrates, ashamed of his own carelessness, and full of resolutions to live and pursue virtue more seriously when he is in Socrates' presence, but this experience repeatedly fades away in the absence of the man himself (*Symposium* 215a–222b). Alcibiades is under the spell of Socrates in a way that he does not understand; he is in awe of something in Socrates that seems to him infinitely noble but also so mysterious that he cannot carry a clear conception of it away with him. This experience is only hinted at by Xenophon, but it is surely another aspect of what beginners often feel when their desire for virtue is real but still poorly grounded.

Knowledge, then, is sovereign in the soul in this strange sense, that when fully present it will prevail, but that without the right disposition and habits insight itself can disappear, and what appeared good before can cease to appear good at all. For there is a natural tendency to slip back into thoughtlessness and confusion if one fails to keep striving for clarity. Insights can come and go, and there is something in particular about insight into the true human condition that has a tendency to slip away or even to run away (Cf. Plato, *Meno* 97d–98a). The truths that teach moderation are painful ones that admonish rather than flatter our vanities and hopes (1.2.21). Furthermore, Xenophon suggests, there is something disjointed or chaotic in human nature that makes perfect harmony impossible. As he says in a strange formulation, "the pleasures growing in the same body together with the soul persuade the soul not to be moderate but instead to gratify themselves and the body as quickly as possible" (1.2.23). That is to say, physical pleasure has a certain elemental force that is never wholly amenable to reason and does not even completely belong to the soul.

Xenophon says that Critias and Alcibiades, as long as they were with Socrates, "were able to overpower their ignoble desires by using him as an ally," but later they were corrupted by worse company. In particular,

Alcibiades, petted and spoiled by fine ladies and by the flattery of the demos, "neglected himself, just as athletes in gymnastics contests who easily win first place neglect their training" (1.2.24). Alcibiades and Critias used the example and exhortations of Socrates, like a foreign army, to give their souls a semblance of order, and like all such extraneous reasons for cultivating excellence, Socrates' presence was helpful to a degree. We might think the problem was that these two were corrupted by their love of honor, yet Socrates does not treat the love of honor as an obstacle to progress but rather as an essential tool of education, appealing to and even encouraging it in his followers (e.g., 1.2.55). In fact, Alcibiades' and Critias's deepest flaw may well have been an insufficient love of honor. They were contented with popular acclaim rather than striving for the respect of worthy judges and above all the self-respect that comes with becoming as good as one possibly can be. In this connection it is significant that Socrates' final criticism of Critias is that he is slavish in his indulgence of sensual desires (1.2.29).

True moderation, then, requires self-control to sustain intellectual insight; without it one may have scattered glimpses of the truth but no steadiness of judgment (4.5.6, 11–12). Socrates sheds more light on the power of desire to overturn clarity in his half-jesting remark that indulgence in pleasure turns men into swine as Circe did to Odysseus's companions (Xenophon, *Memorabilia* 1.3.7; Homer, *Odyssey* 10.210 ff.). To avoid their fate, Odysseus needs both the knowledge that Hermes' root gives him (and that Socrates' daimonic insight gives Socrates) and the self-control to resist Circe's erotic charms. Erotic desires have an especially insidious power to overturn insights that are not backed up by self-control, for they tend either to pull us downwards to the subhuman level, into ever greater indulgence and forgetfulness of our higher natures and enslavement to what is low, or else to make us forget or try to transcend our human limits altogether. If the first tendency presents little danger to the noble souls that are capable of loving philosophy, an intoxicated attempt at self-overcoming and self-forgetting remains a danger and carries with it an enslavement of its own, such as that with which the divine Circe threatens Odysseus himself. Moderation is about finding the properly human middle course that begins with mastering pleasures and aims at constant, wakeful awareness of our true condition.

Like Odysseus, Socrates refuses to indulge in erotic affairs until he has become immune to their enchantment, and he is unwilling to allow any pleasures whatsoever to lull him into forgetfulness.

Socrates appeals especially to his students' concern with freedom and dignity in trying to persuade them to exercise self-control against the intoxicating poison of love. He advises Xenophon to avoid at all costs kissing beautiful boys, lest he become the slave of harmful pleasures (1.3.8–15; cf. 4.5.3–5). In the only conversation Xenophon reports between himself and Socrates, Socrates calls him a wretch (*tlemon*) and a fool (*moron*) for failing to see the terrible power of eros.[4] He abuses Xenophon as roundly and in virtually the same words as Aristophanes' Socrates abuses the thoroughly foolish and dishonest Strepsiades (Aristophanes, *Clouds* 398, 686; cf. Strauss 1972, 21). This treatment of Xenophon is clearly unjust but perhaps not altogether unjust: Xenophon in his imperviousness to this part of Socrates' teaching does bear a certain resemblance to the uneducable Strepsiades and much more to Strepsiades' son Pheidippides, a horseman like himself, who like him learns much from Socrates but rejects Socrates' way of life for one that gives central place to more ordinary human attachments and pleasures.[5] On the other hand, the tone Socrates takes with Xenophon also resembles the tone Socrates' alter egos in the *Symposium* and *Greater Hippias* take towards Socrates himself (see esp. *Symposium* 204b; *Greater Hippias* 286c–d). Perhaps Socrates reserves his roughest abuse for both his most hopeless and his most promising students, and Xenophon is a bit of the former while being a great deal of the latter. Might this playful conversation then reflect a deep kinship and affection but also a lasting disagreement between Socrates and Xenophon, if not about the best way of life for those with the best natures like Socrates, then about the proper place of eros and other pursuits for lesser men like Xenophon? Xenophon clearly admires Socrates and even calls him "blessed" (1.6.14), but he may also think Socrates is not quite fair in assuming that anyone who takes great pleasure in love affairs must remain seriously confused. For the more lighthearted Xenophon, eros may have much more to do with simple pleasure and affection and less to do with the yearning to escape death and oblivion than in the soul of the more profoundly erotic Socrates. At the same time, for the less talented Xenophon, philosophy may not have the compelling power to cast all other pleasures into the shade. Thus ordinary human affections might retain a stronger grip upon him, without that grip necessarily entailing any serious confusion.

SELF-CONTROL AND PLEASURE

But even if every philosophic beginner must take his erotic yearnings firmly in hand and exert immense self-control to resist the charms of unfounded hopes and moral confusions, surely that is not the case with Socrates. Surely Socrates, having once left the cave, is not seriously tempted to fall prey again to its illusions. Why, then, does he live a life of such vigilant austerity regarding sex and food, heat, cold, sleep, and physical labor? Why does he school himself in such frugality that as Xenophon says it would be hard for anyone to "earn so little as not to secure what is sufficient for Socrates" (1.2.1, 1.3.5, 2.1.1–3)?

Socrates' initial answer to this question, at 1.5, is that self-control is the essential foundation for all virtue in the soul. But the argument has a strange character. Self-control comes to sight as such a low-level virtue or mere precondition for virtue that it is available to slaves, and most of the arguments that recommend it come down to ways in which it makes one useful in serving the purposes of others. To be sure, Socrates asserts that it is even more beneficial to oneself, but he says little to explain this statement. Is self-control the necessary foundation for virtue only in the limited sense that one needs the capacity to carry out whatever one's mind determines is good, which might include an extensive pursuit of all sorts of pleasures once one has gained clarity about them? Or is an ongoing effort of self-overcoming needed, especially with regard to pleasure? Must one even subjugate the lower parts of one's nature as a master subjugates his slaves, if one is ever to amount to anything? Xenophon remarks that "Socrates displayed himself to be even more self-controlled in his deeds than in his speeches" (1.5.6), pointing to the incompleteness in his argument, for Socrates certainly makes the case for being in full command of oneself, but not yet for such austerity as he himself practiced.

In the next chapter, however, Socrates defends self-control on very different grounds, now insisting that this is the way to gain the most enjoyment even from life's simplest pleasures (1.6; cf. 2.1.30). Socrates thus poses, improbably, as the ultimate Epicurean. Accused by Antiphon the Sophist of living and teaching a life of misery because of his poverty, Socrates replies that his self-schooled toughness saves him from many discomforts that others suffer, while his meager provisions are as pleasant for him as Antiphon's luxurious ones are for him (1.6.5). He makes the claim even more strongly in a later exchange with Euthydemus: only when one has the self-control to resist and endure physical desires until they become as pleasant as possible can one get any pleasure worth mentioning from food, drink, sex, or sleep (4.5.9).

Now even if we concede that the optimal delay (whatever that turns out to be) brings the maximum pleasure, is it really the case that such extreme austerity as Socrates exercises is required? It does not seem obvious that life is on balance more pleasant if one abstains from water until one is parched, or that sex is more dull for lovers who make love every day than for those who only get around to it now and then. Nor does it explain why Socrates chooses to live in ten-thousand-fold poverty, or why he scorns all the graceful accoutrements of life, such as Xenophon was later to acquire on his country estate, as necessarily more trouble than they are worth (3.8.10). The economy of pleasures in Socrates' own life becomes clear in his conversation with Antiphon: he loves to think with such a passion that all other pleasures are by comparison just extraneous noise (1.6.8). To indulge them, to begin to think about them and plan for them and worry about securing them, is as clearly irrational for him as fertilizing the weeds in the garden.

But if philosophy is not so engrossing for his followers, why does he still enjoin upon them such austerity? Socrates' most serious defense of austerity is not that it magnifies pleasures but that it avoids heavy costs. He judges that all refined pleasures and possessions, if we give them any more of our soul than is absolutely necessary, are traps that prevent our pursuit of what is best. He claims that wealth comes to own us rather than we it. Thus he says it would be bad luck to receive a great inheritance; one would do better to leave it lying in the street (1.5.6). But why is it not possible, pursuing Aristotle's ideal of moderation and the Pythian injunction "nothing in excess," to give a reasonably small corner of one's attention to beautiful possessions and the other refined enjoyments that wealth makes possible, with the determination that only a small corner of one's happiness should be allowed to rest there? Socrates argues that human pleasures and interests have such a fluidity and such a life of their own that whatever we give our attention to comes to possess a part of us, and this is especially true of the desires that are most susceptible of instant gratification. Our higher and more austere pleasures and interests are forever in danger of being swamped by coarser and easier ones, unless the latter are vigilantly kept in check. And as Socrates says to Epigenes (3.12), the habits either of self-control and self-sufficiency or self-indulgence and fecklessness that we cultivate in one area of our lives spill over into others. Hence any indulgence of the body and its pleasures leads to a mushrooming of difficult-to-satisfy desires and a slackening of the moral strength needed for better things. Thus the proper enjoyment of physical pleasures—their only enjoyment that is simply sweet and harmless—is the pleasure of meeting keenly felt desires for sustenance, for rest, or for recreation from great, all-absorbing exertions. Here as always, Socrates insists on the connection between pleasure and need. When we treat physical pleasures as ends rather than as restorative remedies, they sap the powers of the soul for anything better. But when the balance is right between serious endeavors and physical pleasures, then indeed we will not stop to eat or drink until the need becomes pressing, not because we have calculated that this is the best way to enhance those pleasures, but because the desires for them will have to become clamorous to get our attention.

Conversely, just as one indulgence easily leads to others, so one form of exercise lays the foundation for others. Accustoming oneself to strenuous exertion is essential, Socrates argues, both because of nature's stinginess and because of the character of human happiness. As he explains in the story of Hercules' encounter with Virtue and Vice that he borrows from Prodicus, the gods or nature have made it such that nothing truly good or noble comes to human beings without labor and vigilance (2.1.28). At the core of any solid happiness is a firm conviction that we are captains of our own ships and masters of our own fates. If good things fell into our laps, they would never be as sweet, for as Virtue says and Socrates agrees, the most pleasant of all sights is a noble work of one's own (2.1.31).

Socrates demonstrates the importance of well-founded pride in his cross-examination of Aristippus. Aristippus scorns the political life and counts himself among those who want to live as easily and pleasantly as possible. But Socrates is able to show that Aristippus's happiness, like his own, rests in no small part on his own good opinion of himself, although he is not fully aware of how important that pride is for him or how poorly grounded it is.[6] Aristippus imagines that he has found a freedom from the delusions of conventional morality and a uniquely free cosmopolitan way of life that avoids both the burdens of rule and the miseries of subjugation. Socrates gently shows that instead of finding a viable middle course between ruling and slavery, Aristippus has merely fallen between two stools. He has neither the justified pride of the citizen who knows that his happiness depends on the well-being of his polis and is willing and able to fight for its freedom nor the self-sufficiency of a hermit who can find happiness anywhere in a life of complete obscurity. Socrates indeed raises doubts as to whether even a hermit can be self-sufficient, or whether everyone who shares a world with other human beings does not need to give considerable attention to cultivating friends and allies to protect him. But Aristippus is especially in need of allies and legal protection, for his pleasures depend on holding slaves. Aristippus, like many modern hedonists, would doubtless find his life dissatisfying were it not for the pride he takes in his own cleverness and daring, but Socrates shows that he is neither so wise nor so brave as he imagines.

Since Aristippus is Socrates' companion and disciple, we must wonder whether Socrates is not largely responsible for Aristippus's corruption. In particular, it cannot help that Socrates has said so much about how self-control makes one a good servant and how political communities use the virtues of their most gifted citizens for their own ends (3.1–7). Aristippus observes that political communities treat their rulers as he treats his slaves, expecting benefits for themselves and self-sacrifice from those who serve them (2.1.9), and he thinks he has no need for the honors that those communities offer as the chief reward for service. He understands the utility of self-control for all ordinary purposes and is adept at exploiting that of his slaves, but he barely perceives and does not share the higher purposes of Socrates for which only complete self-mastery will suffice, and in particular the love of wisdom so intense that it takes the sting out of a life that lacks dignity by conventional standards. With Aristippus as with all his companions, Socrates attempts to instill a critical stance towards received opinion and a powerful, autonomous desire for excellence and self-admiration. The panoply of fascinating characters who parade through the *Memorabilia* shows us more about the failures of this project than the successes, and as much about the ease of beginning the liberation from opinion as about the profound difficulty of completing it or fostering true autonomy. Through this ambiguous defense of Socrates, Xenophon aptly reveals the many barriers to genuine self-control, and hence the essential nature of virtue's foundation. In the end, men like Aristippus lack the strength and toughness for the most rewarding pursuits, which are also the most difficult (2.1.19–20).

With building strength as with resisting pleasure, Socrates presents the mastery of the body as the essential foundation for the excellence of the soul. Rebuking Epigenes for his poor physical condition, he argues that forgetfulness, dispiritedness, discontent, and madness result from physical unfitness. Forgetfulness is the only element in this list that seems rather surprising, but perhaps the context shows that it is forgetfulness of a particular kind that Socrates is thinking of. For he upbraids Epigenes for imagining that he can avoid death and enslavement in battle if he does not practice, for thinking he will be able to bear the fatigues of campaigning easily, and, in general, for holding in contempt what comes about through fitness. The forgetfulness that unfit intellectuals are especially prone to is a forgetfulness about the body and the vulnerability, neediness, and mortality it brings us. It is all too easy for a high-minded student of philosophy to imagine abstractly that he has risen to a higher plane and transcended the concern with his bodily welfare and even with his own personal existence altogether, but such a movement is not an ascent in wisdom.

Yet if we may consider for a moment the experience of those who do try to follow Socrates' advice, we find something odd. As vexingly hard as it is to overcome lazy habits and establish good ones, when people succeed they often slip to the opposite extreme and begin spending long hours in the weight room, on the tennis courts, or preparing to run marathons. Self-control itself becomes a new source of immoderation. And Socrates has an explanation for this, too. The problem is that a moderate routine of jogging and push-ups, performed daily, gives no more satisfaction than polishing one's shoes. Human pleasures and interests are immensely fluid and can develop and burgeon around almost anything, but they need novelty, change, and movement. And by far the greatest pleasure, Socrates says, arises when one sees oneself "nobly progressing" in whatever one makes one's pursuit (1.6.8). Or as he puts it in summing up his life, "those live best who best attend to becoming as good as possible, and those live most pleasantly who most perceive that they are becoming better" (4.8.6). What is best and what is most pleasant do not quite completely converge, then, even for Socrates, and the gap is worse for most of us, since the pursuits in which we can most easily get the pleasure of progress are often not those that provide what is best for us.

What is more, improvement itself can easily become its own trap and its own source of illusions, as we begin to imagine that we are on an endless upward trajectory, becoming stronger, richer, better connected, more powerful, better known, and more secure: for all of this must necessarily end in death.[7] This danger is hinted at in Socrates' rhetorical question at 1.6.8: "Do you think that anything is more responsible for my not being enslaved to stomach or sleep or lust than that I have other things more pleasant than these that delight not only in their use but also by providing hopes that they will benefit always?" The "always" here no doubt means for Socrates himself only "as long as I have need of them," but in the present contest with Antiphon for the admiration of Socrates' students, Socrates is perhaps willing to give the impression that his way of life will provide endless progress and eternal happiness. Socrates' own clarity on this point is attested by the fact that in his other two statements on the pleasure of progress in Xenophon, in *Memorabilia* 4.8 and the *Apology of Socrates to the Jury* 6, he explicitly links this theme to the subject of death.[8]

Thus just as we need self-control to resist the allure of instant gratification for the greater satisfactions of hard work and improvement, we must exert self-control to keep focusing on becoming better in the ways that matter most, in depth and clarity of understanding and in vigilant wakefulness. If even Socrates found less pleasure in knowing itself than in his own progress in knowing, it is only reasonable that our own pleasure in philosophy would be thin and faltering as long as we give it less than our all. And so it is that the balanced life Aristotle tempts us to aspire to, the life that finds a satisfying place for art and history and music and family and wealth and travel and movies and golf and skiing and philosophy, too, may be in the end an illusion. Balance is attractive in the abstract, but it is intensity and focus and steady progress that satisfy most in actuality. It is an occasion for some regret, however, that Xenophon did not reveal more about his own resolution to the tension between our manifold natural desires and the single-mindedness needed for our greatest fulfillment, which he presents so powerfully in the *Memorabilia.*

PHILOSOPHIC SELF-CONTROL AND MORTALITY

And yet again we must ask, does the intensely philosophic life of Socrates remain a life of self-overcoming, or does it ultimately reach a harmony in which needs and inclinations fall into perfect accord? It does seem that Socrates advises austere self-control for his students and practices it himself in two different spirits, urging the students to pull hard on the leash of every other desire for the sake of their noble goal while himself avoiding other distractions as we would avoid a garrulous bore. If Socrates does remain in need of self-control, it cannot be because other pleasures rival that of thinking, and surely not because he is seriously tempted to return to the moral fog of the cave he once so laboriously left. It can only be because the effort required to keep progressing is so strenuous that he must fight the allure of easy relaxation, or more seriously, because the truth he finds is in some ways such a hard one that it is forever tempting to slide into abstraction or a degree of forgetfulness, pursuing with gusto the fine points of logic or physics and pleasantly forgetting to remember that he must die. In this way philosophy has its own version of the distraction that more often takes the form of frenetic pleasure seeking or empire building. It is interesting in this regard that Socrates more than once puts wakefulness regarding sleep as the central item in his summations of things that require self-control (2.1.1, 2.1.2–3). Similarly, in speaking of the decline that would await him in old age if he continued to live, Socrates says that the awareness of his decline would cause him to live worse as well as unpleasantly, whereas a life in which one was unconscious of one's decline—a life, as it were, spent sleepwalking towards oblivion—might be less palpably unpleasant, but it would not be worth living (4.8.8).

How serious the temptation to distraction and forgetfulness is, and hence how much self-control is permanently required, will depend on the answer to the question of how death looks to the philosopher. Does it remain terrifying? Does it cease to frighten one who has accustomed himself to thinking of it and yet cast such a pall of sadness on everything that it requires a painful effort to keep it in view and not to fall into self-deception? Xenophon's account of the end of Socrates' life suggests, at least, that death does not need to be a terror or a depressing blight. For he relates that in the thirty days between Socrates' condemnation and his execution, Socrates lived exactly as he had always lived. The imminence of death changed nothing for him about its aspect or its importance, for it was the same inevitability that he had always known it to be. Such steadiness in the face of death suggests that it had ceased to be an object of fear to Socrates. In this connection, it is striking that although Xenophon reports that Socrates acquired fame for his courageous death (4.8.1), Xenophon himself never attributes courage to Socrates, nor does Socrates call courage a virtue in his one brief thematic discussion of it in 3.9.1–3, as if he thought the wise man did not need courage to remain clear-sighted.

Indeed, far from presenting death as necessarily a source of overwhelming sorrow, Xenophon makes the remarkable suggestion that a thorough acceptance and even constant awareness of the inevitability of death makes life as happy as it is possible for it to be. For the way of life that did not change after Socrates' condemnation, Xenophon says, was a life supremely admirable for its cheerfulness and contentment (4.8.2). What Xenophon presents as remarkable is not only that Socrates managed to bear up well under the sentence of death (which one might do for the sake of one's friends or reputation while feeling despair inside), but that his whole life was one of exceptional good cheer, and not only of good cheer (which one might school oneself to muster in the face of a grim inevitability), but of true inner contentment. Although death surely still evokes sadness, Socrates' example teaches that it need never make satisfying activity and happiness impossible, even at the end. Thus Socrates' stance towards death seems subtly but decisively different from that of Lucretius, who also lays great importance on coming to terms with mortality. For Lucretius depicts death as casting a grim and perhaps always frightening pall over all of life, so that facing it courageously remains a great challenge, and the self-respect that comes of facing it well is a central source of what solid happiness Lucretius thinks is attainable.

In conclusion, if the strength of all desires could be brought to match the strength of the pleasure that would come from their satisfaction, and if the strength of the true pleasures to be gotten were in perfect proportion to the benefit of each thing for us, then no self-control would be needed. As it is, the best soul will initially need Herculean self-control to attain the clarity of perfect self-understanding, and it will require continual, high-level exertion and concentration to stay focused on the things that matter and to keep progressing in them. The best life remains the life of an athlete in training and not that of an Aristotelian gentleman sipping mint juleps on his porch, and the self-control that consists in continually mustering all one's powers will always be needed as the basis for true moderation. Yet such exertion is precisely what the healthy soul will come to cherish. If Socrates' important pleasures are all of the best sort, the pleasure of reaching ever new heights of insight, of handling interlocutors masterfully, of hard exertion and the perception of constant progress, then an old age of relaxation and gradual decline will never, for him, constitute a life worth having.[9]

Xenophon recognizes the rarity of perfect self-control, and hence the rarity of true virtue, in almost the last words of the *Memorabilia,* as he praises Socrates for being so self-controlled as never to choose what was more pleasant in place of what was better. Because this simple thing remains such a difficult feat, the complete virtue that is summed up in Socratic moderation remains beyond the reach even of most of Socrates' ardent followers. It was no small part of Socratic moderation that he pondered and grasped the full political significance of the elusiveness of such moderation, that he understood that folly and fanaticism could never be bleached from the cloth of political life, that he showed such respect for lawfulness and for simple law-abiding citizens and soldiers (see esp. 4.4), and that he therefore modestly refrained from making things worse by attempting to remake the world in the image of philosophy.

NOTES

An earlier version of this chapter was presented at the Annual Meeting of the American Political Science Association, Boston, MA, September 2002. Unless otherwise noted, all quotations from Xenophon are taken from the Bonnette translation, with occasional modifications.

1. What is missing from this argument is, of course, a full defense of the proposition that the just is always beneficial—and beneficial for the just man himself.

2. Socrates' knowledge of the art of stirring up longings is amply displayed in 3.11, where he instructs the courtesan Theodote in the fine points of ensnaring others in one's web. See also 2.6.8–13 and 28–31; cf. Plato *Alcibiades I,* esp. 104e–106a.

3. For a good account of the confusions about virtue, honor, and public service that Socrates finds in highly ambitious youth and that Critias and Alcibiades would have to resolve to come to a stable commitment to pursuing the excellence of Socrates, see Lorch 2010.

4. Strauss (1972) notes that the phrase "you wretch" occurs elsewhere in Xenophon's Socrates writings only where virtue calls vice a wretch. As Strauss says, "How could Xenophon correspond to vice? Unless indeed the care bestowed upon virtue is corruption" (21). One possible meaning is that Socrates' education of Xenophon has resulted in a successful liberation from conventional morality but an incomplete turn to the philosophic life, so that the consequence of Socrates' care for his virtue is a kind of corruption that leaves Xenophon still somewhat hedonistic, acquisitive, and politically ambitious. Perhaps it is more likely that Xenophon considers his conversion to have been complete but means to hint that Socrates' education of his soul in virtue entailed its corruption as ordinarily understood.

5. As Christopher Bruell observes, Xenophon indicates Socrates' uncharacteristic lack of persuasiveness on this point with a characteristically light-handed silence (Bruell 1994, ix).

6. According to Diogenes Laertius (*Lives of Eminent Philosophers* 2.65 ff.), Aristippus was a thoroughgoing hedonist, not even much concerned with dignity. Xenophon's subtler presentation suggests that beneath this exterior lies a deep pride, a pride that consists precisely in rejecting conventional political standards of dignity, and about which Aristippus is insufficiently thoughtful. Signs that Socrates perceives this pride as a key to Aristippus's character are his elaboration on the shamefulness of being caught in adultery and his stress at the end of the discussion on the significance of one's good opinion of oneself, to which Aristippus has no reply. The point is echoed poetically in the subsequent allegory of Virtue and Vice, in which Vice is depicted as surprisingly vain.

7. The founders of the modern political economy, beginning with Hobbes, understood well how absorbing this project of self-improvement and self-fortification

could become, although Socrates would doubtless say that they still overestimated the extent to which it could eclipse the yearning for immortality.

8. Socrates does not spell out the implications of this analysis for the possibility or impossibility of eternal happiness for beings such as ourselves, should we be granted immortality. Would it be necessary always to find new fields in which to make progress to keep life from growing insipid? Or is the pleasure we take in progress only a second best to the fully developed capacities and complete understanding that would satisfy us most?

9. On the other hand, Xenophon does not present the unattractiveness of life in decline as in itself sufficient reason to end one's life. He indicates at 4.8.1 that Socrates was also moved by the prospect of fame, which he no doubt sought mainly for the sake of the followers who would thereby be protected and even drawn to philosophy. If philosophy were not in such danger in Athens, Socrates might well have learned to find his chief pleasure in things other than his own progress, especially in watching the progress of his students, which would of course also be seeing his own "noble work" (2.1.31).

REFERENCES

Bruell, Christopher. 1994. Introduction to Xenophon, *Memorabilia,* trans. Amy L. Bonnette. Ithaca, NY: Cornell University Press.

Lorch, Benjamin. 2010. "Xenophon's Socrates on Political Ambition and Political Philosophy." *Review of Politics* 72: 189–211.

Strauss, Leo. 1972. *Xenophon's Socrates.* Ithaca, NY: Cornell University Press. Reprint, South Bend, IN: St. Augustine's Press, 1998.

Xenophon. 1994. *Memorabilia.* Trans. and annot. Amy L. Bonnette. Ithaca, NY: Cornell University Press.

Chapter Two

The Complexity of Divine Speech and the Quest for the Ideas in Plato's *Euthyphro*

Ann Ward

The postmodern political philosopher Richard Rorty accuses religion of taking the "God's-eye point of view." Positing universal moral truths that transcend particular historical and cultural contexts, the religious view is problematic according to Rorty because "when we gave up on God" we also gave up on "tru[th] in an unconditional sense" (Rorty 1990, 633–36). The absence of divine presence is crucial to Rorty's rejection of the notion of an absolute truth unconditioned by particular time and place, because he does not believe that reason alone in abstraction from the divine can give us certainty of any such universals. Given reason's inability to rise above the particularities of cultural and historical context, Rorty turns to the concept of "redescription," which he associates with Kundera's understanding of the "wisdom of the novel," as a more authentic means for individual engagement with the world.

Rorty, like Kundera, rejects the tendency of religion and philosophy to claim absolute truths in favor of the novelist's tendency toward "relative truths" or different perspectives of different individuals, societies, and cultures. The novelist gives full hearing to all particular persons, actions, and situations; they are not right or wrong but merely different. The "wisdom of the novel," therefore, lies in its ability to include or "redescribe" every possible perspective of every particular situation and person (Rorty 1990, 638–39).

Classical political philosophy has much to contribute to this contemporary debate concerning human access to unconditioned moral truth. In her monumental work, *Plato's Philosophers: The Coherence of the Dialogues,* Catherine Zuckert argues that in the first three of the eight Platonic dialogues leading up to Socrates' trial and death, Socrates, like Rorty, seeks to demonstrate how difficult it is for human beings to acquire knowledge (Zuckert 2009, 596). In the *Theaetetus, Euthyphro,* and *Cratylus,* Socrates illustrates how neither geometry, nor piety, nor language gives wisdom to human beings (596, 639–40). In the *Euthyphro* in particular, Socrates tries to show his interlocutor that he does not have knowledge of divine things, thus bringing to light the limits of reason in its attempt to understand the gods. Zuckert denies, however, that Socrates goes as far as Rorty to give up the philosophical life and rational pursuit of truth altogether. Rather, Socrates, as Zuckert argues, shows that human reason, through investigation of moral opinion, can discover things about the world in which it lives. For instance, in rationally demonstrating Euthyphro's inability to give a satisfactory definition of piety, Socrates reveals the contradiction at the heart of the traditional understanding of the gods in ancient Greece. Euthyphro and his fellow Athenians believe simultaneously that the gods are enforcers of justice and that they can be corrupted, through prayers and sacrifices, into favoring particular communities and human beings (644–46, 648–49).

In this chapter I argue that Plato, through the *Euthyphro,* illustrates and explores positions on truth and morality similar to the claims of relativity and objectivity in the contemporary debate concerning knowledge of moral truth. Euthyphro's father believes that pious obedience to the gods requires that we punish those guilty of murder. However, the complexity of the unique contexts in which human wrongdoing occurs makes interpretation of divine will, although necessary, impossible to confirm. Euthyphro, on the other hand, in his wish to prosecute his father for murder, believes that piety is imitation of rather than simply obedience to the divine. Interpretation of divine will is unnecessary as the particulars can be ignored in the application of universal principles. Euthyphro's father thus suffers from a moral paralysis arising out of the particularities of the situation, whereas his son is possessed of a moral certainty that results from his moral absolutism.

Through the action of the dialogue Plato suggests that both moral absolutism and moral paralysis can be destructive of human life. I argue, therefore, like Zuckert, that Plato encourages a moral perspective that mediates between certainty of moral knowledge and suspicion of moral ignorance. Socrates is seen pushing Euthyphro toward such a median position by pointing to the complex way in which divine things, such as the "idea" of the pious, reveal themselves to human beings. Socrates' moderation of Euthyphro reaffirms the value of the family in grounding human life. Yet Socrates also suggests that in our confrontation with the apparent injustices of life, pious love of the gods can be transcended by the philosophic quest for the "ideas."

MORAL PARALYSIS VERSUS MORAL ABSOLUTISM

The positions of moral paralysis and moral absolutism appear at the beginning of the dialogue. They are first revealed when we learn why Euthyphro, like Socrates, is at the "Porch of the King," the public building in Athens where judicial cases involving impiety were tried. Euthyphro, who characterizes himself as a prophet with perfect knowledge of divine things, informs Socrates that he has brought a lawsuit against his own father (3c, 4a).[1] The crime for which Euthyphro thinks his father deserves punishment is the "murder" of a hired laborer working for the family when they were farming on Naxos. According to Euthyphro, in a drunken rage this hired man slit the throat of one of the family's servants. In response, Euthyphro's father bound the man and threw him into a ditch, meanwhile sending to Athens for an "exegete" to give him guidance on how to proceed according to the sacred and ancestral laws of the city (see West 1998, 44; Allen 1970, 18). While waiting, Euthyphro's father neglected the man, and he died from exposure before the exegete could reach Naxos from Athens (4c–d).

Socrates' initial reaction to Euthyphro's lawsuit is one of shock. He expresses doubts as to the wisdom of Euthyphro's course of action against his father, saying, "Surely you wouldn't proceed against him for murder on behalf of an outsider" (4b). Socrates' doubts are confirmed as Euthyphro, showing a positive hostility to the principles that underlie the private family, responds:

> It's laughable, Socrates, that you suppose that it makes any difference whether the dead man is an outsider or of the family, rather than that one should be on guard only for whether the killer killed with justice or not; and if it was with justice, to let it go, but if not, to proceed against him—if, that is, the killer shares your hearth and table. For the pollution turns out to be equal if you knowingly associate with such a man and do not purify yourself, as well as him, by proceeding against him in a lawsuit. (4c)

Euthyphro's assumptions in this response are indeed destructive to the private family (see Edwards 2002, 213, 221; but also Saxonhouse 1988, 283–85). He assumes equality between parent and child that allows the son to punish the errant father, reversing the familial order of power and respect. He disregards the bodily connections between parent and child that normally give the father authority over the son; he expresses a belief in a radical individualism that facilitates the prosecution of wrongdoers even if they are parents. Euthyphro's implicit justification for assuming this superiority over the father is his superior knowledge not simply of the pious things but of justice as well (4e). Only knowledge, Euthyphro implies, grants title to rule. The justice that Euthyphro believes he has knowledge of is universal and unchanging. For Euthyphro, the standards of justice, required by the gods, apply equally to all; the gods demand "equality before the law," with no special exemptions (see Saxonhouse 1988, 288–89).

With Euthyphro's response the contrary moral positions of Euthyphro's father and Euthyphro himself are clearly brought to light. For Euthyphro's father, the most important fact is that the hired man killed one of his family's servants. Yet he doesn't know what to do and is unclear about what the sacred and ancestral laws prescribe in this case; after all, the man was drunk at the time he committed the murder. Due to his lack of clarity, he sends for an exegete, thus suggesting that there is no simple answer to the situation; life as immediately experienced is complex and ambiguous and requires expert interpretation. When the exegete fails to arrive and Euthyphro's father is unable to act, the hired man dies. Euthyphro's father thus symbolizes the moral paralysis that follows from moral ignorance. His ignorance consists in the fact that although he believes pious adherence to the gods' will requires that the guilty be punished, the complexity of the various contexts in which human wrongdoing occurs means that universal standards of justice cannot be equally applied in every case. The particular thwarts the universal and conditions what piety would be.

For Euthyphro, on the other hand, moral decision making is easy: the hired man died because of the father's neglect, and he knows exactly what to do. For Euthyphro, there is no ambiguity about what divine will prescribes in individual cases. As a result of such certainty, he does not send for an exegete; there is no need for interpretation because life is simple rather than complex and can be clearly understood. Unlike his father, Euthyphro is a man of action, driven by moral certainty issuing from moral absolutism. For Euthyphro, divine will is easily understood because it commands universal, absolute standards that transcend the various contexts in which human action takes place. The requirements of piety are simple because particulars can be ignored in favor of universal principles, rendering interpretation of divine intention superfluous (but see Burt 2002, 153; Allen 1970, 22–23; also see Egan 1983, 20–23, 26).

SOCRATES' MEDIATION: THE IDEA OF THE PIOUS

Plato, through the action of the dialogue, suggests that both the moral ignorance of Euthyphro's father, which results in the death of the hired man, and the moral absolutism of Euthyphro, which leads to the prosecution of his father and hostility within the family, are destructive to human life and hence morally problematic. It would appear, therefore, that Plato encourages a moral perspective that takes account of both the universal and the particular, or a middle position between the harsh certainty of moral knowledge and the paralyzing humility of moral ignorance. Plato presents Socrates pushing Euthyphro toward this middle position. Socrates begins this mediation when he requests that Euthyphro teach him what the pious and impious are (4e–5a). Socrates asks not simply for an example of the pious, but for the pious "itself" or the "idea" of the pious (6e). Socrates wants to know from Euthyphro:

> What sort of things do you say the pious and impious are, concerning murder and concerning other things? Or isn't the pious itself the same as itself in every action, and again, isn't the impious opposite to everything pious, while it itself is similar to itself and has one certain *idea* in accordance with impiety—everything, that is, that is going to be impious (5d).

Socrates, in asking for the idea of the pious, wants to know the universal characteristic that each act of piety shares (see Plato, *Republic* 476a–b; Nichols 1988, 112; Allen 1970, 28–29, 67–69). He wants the "definition," as it were, of piety, not a specific example of a pious action such as obeying one's elders, sacrificing to the gods, or abstaining from murder (see Mann 1998, 129–31; Furley 1985, 201). By requesting that the universal characteristic shared by all the different instances of a thing, in this case the pious, be articulated, Socrates illustrates that his main interest is in the "nature" of the things themselves. Euthyphro's struggle to comply with Socrates' request demonstrates that the nature or idea of the pious is not readily apparent but rather reveals and conceals itself simultaneously.

The complex way in which the ideas manifest themselves is illustrated in Socrates' refutation of Euthyphro's first attempt to give a definition of piety. According to Euthyphro, the pious is "what I am doing now," to proceed against a wrongdoer regardless of whether he or she is a father or a mother (5e). The source of Euthyphro's certainty is the actions of the gods themselves, as the poets maintain that Zeus punished his father, Kronos, for injustice and that Kronos in turn punished his father, Ouronos, for injustice (5e–6a). Thus, for Euthyphro, proceeding against wrongdoers, even if they are one's familial superiors, is imitating the gods (see Zuckert 2009, 649; Desjardins 2004, 179; Bruell 1999, 123; West 1998, 13; Furley 1985, 203–5; Strauss 1989, 197–99; Egan 1983, 18–19, 29–31). However, in response to Socrates' question whether he really believes that the stories of the gods warring among themselves are true, Euthyphro says, "Not only these, Socrates, but as I said just now, I will also explain many other things to you . . . about the divine things; and . . . I know well that you will be astounded" (6c). If the pious is imitating the gods, but the gods do more things than proceed against wrongdoers, then Euthyphro has given only a particular example of the pious, not the idea of the pious itself. Socrates chides Euthyphro for this error when he says:

> Do you remember that I didn't bid you to teach me some one or two of the many pious things, but that *eidos* itself by which all the pious things are pious? For surely you were saying that it is by one *idea* that the impious things are impious and the pious things pious. Or don't you remember? (6e)

Euthyphro's first example of piety—proceeding against wrongdoers—which he intended to serve as the definition of the pious, illustrates the way in which the idea of the pious simultaneously reveals and conceals itself in the particular. Euthyphro can call "proceeding against wrongdoers" pious because it possesses that common characteristic that all other pious acts share. The idea of the pious is in the example, or reveals itself to us when we proceed against wrongdoers (Burger 2000, 45). Yet the idea of the pious also conceals itself in the example of "proceeding against wrongdoers." The latter is only an example of piety and not the pious itself; it is only an incomplete part of the whole that is the idea of piety, or only a half truth, so to speak, rather than the whole truth. The idea of the pious, therefore, in its particular examples reveals and conceals itself at the same time.

Socrates' request for the idea of the pious pushes Euthyphro toward a middle position between the paralysis of his father and the absolutism of his moral universals (Burger 2000, 57–58). The remarkable aspect of Socrates' method is that in asking for the idea, Socrates, like Euthyphro, looks to the universal (but see Saxonhouse 1988, 289–90, 292). Yet Plato presents Socrates' search for the universal in a way that undermines rather than reaffirms Euthyphro's moral certainty. In showing Euthyphro that he does not indeed know what the pious is, Socrates appears to erode Euthyphro's confidence in proceeding against his father (but see Burt 2002, 154).

After failing at the first attempt to define piety, Euthyphro tries again, asserting that "what is dear to the gods is pious, and what is not dear is impious" (7a). Socrates, however, points to the fact that they have just agreed that the gods war with each other over definitions of the just, the noble, and the good (7d–e). Thus "punishing your father" is something "dear to Zeus but hateful to Kronos and Ouronos" (8b) (see Bruell 1999, 131; Strauss 1989, 199). Socrates refutes Euthyphro by illustrating that according to the latter's second definition an act (punishing one's father) can be both pious and impious at the same time. This is illogical, and the definition fails. Ironically, Euthyphro, the one wedded to universals, has again given an example of the pious and not its universal idea.

THE IDEAS AS ALTERNATIVE TO THE GODS?

On Socrates' insistence Euthyphro tries a third time to articulate the idea of the pious. According to Euthyphro, "the pious is whatever all the gods love, and . . . whatever all the gods hate, is impious" (9e) (see Mann 1998, 125). Socrates' third refutation takes the form of the following question:

> Is the pious loved by the gods because it is pious,
> Or is it pious because it is loved [by the gods]? (10a)

The first alternative posed by Socrates' question—the pious is loved by the gods because it *is pious*—suggests that there is something intrinsic to the pious itself that makes it lovable to the gods (Alston 2002, 290–91; Bruell 1999, 129; but see Paxson 1972, 175–76). The focus is on the object loved and not the will of the gods. If this alternative is true, then piety is a universal, objective standard, independent of the particular wills of the gods. The second alternative posed by Socrates' question—the pious is pious because it *is loved by the gods*—suggests that there is nothing intrinsic to the pious itself that makes it lovable. Rather standards of piety come in an arbitrary way from the particular wills of the gods. The focus is on the subject doing the loving and not the loved object itself. If this alternative is true, then piety is a particular, subjective standard, dependent on the wills of the gods (see Zuckert 2009, 646–47; Burger 2000, 50; Wainwright 2005, 73–75, 80; Alston 2002, 285; Burt 2002, 153–54; but see Macbeath 1982, 566–67; Hall 1968, 8).

The tension that Socrates is trying to bring to light with his question is that between love of the good and love of one's own. For instance, if the gods love the pious because of something intrinsic to the latter, perhaps that intrinsic thing is its goodness, such goodness being the idea of the pious that Socrates is looking for (see Plato, *Republic* 509b–c; MacKinnon and Meynell 1972, 215–16; but see Macbeath 1982, 567–68; MacKinnon and Meynell 1972, 228). If, however, the gods love the pious because it is dear to them, and hence because it is theirs, then what the gods really love is their own will (see Strauss 1989, 201–2; Cohen 1971, 173, 175). As this tension concerning what the gods actually love makes clear, the answer to Socrates' question is not neutral with regard to piety. The pious answer to Socrates' question about the pious appears to be the second alternative (see Wisdo 1987, 222–24; MacKinnon and Meynell 1972, 224; but see Macbeath 1982, 568–69; MacKinnon and Meynell 1972, 212, 215). If something is pious because it is *loved by the gods,* then human beings wishing to be pious must rely on the gods to reveal their passionate will to them. Hence one cannot be and love the pious without loving and knowing the gods. The first alternative, however, appears to make the gods inessential. If the gods love the pious because it *is pious,* because there is something intrinsic to the pious itself that makes it lovable, then the pious is independent of the gods' love. Thus the gods would be unnecessary with respect to piety, as we too could love the pious without knowledge of what the gods love or even of the gods themselves. We would then love the idea of the pious, not the gods; the idea would replace the gods as the object of our affection (see Wainwright 2005, 291; Burger 2000, 51; Bruell 1999, 127, 129–30; West 1998, 14–15; Wisdo 1987, 222–23; Strauss 1989, 291; Paxson 1972, 189; Sharvy 1972, 127–30; MacKinnon and Meynell 1972, 223–24; but see Macbeath 1982, 568–69; Hall 1968, 9, 11). Socrates opens up this possibility when he poses his question in response to Euthyphro's third definition of piety.

Euthyphro fails again to define the pious when, confused by Socrates, he affirms both alternatives. In response to Socrates' persistent questioning, Euthyphro at first maintains that the pious is loved by the gods because it *is pious* and then maintains the opposite, that the pious is pious because it is *loved by the gods* (10d–e). In contradicting himself, Euthyphro again speaks illogically (but see Cohen 1971, 162). However, in getting Euthyphro to affirm both alternatives—the pious is an intrinsic quality of the object loved by the gods, and the pious is obeying the particular will of the gods who love—Socrates has begun to move Euthyphro into a middle position between his original adherence to universality and the moral absolutism that flows from it, and the moderating affect of particularity. Socrates' mediation between these two extremes will continue in his refutation of Euthyphro's fourth attempt to define what the pious is.

THE FAMILY REAFFIRMED

In his fourth and final attempt to say what the idea of the pious is, Euthyphro defines piety as that part of justice which involves "tendance of the gods" through sacrifice and prayer (12d, 13a, 14d). This definition is more compatible with the second alternative above, that the pious is pious because it is *loved by the gods* (see Zuckert 2009, 646–47, 649). Moreover, in tending to the gods, the pious human being is like a slave who provides "skillful service to gods" to help the latter do better their proper work (13d, 14d). This claim begs the question that Socrates then asks: what proper work or product does skillful human service help the gods provide? (13e, 14a). Euthyphro's answer to this question is remarkable considering his lawsuit against his father; indeed Socrates implies that he shames himself in articulating it (14c). According to Euthyphro:

> If someone has knowledge of how to say and do things gratifying to the gods by praying and sacrificing, these are the pious things. And such things preserve private families as well as the communities of cities. The opposite of the things gratifying are impious, and they overturn and destroy everything. (14b)

The proper work of the gods is to preserve private families and cities. Why is Euthyphro shamed by this answer? Because he is forced to admit that proceeding against his father may actually be impious (but see Desjardins 2004, 181, 185). Thus Euthyphro maintains two things that he had previously denied. First, he implies the sacredness of the family, or of the special bodily connections between parents and children. Knowledge, therefore, in abstraction from the body, does not now for Euthyphro grant sole title to rule and does not give the son the right to proceed against his father. Second, Euthyphro has admitted a harmony between the family and the city. The family is part of the city, and the gods, in helping human beings preserve private families, also help them preserve cities. Euthyphro is embarrassed in having to affirm this because it contradicts the assumptions underlying his first definition of piety. When he had said that the pious is proceeding against wrongdoers regardless of whether they are family members, Euthyphro took the perspective of the city. The city, which regards both fathers and sons as equal citizens and treats criminals equally regardless of their familial status, applies universal standards of justice equally to all. The city aims to "equality before the law" regardless of family relations or connections. The family and the city seem to be at odds (see Saxonhouse 1988, 283–85, 288–89). Now, however, Euthyphro presents the family and the city as consonant.

Although still taking the perspective of the city that he believes is supported by the gods, Euthyphro now allows both aspects of the city to come to the surface. The city emphasizes particularity and universality simultaneously, as the city recognizes that it is composed of private families that are its parts at the same time that it tries to be more than its parts; individuals are not just members of families, but equal citizens. Hence the city recognizes its reliance on the particular attachments that exist between members of private families at the same time that it aims for universal standards or laws that apply equally to all. These two sides of the city also point to the need to combine love of one's own with love of the good, the discussion of which surfaced in response to Euthyphro's third definition of piety. When the city recognizes that it is composed of particular families, it permits persons, such as Euthyphro, to love their family because it is theirs; we respect and cherish the private bodily connections that unite us as family members. However, when the city aspires to be more than the parts that compose it and applies universal standards to all, it implies that persons should love family members only if they are good; we should want to love family members because they are good or worthy of love and not simply because they are ours.

It appears that by the end of the dialogue Euthyphro has been pushed by Socrates into a middle position between the moral paralysis of his father and the moral absolutism with which he began, thereby undermining his confidence in his prosecution. Thus we see Euthyphro leave the "Porch of the King" at the end of the dialogue rather than continue with the public proceeding against his father as he had originally planned (15d–e). Socrates shakes Euthyphro's confidence by turning to the question of the idea of the pious and hence implicitly raising the issue of the complex way in which the ideas reveal themselves to human beings. He attempts to illustrate to Euthyphro that in the particular examples of piety the idea of the pious both reveals and conceals itself at the same time. The deceptive side of the idea of the pious manifests itself in Euthyphro's first two attempts to define or say what the pious is. Both attempts fail because they turn out to be particular examples of piety, or "half truths," rather than piety itself or the "whole truth" that is the idea of the pious. In his third attempt to define the pious, Euthyphro, confused, affirms that piety is both an idea or an intrinsic quality and contingent on the particular wills of the gods.

Socrates makes Euthyphro aware that he lacks knowledge of what the pious and the impious actually are. The immediate effect on Euthyphro of this newly gained knowledge of ignorance is to reaffirm the value of the family in its relationship to the city. Yet, although the family may enmesh us in a web of biological and civic relationships that can give grounding to our lives, Socrates' methodology also points us to the life of philosophy. The philosophic life engages with and confronts the potential groundlessness of life not simply by seeking to discover and love the gods but also by seeking to discover and love the ideas or the nature of things.

NOTE

1. Plato, *Euthyphro*, in *Four Texts on Socrates*, trans. Thomas G. West and Grace Starry West (Ithaca, NY: Cornell University Press, 1998). All subsequent citations are from this edition.

REFERENCES

Allen, R. E. 1970. *Plato's Euthyphro and the Earlier Theory of Forms.* New York: Humanities Press.

Alston, William P. 2002. "What Euthyphro Should Have Said." In *Philosophy of Religion: A Reader and Guide,* ed. William Lane Craig, 283–302. New Brunswick, NJ: Rutgers University Press.

Bruell, Christopher. 1999. *On the Socratic Education: An Introduction to the Shorter Platonic Dialogues.* Lanham, MD: Rowman & Littlefield.

Burger, Ronna. 2000. "Making New Gods: On Plato's Euthyphro." In *Plato and Platonism,* ed. Johannes M. Van Ophuijsen, 35–39. Washington, DC: Catholic University of America Press.

Burt, John. 2002. "Reason Also Is Choice: Reflection, Freedom, and the Euthyphro Problem." In *Never Again Would Birds' Song Be the Same: New Essays on Poetry and Poetics, Renaissance to Modern,* 147–89. New Haven: Yale University Press.

Cohen, S. Marc. 1971. "Socrates on the Definition of Piety: *Euthyphro* 10A–11B." In *The Philosophy of Socrates: A Collection of Critical Essays,* ed. Gregory Vlastos, 158–76. Garden City, NY: Anchor Books.

Desjardins, Rosemary. 2004. *Plato and the Good: Illuminating the Darkling Vision.* Leiden: Brill.

Edwards, M. J. 2002. "In Defense of Euthyphro." *American Journal of Philology* 121: 213–24.

Egan, Rory B. 1983. "Tragic Piety in Plato's *Euthyphro.*" *Dionysius* 7 (Dec.): 17–32.

Furley, William D. 1985. "The Figure of Euthyphro in Plato's 'Dialogue.'" *Phronesis* 30 (2): 201–8.

Hall, John C. 1968. "Euthyphro 10a1–11a10." *Philosophical Quarterly* 8, no. 70 (Jan.): 1–11.

Macbeath, Murray. 1982. "The Euthyphro Dilemma." *Mind,* n.s., 91, no. 364 (Oct.): 565–71.

MacKinnon, D. M., and Hugo Meynell. 1972. "The Euthyphro Dilemma." *Proceedings of the Aristotelian Society, Supplementary Volumes,* vol. 46: 211–21, 223–34.

Mann, William E. 1998. "Piety: Lending a Hand to Euthyphro." *Philology and Phenomenological Research* 58, no. 1 (Mar.): 123–42.

Nichols, Mary P. 1988. *Socrates and the Political Community: An Ancient Debate.* Albany: State University of New York Press.

Owen, J. Judd. 2003. *Religion and the Demise of Liberal Rationalism: The Foundational Crisis in the Separation of Church and State.* Chicago: University of Chicago Press.

Paxson, Thomas D., Jr. 1972. "Plato's 'Euthyphro' 10a–11b." *Phronesis* 17 (2): 171–90.

Plato. 1968. *Republic.* Trans. Allan Bloom. New York: Basic Books.

Rorty, Richard. 1990. "On Truth, Freedom, and Politics." *Critical Inquiry* 16, no. 3 (Spring): 633–43.

Saxonhouse, Arlene W. 1988. "The Philosophy of the Particular and the Universality of the City: Socrates' Education of Euthyphro." *Political Theory* 16, no. 2 (May): 281–99.

Sharvy, Richard. 1972. "*Euthyphro* 9d–11b: Analysis and Definition in Plato and Others." *Nous* 6, no. 2 (May): 119–37.

Strauss, Leo. 1989. "On the Euthyphron." In *The Rebirth of Classical Political Rationalism: An Introduction to the Thought of Leo Strauss,* 187–206. Chicago: University of Chicago Press.

Wainwright, William J. 2005. *Religion and Morality.* Aldershot: Ashgate.

West, Thomas G. 1998. *Four Texts on Socrates.* Trans. Thomas G. West and Grace Starry West. Ithaca, NY: Cornell University Press.

Wisdo, David. 1987. "Kierkegaard and Euthyphro." *Philosophy* 62, no. 240 (Apr.): 221–26.

Zuckert, Catherine. 2009. *Plato's Philosophers: The Coherence of the Dialogues.* Chicago: University of Chicago Press.

Chapter Three

Politics and Philosophy in Aristotle's Critique of Plato's *Laws*

KEVIN M. CHERRY

Whether on matters of politics or physics, Aristotle's criticism of his predecessors is not generally considered a model of charitable interpretation. He seems to prefer, as Christopher Rowe puts it, "polemic over accuracy" (2003, 90). His criticism of the *Laws* is particularly puzzling: It is much shorter than his discussion of the *Republic* and raises primarily technical objections of questionable validity. Indeed, some well-known commentators have concluded the criticisms, as we have them in the *Politics,* were made of an earlier draft of the *Laws* and that Plato, in light of these criticisms, revised the final version.[1] I hope to suggest, however, that these incongruities should lead us to look beyond Aristotle's explicit criticisms to an issue he also omits while discussing the *Republic,* namely, the character of philosophy and its place in political life.

Before turning to examine the *Laws* itself, Aristotle makes a curious remark, often read as stating that Socrates is the principal philosopher of the *Laws*.[2] Discussing the differences between the *Republic* and the *Laws*, Aristotle says that "all the speeches of Socrates [πάντες οἱ τοῦ Σοκράτους λόγοι] are extraordinary; they are sophisticated, original, and searching [τὸ ζητητικόν]. But it is perhaps difficult to do everything finely" (*Politics* 1265a10–13).[3]

By referring to "all" the Socratic speeches, Aristotle is obviously including more than one dialogue, and it is perhaps tempting to assume that he intends to include the *Laws*. Yet Aristotle never states that the Athenian Stranger is Socrates or that Socrates appears in the *Laws*. Indeed, given the context, Aristotle may well be contrasting Socrates and the Athenian. For what he finds most praiseworthy about the Socratic dialogues—their searching, or zetetic, character—seems to be wholly absent from the *Laws*. Sinclair and Saunders thus wonder whether Aristotle's reference is "an ironic joke, the ponderous lecturing being a poor replacement for the scintillating conversation of Socrates" (in Aristotle 1992, 120).

What Aristotle suggests here is that there is a difference between Socrates and the Athenian, a difference that is as philosophic as it is political.[4] While Aristotle's explicit account focuses on the political institutions proposed by the Athenian, these criticisms bring us around to the philosophic dispute. That is, we must consider how zetetic the Athenian Stranger is.

THE MIXED REGIME

Aristotle is quite clear that neither the *Republic* nor the *Laws* offers proper guidance for political life, yet his *Politics* has far more in common with the institutions prescribed by the Athenian Stranger. This should not be surprising, for both emphasize learning from the successes, and more frequently failures, of other cities (e.g., *Laws* 691b–92c, 722b, 892de, 968b; *Politics* V–VI). Unlike Plato's Socrates, the Athenian claims to have traveled extensively and engaged in the study of existing constitutions recommended by Aristotle at the conclusion of the *Nicomachean Ethics* (1181a10 ff.), and he recommends that the rulers of the city do the same and incorporate their own experiences into law (639d–e, 772b, 846c, 951bc, 957b).[5]

Perhaps as a result of this shared reliance on political experience, both the Athenian Stranger and Aristotle recommend a mixed, or moderate, regime.[6] There are, however, significant differences in how each understands such a mixture. Given the pious character of the *Laws,* it is unsurprising that the Athenian divinizes the argument for the mixed regime.[7] He ascribes the development of the mixed regime in Sparta to a god (691d–92c, 691d8) and relies on a myth about the age of Kronos to justify the rule of law (713c ff.).[8] A god facilitated the development of a mixed regime in Sparta, allowing her to avoid the evils that befell her fellow cities, and the Athenian suggests that we need only learn from the god's work (692b–c).[9] In the age of Kronos gods cared for human beings, and so we should recognize that in the absence of a god we must subordinate our rulers to laws, the closest thing to the divine we have (714a).

For the Athenian Stranger, the conflict between the various kinds of rule is ultimately irreconcilable.[10] He identifies seven different claims to rule: that of parents over children, the well born over the not well born, the elder over the younger, masters over slaves, the strong over the weak (which elicits an enthusiastic affirmation from the Cretan Clinias, cf. 625b–26c), the prudent over the ignorant (which the Athenian praises), and that of the lucky or, more charitably, the dear to the gods (690a–d). A lawgiver must somehow incorporate them all in order to avoid faction, the great evil in cities (628a–c). In determining what regime would be appropriate for their colony, the Athenian asks his Dorian counterparts whether they live in monarchies, tyrannies, democracies, oligarchies, or tyrannies. They are unable to answer, for they find elements of the different kinds of regimes—save oligarchy—within their own. The Athenian is pleased, commenting that in most cities one part of the city enslaves the others (712c–13a). Therefore, their laws exist to benefit only a part of the city, and the city is divided into factions [στασιώτης]. Thanks to the intervention of the god, laws in the cities of Clinias and Megillus pursue "what is common to the whole city" (715b), and it is only cities such as these that are worthy of the name "regime" (713a). Indeed, all other cities—democracies, oligarchies, even monarchies—are, effectively, nonregimes [οὐ πολιτείας] (832b10).[11] Aristotle concedes that the city described by the Athenian Stranger is indeed a polity, or regime [πολιτείαν] (1265b26–28).[12]

Aristotle alludes to this discussion in his own division of regimes in Book III of the *Politics.* He initially distinguishes regimes on the basis of whether they pursue the common or private good and the number of rulers, referring to the regime in which the multitude rules for the sake of the common benefit as the one that has "the name common to all regimes" [τὸ κοινὸν ὄνομα πασῶν τῶν πολιτειῶν], that is, polity [πολιτεία] (1279a38–39). This is an odd locution, of course, and has been the subject of much commentary, but in light of the Athenian's comment it makes perfect sense. The "polity," as Aristotle's mixed regime is generally translated, is described by him as the rule of the multitude for the common advantage. Due, however, to the limitations of the multitude—most citizens are incapable of possessing the fullness of virtue—the polity achieves the common advantage only by incorporating the wealthy and virtuous alongside the multitude. Insofar as the polity attempts to secure the genuinely common advantage rather than the advantage of the many poor or few rich it meets the condition the Athenian sets out for being appropriately called a "regime." It is the regime that is, and should be, called regime. From Aristotle's perspective, it is the regime that most fully instantiates the character of political communities as communities of free and equal, though different, citizens, who alternate ruling and being ruled.

Aristotle argues for the mixed regime on the basis of opinions about political equality advanced by oligarchs and democrats; ignoring either opinion would be not only destabilizing but also unjust (1280a9 ff., 1301a25 ff.). The virtuous contribute more to the city's higher, truest, end—that of living well or nobly—and so they have a "greater part" in ruling, but the wealthy and free do make contributions and so should have some, if a lesser, part (1281a2–8). While the Athenian emphasizes the necessity of having checks on people in power and appeasing the many who would not be satisfied with the rule of the virtuous, Aristotle's case for the mixed regime is at least partially based on the positive contributions made by different groups to the polis (1281a40 ff., 1283a24 ff.; cf. 1309B16–19). By contrast, the Athenian's inclusion of democratic institutions such as the lot seems to be due only to the "necessity" fostered by the many's refusal to accept "strict justice" rather than any contribution they make (757de).

Aristotle agrees that reconciling the various claims to rule can be difficult, but he suggests the challenge is less formidable than the Athenian Stranger proposes. Some of the claims belong not in the polis, according to Aristotle, but rather the household, and others, he argues, are solved by nature. Whereas the Athenian suggests that the various claims to rule are "by nature opposed to one another," Aristotle instead asserts that nature helps solve this problem by distinguishing the young from the old (*Laws* 690d2–3; *Politics* 1332b35 ff.). Young citizens, endowed with strength, are well suited for military service, which enables them to acquire the necessary experience of being ruled, as well as some familiarity with the advantageous and just, before they become rulers (1329a2 ff.). Later in life they will serve as priests, for it would be improper for anyone other than citizens to honor the gods (1329a26 ff.). The tensions within the mixed regime are less pronounced for Aristotle than for the Athenian Stranger.[13]

THE RULE OF *NOUS* AND THE NOCTURNAL COUNCIL

In order to avoid having one class ruling, the Athenian Stranger insists that the city ought to be ruled by "whatever within us partakes of immortality, giving the name 'law' to the distribution ordained by intelligence" (714a). It is difficult to see how the various offices within the city will reflect intelligence until the Athenian introduces the Nocturnal Council in Books X and XII. The Council comprises many of the most important officials in the city, and its ability to alter the laws (whether explicitly or, more likely, through interpretation) means that its members, in fact, rule.[14] The rule of law may be the closest parallel to the rule of *nous,* but *nous* comes to be in the laws only through the actions of the Nocturnal Council. As the Athenian says, once in place the Council will have the city turned over to it (969b).

To be sure, the presence of philosophy is muted in the *Laws.* The word occurs only twice (857d2, 967c8).[15] That is, at least in part, because the Athenian's interlocutors show little capacity for it. They do, however, show a willingness to accept it in their polis: Clinias accepts transcending the laws in order to prove the existence of the gods, and the Athenian indicates that "unfamiliar arguments" will be necessary (891d–e)—the very arguments to be studied by the Nocturnal Council (966e). This is not to suggest that all the members of the Council will be philosophers. Rather, it is to highlight the requirement that members of the Council receive an advanced education in order to pursue philosophical questions of a certain kind (818a), even if for practical purposes rather than the love and acquisition of wisdom (968c ff.).[16] Most citizens, by contrast, will accept these teachings almost as if they were slaves, without being able to explain them (966b, 967d–68a).

As in the *Republic,* philosophy thus comes to rule in the city.[17] Both Socrates and the Athenian Stranger claim that rulers must philosophize if politics is to be successful (cf. *Republic* 473d) and that the city's institutions must provide a place for philosophizing. Indeed, from Aristotle's perspective, the Athenian's reliance on philosophy is more problematic than that of Socrates, insofar as the Athenian turns the city over to philosophy without saying so explicitly. Aristotle is skeptical of efforts to deceive the people (1297a7–10).[18] However, I would suggest that Aristotle also finds the content of the Athenian's philosophy more problematic than that of Socrates.

As Catherine Zuckert has shown, the two investigations the Athenian Stranger assigns to the Nocturnal Council are ultimately incompatible (2009, 143–46). The first task described by the Athenian Stranger is to come to understand the nature of virtue: How is it both one and four—that is, how is there "virtue" but also courage, moderation, justice, and prudence (965d)? How does virtue relate to what is beautiful and good (966a)? These inquiries point, of course, to the Socratic investigations recounted in Plato's dialogues, searching for the unchanging ideas. However, the Athenian also insists that the Nocturnal Council investigate the motion of the heavenly bodies on which he based his theology in Book X of the *Laws.* These bodies, as we shall see, are not only in constant motion—and thus not unchanging—but also are, at least in part, in irregular motion. The Athenian's account points in both Socratic and pre-Socratic directions and is ultimately incoherent.[19]

Aristotle would doubt whether either of these inquiries is necessary or useful for statesmen. His criticism of the form or idea of the Good in the *Nicomachean Ethics* (1096a11 ff.) suggests that a similar knowledge of virtue, or the various forms it takes, might be equally unhelpful in helping us become virtuous. In addition to his own catalog of virtues in the *Nicomachean Ethics,* Aristotle praises Socrates' sparring partner Gorgias for enumerating the variety, rather than investigating the unity, of the virtues (*Politics* 1260a24–28), particularly insofar as virtuous action differs for each kind of person (1259b18 ff.). It is not that virtue is unimportant for political life but rather that making people virtuous might not require philosophic knowledge of the virtues.

The more critical error for Aristotle, I think, is the Athenian's emphasis on cosmology as the basis for political order. It is clear throughout the *Laws* that the Athenian's argument for the existence and providence of the gods is central to his enterprise. While it is Clinias who states that the proof of the gods' existence and providence would be the best and noblest [κάλλιστόν τε καὶ ἄριστον] of the preludes (887c1–2; cf. 726a ff., 907d1–2), the Athenian does not disagree—and given the emphasis on piety throughout the dialogue, it is hard to see how he could. Aristotle, however, suggests that such knowledge might be unnecessary for, if not dangerous to, political life. In his treatment of the intellectual virtues in Book VI of the *Nicomachean Ethics,* he draws a careful yet firm distinction between the virtues of *phronēsis* and *sophia.* The former involves human action, that which can be otherwise, and it takes a variety of forms, including acting for one's own end as well as legislating for a city (1140a1 ff., 1141b23–34). *Sophia,* by contrast, is the most precise kind of knowledge insofar as it is directed at the highest objects (1141a9 ff.) and seems to provide little guidance in the exercise of *phronēsis,* which may be why people with experience often make better choices than those with wisdom. Popular views about the soul, for instance, are sufficient for guiding legislators in their effort to guide citizens to virtue. The prospective legislator must know that humans possess both rational and irrational parts of the soul, in order to employ both parts in leading citizens to virtue (*NE* 1102a18–26). He would not need to know what is argued in the *De Anima,* in which Aristotle denies that the soul is divided or even divisible (411b5 ff.; cf. *NE* 1102a30–31).

Moreover, to base a political community on these arguments about the gods is to place politics on an unstable foundation, for Aristotle emphasizes that, due to their distance from us, our knowledge of the heavenly bodies is, and must remain, uncertain.[20] The best that we can do is offer arguments that are likely (e.g., *De Caelo* 286a3 ff., 291b24 ff.). The Athenian Stranger also acknowledges this, indicating that his argument will go only so far as human power is capable of knowing these things (966c; cf. *Timaeus* 28c). Despite this, the Athenian proceeds as though the truth about the soul and the gods can be grasped on the basis of arguments that are not particularly difficult or lengthy (821e). By contrast, Aristotle contends that "in every way the soul is one of the most difficult things to get any assurance about" (*De Anima* 402a11–12).[21]

ORDER AND DISORDER IN NATURE AND POLITICS

The "unstable" foundation of a regime based on cosmology is compounded by the way in which the Athenian's inquiry into gods and soul reveals the universe to be at least partially disordered. The result of this is not only, as I noted earlier, a belief that the various claims to rule cannot be reconciled; it also implies a conception of nature that places human beings in a world that is at the very least unconcerned with human flourishing, if not survival.[22]

The argument about divine providence that fills most of Book X of the *Laws* is primarily intended to show the existence and priority of soul over body (892a–c). The Athenian discusses several kinds of motion, but these seem to be reducible to two fundamental kinds: motion that is capable of moving others but not itself and motion capable of moving itself as well as others (894b).[23] The latter motion is obviously eldest and strongest, and such a motion must be characteristic of soul (894d–96a). Insofar as this motion must be first, soul must be prior and superior to body (896c). What is surprising is that the Athenian makes soul the cause of all the motions—"good and bad, noble and shameful, just and unjust"—that we see in the universe (896d). It is only when soul is joined with intelligence (*nous*) that it produces what we usually call good, for example, happiness and order, while it produces the opposite when it lacks intelligence (897b).

The Athenian Stranger asserts that insofar as there are souls that possess every virtue, there must be gods, for what else could such souls be (899b)?[24] The argument continues to show that the gods display care [ἐπιμέλειαν] about human affairs, both great and small, because the gods could not lack any virtue, much less the knowledge necessary to order things (900d). The Athenian himself acknowledges that their argument is not entirely convincing and that some "mythic incantations" [ἐπῳδῶν . . . μύθων ἔτι τινῶν] are also necessary to persuade those who doubt the gods (903a–b; cf. 905d). However, while their myths assert that the gods "contrived" the universe so that virtue would triumph over vice, the Athenian compares the gods to doctors fighting disease or farmers faced with crop shortages (905e–6a). Such conflicts arise because heaven is full of both good and bad things, and, indeed, "there are more of the latter." The result is a universe characterized by "an immortal battle" [μάχη . . . ἀθάνατός] between good and evil (906a–b; cf. *Statesman* 273b–d). The gods may try to care for us, but their success is uncertain. Myths, therefore, are precisely what is necessary to convince the atheists of the second and third, if not the first, truths about the gods—that they care for human beings and cannot be bribed (903a–b).[25] The arguments offered by the Athenian seem to be insufficient for this purpose. Aristotle would not be surprised: The divine beings, or gods, must, according to his arguments, be uninterested in human life.

The philosophic view that the cosmos is characterized by disorderly as well as orderly motion is evident throughout the *Laws,* and it has more significance than being incompatible with the investigation into the being of the various virtues. The Athenian, for instance, claims that "almost all human affairs are matters of chance," due to the frequency of "accidents of every sort," such as war, poverty, disease, or bad weather (709a–b).[26] The account of the origins of cities that he provides in Book III is equally suggestive of "many disasters," such as floods and plagues, that befall and periodically destroy almost all human beings (678e–79a).[27] The Athenian's account of the universe places human beings in a precarious position.

Rather than beginning from abstract, and problematic, speculations about the gods, Aristotle instead begins, and believes philosophy should begin, with what is familiar to us and proceed from there (*Physics* 184a16–21).[28] Nature for Aristotle is not the product of a divine craftsman (cf. *Laws* 967b), although it is sufficiently analogous that Aristotle frequently speaks of nature itself as a craftsman with respect to the way that it regularly achieves its ends (e.g., *Physics* 199a12 ff.). Nature is sufficiently consistent that it achieves its ends either always or for the most part (*Physics* 199a1). Like the Athenian, Aristotle recognizes that there is disorder in the universe. Rather than posit a fundamental conflict between order and disorder, however, Aristotle suggests that the whole is, by and large, orderly and thus intelligible.

Both the Athenian Stranger and Aristotle admit three possibilities with respect to motion: Either all things are in motion, all things are at rest, or some things are in motion and some at rest (*Laws* 893bc; *Physics* 253a23 ff., 254a15 ff.). Both accept the last alternative, but Aristotle indicates that this answer is inadequate. We also must learn whether those things in motion are always in motion and those things at rest always at rest, whether all things are capable of being in motion and at rest or whether some things are always in motion, some things are always at rest and others capable of rest as well as motion. Aristotle, of course, opts for the last of these, and what is noteworthy in light of the Athenian's argument is Aristotle's effort to show that, in addition to things always in motion, some things are always at rest (*Physics* 254b3 ff.).

For Aristotle, that which is always at rest is the unmoved, or prime, mover. While the Athenian Stranger highlights soul as the first motion, Aristotle argues instead that the presence of something always in motion is reflective of the fact that there is something that causes motion without itself moving (*Physics* 257a27–32, 258b10–16; cf. *Metaphysics* 1071b3–6).[29] The unmoved mover moves other things not by moving itself but by being an object of desire and thought (*Metaphysics* 1071b20, 1072a26). In contrast to the views of the Athenian, this unmoved mover—which Aristotle identifies as god—is intellect, or thought, that thinks about only that which is "most divine and precious" without changing (1074b26). It contemplates itself and has no providential or creative purpose, nor does it possess the virtues (*NE* 1178b7 ff.).

In addition to arguing that motion depends on something that does not move, Aristotle doubts whether the soul can properly be said to move at all, although it can effect change and thus cause motion in other beings (*De Anima* 408b30 ff.). The highest characteristic of souls, Aristotle suggests, is the capacity to engage in thought (414b16–415a13) and thus achieve a higher level of perfection insofar as it more closely resembles the activity of the unmoved, and unmoving, mover (*Metaphysics* 1072b14 ff.). It is not humans but those beings which cannot be otherwise than they are, which exist unchanging and by necessity, that are by nature "most honorable" (*NE* 1139b18–24, 1141b3). We exercise our highest capacities to their fullest in coming to know them. The stability of those beings leads to stability throughout the universe.[30]

In Book I of his *Politics* Aristotle begins with what is familiar and obvious to both citizens and philosophers. He emphasizes not abstract cosmological speculations but the orderly and hospitable character of nature we encounter every day. The polis, he famously (though not uncontroversially) asserts, exists by nature (1252b30), and we are by nature political animals (1253a1–3). Indeed, he emphasizes that nature provides human beings with the capacity for reason and speech (*logos*) that makes political communities, to say nothing of human flourishing, possible (1253a14–19; *De Anima* 414a29 ff.). Moreover, according to Aristotle, what human beings need for their survival—such as food—is provided by nature (1256b15–23). Aristotle seems to be suggesting that the regularity of nature, combined with the human ability to deliberate, enables us to make use of what is found in nature for the sake of our self-preservation. And at the end of the day, our ability to know these necessary and everlasting beings through wisdom, the most precise and the most honored kind of knowledge, offers us the potential for the highest happiness (*NE* 1141a17–20, 1179b8 ff.). Having indicated that truths about the soul are difficult, Aristotle, in his defense of the priority of the goods of the soul, refers to his other arguments about happiness (*Politics* 1323a21–23).

PHILOSOPHY AND POLITICS

For all his disagreement with the Athenian Stranger—and Socrates—about the nature and usefulness of philosophy, Aristotle only intimates such criticisms in his *Politics.* One reason may be that for Aristotle philosophy does serve a purpose in politics, but it is a particular kind of philosophy: political philosophy, the study of what is just, what is equal, in the context of the political (*Politics* 1282b20 ff.). This opens the door to philosophy in the full sense, but it is not philosophy in the full sense. Nor does it need to be, for its truncated character means that more people can share in conversations about what is just and so share in the regime (1253a14–18). Political philosophy need not be the exclusive preserve of a few.

This kind of philosophy is employed by Aristotle to resolve the conflict between the various claims to rule. Unlike those who would define oligarchs and democrats only on the basis of their wealth or poverty and would thus point, like the Athenian, to an irreconcilable division between them, Aristotle suggests that a more philosophic understanding reveals that these groups are truly distinguished on the basis of their opinions, however partial or incomplete, about justice and equality (1279b11 ff.). Aristotle brings out in his *Politics* the numerous difficulties with trying to eliminate class tensions. A turn to the *doxai,* however, enables Aristotle to reconcile these political partisans by showing each group the partial truth about their opinions as well as the partial truth about their opponents' opinions. An appreciation for the different contributions and claims could easily be reflected in the political institutions of a mixed regime. Such a regime, which I take to be Aristotle's polity, would be more than a Rawlsian modus vivendi; it would represent a shared and mutual recognition of the contributions various groups make to the city. Only a philosophic understanding of politics which defines the partisans within the city on the basis of their opinion about justice enables those opinions to be reconciled and ameliorates the conflict between them.

Insofar as Aristotle envisions philosophy playing a role in politics, he is unwilling to criticize explicitly Socrates or the Athenian Stranger for suggesting the same thing. Because he disagrees with the ways in which they employ philosophy in the city, however, he criticizes the institutions on which they rely to bring philosophy into the city and, more subtly, the kind of philosophy that characterizes those institutions. For instance, instead of examining the opinions about the various claims to rule in an attempt to reconcile them, the Athenian turns to divine providence to provide the necessary stability for the regime. The Athenian's arguments for this are, however, exceptionally problematic: By making abstract cosmological speculations that undermine the order of nature, he places human life on shaky ground; by denying that there is anything stable and unchanging, he makes impossible what Aristotle identifies as the highest form of human activity.

From Aristotle's perspective, any sound investigation into the heavenly bodies must be not only humble and tentative—and thus unsuited as a foundation for politics—but also deeply rooted in the study of the natural world around us (e.g., *De Caelo* 268a1, 298b2–3). It is only after investigating the physical world with which we are intimately familiar that we can develop the basic framework—such as teleology—necessary for trying to understand that which is far removed from our experience.[31] The Athenian's arguments proceed without any of this background. They seem, therefore, to be less an attempt at seriously understanding the universe than an attempt to foster adherence to the laws he and his interlocutors have set down. They resemble, in short, "what modern thinkers call 'ideology,' that is, the use of philosophically derived concepts and arguments to support a specific political order" (Zuckert 2009, 143). While Socrates and the Athenian both err by making politics dependent on philosophy, Socratic philosophizing alone retains its zetetic character and is thus worthy of praise.

NOTES

1. See, e.g., Morrow 1960.

2. Thomas Pangle claims "Aristotle (*Politics* 1265a12) identifies him as Socrates" (in Plato 1988, 511). Like Pangle, Leo Strauss suggests that the Athenian Stranger represents Socrates having fled his prison in Athens (1975, 2). Others suggest that the Athenian Stranger represents Plato's own mature views (e.g., Halverson 1997).

3. Peter Simpson observes that while "Aristotle refrains from expressly naming Socrates in this chapter about the *Laws* (instead he uses 'he' or 'in the *Laws*' or something similar) . . . he names Socrates many times in his preceding discussion of the *Republic*" (Simpson 1998, 93). In the same way, Aristotle never names—perhaps he could never name—the Eleatic Stranger of Plato's *Statesman* (e.g., *Politics* 1252a6–16, 1289b5–6).

4. Aristotle later combines the views of Socrates and the Athenian Stranger into those of Plato, arguing that Plato's originality consisted in "having in common women and children as well as property; and further the law concerning drinking . . . ; and also that aspect of military training which has them develop ambidexterity" (1274b10 ff.).

5. Morrow (1993) argues that many of the Athenian Stranger's recommendations are variations of institutions found in Solonic Athens. Given Aristotle's praise, however qualified, of Solon (1273b25 ff.), it is unsurprising that there is significant overlap with the laws discussed by the Athenian.

6. This is at least the case with regard to the best attainable regime. Aristotle's regime according to prayer in Books VII and VIII is an aristocracy insofar as it represents the rule of the best, but it is an aristocracy that includes a multitude of, rather than few, citizens. The Athenian Stranger acknowledges that he is legislating for human beings rather than children of gods, but he does not indicate what kind of regime such divine offspring would warrant, save for the community of women, children, and property (739a–e).

7. The Athenian himself refers to their city as a "divine regime" [θείας πολιτείας] (965c).

8. Both the Athenian Stranger and Aristotle criticize and so correct the Spartan regime. The Athenian incorporates more of the Spartan model, perhaps due to the interlocutors with whom he is conversing and the colony he is helping to found in speech if not deed. Aristotle notes that someone—though perhaps not he himself—could object to the Athenian's claim that his mixture is the second-best regime, preferring instead the Spartan or another more aristocratic regime. Might Aristotle here be referring to Socrates (*Republic* 545b ff.)?

9. The Athenian Stranger acknowledges that humans, too, played a part in the Spartan mixture (691e2, 692a3), but he deemphasizes their role in his summary, ascribing it only to a god (692b6) and not mentioning Lycurgus.

10. Jaffa (1963) argues that the central theoretical difficulty confronted by Aristotle in the *Politics*—the incommensurability of the various claims to rule—is resolved by the mixed regime and its inclusion of the multitude, which serves "as the formula for the commensuration of excellences different in kind" (113).

11. Aristotle is rarely so explicit; he generally considers the deviant regimes to be "less regimes" and not nonregimes (1293b29). However, when discussing the mixture of "tyranny" and democracy in the *Laws,* Aristotle suggests first that they may not be regimes at all but then only that they are the "worst" of regimes (1266a1 ff.).

12. Curiously, Aristotle will later fault, among others, Plato for failing to include polity in the enumeration of regimes (1293a42–b1). In the famous degeneration of regimes in the *Republic,* polity is not mentioned.

13. One reason this may be so is that for Aristotle while the polis exists for the sake of living well, it comes into existence for the sake of living, and so those who contribute to that lower, yet still essential, end—through, for instance, military service—ought to have some share in ruling, even if their contribution to living well is negligible (1252b27–30). The Athenian, by contrast, argues that nothing should take priority to the acquisition of virtue, not even the defense of the city (770d–e).

14. As is acknowledged by Simpson, who suggests that Aristotle's real reason for disagreeing with the rule of philosophers is that he believes "virtue can be found in the mass" (2003, 302). Lewis (1998b) persuasively argues that the Nocturnal Council does not undermine the regime outlined in the preceding books but rather meets some of its needs.

15. Cf. Strauss, who identifies "the most philosophic, the only philosophic, part of the *Laws*" as the theology of Book X (1975, 129).

16. Cf. Zuckert 2009, 138–39.

17. Contending that Plato altered his preferred political views after the disastrous events of Syracuse (196–200), George Klosko insists that the *Laws* "more or less explicitly turns away from the ideal of the *Republic*." Its culmination in the rule of the "sinister sounding" Nocturnal Council that "recalls the Guardians of the *Republic*" thus requires explanation (Klosko 2006, 218, 236, 252), which Klosko suggests is due to Plato's death before completing revisions to the text (2008). Against this, see Lewis 1998a, 1998b; Marquez 2011.

18. The Athenian recognizes that not all officeholders will be virtuous, which is why the institutions of the audit and the scrutiny play such an important role.

19. Lewis suggests that the Nocturnal Council, far from simply accepting the Athenian's argument, will instead pursue these questions as they best see fit (2009, 88).

20. Cf. Strauss's criticism of Thomistic natural law as "practically inseparable" from "natural theology" as well as the Bible (1953, 164).

21. Aristotle's account of the heavenly bodies in *De Caelo* says little about the soul (the word [ψυχῆ] occurs only three times, 284a27, 28, 32).

22. The tension between the human good and "the observed, intelligible characteristics of the universe" brought out by Plato in the *Laws* reflects the contemporary feeling that we are "adrift in a fundamentally indifferent, if not hostile environment" (Zuckert 2009, 145). Pangle, too, notes that the "problematic, if not disorderly, character of the relation between the human and the nonhuman . . . places man much more at the mercy of indifferent or alien forces" (1976, 1076). The contrast with Aristotle, as I suggest above, is apparent.

23. I follow Mayhew's commentary in reading the former of these as the genus of which the previously enumerated motions (893b–94b) are species (Mayhew 2008, 117 ff.)

24. Benardete contends that the Athenian Stranger "asserts that souls with complete virtue are gods, but he never shows that such souls are, . . . and he admits he does not know how they are and are causes (899b4–8)" (2000, 299).

25. Pangle suggests that the Athenian's conception of a universe divided between good and evil will make for rich mythology among the citizens of Magnesia (1976, 1076).

26. The Athenian here connects chance and the gods. On the account in Book X, this would represent disorder and order, respectively (709bc). They are joined by a third thing, art, which is "gentler" but seems to be necessary in times of disorder.

27. Such disasters reflect the disorder in the universe. By contrast, the relative ease of procuring food suggests the order in the universe (678e–79a).

28. While Aristotle envisions priests in his city according to prayer, he says little about their duties and provides no specific theological doctrines save those useful to the city. Piety is not among the virtues in the *Nicomachean Ethics*. Cf. *Politics* 1328b11–13, 1335b12–16.

29. Aristotle explicitly criticizes the Athenian's account in the *Metaphysics*, asserting that Plato errs by claiming that all things are in motion without identifying

the cause of this motion. Insofar as Plato conflates soul and the heavenly motions, he cannot point to a first cause: That which moves itself is not truly first (1071b31–72a3).

30. Bodnár and Pellegrin assert that Aristotle's account of the order found in the cosmos depends on "the causal influence of immutable entities" (2009, 270).

31. See Leunissen 2010, chap. 6.

REFERENCES

Aristotle. 1939. *On the Heavens.* Trans. W. K. C. Guthrie. Cambridge, MA: Harvard University Press.

———. 1941a. *Metaphysics.* In *The Basic Works of Aristotle,* ed. Richard McKeon, trans. W. D. Ross, 681–926. New York: Random House.

———. 1941b. *Physics.* In *The Basic Works of Aristotle,* ed. Richard McKeon, trans. R. P. Hardie and R. K. Gaye, 213–394. New York: Random House.

———. 1984. *Politics.* Trans. Carnes Lord. Chicago: University of Chicago Press.

———. 1992. *Politics.* Trans. T.A. Sinclair and Trevor J. Saunders. New York: Penguin.

———. 2001. *On the Soul.* Trans. Joe Sachs. Santa Fe, NM: Green Lion Press.

———. 2004. *Nicomachean Ethics.* Trans. Joe Sachs. Newburyport, MA: Focus.

Benardete, Seth. 2000. *Plato's Laws: The Discovery of Being.* Chicago: University of Chicago Press.

Bodnár, István, and Pierre Pellegrin. 2009. "Aristotle's Physics and Cosmology." In *A Companion to Ancient Philosophy,* ed. Mary Louise Gill and Pierre Pellegrin, 270–91. Malden, MA: Blackwell.

Halverson, John. 1997. "Plato, the Athenian Stranger." *Arethusa* 30 (1): 75–102.

Jaffa, Harry. 1963. "Aristotle." In *History of Political Philosophy,* ed. Leo Strauss and Joseph Cropsey, 64–129. Chicago: University of Chicago Press.

Klosko, George. 2006. *The Development of Plato's Political Theory.* 2nd ed. New York: Cambridge University Press, 2006.

———. 2008. "Knowledge and Law in Plato's *Laws.*" *Political Studies* 56 (2): 456–74.

Leunissen, Mariska. 2010. *Explanation and Teleology in Aristotle's Science of Nature.* New York: Cambridge University Press.

Lewis, V. Bradley. 1998a. "Politeia kai Nomoi: On the Coherence of Plato's Political Philosophy." *Polity* 31, no. 2 (Winter): 331–49.

———. 1998b. "The Nocturnal Council and Plato's Political Philosophy." *History of Political Thought* 19 (1): 1–20.

———. 2009. "'Reason Striving to Become Law': Nature and Law in Plato's *Laws.*" *American Journal of Jurisprudence* 54: 67–91.

Marquez, Xavier. 2011. "Knowledge and Law in Plato's *Statesman* and *Laws:* A Response to Klosko." *Political Studies* 59 (1): 188–203.

Mayhew, Robert, ed. 2008. *Plato: Laws 10.* Oxford: Clarendon Press.

Morrow, Glenn R. 1960. "Aristotle Comments on Plato's Laws." In *Aristotle and Plato in the Mid Fourth Century,* ed. I. Duhring and G. E. L. Owen. Göteborg: Studia Graeca et Latina Gotoburgensia.

———. 1993. *Plato's Cretan City.* Princeton: Princeton University Press.

Pangle, Thomas L. 1976. "The Political Psychology of Religion in Plato's Laws." *American Political Science Review* 70 (4): 1059–77.

Plato. 1961. *Nomoi.* In *Platonis Opera v. 5,* ed. J. Burnet. Oxford: Oxford University Press.

———. 1988. *Laws.* Trans. with Notes and Interpretive Essay by Thomas L. Pangle. Chicago: University of Chicago Press.

Rowe, Christopher. 2003. "Socrates, the Laws, and the *Laws.*" In *Plato's Laws: From Theory into Practice,* ed. Luc Brisson and Samuel Scolnicov, 87–97. Sankt Augustin: Academia Verlag.

Simpson, Peter L. Philips. 1998. *A Philosophical Commentary on the Politics of Aristotle.* Chapel Hill: University of North Carolina Press.

———. 2003. "Plato's *Laws* in the Hands of Aristotle." In *Plato's Laws: From Theory into Practice,* ed. Luc Brisson and Samuel Scolnicov, 298–303. Sankt Augustin: Academia Verlag.

Strauss, Leo. 1953. *Natural Right and History.* Chicago: University of Chicago Press.

———. 1975. *The Argument and Action of Plato's Laws.* Chicago: University of Chicago Press.

Zuckert, Catherine. 2009. *Plato's Philosophers.* Chicago: University of Chicago Press.

Chapter Four

Both Friends and Truth Are Dear

Aristotle's Political Thought as a Response to Plato

MARY P. NICHOLS

Aristotle's criticisms of Plato's political thought are well known. He begins his *Politics,* for example, by criticizing those who fail to distinguish the kind of rule appropriate to political communities from that of masters over slaves, kings over subjects, and even heads of families over their members (1257a ff.). Whereas a master is defined in relation to a slave, and a king in relation to subjects, the individual who engages in political rule, the statesman, is defined in relation to citizens. The statesman (*politikos*) is, literally in Greek, skilled in doing what a citizen does, which is acting in matters related to the political community or, in the Greek, the *polis.* Just as the statesman rules "in turn" or "in part," the citizen, Aristotle says, shares in ruling and being ruled (*Politics* 1261b2–5, 1279a8–10, 1283b42–84a1).[1] Whereas statesmen and heads of families belong to different classes, statesmen and citizens do not. Skilled in political matters, the statesman is a good citizen, an exemplary member of his class but a member of his class.

While Aristotle does not mention anyone by name when he criticizes those who ignore the distinctions between different kinds of rule, Plato's *Statesman* refers interchangeably to the statesman and the king, and even suggests that the four kinds of rule that Aristotle distinguishes are essentially the same. Indeed, the principal interlocutor in that dialogue claims that there is no difference between a large household and a small city (*Statesman* 258e–259b). And when Aristotle turns at the beginning of Book II to the thoughts of his predecessors about politics, his criticism of Plato's political thought becomes explicit, for he criticizes the *Republic,* especially its community of wives, children, and property. Once again, it seems, Plato has collapsed the political community into a large family, and neglected the kind of sharing in rule that Aristotle presents as definitive of politics. The city Socrates describes in the *Republic,* moreover, is ruled by a king or kings (although philosophic ones) who do not share their rule with other parts of the community. They do not participate in the shared rule that Aristotle identifies as politics.

Aristotle's criticisms of Plato's political thought have often been discussed in the literature (e.g., Nussbaum 1981; Zuckert 1983; Saxonhouse 1986, 1992; Nichols 1992; Dobbs 2000), but less attention has been given to the ways in which Aristotle's *Nicomachean Ethics* prepares for his political critique of Plato in the *Politics* (but see Salkever 2009). Aristotle presents the *Politics* as a sequel to the *Ethics.* He begins the *Ethics* with a description of political science or statesmanship (*politikē*) as the architectonic or commanding art that aims at the highest good, calls his own inquiry in the *Ethics* a "kind of *politikē,*"[2] and concludes his *Ethics* by discussing the need for another work on politics and by outlining his own *Politics.* In this essay I focus on how the *Ethics,* not only Aristotle's explicit criticisms of Plato there, but also his discussion of happiness, virtue, and friendship, support his criticism of Plato in the *Politics* and his own alternative approach to political life.

I begin with ways in which Aristotle distinguishes himself from Plato in Book I of the *Ethics,* especially his specific criticisms of Plato's idea of the good. Consistent with the prominent place occupied by friendship in the *Nicomachean Ethics,*[3] Aristotle introduces his discussion of the ideas by acknowledging that he and those who introduced the ideas are friends. Although truth and friends are both dear, a philosopher must honor the truth most of all (1096a10–16). Aristotle's rejection of Plato's ideas here, I argue, is in fact demanded by friendship and the good for human beings, as he presents them in the *Ethics.* Turning then to Aristotle's *Politics,* I show how the *Ethics* is consistent with Aristotle's political critique of the *Republic* as well as with his own political thought. The community of wives and children and community of property, like the idea of the good, reduce individuals to the class of which they are members. Without the diversity of goods for which human beings strive and without the distinct contributions made by members of a community, there is no politics in Aristotle's sense, where differences justify participation.

ARISTOTLE'S RESPONSE TO PLATO IN THE *NICOMACHEAN ETHICS*

At first glance Plato's and Aristotle's political thought do not seem comparable. Plato's *Republic* describes a utopia, where philosophers rule, families and property are abolished, and there is little conflict because all are "friends." Even Socrates himself acknowledges that he may be presenting a model in the *Republic* that is more theoretical than practical (*Republic* 472e–472a). Centuries later, when Machiavelli complained of imaginary principalities and republics that are so far from what is seen or done in the world as to be useless, he surely had Plato among others in mind. Twentieth-century scholars such as Leo Strauss implicitly agree that the *Republic* is useless as a guide for political practice when they argue that Plato is an antiutopian thinker: insofar as actual politics falls short of the ideal, the *Republic* demonstrates the limits of politics (Strauss 1964, 127, 138). Although drawing conclusions different from Machiavelli's, Socrates acknowledges that if a good man were to go into politics he would likely come to ruin among so many who are not good (*Apology* 31e–32a). From this perspective, Plato's political theory, if it can be called by this name, is apolitical, as it turns talented and politically ambitious youth away from politics to a private life of philosophy.[4] Socrates' account of why one might engage in politics in the *Republic*—as a matter of drudgery and necessity (*Republic* 520e)—could only support such a conversion of the young. When Socrates insists in the *Gorgias* that he may be the only Athenian practicing "the true political art," he is boldly claiming the name of politics for his own private conversations (521d).

Aristotle, in contrast, seems very much of this world, at least in his political or practical works. He introduces his *Nicomachean Ethics* with an account of political science or statesmanship as the ruling art in political communities, which aims at the highest or most comprehensive good for human beings. When he says that his own inquiry in the *Ethics* is a kind of political science or statesmanship, he does so in the context of examining not just the good of individuals, but of political communities (1094b11–12), almost as if he were answering Socrates' assertion in the *Gorgias.* When he declares that securing the good for cities or nations is a nobler and more divine accomplishment than securing that of an individual (1094b10–11), he again addresses Plato, insofar as the latter's dialogues aim not at political reform but at educating the young. He does so as well when he insists throughout the *Ethics* that his goal is not knowledge but action (e.g., 1095a6). The highest good, at which politics aims, that for the sake of which we do everything else, is "a practical good," that is, "a good attainable by action" (1097a24).

Consistent with his practical purpose in the *Ethics,* Aristotle addresses those "experienced in the deeds of life," inasmuch as his political science is "based on these" (*NE* 1095a4–5). When he infers from this that his political science is not fit for the young, who lack such experience, he can be heard reproaching Plato's Socrates, who is famous for conversing with the young and was charged with corrupting them. So too does Aristotle address the *Republic* when he investigates the soul in the *Ethics,* as he claims, only to the extent such discussion is necessary to the statesman (1102a16–26). And we must expect, Aristotle also cautions, only so much precision as the subject matter warrants: the just and the noble involve much variation and uncertainty, he points out, and good things themselves can cause harm. Aristotle therefore maintains that we should accept in studying politics only what holds "for the most part" rather than in all cases. Just as we should not accept merely probable statements from a mathematician, we should not demand strict demonstrations when it comes to ethics and politics (1094b12–32). The implications seem clear: if one were to pursue what is universally or simply just, noble, or good, which does not change with the circumstances but which is always the same in all respects, as Socrates describes the ideas that philosophers love in the *Republic* (478e–479a, 479d–e), one would confuse political science with mathematics. Aristotle implies that Plato seeks a precise science where it is impossible to do so. This leads not only to unreasonable expectations about politics but also to cynicism about political life when it fails to meet those expectations.

In addition to these implicit responses to Plato at the outset of the *Ethics,* Aristotle offers a critique of the idea of the good later in Book I, when he discusses different views of happiness. In this context he examines "the universal good," and those who "introduce the ideas" even though they are friends. Such a critique of friends, he admits, "goes against the grain," but while friends and the truth are both dear, it belongs to the philosopher to reject his "own" for "the preservation of the truth" and "to honor" the truth most of all (1096a11–17).

Although Aristotle offers critiques of Plato in many other works, from his *Politics* to his *Metaphysics,* such a preface about truth and friendship is unique to the *Ethics,* as is his referring to those he criticizes as friends. Aquinas, in his commentary on Aristotle's *Ethics,* explains why it is in this work that Aristotle prefaces his criticism of Plato in this way: while repudiating a friend's opinion is not contrary to truth, it might seem to be contrary "to good morals," and so Aristotle must defend his action in his *Ethics*—since it is a work about "good morals" (Aquinas 1993, 24). Choosing friendship over truth, Aquinas continues, would undermine friendship itself, because one owes one's friend the truth.[5] Aquinas here calls attention to the extent to which Aristotle does not simply reject friendship in favor of truth, but finds a way to reconcile the two. After all, Aristotle does admit that both truth and friends are "dear" to him, or, literally, that "both are friends."

In his reference to those who "introduce the ideas," Aristotle does not refer to Plato by name, as he does in other works such as the *Metaphysics* where he offers a similar critique (*Metaphysics* 987a30 ff.). Following Aquinas, we might suppose that this is another concession to friendship appropriate to an *Ethics,* for in criticizing the argument of a friend we would spare him by not mentioning his name. But Aristotle reduces his friend Plato to a class of philosophers—"men who introduced the ideas"—obscuring the individual who formulated an account of them in his writings. When Aristotle proceeds to criticize Plato's theory, curiously, he does so on the ground that it reduces particular individuals to their class: the simple, universal idea absorbs the individual, what is his own or what is particular to him, and by implication leaves no room for particular friends. By leaving the "authors" of the theory anonymous and by referring to them as a class, Aristotle's deeds illustrate not his own theory of friendship but the theory of his friend, which in its recourse to universal ideas undermines friendship itself. Aristotle is demonstrating to Plato—and of course to us—the need of a philosophic understanding of the world consistent with their own friendship.

Aristotle proceeds to argue that the phrase "the good in itself" or "the good as such," as used by these philosophers, can have no meaning. How would the good as such, he asks, differ from other goods insofar as they are good? If it is the same as other goods, there could be no appeal to it to explain what all good things, itself included, have in common. On the other hand, Aristotle's argument goes, if the good as such differs radically from all other goods, how could they have anything in common with it? How, then, Aristotle asks, could all the things we consider good be really good? Would the good not end up being an empty class? There is a certain resemblance between Aristotle's argument against the ideas here and the one that Plato himself gives to his character Parmenides in the dialogue bearing his name (*Parmenides* 132d–134c). Aristotle has learned the problems with the ideas from Plato himself. His apparent "critique" implicitly acknowledges Plato's insight into the difficulty of connecting the permanent ideas or classes that make sense of our experience with the very experience of imperfect and changing goods we are trying to understand.[6] We want to know that the many things we desire are good, and why they are so, so that we can choose among them, and become happy by attaining what is good for ourselves.

By implication of Aristotle's critique, Plato's "idea of the good" would deny satisfaction to the statesman Aristotle describes, who seeks honor out of a desire to have his goodness confirmed (1095b27–28). Either he is not good, because only the idea of the good is good; or his goodness is identical to the idea of goodness, and hence is not his own. Moreover, if all goods are identical insofar as they are good, we have no cause to single anyone out as an object of love. Or if only the idea of the good is good, we have no cause to love anyone or anything except it. But Aristotle has just said that both the truth and *friends* are dear. His statement thus anticipates his need to explain the good in a way that does not undermine our experience of what is dear, of what we love. The irony of Aristotle's discussion is that what he presents as going against the grain of friendship, his critique of the idea of the good, is also required for the sake of friendship. That is, the critique of Plato's theory is required by friendship because the very theory makes friendship impossible, at least insofar as friends are loved in their own right and not just as an expression of a universal idea in which others also share. The critique of Plato's theory also serves a political community in which diverse human beings participate, in contrast to one in which there is a single ruler, who either knows or embodies the good common to all.

Aristotle concludes his critique of the ideas with a final argument: even if the idea of the good existed, how could it be useful to human life? For example, Aristotle asks, what good would it be to the carpenter, or weaver, in his art? Or how will anyone be a better doctor or general from having contemplated the idea? Aristotle observes that even the physician does not investigate "health" but rather the health of particular human beings, for they are the ones he must cure (1097a6–14). Aristotle ends the discussion of the idea of the good, of the "universal" as he said at the beginning, with a return to what is merely particular or idiosyncratic. But his concluding observation denies the very possibility of art, as it makes experience irreducible to any common elements. We would have only a doctor for Tom, and a doctor for Harry, and so on. It would therefore be left to chance whether there would be a doctor for any one of us should we need one. Not only would the arts be impossible, but so would politics, inasmuch as politics requires speech to others about matters of justice and the common good. And, as Parmenides pointed out in Plato's dialogue named for him, if there are no ideas or classes to which particular things belong, we will have no basis for speech or conversation about anything (*Parmenides* 135b–c). We need some middle way that links experience with thought, which connects, for example, a doctor's experience of a particular patient with rules that hold more generally and can be taught to others.[7] What Aristotle insists of political communities applies more generally to human life, including our understanding, our arts, and our actions: it is necessary "to hold some things in common, others not" (*Politics* 1261a4).

ARISTOTLE'S MIDDLE WAY IN THE *NICOMACHEAN ETHICS:* HAPPINESS AND THE VIRTUES

Aristotle's account of ethical virtue as a mean between extremes that we must resist is his most obvious statement in the *Ethics* of a "middle way." And that mean itself, Aristotle tells us, varies from person to person, for "what is too much and too little is not the same for everyone" (1106a26–b8). Aristotle must illustrate that ethical virtue is a mean not only in general (*katholou*), he admits, but with reference to each of the virtues, for while "the universal is more common, in speeches concerning actions what pertains to the part is more true, for actions involve particulars" (1107a28–32). And so Aristotle begins the *Ethics* by observing the diversity of goods at which we aim: "every art and every inquiry, every action and every choice seem to aim at some good, and therefore it is well said that the good is that at which all things aim" (1094b1–3). His opening statement does not require that there is one good in common to all the goods we seek or that constitutes the end to which all the other goods are instrumental or even subordinate. And when Aristotle proceeds to search for one such "highest good" that serves this purpose, difficulties mount.

Aristotle approaches this highest good by looking at the arts: some arts are subordinate to others, such as bridle making to horsemanship and horsemanship to military strategy, which is therefore an "architectonic" or commanding art. Because politics or statesmanship orders everything in the city, it is the most architectonic of all, and its goal is the good that comprehends all the rest. But Aristotle indicates problems with his argument from the outset. For example, he distinguishes activities that have their ends in products outside themselves from those that have their ends in their own activities. In the case of those that have their ends in their own activity rather than in a product, however, it is difficult to maintain that the end, which lies in the activity itself, is subordinate to another or finds its place in a larger whole.[8] Activities or practices that we choose for their own sakes have an independence or integrity of their own, and call into question the view that there is one and only one final good for all our activities, for which all other goods are only instrumental.

Moreover, Aristotle argues that politics has an end that encompasses other goods, inasmuch as it legislates about what is to be done and not done in cities, and even "commands which kinds of knowledge must exist in cities, and what sort each person must learn and up to what point" (1094a29–b7). But Aristotle soon claims that his own pursuit or inquiry (*methodos*) in the *Ethics* is itself "a kind of political art (*politikē tis*)" (1094b11). Aristotle's is obviously not one legislated by the laws of his community. He suggests that his political art is less than architectonic when he explains that he is leaving many things open for further development, for the account of the good he gives is only the "rough edges" to be filled in later. "A good sketch can be carried forward and articulated by everyone," he admits, "and time is a good discoverer of such things and a fellow worker (*sunergos*)" (1098a21–25). Aristotle's rough sketch or outline (*tupos*) is nothing other than his definition of happiness as our highest good, which he derives from what he identifies as the human work—the virtuous activity of an animal having reason or speech (1098a1–20). And while he himself helps us to understand what this entails in his accounts of the many ethical and intellectual virtues in the *Ethics,* his account must remain imprecise because he is dealing with matters that admit of variation.[9] Moreover, politics aims at action, as we have seen, and actions involve particulars. Aristotle's *politikē,* his political inquiry or art, is one that requires the contributions of others over time.

Having distinguished two sets of virtues, the ethical and the intellectual, as pertaining to the human work whose excellence constitutes happiness for human beings, Aristotle discusses the former in Books II through V of the *Ethics.* While the ethical virtues (*ēthikai,* lit., "the virtues of character") are not contrary to nature, Aristotle explains, we do not possess them by nature but acquire them by habit. It is by repeating certain acts that we acquire the virtues: we become just, for example, by performing just acts, moderate and courageous by acting so. And habit (*ethos*) eventually produces character (*ēthos*), Aristotle says, tracing the Greek word for "character" to that for "habit." We are able to make our own the habits imparted to us by our parents and teachers through their exhortations and by our political communities and their laws, and even the habits we seek for ourselves (1103a16–b5, b26–31; 1109b1–12, 1114b22–25). Once our habits take hold and impart character, we can make choices and voluntarily (*ekouiōs*) act in conformity with who we are (*NE* 1109b33 ff.). Or we can undertake actions that "go against the grain" (*prosantēs*), as Aristotle does in his criticism of Plato (*NE* 1096a10). The education that attempts to make us good citizens by inculcating virtuous habits paradoxically fosters an independence from our families and cities that allows us to stand apart from and even against them. Without the move from habit to character, there would be no *Ethics*. The responsibility necessary for ethical action thus calls into question our being merely parts of a whole, subject to an art that arranges everything in the city.

According to Aristotle, ethical virtue involves action chosen for its own sake, because it is noble (1115b12–13; 1116b1–3; 1117a, b8)—and not, for example, for the sake of some consequence outside itself, or even for the sake of others. In other words, the noble, at which ethical virtue aims, is not an end subordinate to another further end in a chain of goods that culminates in one final comprehensive good. The noble is not subordinate even to the political community, as Aristotle makes clear in his discussion of courage. There he distinguishes the true courage that acts for the sake of the noble from what he calls "political" or civic courage, which is based on a love of honor or fear of shame—passions that tie one to a political community (1116a17–30).[10] Aristotle's ethical virtues that aim at the noble, activities chosen for their own sake, fall among those activities that have their ends in themselves that Aristotle mentions at the outset of the *Ethics*. The political art or statesmanship becomes less—or perhaps more—complete when it encompasses such activities. It rules, we could say, only "in part" or "in turn," as Aristotle describes in the *Politics* the rule appropriate to political communities. Although in Book V Aristotle describes the justice embodied in the laws to be "the perfect [or complete] virtue because the laws command every virtue and forbid every vice" (1129b19–32), by the end of that book he moves to a discussion of equity, "a kind of justice," which must correct the law when its universal commands do not accomplish justice in particular situations (1137b25–38a3; also *Politics* 1284a4–25). Plato includes a similar observation in the *Statesman* about the defect of the law due to its generality (294a–c), but instead of anything like equity he recommends the rule of a statesman without laws, and in the absence of that statesman the rule of laws as second best (300a–e). What the *Statesman* leaves as alternatives, law and discretion, Aristotle brings together in equity.

In his discussion of the intellectual virtues in Book VI, Aristotle gives us another glimpse of a consummate virtue, wisdom (*sophia*), which is the most precise knowledge of the most exalted things, which exist of necessity and could not be otherwise (1139a8, 1141a20). And yet wisdom is only one intellectual virtue among others that Aristotle discusses. Prudence (*phronēsis*) deliberates about the just, the noble, and the good, those things for which we act and which do not exist of necessity (11141b10–14, 143b2–3). We choose both wisdom and prudence for their own sake, for as parts of virtue they constitute happiness (1144a5, 1143b16, 1144a1–5). But unlike wisdom, prudence also serves ends outside itself, both the ethical virtues, which provide the ends whereas prudence finds the means (1144a6–9), and wisdom, which prudence serves by "looking to how it comes into being," as medicine serves health (1145a6–12).[11] Whatever Aristotle means by wisdom—and a fuller discussion presumably belongs to another work (1294b13–14)—it is unlike the wisdom of the *Republic*'s philosopher-kings: it is not self-sufficient, inasmuch as it depends in some way on the prudence of the statesman. Neither does it rule in the political community. Wisdom is, after all, only "part of virtue," the virtue of only "a part" of the soul (1144a2, 1143b16–17).

Human happiness comprehends a variety of goods, which cannot be reduced or simply subordinated to one other. Happiness, Aristotle said in Book I, is self-sufficient, but by self-sufficient we mean lacking in none of the goods that constitute happiness, including parents, wife, children, friends, and fellow citizens (1097b9–12). And Aristotle concludes his discussion of the intellectual virtues, including wisdom, with reference to the divine that no art of politics, however powerful, can contain, for politics does not "rule the gods by arranging everything in the political community" (1145a11–12).

ARISTOTLE'S MIDDLE WAY IN THE *NICOMACHEAN ETHICS:* HAPPINESS AND FRIENDSHIP

After discussing the ethical and intellectual virtues, Aristotle declares that his work requires "another beginning" (1145a15). Happiness, it appears, is not constituted by the activity of virtue alone but requires friendship (Books VIII, IX) and the self-restraint (Book VII) that makes friendship possible. Self-restraint is necessary because friends are those whom we love not simply for our own sake but for theirs as well (1155b25, 32; 1156b7–12; 1159a; 1166a5–7). They not only have goodwill toward each other, but each is aware of the other's goodwill toward him (1156a5). Friendship is reciprocal. And the self-awareness of each friend is fostered by their friendship: since we are better able to contemplate our neighbors than ourselves, and their actions better than our own, friends who are themselves good can better see themselves in the good deeds done by each other (1169b34–70a2).

Although friends are like each other (e.g., 1159b2–4), they can become more alike over time, or less so. When the disparity becomes too great, because one or another of the friends changes, whether for better or worse, the friendship cannot last (1165b17–27). But it is also possible that friends become better through their association, and their goodness "increases together" (*sunauxazanesthai*) when they "correct each other" and "take upon the impress from the other of [those aspects of the other's character] they take pleasure in" (1172a14). We become like what we love, and friends therefore become better by loving each other when they are good. So too do friends contribute to each other's activity because activities performed together—whether it is drinking together, hunting together, or philosophizing together, to use Aristotle's examples—can be performed more continuously than when one engages in them alone (1170a5–8, 1172a2–7). Friends see themselves in each other, then, not only because they are alike, and share in the same activities, but because they themselves play a part in their friend's becoming good.[12] We see our deeds in those of our friend, not merely because they are like our own, but because we are in part their cause, as our friend is of ours (see 1167b28–33). As Aristotle says, the actions of a good friend are both good and one's own (*to oikeion*), and "both are by nature pleasant" (1169b31–1170a2). Because we can see our goodness in the deeds of our friend, and know it to be ours, the desire that Aristotle identifies in the love of honor—to be able to trust one's own goodness (1095b26–29)—can find satisfaction in friendship. The goodness of friends cannot therefore be measured by a good that is the same in each of them but rather by the ways in which they contribute to their friend's goodness and the ways in which they respond to their friend, both in accepting his correction and in changing in the course of loving him. If friends were merely parts of wholes that they form with each other, or identical insofar as they are members of a class, they would have very little if anything to offer each other.

Because friendship at its best is based on the difference as well as the similarity between friends, it finds its clearest expression in the relation between a man and a woman in marriage. In the first place, men and women have different tasks and virtues (1158b18–19, 1162a22; see also *Pol.* 1277b25). Aristotle finds in the relation of husband and wife in families a reflection of "aristocratic" government: "the husband rules on account of his worth, and over those things a man should rule, while he yields to his wife as much as is fitting. And when the man is sovereign in everything, he renders the relation oligarchic" (1160b32–35). Their relation is "aristocratic," then, not because the better, the man, rules but because the "best" relationship involves sharing in the rule appropriate to each, "with each contributing what is his or her own (*ta idia*) toward their common lives (*to koinon*)" (1162a23). In the family, the manifest difference between husband and wife illustrates that a friend is not just another "self" but "another" self (1166a32, 1170b6).[13] Without the former, there would be no sharing; without the latter, friendship would be simply a manifestation of self-love. Aristotle allows that the friendship between husband and wife is useful and pleasant but observes that it might also be based on virtue, if they are "good" or "equitable" (*epieikeis*), "for there is a virtue for each of them, and they delight in that" (1162a23–26).

As Aristotle observes in his discussion of equity, we often use *equitable* in the place of *good* in order to praise someone (1137a35–b2). But Aristotle means something more precise by the word. He uses it to refer to the justice that corrects the law when the law is too general to apply to the particular case. And an equitable man "is inclined to choose and to do the equitable, not to insist on precise justice (*akribodikaios*) to a fault, and to take less even when he has the law as a help" (1137b35–38a3).[14] Like Aristotle's political science itself, equity does not insist on too much precision where justice is concerned. In particular, it inclines toward accepting less than the law permits rather than toward insisting on more than it gives. Aristotle suggests the basis of equity when discussing the intellectual capacities in Book VI: "forgiveness" or "pardon" (*suggnōmē*) is a judgment belonging to equity (1143b20–21). Like equity, forgiving exacts less than what is due in the strict sense, and is possible because as the name suggests we are able "to know together" with another, or to understand how things looked to him or her when he or she acted. The equity that Aristotle attributes to the relationship between husband and wife serves as a model for friendship altogether, and also provides an antidote to the desire for "precise justice" in politics.[15]

As Aristotle approaches the conclusion of his discussion of friendship, he points to a difficulty for friends in sharing each other's joys and sorrows. Because it is "noble to do good deeds" and "ignoble to pursue benefits" (1171b17, 25–26; see also 1124b10–13), a noble person is eager to share his good fortune with his friend but shrinks from sharing his suffering. He wants to give rather than to receive. But so too would his noble friend, who wants to relieve his friend's suffering when he is in pain but who resists the benefits his friend tries to bestow (1171a34–b28). This impasse between friends is much like that of the two noble men whom Aristotle describes, each holding back from the noble deed so that the other can undertake it (1169a18–b1) (see Cropsey 1977, 271–72; Pangle 2003, 175; Burger 2008, 176).[16] Aristotle suggests a way through the impasse when he distinguishes "manly types" from "women and men who are like them." Like the model that Socrates proposes for citizens in the *Republic* (387d–e), manly types do not want others to grieve with them, because they do not do so themselves. Women and those like them, in contrast, take comfort in sharing their grief with others and love as friends those who share their grief. Able to share their suffering with their friends, they are presumably able to share the good fortunes of their friends as well. Speaking of these two different types, Aristotle says merely that "one must imitate the better in all things" (1171b12). Unlike Socrates in the *Republic,* who relegates lamentations to "women—and not to serious ones among them—and to all bad men" (387e–88a), Aristotle does not say explicitly which is better.[17] He does conclude, however, that "being with friends is to be chosen in every case" (1171b29). One cannot of course choose to be with friends in their good fortunes and in one's own misfortunes unless one is willing to receive benefits from one's friend. Friendship requires the latter as much as it requires an eagerness to give.

The different inclinations that Aristotle attributes to men and women are both necessary for friendship.

Toward the end of his *Ethics* Aristotle judges between the theoretical or contemplative activity (*theōretikē*) and practical or political virtues (*praktikai*) (Book X). He argues that "perfect [or complete] happiness" is found in the former, because it is the only activity chosen for its own sake and not for anything else as well. So too is it in need of nothing and self-sufficient. It is also the activity in accordance with the best and most divine thing we have, our minds, and we are able to engage in it more continuously than in action (1176b1–6, 1177a11–71b1). He also argues that contemplative activity is the only activity we can conceive as belonging to the gods, for what actions could we attribute to them? Not courage or liberality, for what would they fear, and to whom would they give? Nor justice, for with whom would they make agreements or pay back deposits? (1178b7–15). Aristotle's series of rhetorical questions prepares us for the concluding turn he gives to his treatment of this issue in the *Ethics*. He reminds us that in practical matters although arguments or speeches are to be trusted to a certain extent, "the truth must be judged on the basis of the deeds of life." The arguments must harmonize with deeds, with what happens, if they are to be acceptable (1179a17–23; see also 1168a35–b1; *Pol.* 1254a20–21). Aristotle proceeds to refer to the deeds of gods, "good deeds they do in turn" for those who contemplate, inasmuch as those are most like themselves (1179a25–32). But if such deeds contribute to the happiness of those who contemplate, their contemplation is not sufficient for happiness, nor are the gods who so benefit human beings characterized merely by contemplative activity. Deeds that benefit those who deserve benefit serve as the last example of divine activity in this section. Aristotle's appeal to this activity of the gods occurs near the end of the *Ethics,* just before the concluding section in which Aristotle explains why he must write a *Politics*. In this Aristotle imitates the gods to whom he attributes good deeds for those like themselves, and the friends whom he described in his books on friendship. And in another way, his speeches turn to the deeds of life—to the various polities or regimes and the ways in which they can be safeguarded and improved.

Although Aristotle has given a rough sketch of perfect (or complete) (*teleia*) happiness, his inquiry has not reached an end (*telos*) for the end "in practical matters is not contemplating and knowing but action. And so . . . we must attempt to acquire virtue and use it, if we are somehow to become good" (1179a33–79b4). This time Aristotle points out the insufficiency of "contemplating" along with "knowing." His words recall his warning that one becomes good by performing virtuous deeds, not by "taking refuge in words and believing that one is philosophizing" (1105b11–15). But instead of renewing his implicit criticism of Socrates, who indeed claims to have "taken refuge in words" as a way of pursuing the truth (*Phaedo* 99e), Aristotle now acknowledges that words (such as his own words in the *Ethics*) can have an effect on "the liberal (*eleutherioi*) among the young" (1179b7–11). It is "the many," who are too eager to take refuge in words in Aristotle's earlier statement, that are the source of the difficulty, for words have little effect on turning them to nobility and goodness (*kalokagathia*), inasmuch as they live by their passions. It is because they require education by the force of the laws that Aristotle's work is not done (1179b32–a6; cf. Aristotle's reference to the need for punishment in this passage with *Apology* 26a) and that he must write another work, the *Politics,* to address this issue. His criticism of Socrates for taking refuge in words (and of Plato, by implication, for not writing a work like Aristotle's *Politics*) is not for teaching the young but for not proceeding to integrate that teaching with the political life of the majority of human beings.

Aristotle must write the *Politics,* specifically, because experience yields insufficient guidance. Statesmen engage in politics, but unlike the practitioners of the others arts, they cannot give an account of what they do and thereby teach it to others. On the other hand, those who claim to teach politics, the Sophists, do not practice it, and as a result their understanding is inadequate (1179b28 ff.). This split that Aristotle finds between the statesmen and the Sophists is a version of the one he claims that Plato leaves between the world in which we act and the ideas, or between our experience and what explains it. It is also a version of the split between Aristotle and Plato that Aristotle indicated in his criticism of the friends who introduced the ideas. Aristotle thinks that he "does politics" in a way that Plato did not. This becomes even clearer in the *Politics,* where he says that human beings are political animals, because they have a capacity for speech and can therefore address the advantageous and disadvantageous, and hence the just and the unjust (1253a10–16). In spite of the limits of speech to move the many, speech makes community possible. Through its advocacy of the advantageous and the just, speech also makes differences manifest. In the *Politics* Aristotle is still responding to his friend, as he addresses the problems that Plato set forth.[18] It is to that work we now turn.

ARISTOTLE'S RESPONSE TO PLATO IN THE *POLITICS*

When in Book II of the *Politics* Aristotle turns to the work of his predecessors, he gives the most time to a critique of the *Republic,* especially to Socrates' proposals for a community of wives and children, in which there are no "private" families but in which each member of the city says "mine" and "not mine" of the same people.[19] All fathers and mothers, for example, are addressed as "father" and "mother" by all sons and daughters, and vice versa, just as any brother or sister is considered the brother and sister of all. Individuals are simply members of a class. Such unity, Aristotle claims, is not a proper goal for a political community, which is constituted out of dissimilar or diverse elements (1260b40, 1261a21–24). Just as Aristotle's predecessors miss what is unique about the city in their failure to distinguish political communities from families, and statesmanship from despotism, Socrates turns the city into a family, and even into an individual. A "family is more of a unity than a city," Aristotle explains, "and an individual more than a family" (1261a21). As the city Socrates describes approaches an individual, the individuals within it approach an idea—the idea of mother rather than the mother of some particular son or daughter. The community of wives and children reduces individuals to their class, just as the ideas its philosophic rulers contemplate reduce members of a class to their class characteristic.

If the political community is composed "out of a diversity," as Aristotle insists, rather than reduced to the unity of an idea, there are differences among those who share in rule that make their participation useful to the community as a whole. Aristotle finds those differences grounded in the family, as he makes clear when he traces its development in Book I of his *Politics.* Men and women initially come together, he says, for the sake of the preservation of the species. Life in families therefore teaches men and women that they are incomplete, insofar as they need each other for reproduction. Families do not merely teach limits, however, for men and women in families develop virtues in common, such as courage and moderation, although virtues that have different manifestations in each of them. The courage of a man, Aristotle says, differs from that of a woman, as does a woman's moderation differ from that of a man. So too does their justice (1260a20–31, 1277b18–23), as do their tasks within the family. It is the work of a man to acquire, Aristotle observes, and of a woman to preserve (1277b124–25). Moreover, Aristotle indicates that the deliberative capacities of women are useful, and even necessary, to men (1260a27–30). Moral and intellectual virtues, as well as different capacities of body and soul, which develop through relations within families, constitute the diversity out of which political communities develop and which are fostered by them in turn.

Aristotle's criticisms of the *Republic*'s political arrangements defend friendship as well as family life. In explaining the community of wives and children in the *Republic,* Socrates quotes the proverb that "friends have all things in common" (423e). Aristotle points out the resemblance between Socrates' application of the proverb in the *Republic* and the friendship that Plato has Aristophanes describe in the *Symposium,* in which lovers desire to become one. Should this happen, Aristotle says, "both or at least one must be destroyed" (1262b7–14). The "friendship" of the *Republic*'s institutions destroys the differences between friends that Aristotle shows in his *Ethics* make friendship possible.

When Socrates introduces the rule of philosophers or lovers of wisdom (*philosophoi*) in the city, which he claims is necessary for the sake of its coming into being (472e–473d), he describes what it means for someone "to love" (or "befriend," *philein*) someone or something, like wisdom. Socrates explains that when someone loves, he "does not show a love [or friendship] for one part of it and not for another, but cherishes all of it" (474c). Socrates means not that we love the whole person, but rather we love all the members of a class. He offers examples: wine lovers (*philoinoi*) "delight in every kind of wine," lovers of honor (*philotimoi*) love honor regardless of who bestows it, and all boys in the bloom of youth arouse the boy lover (*philopais*) and erotic man (474d–475b).

Aristotle, in contrast, indicates that lovers of honor do not love honor indiscriminately. The statesman who seeks honor in order to confirm his own goodness, for example, seeks honor from those in a position to do so—"those who are prudent and who know him" (1095b22–29). So too the magnanimous man takes moderate pleasure in honors bestowed by the worthy while despising those coming from any chance person and for trivial matters, for they are not worthy of him (1124a5–12). As to the boy lover who loves all boys, Plato himself suggests reservations about such lovers (*erōtikoi*) when Glaucon agrees with Socrates' description of what lovers do only "for the sake of the argument" (475a). It is Socrates' account of friendship in the *Republic* that is "for the sake of the argument," for the friendship he describes is the one at work in the community of women and children, where guardians of the city love all members of their class. Socrates' young interlocutors, however, do not raise any of the objections that Aristotle would to this account of friendship. As Aristotle indicates in his discussions of friends, as we have seen, one loves one's friends because they are both "one's own" and "good" (1169b31–1170a2; see also *Politics* 1262b22).

Aristotle finds faults as well with the arrangements for the community of property that Socrates recommends. As an alternative, he suggests the private ownership of property combined with common use, which occurs among friends. To this common use, Aristotle applies the very saying to which Socrates appeals in the *Republic* for communal property, "the things of friends are common" (1263a22–40). Private families and property, moreover, are the conditions for the practice of the virtues of moderation and liberality as well as the activity of friends. For it is a noble deed, Aristotle says, to hold oneself back from the wife of another while liberality occurs in the use of one's possessions (1263b7–14).[20] The former acknowledges what belongs to another; the latter demonstrates what one is able to share of one's own. In Aristotle's defense of these virtues against the community of property, one can see the two meanings of Aristotle's reference to the friend as "another self."

Aristotle offers another practical criticism of the city Socrates describes in the *Republic:* Socrates has not clarified whether community of women, children, and property applies to the city's lowest classes. If it does, they will not be sufficiently different from the upper classes and consequently will not submit to their rule. On the other hand, if the community of wives and children and property, Aristotle continues, does not apply to the city's lower classes, the city will be two cities, antagonistic to each other because they have little in common (1264a13–26). In either case, like the idea of the good that Aristotle discusses in the *Ethics,* the principle that is intended to confer unity on the whole fails to do so. If the rulers are no different from the ruled, they cannot rule them. Difference is needed for authority or rule. Too much in common undermines rule. But neither could rulers rule if they are radically different from the ruled. They would share no community in which they could interact with them. Too much difference undermines rule.

In other words, Aristotle is bringing his criticism of the theory of the ideas to his discussion of politics, just as he had done in his discussion of the relation between men and women in the *Ethics.* It is in families and political communities that Aristotle finds that experience that indicates the middle way that addresses the problems he identifies with the ideas. Socrates of course is famous for directing philosophy to political and family life. In the words of Cicero, whereas previous philosophers investigated the things in the heavens, Socrates brings philosophy into the cities and the homes, and inquires into good and bad (*Tusculan Disputations* v. 10; see also Xenophon, *Memorabilia* I.i.11–16; Aristotle, *Metaphysics* 987b1–4). Aristotle takes Socrates' turn to the human things one step further—from the speeches or dialogues through which Socrates makes his inquiries with others to the deeds of politics, which he intends to influence and in which he himself engages by his attempt to have such an influence.

It is not that Aristotle is more practical than Plato or Socrates, or more concerned with improving political life. Rather, he sees how politics, understood and brought to fruition by his political science, allows him to respond to the dilemmas that Plato and Socrates explore. One of the words that Socrates uses to refer to how the complex beings in the world "participate" or "share in" the ideas, *koinōnia* (*Phaedo* 100d), is the same word that Socrates uses in the *Republic* to refer to the "community" of women and children (e.g., 449c, d, 450c, 461e, etc.). Almost as if in reply, Aristotle uses the word to refer to the range of human associations, including friendships, families, and political communities, which he insists differ in kind, just as he insists on the differences among their members (*NE* 1171b33, 1160a25–32; *Politics* 1252a1–7). In such associations Aristotle finds the "unity out of a diversity" of which the theory of the ideas falls short. That is why Aristotle can pronounce, as neither Plato nor Socrates does, that human beings are political by nature (1097b12; see also *Politics* 1253a8–9).

It has been noticed that Aristotle's critique of the institutions of the *Republic* ignores one of its more prominent institutions, the philosopher-kings.[21] While it might seem that his silence implies agreement with Plato on this point, his criticism of the idea of the good in the *Ethics* has made clear that such ideas if known to the philosopher cannot be a basis for ruling a city. But this is Socrates' justification of their rule. That Aristotle's criticism of the ideas applies to the philosopher-kings, moreover, is confirmed by Socrates' explanation of what the philosophers love in the *Republic:* when arguing that love is directed to all members of a class, Socrates refines the statement even further: philosophers or lovers of learning (*philomatheis*) do not really approach "every kind of learning with delight," as his analogy with other lovers at first suggests. The philosophers do not love all kinds of learning, all the members of the class of "learnings," but only the class or idea itself (475e–476d). Socrates' qualification is only a refinement, for if one loves all the members of a class one does so because of some common or class characteristic rather than because of what distinguishes them from one another. Only then could they all seem worthy of attention and delight. Aristotle need not criticize the philosopher-kings in his discussion of the *Republic,* because he has already done so in his critique of the idea of the good in the *Ethics.* He needed to do so there before proceeding with his own account of happiness, the virtues, and friendship.

ARISTOTLE'S MIDDLE WAY IN THE *POLITICS*

Following through on his observation that political life requires some things to be held in common but not everything (*Politics* 1260b37–61a9), Aristotle explores in great detail and complexity different ways, some better and some worse, in which this might occur, as circumstances permit.

In Book III, after defining the citizen as the one who participates in (or has in common, *koinōnein*) the deliberative and judicial offices of the city (1275b19–20), Aristotle provides his famous classification of polities or regimes (*politeiai*). The correct ones aim at the common advantage, whether one, or few, or many hold sovereign authority, whereas the deviant ones aim at the private advantage of the ruler or rulers (1279b16–30). The correct forms of the rule of the one and the few are kingship and aristocracy; when the many rule with a view to the common advantage, Aristotle says, it is "called by the name common to all polities, polity" (1279b35–39). Aristotle has given the name common to a class to one of the members of the class.[22] He is not, however, reducing all members of the class to the one form. Rather, the polity that Aristotle designates with the class name is the most exemplary member of the class, but the exemplary can either illustrate a type, what all members of a class have in common, or serve as a model, the best of the kind, that to which they might aspire. Numerous polities can be properly given that name. And, indeed, what Aristotle means by polity, the name he gives to the correct form of the rule of the many, undergoes development in the course of the *Politics,* from a polity or regime based on the military virtue of those who defend their city to a polity mixed of democratic and oligarchic elements, wealth and numbers, or even to a polity that gives a part to wealth, numbers, and virtue (1279a40–b2, 1293b33–34, 1295b3–33, 1293b14–20).

The inclusive character of the polity, as Aristotle suggests by giving the generic name to a specific form of the rule of the many, is illustrated in two prominent discussions in the last half of Book III. Aristotle defends the rule of the many on the basis of the ability of each to judge the parts with which he is familiar rather than an ability to judge the good of the whole. The particular contributions of the many, including their virtues and judgments, give them a title to participate in rule that goes beyond their numbers or their collective wealth (1281b4–10). So too does Aristotle suggest the inclusive character of politics by his reservations concerning the king "over all" (*pambasileus*), who deserves to rule because of his outstanding virtue. He is like "a god among human beings" and therefore is "no part of a political community" (1284a4–14). He rules more like a father does in his own family than a ruler who rules and is ruled in turn (1285b31–33).[23]

In the middle books of the *Politics,* IV through VI, Aristotle demonstrates how small changes in existing polities, which suffer more or less from the oppression either of the majority or of the few, can move them toward more just conditions by expanding participation. Indeed, it is the task of the skilled citizen, or the statesman, to do so. As Aristotle observes, "to reform a polity is no less a task than to form one from the beginning" (*Politics* 1298a3–4). Aristotle is still implicitly criticizing the *Republic,* where Socrates forms a polity "in speech" from the beginning, just as his philosopher-kings "take the city and the dispositions of human beings, as though they were a tablet," and "wipe [them] clean" (*Republic* 501a). But in politics, for Aristotle, there are no clean slates.[24] In Book III of the *Politics* Aristotle asks whether a new polity owes the debts incurred by the old (1274b30–35). But even in the clearest case, where a revolution overthrows a tyranny and establishes a more just government and thus repudiates its past, Aristotle avoids answering his explicit question (1276b13–15): There is no explicit answer, because the new is never wholly new but is indebted to the past.

Aristotle's emphasis on reform does not merely recognize debts from the past and the limits they impose on what can be done, however. It supports—and shows the way toward— improvement. In this as well Aristotle distinguishes himself from Socrates, who in the *Republic* describes an inevitable decline of polities, each polity deteriorating into a worse form, from the "the best polity" to timocracy to oligarchy to democracy, culminating in tyranny. Aristotle sees little merit in Socrates' exposition, although he acknowledges that Socrates "perhaps is not wrong" when he supposes that there will arise those who are mean-spirited and beyond education. But this can happen in any polity. Socrates does not mention any change "proper" (*idiōs*) to the best polity but simply says that "nothing lasts" (1361a1–12). Once again Aristotle suggests that Socrates has bypassed what is "private" or "proper" in his search for a common cause, even of change itself.

Given the peculiar character of each polity, polities can change into their opposite forms as well as into one near them on Socrates' scale, Aristotle says; contra Socrates, an oligarchy could change into an aristocracy, for example. And they may also go "in the other direction"—a democracy to an oligarchy, for example, rather than an oligarchy into a democracy

(1316a18–24). Nor does Socrates say what happens to tyranny, whether it too will undergo revolution, and if not, why not (1316a24–34). Aristotle is well aware of the harshness of tyrants, who to preserve themselves attempt to prevent leisured conversation (*sullogoi*) and trust among their subjects; tyrants "set friends at odds with friends, the people with the notables, and the wealthy among themselves," inasmuch as friendship and trust among subjects could lead to their overthrow. So they too must "distrust their own friends" (1313bb1–2, 16–18, 29–33). Aristotle has nevertheless spent some time when discussing tyranny showing how tyrants can improve their polities: for the sake of their own preservation they should moderate their tyrannical rule by serving their city and seeking the approval of both the notables and the many. Thus their rule will last longer if it is over willing subjects, and they will become "more disposed in character toward virtue" (1315a40–b9, 10).[25] And now Aristotle demonstrates by examples from experience specific polities that underwent changes in a variety of directions for which Socrates' exposition would have no account (1316a30–34). Aristotle relies not only on the experience of Greek cities for his case against Socrates, but on the human capacity for deliberation and choice, for speech about the advantageous and the just, which his political art or statesmanship demonstrates.

Aristotle concludes his *Politics* in Books VII and VIII by describing the best polity or regime, literally, a polity "according to prayer" (1325b37–40). That polity assigns citizenship, participating in deciding matters of advantage and justice, to those who have served in the military when young. It is therefore to some extent an inclusive regime, although it excludes farmers and mechanics, inasmuch as leisure is required for the development of virtue and political participation (1328b35–29a16). It is a polity plagued with tensions (e.g., between foreign affairs and internal politics [1330a9–23], between security and both beauty and virtue [1330b22–31, 1330b35–31a2, 1331a10–14]), and even injustices, the most obvious becoming clear when Aristotle advises that slaves be promised their freedom as a reward (1330a32–33). That is, the polity enslaves those who are capable of exercising freedom. Even the best polity is therefore unjust, although Aristotle recommends its improvement. The *Politics* therefore does not end in proposing a static, hierarchical political structure, like that found in the *Republic*'s city, but rather one that changes over time, whether for better or worse (see 1330b14–17). It is the very diversity out of which a city is composed from which change stems, including the capacities of the enslaved who demonstrate behavior that deserves freedom and of the masters who can be persuaded to reward it to them. And it is that very diversity that both demands and justifies shared governance.

Socrates insists in the *Republic* that the polity or regime he describes is one that is possible and "is not wholly a prayer," even though he has already admitted that it is unlikely to ever come into being, human nature being what it is (540c, 472e–473a). Aristotle, in contrast, does not hesitate to call his best polity "a prayer," even if he too means that it is not wholly a prayer. It is not wholly a prayer because it is an imperfect polity, precisely because it is one in which rule is shared. It is not wholly a prayer, in the second place, because it is one that we ourselves can seek by reforming our own political arrangements through deliberation and choice. It is therefore a polity for which we can pray, and do more than pray, because it—or something like it, depending on circumstances—is both possible and good.

Aristotle's criticisms of Plato, which provide an introduction to his own approach to human life in both the *Ethics* and the *Politics,* can be reduced to the simple statement this essay attempts to amplify: Plato treats friends as if they were merely parts of a whole rather than independent objects of love. Aristotle knows the contrary from the experience of friendship, as he describes it in Books VIII and IX of the *Ethics,* and an experience which he claims to have had with "those who introduced the ideas," and which I have argued calls those very ideas into question. Aristotle's statement thus bears repeating: both the truth and friends are dear. If friends as well as the truth are dear, the truth that fails to incorporate this truth falls short of itself, and the philosopher who supposes otherwise fails in self-reflection.

NOTES

1. Translations from Aristotle's *Politics* are my own, although I have consulted the translation of Carnes Lord (1984) and the Loeb Classical Library's translation by H. Rackham (1932). I have used the Greek text in the Loeb edition.

2. The Greek *politikē* is a feminine adjective used as a noun and thus might modify a feminine noun such as art (*technē*) or science or knowledge (*epistēmē*). It thus refers at the same time both to political science and to political art or statesmanship.

3. Aristotle devotes two books of the *Ethics* to a discussion of friendship. He gives more space to friendship than to any moral virtue, more than to justice and more than to all the intellectual virtues taken together.

4. "Certain it is that the *Republic* supplies the most magnificent cure ever devised for every form of political ambition" (Strauss 1964, 65).

5. Aquinas also says, "Unless a man prefer truth to his friends, it follows that he will make false judgment and bear false witness against them" (1993, 24). Ronna Burger comments that "'the things of one's own' that might have to be sacrificed could refer [not to allegiance to a friend but] to one's own opinion, whose inadequacy could be uncovered precisely through dialogue with a friend" (2008, 24, 159–60). See her pathbreaking argument that Aristotle understood the highest friendship as existing not between two self-sufficient friends, joined by their perfect goodness and wisdom, but between two who "philosophize together" and thus help each other pursue what they lack. Thus Aristotle is able to incorporate *eros* into *philia,* and what she calls "the dialogic self" that emerges in friendship becomes "the joint realization of our rational nature and our political nature" (Burger 2008, 182–89).

6. As Aristotle observes, Plato claims that the many things that have the same name as the ideas exist by participation in them, but he left it open as to what this participation means (*Metaphysics* 987b10–15). See *The Phaedo: A Platonic Labyrinth* (Burger 1984, 150); "The Socratic Turn" (Zuckert 2004, 196–98); and *Plato's Philosophers: The Coherence of the Dialogues* (Zuckert 2009, 185–89).

7. In discussing the intellectual virtues in Book VI of the *Ethics,* Aristide Tessitore articulates Aristotle's middle way in a manner that parallels my own: "Between the two extremes of philosophers without prudence [Thales and Anaxagoras] and statesmen without philosophy [Pericles] stands an unarticulated middle ground occupied by Aristotle himself" (1996, 50). Burger observes the absence of Socrates in Aristotle's contrast between the representatives of theory and those of practice (2008, 111–12).

8. The problem arises even with those arts that Aristotle himself mentions as examples that serve an architectonic art; for example, horseback riding may have ends other than military strategy, or it may simply be enjoyed for its own sake. See Davis, *The Soul of the Greeks* (2011, 62–63); and Burger 2008, 15 and note 5, 231–32.

9. Even near the end of Book X, Aristotle refers to his work as a rough sketch or outline (1176a30–31, 1179a34–35). This should not surprise us.

10. See Susan D. Collins's exploration of the status of virtue for Aristotle as "an independent end": 2004, 47–61, esp. 49. It is, however, a question whether this independence of the noble, as Aristotle presents it, can be maintained, even by Aristotle's own account. See Ward 2001, 71–83.

11. On a related issue, Burger observes that "action" (*praxis*), "in contrast with *technē*, has its end in itself; when contrasted with *theoria* at the end of Book X, it will

be found to have an end outside itself" (2008, 117). For discussion of the relation between prudence and wisdom, and the intellectual virtues in Aristotle in general, see Burger 2008, 109–30, esp. 127–30.

12. Even though Lorraine Smith Pangle acknowledges that there is pleasure in contemplating another who is good, especially if he is our friend and especially if we helped to form him, she questions whether "the pleasure of watching good activity [is] ever as great as the pleasure of engaging in it," and whether "the actions of one's friends [can] ever be one's own except in a weak and derivative sense." Consequently, she suggests that Aristotle's argument that we take pleasure in contemplating the deeds of our friend as our own applies to the young and immature and "points to the fact that people are often more inclined to claim others as their own, or rest upon the laurels of others, or try to live through others, than is reasonably justified" (Pangle 2003, 187). Her interpretation assumes that "the most blessed, being wisest," have a "more sensible recognition of their own separateness" (187). It is nevertheless the case that Aristotle does not explicitly restrict his observations about friends to the young and immature. Moreover, Aristotle "includes such factors [as contemplating oneself in the activities of one's friend] even in his final statement on the goodness of friendship." Pangle understands this as "evidence" that friendship has more to do with the ascent to the best life than with the best life itself (188–89).

13. For discussions of Aristotle's use of "another self," see Davis 2011, 72–74; Burger 2008, 182; Pangle 2003, 152–53.

14. The word Aristotle uses to describe what the equitable person is not, *akribodikaios,* occurs only here in extant Greek literature. It is possible that Aristotle coined it to contrast it with equity.

15. This is related to Aristotle's omission of righteous indignation (*nemesis*) from his discussion of ethical virtues in Book IV, after listing it in Book II as one of the mean conditions he plans to discuss (1108b1–7). As Burger observes, "Had it not been eliminated, righteous indignation would have occupied the culminating position in the discussion of the virtues of character and cast [its shadow] on the set as a whole" (2008, 92).

16. Pangle points out that while the noble friend feels pain from his friend's misfortune, he also "welcomes" it since it is the occasion for his acting as a benefactor. She argues that Aristotle finds a way around this impasse through philosophy: "In revealing these fissures that lie beneath the surface of ordinary friendship," she argues, "Aristotle indicates that it is not in the sharing either of fortune's blows or fortune's smiles that friendship is in fact at its best." Rather "it is in the life lived according to Socratic wisdom," she argues, attributing such wisdom to Aristotle, that there is "little mourning of misfortune, whether one's own or another's, and indeed little rejoicing at good fortune, since so little is required of fortune," but rather common pleasure in a shared pursuit of knowledge (2003, 194–95; see also Cropsey 1977, 273).

17. Assuming it from the context, Rackham translates, "we must copy the example of the man of nobler nature" (1926, 571).

18. For further discussion of how Aristotle's *Ethics* prepares for his *Politics,* see Tessitore 1996, 85–90; and Ann Ward's exploration of "political friendship" in the *Ethics,* including the reflection in different regimes of the friendships in the family, and concord or "like-mindedness" (*homonoia*) among citizens, in "Friendship and Politics in Aristotle's *Nicomachean Ethics*" (2011, 446, 454–59, 459–60). Aristotle describes *homonoia* as agreement among citizens about some things but not all things (1167a22–b4). My argument that Aristotle's understanding of friendship, as elaborated in the *Ethics,* prepares for Aristotle's understanding of political communities in the *Politics* also finds support in Smith 2001, 206–11; Frank 2005, 138–80; Collins 2006.

19. For a fuller discussion of Aristotle's *Politics,* including Aristotle's criticism of his predecessors in Book II, see Nichols 1992.

20. Michael Davis comments, "Much of Aristotle's criticism turns on the fact that the communism of the *Republic* in creating conditions under which it is impossible not to be virtuous also creates conditions under which it would be impossible to be virtuous" (1996, 40).

21. Robert C. Bartlett finds that "Aristotle's silence" about the philosopher-king in his discussion of Plato's *Republic* is to some extent compensated for by his treatment of the "absolute king" in the third book of his *Politics,* which "is, in short the rule of a 'philosopher-king'" (1994, 148). According to Bartlett, for Aristotle, "wisdom is in a sense the supreme title to rule" (148). See also my response to Bartlett on "Aristotle's Science of the Best Regime" (1995, 152–55). Cropsey finds in Aristotle's account of kingship in his discussion of friendship in the *Ethics* a criticism of Plato's philosopher-king, just as he finds in Aristotle's account of the relation between mother and child a criticism of the community of women and children (1977, 267–68).

22. In Plato's *Statesman* there is also a sixfold classification of polities or regimes, but there is only one term, democracy, for the rule of the many, whether it be the correct or deviant form (302d–e). Aristotle clears up one confusion, due to one word being used in two senses, as it were, only to create another similar confusion, at least for translators, who either must say something like "there are six polities and one of them is polity," or use different words to translate the generic polity and the specific polity. See Lord's use of "regime" for the former and "polity" for the latter, although he is translating the same word (in Aristotle 1984, 96). Rackham translates the generic name as "constitution" and the specific as "constitutional government" (1932, 207).

23. Those who claim a share in his rule, Aristotle says, act as if they deserve "to split the offices with Zeus" (1284b30–31). But in discussing friendship in the *Ethics* he observes that many have claims on us, including our parents, our siblings, our comrades, and our benefactors. We should render what is appropriate and fitting to each, and therefore cannot be expected to give all things to our father, he says, just as even Zeus shares the sacrifices (1165a14–17).

24. See Zuckert's discussion of how Aristotle's work stands "in marked contrast to Plato's *Republic,* at least on the surface" (1983, 203–4).

25. For a fuller discussion of Aristotle's treatment on tyranny in the Book V of the *Politics,* see Nichols 1992, 104–10.

REFERENCES

Aquinas, St. Thomas. 1993. *Commentary on Aristotle's "Nicomachean Ethics."* Trans. C. I. Litzinger, with Foreword by Ralph McInerny. South Bend, IN: St. Augustine's Press.

Aristotle. 1984. *Politics.* Trans. Carnes Lord. Chicago: University of Chicago Press.

———. 2000. *Nichomachean Ethics.* Trans. Joe Sachs. Newburyport, MA: Focus.

Bartlett, Robert. 1994. "Aristotle's Science of the Best Regime." *American Political Science Review* 88, no. 1 (Mar.): 143–55.

Burger, Ronna. 1984. *The Phaedo: A Platonic Labyrinth.* New Haven: Yale University Press.

———. 2008. *Aristotle's Dialogue with Socrates: On the "Nicomachean Ethics."* Chicago: University of Chicago Press.

Collins, Susan D. 2004. "Moral Virtue and the Limits of Political Community in Aristotle's *Nicomachean Ethics.*" *American Journal of Political Science* 48 (1): 47–61.

———. 2006. *Aristotle and the Rediscovery of Citizenship.* Cambridge: Cambridge University Press.

Cropsey, Joseph. 1977. "Justice and Friendship in the *Nicomachean Ethics.*" In *Political Philosophy and the Issues of Politics,* 252–73. Chicago: University of Chicago Press.

Davis, Michael. 1996. *The Politics of Philosophy: A Commentary on Aristotle's Politics.* Lanham, MD: Rowman and Littlefield.

———. 2011. *The Soul of the Greeks.* Chicago: University of Chicago Press.

Dobbs, Darrell. 2000. "Socratic Communism." *Journal of Politics* 62: 491–510.

Frank, Jill. 2005. *A Democracy of Distinction: Aristotle and the Work of Politics.* Chicago: University of Chicago Press.

Nichols, Mary P. 1992. *Citizens and Statesmen: A Study of Aristotle's "Politics."* Lanham, MD: Rowman and Littlefield.

———. 1995. "Aristotle's Science of the Best Regime." *American Political Science Review* 89: 152–55.

Nussbaum, Martha. 1981. "Shame, Separateness, and Political Unity: Aristotle's Criticism of Plato." In *Essays on Aristotle's "Ethics,"* ed. Amelie O. Rorty, 395–435. Berkeley: University of California Press.

Pangle, Lorraine Smith. 2003. *Aristotle and the Philosophy of Friendship.* Cambridge: Cambridge University Press.

Rackham, H., trans. 1926. *Nicomachean Ethics.* Loeb Classical Library. Cambridge, MA: Harvard University Press.

———. 1932. *Politics.* Loeb Classical Library. Cambridge, MA: Harvard University Press.

Salkever, Stephen. 2009. "Reading Aristotle's *Nicomachean Ethics* and *Politics* as a Single Course of Lectures." In *The Cambridge Companion to Ancient Greek Political Thought,* ed. Stephen Salkever. Cambridge: Cambridge University Press.

Saxonhouse, Arlene W. 1986. "Family, Polity, and Unity: Aristotle on Socrates' Community of Wives." *Polity* 15, no. 2 (Winter): 202–19.

———. 1992. *Fear of Diversity: The Birth of Political Science in Ancient Greek Thought.* Chicago: University of Chicago Press.

Smith, Thomas W. 2001. *Revaluing Ethics: Aristotle's Dialectical Pedagogy.* Albany: State University of New York Press.

Strauss, Leo. 1964. *City and Man.* Chicago: Rand McNally.

Tessitore, Aristide. 1996. *Reading Aristotle's "Ethics": Virtue, Rhetoric, and Political Philosophy.* Albany: State University of New York Press.

Ward, Ann. 2011. "Friendship and Politics in Aristotle's *Nicomachean Ethics.*" *European Journal of Political Theory* 10 (4): 443–62.

Ward, Lee. 2001. "Nobility and Necessity: The Problem of Courage in Aristotle's *Nicomachean Ethics.*" *American Political Science Review* 95 (1): 71–83.

Zuckert, Catherine H. 1983. "Aristotle on the Limits and Satisfactions of Political Life." *Interpretation* 11: 185–206.

———. 2004. "The Socratic Turn." *History of Political Thought* 25, no. 2 (Summer): 189–219.

———. 2009. *Plato's Philosophers: The Coherence of the Dialogues.* Chicago: University of Chicago Press.

Chapter Five

Augustinian Humility as Natural Right

MARY M. KEYS

> Most glorious is the City of God. . . . In this work . . . I have undertaken to defend her against those who favor their own gods above her Founder. The work is great and arduous; but God is our helper. I know, however, what efforts are needed to persuade the proud how great is that virtue of humility which, not by dint of any human loftiness, but by divine grace bestowed from on high, raises us above all the earthly pinnacles which sway in this inconstant age. . . . [W]e must not pass over in silence the earthly city also; that city which, when it seeks mastery, is itself mastered by the lust for mastery even though all the nations serve it.
>
> —Augustine, *City of God* I, Preface

Augustine's *City of God* (*CG*) makes an impassioned and dialogically reasoned defense of Christianity against those who claim that the new religion bears chief responsibility for the Roman Empire's decline and fall (ongoing as Augustine wrote and sealed shortly after his death in 430 C.E.). As the passage quoted above from his preface makes clear,

Augustine sees his great *apologia* for Christianity, and more broadly for the community of all who love God more than self, as an *apologia* for the virtue of humility. I argue here that in defending virtuous humility Augustine defends not only the Christian religion and divine grace but also a new account of natural right. The concept of natural right, of course, had played a crucial role in earlier Greek and Roman ethical-political philosophy, with which Augustine is in dialogue throughout his *City of God.* Classical natural right theory seeks to identify the foundation of justice for and among human beings according to their common nature, and Augustine's work continues this quest.

In support of this thesis this chapter offers a reading of key sections in *City of God,* Books I–V. This first complete segment of Augustine's magnum opus argues against the merits of polytheistic worship for personal and political prosperity in this life. In service of this task Augustine must examine closely the nature of right and of human flourishing more broadly, together with key causes supporting or undermining them. In these early books we encounter a microcosm of Augustine's overarching argument in his *City of God* for the excellence of humility (*humilitas*) and the shameful folly of pride (*superbia*). Augustine's analysis embarks in Books I through III from the very great pride of the grandeur of political might, apparently strong and glorious but actually, he argues, intrinsically enslaving and enfeebling. Such *superbia* is enslaving for humans because it is unnatural, a mere creature's individual or collective usurping of the place of God. It therefore results in an unwitting yet quite real enslavement to human finitude, folly, and moral weaknesses. Augustine's argument *contra superbia* thus continues to and peaks with his introduction of a metaphysics or natural theology of creation in Book IV, carrying over into revealed theology and reinforcing it in Book V. These books seek to establish divine governance as the fully just and liberating form of rule, one that is on a far higher plane than free human jurisdictions and thus that undergirds and guides rather than undoes them. In the background is the astounding humility of God, known to an extent through nature and most perfectly through revelation. Augustine's argument in the *City of God,* encapsulated and foreshadowed in its opening section, accompanies its political-philosophic readers on a dialectical journey from *political power and domination* to *pride as unnatural wrong,* and thence via moderation and creation to the *natural* as well as *divine right of humility.*

POLITICAL PRIDE, HUMAN NATURE, AND JUSTICE IN BOOKS I–III

In Books I through V Augustine undertakes to defend the City of God and therewith the virtue of humility from their contemporary and, we may assume, future detractors. Augustine makes it apparent that he considers humility a strong and splendid virtue, conferring on its possessor a transcendent, even divine loftiness and a serene stability amid this tempestuous temporal world. Humility before God is a precept of "divine law" promulgated "in the Scriptures of His people" (*CG* I, Pref.). Yet it is a part of Augustine's endeavor to persuade those who do not yet accept Scripture's authority of the excellence of humility, and so invite them to citizenship in the *Civitas Dei* (see, inter alia, *CG* II.29; cf. Busch 2008, 2009). Since this is so, despite what he admits is the task's daunting difficulty, Augustine must consider humility to have a foothold, a foundation in human nature, notwithstanding its fallen state. Augustine thus relies on divine assistance and also employs copious human argument on humility's behalf in this "great and arduous" dialectic. As we see at the end of his preface, a natural *epistemic* foothold for Augustine's case for humility is the misery of human pride, reaching its pinnacle when it claims divine honors and attributes in the service of its insatiable "lust for mastery" (*libido dominandi*). Augustine may not be able to appeal to the natural goodness and natural right of humility effectively as his first step, but he can begin to demonstrate to the jaded earthly city that "when it seeks mastery, [it] is itself mastered by the lust for mastery even though all the nations serve it" (*CG* I, Pref.). Pride (*superbia*) is not a true foundation for human happiness and greatness, if Augustine is correct, and someone persuaded of this much may begin to investigate with the *City of God*'s author his fuller, constructive case for humility's natural (and divine) justice and goodness.

In the main body of Book I Augustine thus proceeds in what we might term his *apologia pro humilitate* with a dialectical critique of political pride.

This pride, he first aims to show, obscures true social and civic vision. In recent years it has blinded certain pagan citizens to the mitigation of the horrors of war that the Christian religion clearly seems to have effected during Alaric's sack of Rome (*CG* I.1–7). Some who themselves escaped slaughter or slavery through the kindness of (Arian Christian) Goths, or by taking refuge in Christian churches respected by the invaders as "places of mercy and humility" and so of life and liberty (*CG* I.4), still fail *to perceive rightly* the cause of their good fortune. "Ungrateful pride" precludes for them a just recognition of Christian mercy's ameliorating effects in this time of war (*CG* I.1).[1] Prideful callousness has further led some pagan contemporaries of Augustine to blame Christian women who were victims of sexual assault during the city's pillaging instead of rightfully pitying and consoling them (*CG* I.16 ff.). This harsh and unjust response to violence belies the noblesse of pagan righteousness as described by Virgil, requiring of the virtuous great that they "spare the humble and subdue the proud" (*Aeneid* 6, 853). Augustine also finds in Virgil's poetic praise of ancient Rome profound evidence of its unjust pride, its hubris in attributing to human beings and a human city a task of judgment that only God can rightly and equitably fulfill (*CG* I, Pref., I.6).

In Books II and III Augustine continues to encourage humbler, more realistic readings of pre-Christian Roman social and civic life, employing renowned historians and statesmen whose works educated pagans knew well against naive or falsifying claims that the old pagan days were good or even significantly better. Roman *superbia* takes a chastening first through Augustine's survey of ancient historians' accounts of the moral evils and injustices that occurred as far back as the foundation of the city and in its monarchy and early republic. In Book II Augustine follows Sallust in considering the possibility of locating natural right or natural justice in the early Roman citizenry and their polity. At least three times Augustine quotes Sallust's claim concerning the epoch immediately following the expulsion of the Tarquins, that "'*Justice and goodness prevailed* among [the Romans] as *much by nature* as by law'" (*Catiline's War* 9.1, as quoted in *CG* II.17, 18; emphasis added). Augustine questions the truth of this praise by referring to Sallust's own accounts of events, including the abduction of the Sabine women and the war waged afterward against their parents and patria, the exile of Marcus Camillus, and the domineering, unjust actions of the patricians vis-à-vis the plebian class and the resultant civil strife. Roman moral rectitude and civic harmony reached their high point during the period between the second and final Punic Wars, yet not because of any natural goodness or justice. The chief cause, as Sallust himself indicates and Augustine emphasizes, was fear of foreign invasion, just as it had been in earlier periods of relatively "'equitable and moderate [rule of] law.'" After Carthage was destroyed and fear of foreign might assuaged, Sallust concedes, "'the morals of our forefathers were swept away, not by slow degrees, as formerly, but as if by a torrent'" (*CG* II.18, quoting Sallust, *Histories: fragments.* I.11).[2] Augustine indicates in this chapter that in his view "love of justice" for its own sake belongs to human nature *when it is right* (whether unfallen or as justified after the Fall) more properly than does "fear of uncertain peace" (*CG* II.18).

Book III, focusing on the physical and social afflictions that plagued pre-Christian Rome, continues Augustine's unmasking of pride as unnatural evil despite its cloak of glory and grandeur. The heart of Augustine's critique in this book is pride's destructive impact on natural ties of human affection, especially spousal and familial affection. Sallust is again Augustine's chief interlocutor and inspiration, and the incident most illustrative of this evil of *superbia* is the war provoked by the Romans against their mother city, Alba. Despite ties of consanguinity and shared history, Rome embarked on a bloody war to subdue the Albans to their rule and celebrated when the war was won. What rather was *right* for humanity in such circumstances was mourning and sorrow, Augustine begs his readers to realize. The misery and the horror of this military exploit were heightened after its completion, when the weeping of a young Roman woman for her Alban fiancé, dead by her own brother's hand, resulted in her brother slaying her.[3] In this woman's pity and grief (for her deceased betrothed, and perhaps also for her brother who slew his future brother-in-law) we find a great measure of *humanitas,* yet her bellicose brother and proud fatherland tragically could not see it (*CG* III.14). We finally see in her deed, Augustine implies, *an action right by nature;* yet it was rejected as wrongful by Rome. And why was it so rejected? It seems that the prideful lust for domination cannot bear a humble manifestation of natural spousal or kindred affection when it interferes with or dampens the triumph of military progress and political expansion.

After praising this woman for possessing "more humanity than the entire Roman people" (*CG* III.14), Augustine contests both the justice and the grandeur of Rome's triumph. "Why do our adversaries plead the words 'praise' and 'victory' to me? Take off the cloak of vain opinion and let such evil deeds be examined naked." He borrows from Sallust's critique of wars of aggression fueled by the "lust for mastery" (*libido dominandi*), which the ancient Roman historian attributed first to Cyrus and the Athenians and Spartans in their imperial wars (Sallust, *Catiline's War* 2.2). Here, in the lust for domination, again Augustine turns the proud glory of Rome against its own polity and its very humanity: "This 'lust for mastery' disturbs and consumes the human race with great ills. Rome was conquered by this lust when she triumphed over Alba; and, in praising her own crime, she called it glory" (*CG* III.14). The evil of Rome's proud injustice at Alba was only intensified and its horror made manifest by its familial, thus impious, context: "It was because of this wrongful purpose, then, that the great wickedness of war between allies and kinsmen was perpetrated" (*CG* III.14).[4]

The theme of political pride versus familial love and piety continues through the central and concluding chapters of Book III. Junius Brutus ordered and presided over the execution of his rebel sons, according to Virgil out of "love of country . . . and the immense love of praise" (*CG* III.16, quoting Virgil, *Aeneid* 6.820 ff.; cf. *CG* V.18). This too was during the period of "just and equitable" rule of law in the *res publica* according to Sallust. In this same era "the Voconian Law was passed, which forbade anyone to make a woman, not even an only daughter, his heir." Augustine comments poignantly of this proviso, "I do not know of any law that could be said or thought to be more unjust" (*CG* III.21, 130). Here we grasp again that natural right and familial bonds are closely united in Augustine's mind.[5] Pride demotes or even severs these bonds, whereas humility acknowledges them gladly. It is characteristic of Rome's *libido dominandi* to desire a disproportionate share of its citizens' loyalty, their whole hearts and wills and efforts at the expense of other commitments and connections that are also, and even more so, *naturally* right. At its limit, this perverted desire expresses a false *deification* of the political community and its exemplar citizens or rulers, a desire for worship which is emphatically not its natural due.[6] When political societies or their rulers thus turn against the affective and moral ties that give birth to and sustain their citizenry, *superbia* cooperates in and motivates grievous, unnatural wrongs, boding ill in the long run for the regime and rulers that perpetrate them.[7]

FROM POLITICAL PRIDE TO MODERATION AND A METAPHYSICS OF HUMILITY: AUGUSTINE'S DIALECTIC IN BOOK IV

Book IV plays a pivotal role in Augustine's argument *contra superbia* and *pro humilitate.* Augustine now develops his political and moral critique of pride with a dialectic favoring an analogue or close relative of humility: moderation.[8] Augustine inverts Socrates' dialogic methodology in Plato's *Republic* (368c–369b), arguing that virtues and their relation to happiness are easier to identify in a human being's life than in a political society; so he crafts two *human beings in speech.* As a former professor of rhetoric who had political ambitions of his own in his youth, Augustine is acutely sensitive to the power and splendor of language associated with politics on a large scale, probably always and everywhere but certainly in Rome. Sharing Socrates' antisophistry he challenges his readers to look more closely toward reality, to things as they are or at least as we ought rightfully to perceive them, and so avoid becoming overly impressed by grand phrases and magnificent appearances: "Let us not allow the edge of our attention to be dulled by the splendid names of things when we hear of 'peoples,' 'kingdoms' and 'provinces.' Instead, let us form (*constituamus*) two men (for each individual man, like one letter in a text, is, as it were, an element of the city or kingdom, no matter how extensive it is in its occupation of the earth)" (*CG* IV.3; cf. III.14). One of these men is of moderate means (*mediocrem*), possessing enough to live simply and well. He is beloved by his family and dwells in amicable concord with his neighbors. The other is wealthy but feverish, constantly acquiring property but never free from cares, conflicts, and fears that his adversaries' greed may one day overtake his own and strip him of his gains. Augustine's (again seemingly Socratic) answer to the question of which life and ordering of soul should be preferred, the *moderate* one, extends outward along the chain of communities: "so [also in the case of] two families, two peoples, two kingdoms . . . and if we use this principle vigilantly, to guide our search, we shall very easily see where vanity dwells, and where happiness lies." Augustine concludes that the Roman Empire would have been happier—that is, the *human beings* whose *res publica* it is or purports to be would have been happier—if it had remained moderate in size and ambition rather than seek to extend its dominion throughout the world. As it was, "the Romans always lived in fear and cruel lust, surrounded by the disasters of war and the shedding of human blood, which, whether that of fellow citizens or enemies, was human nonetheless." By nature, then, it is right and prudent for men to wish for peace and cultivate civic concord and moderation but not to "glory in the breadth and magnitude of an empire" (*CG* IV.3).

Augustine again appeals to a pagan Roman *auctoritas* to support this claim of the natural goodness of moderation and the wrongful harm of greedy overreaching. Justinus's pre-Roman history claims that at first kings ruled on account of "'the knowledge that good men had of their moderation (*moderatio*). The people were not bound by any laws.'" This all was changed, including the customary moderation of military force (employed only or chiefly in defensive causes), by the Assyrian king Ninus "through a new greed for empire" that led him on a snowballing series of offensive wars.[9] This immoderate love of dominion, Justinus quietly indicates but Augustine shouts for all to hear, is both an instance and a cause of great injustice: "[W]hat else is this to be called other than great robbery?" (*CG* IV. 6; cf. IV.4, with the famous story of Alexander and the pirate).

The key to Augustine's case in this section is therefore its argument for the greater naturalness and goodness of moderation as compared with prideful acquisitiveness; of temperate self-rule extended also to the benefit of others over self-enslaving love of domination over others. Augustine at this point introduces a specifically theological emphasis into his investigation, asking whether gods and goddesses whose example stoked immoderation and whose multiplicity and conflict countered human concord should be praised for their political beneficence. Augustine's argument once again begins with ancient pagan wisdom as recorded by sages, historians, and statesmen and moves thence toward monotheism that is capable of grounding both moderation and humility properly speaking.

Beginning from popular paganism that takes the multiplicity of divine beings at face value, Augustine not unintelligibly wonders just which (one or many) of these competing gods should be held responsible for the breadth of empire and its duration, and why, if their chief aim were the temporal protection and extension of Rome, they so often failed in their charge (*CG* IV.7–8). From here Augustine follows the interpretation of "the *natural* order" and its principles offered by various learned Romans (*CG* IV.11; emphasis added), including the great poet Virgil and a leading intellectual named Varro, who concur with Augustine that plain polytheism is untenable but unlike Augustine argue that it requires only reinterpretation by and for the learned. On their accounts the multiplicity of divine beings are either parts of the one god "Jupiter" or metaphoric expressions of his attributes or natural works. Virgil writes that "all things are full of Jupiter," and "Varro believes that [Jupiter] is worshipped, though called by another name, even by those who worship one God only, without an image" (*CG* IV.9; cf. IV.10–13). Augustine still finds such sophisticated, pantheistic interpretations of the god Jupiter as the soul of the corporeal world unpersuasive, beginning his dialectical theological challenge to them from the perspective of a pious pagan who would not wish to trample on a part of god when stepping on a stone or bug (*CG* IV.12–13).

Augustine now brings his dialectical critique full circle, returning to plain popular polytheism as the heart of the Roman attribution of its grand empire to Jupiter, as the chief god among many: it is "only by the king of the gods . . . that a kingdom of men could have been propagated and increased" (*CG* IV.13). But then why Jupiter and not the Roman goddess Victory, or why not deify "Empire" officially, since the Romans seem to have done so in their aspirations and actions? Here again Augustine pauses his theological-political reasoning to reiterate his critique of imperial expansion and grandeur as intrinsically valuable ends. He echoes his ethical-political appeal, with precedents in pagan histories, for a natural, rational recognition of the wrongness of victory won by aggression against "peaceable neighbors who have done no harm, in order to extend . . . rule" (*CG* IV.14). Chapter 15 radicalizes the inquiry by asking whether even basically just conquests of iniquitous polities are a cause for rejoicing. Augustine rejects them as unqualifiedly good but also admits the reasonableness of a moderate, just pleasure that may be taken in an outcome of better peace than perhaps would have resulted absent such (basically defensive) use of force (*CG* IV.15).[10]

Once again Augustine's dialectical exposition moves from the moderation of political pride to considerations of natural or philosophic theology. His case reaches its climax as he challenges those who worship creatures rather than the Creator, who worship gifts of God as if they were God, to acknowledge humbly the gap separating transcendent, infinite being from finite and contingent beings and the dependence of the latter on the former. Augustine's argument here applies to both plain popular polytheists and sophisticated philosophic or poetic pantheists. To the popular polytheists, Augustine argues that their late introduction of Felicity as a goddess indicates that they did not think their chief god, Jupiter, capable of bestowing true and lasting happiness. Yet happiness must be a gift of a divine being who possesses it and so can give it. The name of this being they did not know, so the name of the gift became their name for the unknown Giver.

> Now . . . we shall, perhaps, be more easily able to persuade as we wish those whose hearts are not already too greatly hardened. For human infirmity has now clearly realized that felicity cannot be given except by some god. . . . [B]y this argument I prove that they believed felicity to be given by some God whom they did not know. Let that God be sought, then; let him be worshipped, and it is enough." (*CG* IV.25)[11]

Augustine's invitation to the popular pagans, intimating that they are groping for the true God and so are closer than they think to finding him, is substantially the same as his word to the sophisticated intellectual Varro and others with a pantheist, world-soul understanding of the Deity. Augustine's admiration for their achievement of a good measure of truth tempers his critique of their public reticence to teach or even act consistently with their philosophic monotheism. Though he does not now elaborate a full metaphysics, Augustine unmistakably refers to a Platonic philosophy of soul and natural theology that might perhaps have persuaded Varro that the one God is transcendent and distinct from his creation. Augustine's assessment of Varro's theology marks the high point of Book IV's philosophic movement and merits quoting here.

> [Varro] . . . also says that . . . the only men who have truly understood what God is are those who have believed Him to be the soul of the world, governing it by movement and reason. And it appears from this that, though Varro still did not hold the correct view (for the true God is not a soul, but the maker and establisher of the soul), yet, if he could have been free to resist the prejudice of custom, he would have confessed, and persuaded others, that only one God is to be worshipped. . . . *The only question then remaining to be debated with him in this connection would be that he had called Him a soul, and not rather the Creator of the soul. . . . [S]o close to the truth, he might perhaps have been easily persuaded of the mutability of the soul, and so have come to understand that the true God is that immutable nature which created the soul itself.* (*CG* IV. 31, emphasis added; cf. VIII.1, VIII.5–9)

Had Varro achieved this final philosophic step, a true ethics of humility beginning from the willing recognition of one's own, one's polity's, and all human beings' *creaturely* status vis-à-vis the divine Creator would have been within his reach and perhaps within all of Rome's as well. As it was, the common people of Rome were left prey to the proud *libido dominandi* of civic elites who tolerated and even fomented false faith, so as to "bind men more tightly . . . in civil society . . . [and] possess them as subjects" (*CG* IV.32).

BOOK V: CREATION, JUSTICE, AND THE PROVIDENTIAL AND HUMAN CAUSES OF ROME'S GREATNESS

Book V completes Augustine's first and most deeply political segment of his *City of God.* It does so by aiming to demonstrate that Rome's political grandeur, might, glory, and fame are consequences of both human and divine causation, or the interplay of Providence and human freedom. Here Augustine seems to return to the concerns with which Book I began, and so to address principally, though not exclusively, his Christian fellows who are attempting to comprehend and come to terms with the causes of their polity's former greatness and current decline. Yet he does not leave his pagan compatriots entirely behind, engaging once again with their great philosophic statesman Cicero and also with the Stoics on the vexed question of the compatibility of divine providence and human free will. In doing so he outlines his theology of creation and its implicit metaphysics of finite and infinite being, thus paving the way for his fullest engagement with the Platonic philosophers, to whose arguments we have seen him appeal already near the end of Book IV, later on in Books VIII through X, and beyond (especially Book XIX). Like Augustine many pagan Platonists of the late classical era argue metaphysically beyond both the pantheism of Varro and the limited theism (perhaps atheism) of Cicero (see *CG* V.9): "[These Platonists] agree that a divine nature exists and concerns itself with human affairs[,] . . . a God Who made not only this visible world . . . but also every soul whatsoever, and Who makes the rational and intelligible soul, of which kind is that of human beings, blessed by participation in His unchangeable and incorporeal light" (*CG* VIII.1).

According to Augustine's argument in this section, it is by no means necessary to choose between providence and freedom in human affairs, once one recognizes all finite beings, including rational and free human beings, as the creatures of an infinitely wise and omnipotent Being. God's authority as the "Author and Creator of all nature" (*CG* V.9) operates on a transcendent level and poses no competition to human freedom. Indeed, the Creator created and sustains human creatures capable of freedom. Thus Augustine implies that human dignity and humility can and must go hand in hand if humans are to achieve full self-knowledge and strive for true justice, and that in their virtuous forms neither of these human attributes is independent of the Creator's providence.

Again in this segment of his argument Augustine provides some evidence supporting the naturalness of social and civic life among humans (see also IV.15 and n. 9 below); of a view of political life that is among the natural realities created and governed by providence, though now doubtless in a form changed and marred by sin and *superbia.*

> The supreme and true God, then[,] . . . [is the] Creator and Maker of every soul and every body. It is by participation in Him that all are happy who are happy in truth and not in emptiness. He made man a rational animal composed of soul and body. . . . Neither heaven nor earth, neither

> angel nor man, not even the inward parts of the smallest and most inconsiderable animal, nor the feather of a bird, nor a tiny flower of a plant nor the leaf on the tree, has God left unprovided with a harmony and, as it were, a peace among its parts. It can in no wise be believed, then, that he has chosen to exclude the kingdoms of men and their lordships and servants from the laws of his providence. (*CG* V.11)

After this theological prelude Augustine speculates that Rome's fame and political grandeur were the result of the justice and mercy of God, respecting the free choices of many ancient Romans to pursue human glory and cultivate justice and virtue in glory's service. Because they did not recognize or worship the one Creator, however, they fell prey by degrees to their own pride, making themselves individually or collectively into self-sufficient gods to whose praise their actions were directed. Love of freedom, natural and noble in itself yet twisted by a proud disdain of humbly serving others, grew into hubristic love of glory; and from there too many Romans plunged headlong into the pit of their own *libido dominandi,* the intensely proud deification of mere mortals as masters of the fates of others (see *CG* V.12–20). In so doing they undid the very freedom Rome had begun by seeking to preserve, both personally and politically becoming enslaved to a lie about their identities and refusing to look up to the Source of their being and so discern their nature's true right.

Only in humility can humans defy public or elite opinion and praise when needed in order to discern and love what is just and right. This apparent lowliness, as Augustine intimated already in the preface to Book I, is the starting point of all paths that lead to true divinization and immortality. Here again, later in Book V, he debates with Cicero on the point the latter makes on glory's behalf: "Honor fosters the arts, and all men are fired in their endeavors by the prospect of glory; whereas men always neglect those things which are held in low esteem" (*Tusculan Disputations* I.2.4; cited in *CG* V.13). Often, Augustine suggests, what is right and good will be found among those apparently lowly realities, where a proud person will not look or where he or she would disdain to go. This proud person is not only the ancient pagan, Augustine is at pains to convince his Christian interlocutors, but in part and perhaps more than in part also those who publicly profess to be seeking citizenship in the City of God: "It may be that in this life, [love of praise] cannot be completely eradicated from the heart. After all, it does not cease to tempt the minds even of those who are well advanced in virtue. But let the lust for glory be at any rate so surpassed by the love of righteousness that, if at any point 'those things which are held in low esteem' should be neglected even if they are good and right, the love of human praise will blush and yield to the love of truth" (*CG* V.14).

Augustine deepens his dialectic of humility, reminding Christian citizens how great the deeds of many ancient Romans were; how impressive was the greatest pagans' self-overcoming (relatively rightly, yet also at times wrongly done) on behalf of temporal, personal, and political glory; and hence how foolish Christians would be to overrate their own efforts of love of God and neighbor with an immortal polity and true glory in view. And for all those persuaded by, or at least open to, the natural and revealed theology of creation and providence, remembering that they are but human beings and thus one more among many fellows and not the cause of their own being, Augustine contrasts social and civic benefits of humility with the injustice and misery stoked by pride. Humility counters false divinization of self and society and so strengthens commitment to moderation and justice among human beings. It opens one to a love of rightful equality among humans, to recognition of true merits in others, to willing personal and public service on behalf of others, and to extension of one's natural familial affection and care to include the poor and abandoned of society (see *CG* V.14, 16, 17). Augustinian humility is thus the foundational virtue of human beings according to their finite, social, and especially created natures; it is Augustine's virtue embodying at its core what is right according to human nature.

CONCLUSION

Augustine's dialectical argument in Books I through V, for the natural wrong of *superbia* and the natural right of *humilitas,* continues and is deepened and developed throughout the remainder of his *City of God.* In Book XIX he expresses his case for humility as natural right in this way: "The task of [justice] is to give each his due. . . . It is for this reason that there is established in man himself a certain just order of nature, such that the soul is subordinated to God and the body to the soul, and thus both the body and the soul are subordinated to God" (*CG* XIX.4). This right order, Augustine also argues, has been weakened and indeed nearly undone by the Fall and personal sin (see *CG* XIV), yet inheres in our nature at least in its yearning for fulfillment and happiness, and may still be recovered. Augustine considers that philosophy can and should play its part in the human quest to recover natural right; yet in his view it too is impeded by the threat of philosophic pride and the finitude of the human mind and will (see *CG* VIII–X). He concludes that this quest for justice in and by philosophy must lead the true lover of wisdom beyond his or her own mind, to seek a Mediator who can purify us from the sin of pride and lead both learned and unlearned persons to salvation. Augustine considers that this Mediator has indeed come, in lowly flesh and "humble of heart" (see Matthew 11:29), to point out the right way of humility[12] and assist humans to follow it, though never with perfection in this *saeculum.*[13] Thus Augustine's dialectic of pride and humility in the *City of God* concludes hopefully that human beings can recover the true order of justice rooted in humility, as written in our common nature and expressed in Scripture: "'He hath shewed thee, O man, what is good; and what does the Lord require of thee, but to do justly, and to love mercy, and to walk humbly with thy God?'" (Micah 6:6; quoted in *CG* X.5).[14]

NOTES

Quotations from Augustine's *City of God* are taken from the translation by R.W. Dyson (Cambridge, 1998), cited with book and chapter numbers. I have occasionally modified Dyson's translation according to my reading of Augustine's Latin.

1. That the barbarian troops' restraint regarding *some* "customs and usages of war," chiefly in the churches, is not enough for a true Christian military ethic becomes clear later in Book I: "[Christians] are bound by no military authority, nor by an oath of military service, to smite *even a conquered enemy.* Who is so grievously in error, then, as to suppose that a man may kill himself because a foe has sinned against him, *yet may not kill the foe himself who has sinned, or in the future may sin against him?*" (*CG* I. 24; emphasis added).

2. Augustine makes an overlapping argument earlier, near the end of Book I, noting how Scipio opposed Cato over the destruction of Carthage "fear[ing] security [and the subsequent absence of fear] as the enemy of weak spirits. . . . [T]he outcome proved how truly he had spoken. For when Carthage was destroyed . . . once it had conquered a few of the mightier men, that *lust for mastery . . . overcame other men also,* worn out and exhausted as they were by the yoke of servitude" and civil strife (*CG* I.30; emphasis added).

3. I am grateful to Ashleen Menchaca Kelly for helping me appreciate more fully the significance of this incident and its protagonist in Augustine's ethics and political science.

4. Augustine continues this critique of rhetorical concealments later in this long chapter: "Away, then, with concealments and deceitful whitewashings! Let these things be examined openly . . . if two gladiators were to enter the arena to fight, one a son and the other his father, who could endure such a spectacle? . . . . How then, could the clash of arms between two cities be glorious when one of the cities was a mother and the other her daughter . . . , and broader battlefields were filled with the bodies, not of two gladiators, but of multitudes belonging to two peoples?" (*CG* III.14).

5. Cf. Michael Zuckert on Polybius's earlier and alternative account of the origin of justice in the natural development of family relationships, specifically in the gratitude that children reasonably and rightly ought to show toward their parents (2011, 8–11).

6. I am grateful to Veronica Roberts for clarifying this connection between the political usurpation of *familial* right and the political usurpation of *divine* right, and for her editorial assistance in preparing this chapter for publication.

7. In this regard Augustine seems quite close to some ancient tragedians' views; consider for instance the narrative interrelatedness of familial, civic, and divine rights in Sophocles' *Antigone.* For thoughtful reflections on imaginative expressions of modern natural right theory in American literature, see Zuckert 1990.

8. Cf. Origen (*Homily on Luke* viii), as quoted by Thomas Aquinas: "'If thou wilt hear the name of this virtue, and what it was called by the philosophers, know that humility which God regards is the same as what they called *metriotes,* i.e., measure or moderation'" (*Summa Theologiae* II–II 161, 4, *sed contra*). A closer examination of Aquinas's analysis shows that he like Augustine considers moderation and humility closely related but not identical virtues.

9. Cf. Augustine's earlier citation of Sallust, with diverse culprits (like Justinus's villains, none of them Roman) but a strikingly similar account of the praiseworthiness of (very) ancient civic moderation and the decline caused by those who "'began . . . to deem lust for mastery a sufficient reason for war, and to hold that the greatest glory belongs to the greatest empire'" (*CG* III.14, quoting Sallust, *Catiline's War* 2.2).

10. In this chapter Augustine notably indicates the naturalness of some sort of political life, marked by moderation and concord, even absent sin and the Fall: "If men were always peaceful and just, human affairs would be happier and all kingdoms would

be small, rejoicing in concord with their neighbors. There would be as many kingdoms among the nations as there are now houses of the citizens of a city" (*CG* IV.15).

11. Augustine's argument here is strongly reminiscent of Paul's speech in the Athenian Areopagus; see Acts 17:22–31.

12. Augustine alludes also to false or *wrong* ways of humility, as for example in *CG* X.5: "Many terms belonging to divine worship are . . . wrongly used in showing honor to human beings, whether out of excessive humility or . . . flattery."

13. See Dodaro 2004 for a study of the relationship between Christ and the just society.

14. For their generous support of my research project on humility, modernity, and the science of politics, of which this chapter forms part, I am grateful to the Earhart Foundation, the Martin Marty Center of the University of Chicago, the National Endowment for the Humanities, Notre Dame's Institute for Scholarship in the Liberal Arts, the Strake Foundation, and the University of Notre Dame.

REFERENCES

Augustine. *De Civitate Dei.* Accessed online at www.thelatinlibrary.com/august.html.

———. 1998. *The City of God against the Pagans.* Trans. and ed. R.W. Dyson. Cambridge: Cambridge University Press.

Busch, Peter. 2008. "On the Use and Disadvantage of History for the Afterlife." In *Augustine and History,* ed. Christopher T. Daly, John Doody, and Kim Paffenroth, 3–30. Lanham, MD: Lexington Books.

———. 2009. "Augustine's Dialogue with Political Philosophy in *City of God* XIX." Paper presented at the Annual Meeting of the Southern Political Science Association, New Orleans, LA, Jan. 7.

Dodaro, Robert. 2004. *Christ and the Just Society in the Thought of Augustine.* Cambridge: Cambridge University Press.

Plato. [1968] 1991. *The Republic.* 2nd ed. Trans. Allan Bloom. New York: Basic Books.

Zuckert, Catherine H. 1990. *Natural Right and the American Imagination.* Savage, MD: Rowman and Littlefield.

Zuckert, Michael P. 2011. "Rome: Machiavelli's New Constitutionalism." Paper presented at the University of Notre Dame's Political Theory Symposium, Notre Dame, IN, Mar. 25.

PART II

Modern Natural Rights

Chapter Six

On the Treatment of Moral Responsibility in Montaigne's *Essays* I.15–16

DAVID LEWIS SCHAEFER

For most of the twentieth century the dominant interpretation of Montaigne's *Essays* viewed it as recording the gradual evolution of its author's thought and attitudes, from the "impersonal" character of the chapters thought to have been composed first, in which the author typically defers to the Stoic wisdom of classical antiquity and says little about himself, through a "skeptical crisis" recorded in the "Apology for Raymond Sebond" (*Essays* II.12), culminating in a more personal style and more hedonistic and libertarian outlook embodied in Book III and in the later additions to Books I and II. (The first two books of the *Essays* were published in 1580; the so-called fourth edition of the work, which appeared in 1588, added Book III and contained hundreds of additions to and emendations of Books I and II. Montaigne then continued to make additions and other changes to the book until his death in 1592, all of which were incorporated into the editions published subsequently.)

The evolutionary interpretation pioneered by Fortunat Strowski (1931) and Pierre Villey (1908) was entirely suppositional, since its proponents acknowledged that the evolution had already been essentially completed by the time the first edition of the *Essays* appeared. In fact, as critics including the present author have pointed out, the interpretation was belied by the presence of thoughts supposedly characteristic of the "late" Montaigne in the allegedly early essays and of thoughts supposedly representative of the first stage in both Book III and the post-1588 editions. (See Schaefer 1990, 26–27.) It is more plausible, I have argued, to understand the broad evolution that Montaigne appears to undergo as he writes as a rhetorical strategy designed to gradually transform the thought and outlook of his readers rather than as a reflection of any change in his own views—particularly in view of his avowals of his consistency and his acknowledgment of the need to read his book with care in order to grasp his meaning (III.9, 942, 973–74 [736, 761];[1] Schaefer 1990, 14, 29–31).

While there was good reason for more recent critics to abandon the evolutionary interpretation, they have failed to offer a satisfactory alternative explanation of the character of a number of what Villey identified as early (usually brief) essays, which typically consist of a series of scattered observations, heavily reliant on quotations from other sources, without expressing a clear authorial point of view (even with the later additions). Prominent among these "problem" essays are the opening chapter, "By Diverse Means We Arrive at the Same End," and three subsequent pairs of essays that are found early in Book I, in which the second of each pair elaborates a theme introduced in the first: I.5–6, I.9–10, and I.15–16. Of these three pairs, the last is perhaps the most obscure and puzzling, leading to its near-neglect in the scholarly literature. Probably still exemplary of the critics' outlook (to the extent that scholars have considered these chapters at all) is Jacob Zeitlin's description of the last pair, along with the two chapters that follow them, as "simple discussions of military and politic questions . . . inspired by Montaigne's reading of Du Bellay's *Mémoires*" (from which the chapters borrow several anecdotes), the "impersonal tone" of which is "scarcely alter[ed]" by the author's "later additions from his classical reading and a few from his own experience" (1934, III, 316–17).

Having explored the first two pairs of chapters along with I.1 in my book *The Political Philosophy of Montaigne* (Schaefer 1990, 19, 219–23, 255–62), I devote the present study to the third pair. I argue that beneath a rambling exterior concerned largely with military matters the two chapters imply a philosophic challenge to conventional views of moral responsibility, and hence also to the Christian doctrine of free will. I elaborate this theme, which harmonizes with Aristotle's subtle treatment of the same issue in his *Nicomachean Ethics* as well as the famous "Socratic paradox" in Plato's dialogues, by citing relevant passages in several other essays. And I connect the theme with Montaigne's broader project of lowering the moral standards against which human beings are judged, in the spirit of Machiavelli's *Prince.*

AN OVERVIEW OF *ESSAYS* I.15–16

Before undertaking an analysis of I.15–16, it is necessary to provide an overview of these chapters. The theme that broadly links the two is courage and cowardice and their simulacra or variants, and the way in which each quality (or its possessor) should be treated. I.15 is titled "One Is Punished for Stubbornly Maintaining a Place (*s'opiniastrer à une place*) without Reason," and Montaigne's initial examples exhibit how the excessively obstinate defense of ultimately indefensible military positions in violation of "the rules of war (*reigles militaires*)" sometimes causes the besiegers to mercilessly punish the defenders once the holdouts have been overcome. This practice is said to illustrate the fact that "valor has its limits, like the other virtues," and that excessive valor turns into "boldness, obstinacy (*obstination*), and folly" for anyone who fails to recognize its limits, which are admittedly "hard . . . to determine (*choisir*)" (68–69 [47]).

Montaigne cites three contemporary examples of French commanders who executed all those who had resisted them on account of the defenders' stubbornness. Then he explains why the line between proper valor and punishable obstinacy may be difficult to discern in such cases: such judgments are inherently circumstantial, requiring that one assess not only "the comparative strength of the forces attacking" a position but also "the greatness of the conquering prince, his reputation, [and] the respect that is owed him," the latter consideration creating the "danger" that the prince will weigh the "balance" of judgment heavily in his own favor (in other words, that he will treat as punishable stubbornness what was actually legitimate courage). And Montaigne adds, "some have so great an opinion of themselves and their power that, since it seems unreasonable to them that there should be anything worthy to stand up against them, they put everyone to the sword wherever they find resistance," a practice characteristic of "Oriental princes" and "their successors." After illustrating this practice by citing the behavior of peoples encountered by the Portuguese in the Indies who had the "universal and inviolable law" that any enemy whom the king vanquished in person "is beyond consideration for ransom or mercy," Montaigne draws the sensible if obvious lesson that "above all, we must beware, if we can, of falling into the hands of an enemy judge who is victorious and armed" (I.15.68–69 [47–48]). He offers no explicit judgment on the justness of punishing stubborn defenders with extreme severity. Not surprisingly, Grace Norton observes in her commentary that "the subject of this *Essay* has so little to do with our own day that the first sentence [regarding the limits of valor] is the only one of general interest" (Ives and Norton 1946, 1575).

The next chapter immediately turns from the penalties sometimes incurred as a result of excessive courage to the opposite case. Its title is "Of the Punishment of Cowardice." Montaigne begins his discussion by citing the remark of "a prince, a very great captain[,] . . . that a soldier could not be condemned to death for faintheartedness," having "just been told the story . . . of the trial of the seigneur de Vervins, who was condemned to death for having surrendered Boulogne" (to Henry VIII of England in 1545). The author immediately lends support to the prince's judgment by stating the need "to make a great distinction between the faults that come from our weakness and those that come from our malice: For in the latter we have tensed ourselves deliberately against the rules (*reigles*) of reason that nature has imprinted in us; and in the former it seems that we can call on this same nature as our warrantor, for having left us in such imperfection and weakness" (70 [48]).

Without elaborating the character of the rules of reason to which he has alluded, Montaigne adds, with a barely veiled boldness that is properly remarked by Norton ("It was hardly safe to do more than to hint at such an opinion" [Ives and Norton 1946, 1576]) that "many people" have consequently "thought that we could not be blamed except for what we do against our conscience; and on this rule (*regle*) is partly based the opinion of those who condemn capital punishment for heretics and unbelievers," as well as the belief "that an advocate or a judge cannot be held responsible for having failed in his charge because of ignorance" (70 [48]).[2]

After this seeming digression, Montaigne returns to the official theme of the chapter by remarking that "it is certain that the commonest way" to punish cowardice is "by shame and ignominy." Drawing on Diodorus Siculus, he attributes the invention of this "rule (*regle*)" to the (sixth century B.C.E.) legislator Charondas, before whose time "the laws of Greece punished by death those who had fled from a battle." By ordaining that the cowards instead simply "be placed in the public square for three days, dressed in women's clothes," Charondas hoped "to use them after having brought back their courage by this shame." Montaigne then notes that "it seems also that in ancient times the Roman laws condemned to death those who had fled," as the emperor Julian once did to ten of his soldiers—though on another occasion the emperor merely condemned the cowards "to stay among the prisoners under the baggage ensign," and under the republic "the harsh sentence passed by the Roman people on the soldiers who had escaped from Cannae and . . . on those who accompanied Cn. Fulvius to his defeat did not go so far as death." (According to Livy both armies were removed to Sicily, where they were compelled to remain as long as enemy soldiers remained on Italian soil. Thus the Roman people in the days of the republic appear to have been milder than Julian, despite the claim that in imposing the death sentence he was following "ancient laws.") But Montaigne adds that "it is to be feared that shame may make [those punished by it] desperate, and not merely cold, but enemies" (71 [49]). Turning to examples drawn from "our fathers' time," Montaigne then reports the "rough sentence" executed against an officer for having surrendered the place he governed to the Spaniards: that he be "deprived of his nobility, and both he and his posterity . . . declared commoners, taxable, and unfit to bear arms." (This case recalls the issue of when a commander should surrender discussed in the previous chapter.) The same punishment was subsequently imposed on other noblemen, Montaigne reports. But he concludes, returning to the question of the relation between malice and ignorance, that "if there should be such gross and apparent ignorance or cowardice as to surpass all the ordinary [examples], it would be right to take it as sufficient proof of wickedness and malice and to punish it as such" (71 [59]). He does not explain how ignorance can rise to the level of wickedness or what the appropriate punishment in such a case would be.[3]

IGNORANCE, MALICE, AND MORAL RESPONSIBILITY

I begin my reconsideration of the two chapters under discussion by noting that each one refers to people being punished for violating a set of "rules"—military ones, in the first case; those of reason, in the second. But the content of these rules is left so vague in the first case as to leave one in the dark as to whether a given action violates them; and in the second instance, their content is entirely unspecified. Bearing in mind the Thomistic precept that human beings can properly be obliged to obey a law only if it has been duly "promulgated" or made known to them, we are led to wonder about the status of both sets of putative rules.

There are, indeed, several passages in the *Essays* that refer to the "laws" of nature, beginning with Montaigne's reference in his preface, "To the Reader," to the "nations which are said to live still in the sweet freedom of nature's first laws" (9 [2]; cf. I.31, 204 [153]; III.13, 1043 [816]). But these laws are not typically depicted as "rules of reason." Rather, "nature's" laws are portrayed as prerational instincts, notably the instinct of self-preservation, and are said to be "known" through feeling rather than reason (II.8, 365 [279]; II.12, 564–65 [439]; III.13, 1050–51 [821–22]). Nor are those laws said to forbid cowardice. Thus the nature and content of the rules alluded to in I.16 remain obscure.

The problem of the knowability of the moral or prudential rules that we are bound to follow is indirectly raised as well by Montaigne's remark at the outset of I.15 that the excess of valor, as with other virtues, amounts to a defect. As every reader of the *Nicomachean Ethics* knows, this is a claim that Aristotle denies. While each moral virtue is a mean between two extremes, he holds, there is no extreme with respect to virtue itself: there cannot be an excess of something that is inherently (not merely instrumentally) good (1107a6–7, 22–26). But Montaigne will repeat his implicit challenge to this claim in a chapter dealing with the other moral virtue in Aristotle's list that concerns the irrational part of the soul: I.30, "Of Moderation." (Given the evidence marshaled by Daniel Martin [1992], among others, suggesting a mathematical plan to the *Essays,* the appearance of the second challenge in a chapter that doubles the number of the first one may not be accidental.)

In "Of Moderation" Montaigne accuses "those who say that there is never any excess in virtue, inasmuch as it is no longer virtue if there is excess in it," of "playing with words" (I.30, 195 [146]). The charge appears to have merit. Even if it is definitionally true that one cannot be too virtuous, in practice Aristotle himself acknowledges—just as Montaigne did in I.15—that to determine the precisely correct course of action on a particular occasion may be no easy feat, depending as it does on a judgment of circumstances (*NE* 1104a1 ff., 1110a4 ff.). By what standard is one to distinguish in a given situation between proper courage and the vices of foolhardiness and cowardice? Aristotle denies that the right course of action can be determined by consulting a fixed set of rules. And in view of the difficulty of identifying the mean he prescribes as a second-best solution that we steer ourselves away from the extreme to which we are naturally inclined, that is, the more pleasant alternative (*NE* 1109b1–12)—though this is not his final answer.[4]

Not until considerably later in the *Ethics* does Aristotle indicate that the true standard of the virtuous mean is supplied by the *phronimos,* the possessor of practical wisdom as distinguished from mere right opinion—and that such wisdom may in turn be inseparable from (Socratic) philosophic wisdom, or knowledge of ignorance (1144b26–1145a6; Burger 2008, 129; Schaefer 1988). But since he gives no reason to expect that most human beings will acquire such wisdom, his seeming practical advice to them to beware of pleasure creates the risk in principle that they will be led to give it less than its due, thereby going to an improper extreme. However unlikely such a result may have seemed to Aristotle, given the naturalness of our attachment to pleasure, Montaigne suggests in I.30 and elsewhere that such was the ultimate effectual truth of classical moral philosophy once it was transformed under the aegis of Christianity with its promise of eternal beatitude to those who successfully resist their carnal appetites while on earth. (See II.2, 329 [250] for the connection between the "holy" frenzy of "our martyrs" and the supposed Stoic preference for pain over sensual pleasure.) Hence in "Of Moderation" Montaigne laments that "human wisdom very stupidly exercises its ingenuity to reduce the number and the sweetness of the sensual pleasures that belong to us" and "that our spiritual and bodily physicians, as if by a conspiracy, find . . . no remedy for the diseases of the body and the soul, but by torment, misery, and pain" (198 [148]). And he links that attitude with "the belief universally embraced in all religions" that "we gratify heaven and nature by committing massacre and homicide" (199 [149]; for further discussion of this chapter, see Schaefer 1990, 237–40).

The defense of pleasure in I.30 thus harmonizes with Montaigne's warning of the risks of excessive valor in I.15: both courage and moderation are putative virtues that are susceptible of excess. But there is another major point in I.15 that connects with discussions in both the opening and closing chapters of the *Essays* and elsewhere: the theme of conquerors whose excessive estimation of their own greatness leads to the merciless slaughter of anyone who stands in their way. The first and last essays address the cruelty of Alexander the Great in this regard; in each Montaigne juxtaposes Alexander's harshness with his own disposition to compassion, an attribute he also contrasts with the "heroic" virtue of Cato the Younger in the essay "Of Cruelty" (I.1.12–14 [4–5]; II.11; III.13, 1079 [844], 1096 [856–57]). (See, on the significance of these comparisons, Quint 1998; Schaefer 1990, 232–33.) Montaigne's critique of Alexandrian cruelty is in turn connected with his defense of sensual pleasure in I.30 by the fact that both cruelty and contempt for sensual indulgence are rooted in what the essayist terms, in the chapter "Of Presumption," man's "over-good opinion of himself" (II.17, 617 [480–81]). That outlook made Alexander, as Montaigne observes at the conclusion of the book, unable to accept his own humanity (III.13, 1096 [857]). By contrast Montaigne claims to embrace those opinions that "despise, humiliate, and nullify us the most" (II.17, 617 [480])[5] and suggests in "Of Cruelty" that only if human beings are taught to understand themselves in light of the sensitivity to bodily pleasure and pain that they share with the beasts, rather than in light of the divine, can they be induced to treat one another with proper humanity (II.11, 412–15 [316–18]; Schaefer

1990, 231–32; contrast Aristotle, *NE* 1177a32–1178a8). My suggestion is that the real "stubbornness" or obstinacy that Montaigne means to criticize in I.15 is not that of defenders of besieged fortifications—since by his account there is no sort of defense that will not be punished most severely by conquerors whose opinion of themselves is sufficiently elevated—but rather that of the conquerors themselves, who, like Alexander, are unwilling to be "content" "with a man's proportions" (III.13, 1096 [857]) or to accept "the laws of our condition" (III.13, 1067 [835]).

Here is the crucial link between I.15 and I.16: in questioning how far, if at all, human beings should be held accountable for the faults that derive from their natural weakness, as distinguished from "malice," Montaigne is implying the need to correct the excessively high standards against which they are commonly judged. As the reference to the punishment of heretics indicates, the theme has a much broader bearing than the merely military one. Montaigne's additional suggested exoneration of lawyers and judges from responsibility for failures that result from ignorance implies the further question of whether or how far *anyone* should be blamed for such failings. Most important, the chapter offers no criterion for distinguishing between pardonable ignorance and malice. And in I.3 Montaigne blamed nature, "more zealous for our action than for our knowledge," for "imprint[ing]" many "errors" in us (such as that of "always gaping after future things" instead of learning to content ourselves with "present goods") (18 [8]). Nature, then, is not simply the benign force that Montaigne's periodic appeals to her "laws" make it seem. If nature fills us with erroneous tendencies rather than rules of reason, how far can we be held accountable for departing from the path of virtue? Is malice, however defined, any more a quality that the individual can be said to have chosen, and thus be "responsible" for, than any other form of "error" induced by nature?

This challenge to the notion of moral responsibility is buttressed in another early chapter titled "That Intention Is Judge of Our Actions" (I.7), which like I.15 is ostensibly devoted largely to recent political and military events. In that essay Montaigne states the principle that "we cannot be bound beyond our powers and means," adding that "there is nothing really in our power but will," on which "all the rules of man's duty" are necessarily founded (I.7, 32 [20]). But this only raises the question of to what extent even our will is truly in our power, or the extent to which having a good will is a matter of choice. Montaigne challenges the doctrine of free will itself in the chapter "Of the Power of the Imagination." There, responding to Saint Augustine's attribution of "omnipotence" to the will, the essayist suggests that it might legitimately be charged with "rebellion and sedition" for its "disorderliness and disobedience": "Does it always will what we would will it to will? Doesn't it often will what we forbid it to will, and that to our evident disadvantage? Is it any more amenable than our other parts to the decisions of our reason?" (I.21, 100–101 [73]).

In other words, Montaigne implies that the very notion of holding people responsible for "willing" to do evil is an incoherent one: in answer to any such assignment of blame, one might respond, with Socrates, that no one "wills" to do what he truly believes to be bad. Hence wrong actions are the result either of weakness of will, which no one chooses to possess, or of an ignorance of what is truly good for oneself, which is similarly unchosen.

We are led by these successive mitigations of human responsibility toward the position of self-acceptance that Montaigne espouses in III.2, "Of Repentance," wherein he remarks, ostensibly of himself but in fact of the human race as a whole, that while he is "ill-formed," and eminently worthy of remaking if that were possible, "now it is done" (782 [610]), and later acknowledges that while "I may condemn and dislike my nature as a whole, and implore God to reform me completely and to pardon my natural weakness," this is far from repentance, since "my actions are in order and conformity with what I am and with my condition. I can do no better" (791 [617]). In sum, just as Aristotle counteracts his original exaggeration of human moral responsibility when he addresses the subject in the context of justice, the sphere in which legal punishments are imposed for deviations from one's duty (*NE* V.8–9; Burger 2008, 97–98; Faulkner 1972, 92), Montaigne suggests that it is nature herself that is the cause of our "imperfection and weakness," and awareness of this fact ought at least to moderate the vengefulness of those whose high self-estimation leads them to think that in punishing heretics and others who deviate from God's supposed commands they are doing God's work. (In contemplating Montaigne's reference to the cruelty practiced by "Oriental princes" and "their successors," one should perhaps bear in mind the Asiatic origins of Christianity.)

PHILOSOPHY AND POPULAR ENLIGHTENMENT

There remains to be considered the puzzling conclusion of I.16, to the effect that extraordinary instances of ignorance as well as cowardice should be regarded as "proof of wickedness and malice" and punished as such. In harmony with the textual evidence cited in the preceding section, there are at least three passages in other chapters of the *Essays* that suggest Montaigne's judgment that vice is itself the result of ignorance rather than of a "will" to do evil—leaving it obscure how even extreme ignorance could be a sign of wickedness rather than the other way around. In "Of Democritus and Heraclitus" he remarks that human beings are characterized less by "malice" than by "stupidity (*sotise*)" (I.50, 291 [221]). In "Of Repentance" he adds, "perhaps the people are right who say that [vice] is principally produced by stupidity and ignorance" (III.2, 784 [612]). And at the beginning of the "Apology of Raymond Sebond," after expressing his high regard for knowledge while refusing to set the "extreme" valuation that the Stoic philosopher Herillus placed on it as "the sovereign good," Montaigne first professes not to believe "that knowledge is the mother of all virtue, and that all vice is produced by ignorance," but then backtracks by adding, "if that is true, it is subject to a long interpretation" (II.12, 415 [319]). The view that the supreme good is to be found in wisdom, or the quest for it, is of course a core teaching of the Platonic Socrates and Aristotle, no less than of the relatively obscure Herillus. And the "long interpretation" of the thesis that virtue is knowledge might be an apt description of the process of studying the Platonic corpus. But if vice is truly the result of ignorance, then the only appropriate "punishment" that it merits would presumably be an education that remedies the ignorance, as Socrates suggests, for instance, in Plato's *Apology of Socrates* (26a).

It is for the sake of combating the sort of ignorance that encourages inhumanity that Montaigne espouses a moral teaching that differs from that of the classical political philosophers. Again we must look to other essays to see the point developed. Early in I.20, "That to Philosophize Is to Learn How to Die," Montaigne interprets the saying quoted in the title (originally a claim made by Socrates in Plato's *Phaedo,* though Montaigne attributes it to Cicero) to mean that reason's "labors" must serve "to make us live well and at our ease," and adds that "all the opinions in the world agree . . . that pleasure is our goal, though they choose different means to it." He elaborates that "in virtue itself the ultimate goal we aim at is voluptuousness (*volupté*)," judging that "the dissensions of the philosophic sects" on this issue are merely "verbal" (I.20, 79–80 [56]). In other words, he accuses the philosophers here of the same fault of wordplay with which he charges those who deny that there can be an excess of virtue in I.30. This mumbo jumbo reflected the philosophers' endeavor to give public endorsement to the conventional morality of self-restraint, even as their own way of life, based on "nature" and "reason," was one of hedonism (II.12, 567–69 [440–41]; III.9, 967–68 [757]). It is of particular interest that in I.20 Montaigne laments that on the issue of hedonism "there is more stubbornness (*opiniastreté*) and wrangling than begets such a holy profession" as that of philosophy (80 [56]). Thus he attributes to the philosophers as a whole—at least with regard to their public teachings[6]—the same vice of stubbornness that he warned in I.15 may lead to severe "punishment."

The penalty that the philosophic enterprise has incurred in Montaigne's time as a consequence of the verbal "quibblings (*ergotismes*)" that have blocked her "approaches (*avenues*)," he asserts in I.26, "Of the Education of Children," is that philosophy itself has become, "even to people of understanding, a vain and fantastic name." To counteract this image, presumably the product of Scholasticism, the essayist contends that it is "wrong to portray [philosophy] as inaccessible to children," since "she preaches nothing but merrymaking and a good time" (I.26, 159–60 [118]). In direct opposition to Aristotle, who announces early in his *Ethics* that this inquiry has no value for the immature (1095a1–12), Montaigne goes so far as to complain that owing to the deferral of philosophic study until the time of maturity, "a hundred students have caught syphilis before they came to Aristotle's lesson on temperance" (I.26, 162 [120])—as if Aristotle had chiefly intended his treatment of temperance or moderation to have a morally curative effect, when he actually emphasizes that moral virtue is the consequence of habituation rather than teaching (*NE* II.1).

The droll notion that reading Aristotle in one's youth would prevent syphilis indirectly points toward the more serious aspect of Montaigne's project of overcoming certain sorts of vice by a project of popular enlightenment, founded on a principle for which Alexis de Tocqueville would later credit Montaigne: the doctrine of "self-interest rightly understood" (Tocqueville 2000, II.ii.8, 501). Integral to that project, as indicated by the hints in I.16, is an elaboration of the Machiavellian enterprise of lowering the moral standards by which human actions are measured so as to reduce if not eliminate the gap between the "ought" and the "is." If virtue, properly understood, harmonizes with self-interest and pleasure, then its inculcation need not rely exclusively on nonrational habituation: Montaigne's "new lesson" is "that the value and height of true virtue lies in the ease, utility, and pleasure of its practice, [which is] so far from being difficult that children can master it as well as men" (I.26, 161 [120]). Elsewhere, he protests that "the precepts and laws of our life" have often been made "strict beyond universal reason" (III.9, 968 [757]).

Returning to I.15 and 16, in both chapters Montaigne asserts the existence of "rules" the violation of which is subject to punishment (military rules, rules of reason)—but which it is difficult to state precisely in the former case and of which Montaigne supplies no content in the second. In I.16, however, the stated rule is supplemented by two man-made rules that have the effect of softening the treatment of offenders by abolishing capital punishment for them (heretics and atheists in the first instance, cowardly soldiers in the second). What seems to be implied is that while nature herself fails to "imprint" meaningful rules of reason on us any more than she does the supposed "rules" of war (which are "reasonable even at the expense of reason"; I.6, 30 [18]), human art, guided by a consciousness of the "imperfection and weakness" of our nature, ought to formulate rules that limit the moral demands that the law makes on us. At the same time, the redirection of human endeavor from the pursuit of godlike superiority (as sought by Alexander along with the proud conquerors mentioned in I.15) to earthly pleasures might mitigate the inhumanity with which human beings treat one another, in particular, alleged "heretics and unbelievers."

NOTES

1. Parenthetical citations in the text refer successively to book, chapter, and page in Montaigne 1962, followed by a bracketed reference to the Frame translation (1958),

which I have followed with occasional modification. Book and chapter numbers are omitted when the chapter being discussed is obvious from the context.

2. While Zeitlin contrasts the "detached quality" of Montaigne's remark about the capital punishment of heretics with the "warmth" with which the essayist later condemns religious warfare (Zeitlin, 1934: I, 317), this need not reflect a change of outlook. Rather, I suggest that at this early point in his book, Montaigne is still engaged in winning his readers' confidence, and hence is more cautious about directly challenging received opinions about controversial issues.

3. For a comparable difficulty in Aristotle's teaching, concerning the unforgiveableness of actions committed out of ignorance resulting from "a passion that is neither natural nor human," see *Nichomachean Ethics* 1136a7–9.

4. See *Nicomachean Ethics* VII.14 and X.1–6 for the rehabilitation of pleasure, and 1172a29ff. in particular for Aristotle's rejection of the tactic of denouncing pleasure for the sake of curbing its excessive pursuit.

5. However, he expressly renounces such an attitude in discussing suicide: II.3, 334 [254].

6. See II.12, 483 [372] where Montaigne cites the Pyrrhonian Skeptics' profession of ignorance as having freed them from the vice of stubbornness, among other evils; in subsequent pages he implies that this awareness of ignorance was in reality characteristic of all philosophers, some of whom "put on the mask of assurance only to look better," or to have a morally edifying effect on the multitude (II.12.487 [375], 492 [379]).

REFERENCES

Aristotle. 2011. *Nichomachean Ethics.* Trans. Robert C. Bartlett and Susan D. Collins. Chicago: University of Chicago Press.

Burger, Ronna. 2008. *Aristotle's Dialogue with Socrates: On the "Nicomachean Ethics."* Chicago: University of Chicago Press.

Faulkner, Robert. 1972. "Spontaneity, Justice, and Coercion: On *Nicomachean Ethics,* Books III and V." In *Nomos 14: Coercion,* ed. J. Roland Pennock and John W. Chapman, 81–106. Chicago: Aldine/Atherton.

Ives, George B., trans., with commentary by Grace Norton. 1946. *The Essays of Montaigne.* 3 vols. New York: Heritage Press.

Martin, Daniel. 1992. *L'Architecture des Essais de Montaigne.* Paris: A.-G. Nizet.

Montaigne, Michel de. 1958. *The Complete Essays of Montaigne.* Trans. Donald Frame. Palo Alto, CA: Stanford University Press.

———. 1962. *Essais.* In *Oeuvres complètes,* ed. A. Thibaudet and M. Rat. Paris: Gallimard (Bibliothèque de la Pléiade).

Quint, David. 1998. *Montaigne and the Quality of Mercy.* Princeton: Princeton University Press.

Schaefer, David Lewis. 1988. "Wisdom and Morality: Aristotle's Account of *Akrasia.*" *Polity* 21, no. 2 (Winter): 221–52.

———. 1990. *The Political Philosophy of Montaigne.* Ithaca, NY: Cornell University Press.

Strowski, Fortunat. 1931. *Montaigne.* 2nd ed. Paris: Alcan.

Tocqueville, Alexis de. 2000. *Democracy in America.* Trans. Harvey C. Mansfield and Delba Winthrop. Chicago: University of Chicago Press.

Villey, Pierre. 1908. *Les sources et l'évolution des Essais de Montaigne.* 2 vols. Paris: Hachette.

Zeitlin, Jacob, ed. and trans. 1934. *The Essays of Montaigne.* 3 vols. New York: Knopf.

Chapter Seven

Benedict Spinoza and the Problem of Theocracy

LEE WARD

Of all the features of Spinoza's political theory, perhaps none is more perplexing than his account of the Old Testament Hebrew Commonwealth in chapters 17 and 18 of the *Theological-Political Treatise*. In this discussion of the Hebrew polity governed by Mosaic Law, Spinoza presents his fullest analysis of the intersection of religion and politics; that is to say, it is here in his most important political work that Spinoza considers the issue of theocracy. Antonio Negri is perhaps unique in his dismissal of this discussion as meaningless in the general scope of Spinoza's thought (Negri 1981, 116). Most commentators recognize the importance of Spinoza's regime analysis of the biblical Hebrews, yet they often differ as to what it signifies. For some, the Hebrew republic prior to the kings represents a model of Spinoza's best regime, akin to the role that the

Roman republic plays in Machiavelli's *Discourses on Livy* (e.g., Smith 1997, 146–47; Smith 1995, 222; Haitsma and Mulier 1980, 181–82, 186). For others, Spinoza's account of the Hebrew theocracy is primarily a cautionary tale intended to highlight by analogy the dangers that religious orthodoxy and clericalism pose for free government in the context of the seventeenth-century Dutch republic (Rosenthal 1997, 227–30; Feuer 1958, 121, 134–35; Morrison 1980, 189). Whether it is seen as the object of Spinoza's praise or criticism, it is perhaps unavoidable that the most authoritative biblical treatment of politics could not avoid drawing Spinoza's attention.

I propose to reconsider Spinoza's treatment of the Hebrew theocracy by focusing on an important but often neglected aspect of Spinoza's account. This is the explicit parallel Spinoza draws between democracy and theocracy. As is well known, Spinoza praised democracy, setting it as the peak of political possibilities because it was in his view the most natural and most rational form of government. However, less widely recognized is the, at least formal, resemblance or connection between democracy and theocracy, for Spinoza claims that in establishing their theocracy the Hebrews "all gave up their right, equally, as in a democracy."[1] Spinoza's affirmation of the egalitarian foundation of theocracy suggests that our understanding of his praise or criticism of the Hebrew polity must be considered in light of the relation between theocracy and democracy. Thus Spinoza's conception of theocracy either benefits from its resemblance to democracy—his best regime—or suffers from the extent to which it departs from the democratic standard of excellence.

This chapter argues that despite sharing some similar properties, democracy and theocracy actually stand as antitheses in Spinoza's political thought because theocracy represents the radicalization of dangerous and erroneous principles deduced from a misunderstanding of the human relation to, and place in, nature. Spinoza contrasts the theocratic perspective, which places the human relation to the divine as the central organizing principle of reality, with the philosophical or scientific approach to the study of nature, which he identifies as natural right. If democracy is the most natural regime because it immerses inquiry about the human in the study of nature simply, theocracy is, perhaps paradoxically, the most narcissistic and in a sense most unnatural regime because it encourages a false idea about the moral significance of the distinctly human in nature. Democracy logically flows from the principles of natural right, whereas theocracy does not.

Spinoza identifies the problem of theocracy operating in two distinct dimensions of Hebrew political life. First, he criticizes the quasi-separation of powers that emerged in the Hebrew polity after the death of Moses as a source of deep structural instability in the Hebrew state. The perpetual conflict between the Levite priestly class and the military leaders over who governs dramatically illustrates the problem of divided sovereignty, and the dangers attending any institutional effort to make religion acquire the force of law. I argue that Spinoza's account of the Hebrew Commonwealth also signifies a more general critique of the classical republican idea of balanced government, which was seen by many of Spinoza's contemporaries as the cornerstone of civic freedom. In this respect, Spinoza's treatment of the Hebrews was designed to influence the modern but not exclusively Dutch context by reorienting the republican conception of freedom away from classical ideals of balanced or mixed government and toward a clearer notion of the democratic and egalitarian foundations of political liberty.

However, for Spinoza the lesson of the Hebrew Commonwealth is not simply the need to have political control over religious authority. Rather the more fundamental problem of theocracy relates to the intellectual foundations of this type of regime. As Spinoza presents it, theocracy is based on a fundamental contradiction flowing from the proposition that the human relation to the divine is characterized by convention or agreement. On the one hand, theocracy presupposes that God is a legislator; on the other, the Hebrew regime signifies that divine law is the product of human agreement. According to Spinoza, the tension, and indeed contradiction, between the divine and the human origins of religious law created a source of permanent internal instability in the Hebrew polity. Thus the preservation of theocracy requires the suppression of intellectual inquiry about the truth of the prevailing religion, for as Spinoza seeks to demonstrate no plausible account of nature can support the notion of God as legislator or the idea that there is any human agreement or contract that is in principle inviolable. Spinoza's conception of natural right thus reduces every theocratic formulation of divine law into a form of politically enforced mass prejudice. The problem of theocracy, then, is inseparable from the misunderstanding of nature and lack of intellectual freedom that is in principle an essential feature of orthodoxy.

DEFINING THEOCRACY

Before beginning an examination of the Hebrew polity, it is important to locate chapters 17 and 18 in the framework of Spinoza's treatment of the relation of politics and religion in the *Theological-Political Treatise*. In the opening ten chapters of this work the Hebrew Commonwealth is a frequent focus of analysis as Spinoza considers the philosophical meaning and political significance of the Old Testament. His primary concern there is to present sound principles for interpreting Scripture, that is, principles of interpretation that are deducible from reason. In the context of this discussion, two features of Old Testament exegesis assume special significance: namely, the notion of Hebrew election and the role of prophecy in the establishment of Mosaic Law. Together these two propositions stand at the very core of what the Hebrew Commonwealth represents in Scripture.

In the course of offering a rigorously naturalistic account of scriptural interpretation, Spinoza presents a starkly unorthodox reading of the meaning of prophecy and Hebrew election. Prophecy we are told is primarily a product of vivid imagination rather than the superinduction of divine reason. Even in the case of Moses, who Scripture claims was unique among Hebrew prophets inasmuch as God spoke to him directly in a "real voice" (1.8.15), Spinoza identifies serious cognitive limitations that can undermine the coherence of prophecy. Indeed, Spinoza insists that Moses did not "adequately grasp that God is omniscient," and in actuality had only rather rudimentary ideas about God, including the belief that God has his "home in the heavens" like the Olympian gods "among the gentiles" (2.14.36–37). Moreover, Spinoza claims that prophecy was by no means unique to the Hebrews, for as Scripture reveals "all nations have had prophets, and that the prophetic gift was not peculiar to the Jews" (3.8.49).

Spinoza's critical approach to prophecy largely dismissed the importance of the particular features of Hebrew prophecy and focuses rather on a universal standard of moral actions for assessing the authority of prophecy. It is on this basis that Spinoza's critical approach to prophecy has an impact on his interpretation of the biblical idea of election. Insofar as prophecy is a product of human reflection on moral as opposed to speculative matters, it can only be judged by a secular standard of success or failure. Hebrew election had nothing to do with any particular insights about God's essence, for Spinoza insists that the Hebrews (including Moses) "had entirely commonplace notions of God and nature, and, thus they were not chosen by God, above others, for their understanding" (3.6.47). Rather what the Bible meant to indicate by the idea of Hebrew election is the "success and the prosperity at that time of their commonwealth" (3.6.47). This measure of success had to do primarily with the material welfare of the Jewish people and the independence and stability of the Hebrew state—a standard of success that in principle is universal. Moreover, given the secular basis of election, Spinoza claims, it is not a permanent feature of Jewish political life (3.11.54). Thus, according to Spinoza, neither the Old Testament idea of prophecy nor election indicates that Mosaic Law has any application beyond the Hebrew polity in a particular time and determinable by a measurable standard of political success.

Given the centrality of the Old Testament in Spinoza's treatment of scriptural interpretation, it is perhaps inevitable that he would expend considerable effort to examine the Mosaic regime that constituted the direct political manifestation of prophecy. However, when Spinoza turns to analyze the Hebrew Commonwealth in chapters 17 and 18 it soon becomes apparent that this polity does not fit standard categories of regime typology such as the classical idea of rule by one, few, or the many.[2] Rather Spinoza presents his notion of theocracy as something of a new discovery in the political realm, or at least theocracy emerges as Spinoza's attempt to craft a meaningful definition from a decidedly amorphous concept.[3] There are three components to Spinoza's definition of theocracy. First, he identifies a contractual basis of theocracy. When the Hebrews departed from Egypt they were "not bound by compact to anyone," and thus their political obligation came into being only when, on "the advice of Moses," they all agreed "to transfer their right to no mortal man but rather to God alone" (17.7.213). In this sense theocracy appears to be simply a variant of early modern, especially Hobbesian, contract theory. However, the second element of theocracy is the specifically theological content of the social compact for the practical effect of establishing God alone as sovereign is to give religion the force of law. As such, in the Hebrew Commonwealth "religious dogmas were not doctrines but rather laws and decrees," and the Temple was the "palace of government" (17.8.213, 17.15.219).

The third and final element of Spinoza's definition of theocracy is the separation of powers. The striking characteristic of the structure of the Hebrew government was, according to Spinoza, that "the right to interpret the laws and communicate God's responses was assigned to one man while the right and power of administering government according to the laws interpreted by the first and the responses he communicated was given to another" (17.10.215). In practice this meant that authority was divided between the high priest, who interpreted the law, and the civil leadership, who commanded the military. By this account, theocracy differs from monarchy, aristocracy, and democracy precisely because it reflects the antiabsolutist thrust embodied in the classical republican idea of divided or balanced government. That is to say, God rules theocracy almost by default as no other political or religious actors can govern on their own.

Even as Spinoza presents his multidimensional definition of theocracy, it is apparent that this theoretical account is in some sense inseparable from the distinct features of Jewish history and religious experience. While Spinoza argues that the Hebrew Commonwealth is the product of mass compact at a particular point in time during the exodus from Egypt, he also indicates that the Hebrew polity is indistinguishable from the religious rituals and ceremonies that "served to establish and preserve the Jewish state" (5.1.68). The complex dynamic of theocracy appears to flow in part from the tension between habituation and consent, between the deliberative actions of a political community and the ceremonial habits of continual obedience. It is on this basis that the relation between theocracy and democracy assumes particular significance for our purposes.

THE PARALLEL OF THEOCRACY AND DEMOCRACY

Any effort to define Spinoza's conception of theocracy is radically incomplete without careful consideration of the explicit parallel he draws between theocracy and democracy. Spinoza suggests this relation early in chapter 17 when he indicated that while "god alone held the government of the Hebrews, . . . in reality the Hebrews retained absolutely the right of government" (17.8.213–14). The underlying basis for Hebrew self-government was the fact that "the Hebrews did not transfer their right to another person but rather all gave up their right equally, as in a democracy. . . . It follows therefore that they all remained perfectly equal as a result of this agreement" (17.9.214). The common link between theocracy and democracy is the egalitarian basis of each, for in both states it is the "common consent" (19.6.240) to live by the dictates of reason or prophetic revelation respectively that grounds the polity.

The significance of Spinoza's references to the resemblance between democracy and theocracy is immediately apparent when we recall that the superiority of democracy is one of the hallmarks of Spinoza's political philosophy. In chapter 16 of the *Theological-Political Treatise,* just preceding his treatment of the Hebrew Commonwealth in chapters 17 and 18, Spinoza famously argued that democracy is the best regime because it is the most natural regime, that is, the regime in which a community can be formed "without any alienation of the natural right" of individuals (16.8.200). Insofar as in democracy sovereignty is retained by the society as a whole, it is thus the freest and most rational form of government (16.9–10.200–201). The basis for this claim is Spinoza's formulation of natural right. As is well known, by "natural right" Spinoza meant more than just the Hobbesian right of self-preservation inhering in individuals. Rather for Spinoza the principle of natural right extends to the whole of nature, and thus far from being a normative principle distinguishing humanity from the rest of nature, natural right in the Spinozist formulation embeds any consideration of human morality in the context of a non-teleological mechanistic account of nature. In this grand deterministic system, all beings strive to preserve themselves, and "the right of each thing extends so far as its determined power extends" (16.2.195). In other words, it is the natural right of big fish to eat smaller fish. According to Spinoza's natural right, God is nothing less than the totality of nature, "who has supreme right to do all things" (16.2.195). Democracy, then, is the most natural, and hence most God-like, regime because at least in principle it most fully collects the power of all the individuals in society.

When Spinoza refers to the "excellence" of the Hebrew state at the time of Moses, the determination of political excellence must hinge on the theocracy's connection to democracy. That is to say, questions about the political character of Hebrew identity take on greater urgency in the aftermath of the crucial discussion of democracy in chapter 16. Democracy is the political portal Spinoza sets for glimpsing the essential properties of nature. As such, his account of natural right established the preface of sorts for his treatment of the Hebrew Commonwealth. As Spinoza presents it, natural right grounds three basic political problems with which every government must grapple. First, natural right is the basis of human equality insofar as every human being has more or less equal right to preserve themselves. There is simply less natural power differential among humans than among fish. As natural equals, human beings thus resent rule and "will not allow themselves to be ruled" easily (17.4.210). Second, the inexorable preservationist thrust of natural right means that the most fundamental normative principles are essentially self-regarding. One aspect of the political problem, then, is how to make individuals prefer public right to private advantage (17.4.211)? And third, the natural right political problematic is really just the cumulative effect of natural equality and self-interest. Spinoza insists that governments survive or perish on the basis of their ability to secure the loyalty of the subjects or citizens. Every government in history has been "at greater risk from its own citizens" than from foreign enemies (17.1.208). By implication, the great strength of democracy is that its respect for intellectual and political freedom inspires the loyalty of its citizens.

The political "excellence" of the Hebrew theocracy must, then, be understood in the context of Spinoza's praise of democracy. Theoretical discussions of sovereignty, he suggests, point to the practical requirement to limit political power in favor of institutional and legal recognition of individual freedom and equality. Thus the central question animating any attempt to get at the heart of theocracy is, How well or poorly did Spinoza think that the Hebrew Commonwealth dealt with these basic political problems?

THE INSTITUTIONAL PROBLEM OF THEOCRACY

The opening sections of chapter 17 of the *Theological-Political Treatise* surprisingly say nothing about the Hebrew Commonwealth directly.

Rather, here Spinoza moved to correct the abstract treatment of sovereignty from the previous chapter by suggesting that while the logic of sovereignty leads to a form of absolutism, in reality the sovereign power of government is limited seriously by the internal freedom of mind and individual consciousness. The importance of loyalty in Spinoza's conception of political obligation derives from his assessment of this irreducible subjective freedom: citizens and subjects are not animals or machines. The structural component of Spinoza's definition of theocracy suggests that the excellence of the Hebrew polity would depend, at least in part, on its capacity to do two things, namely, secure the loyalty of the citizens and limit the power of government through a system of divided sovereignty. While Spinoza lists among the strengths of the Hebrew polity its ability to protect the property of individuals and the manner in which the citizen militias of the tribes encouraged civic virtue among the people, his idea of excellence also perhaps connects to the technical sense of a compound thing's excellence lying in its capacity to sustain its original complex structure over time (17.25.224, 17.18.220–21). In this case Spinoza's definition of excellence would resemble the classical republican principle of hostility to monarchy; that is to say, for centuries the separation of powers successfully moderated or checked Hebrew leaders after Moses who sought to establish one-man rule. But does Spinoza's account of the Hebrew Commonwealth prior to the kings actually signify its excellence in terms of either civic virtue or structural stability?

An examination of Spinoza's account of the Hebrew separation of powers suggests that far from lauding its virtues, he actually saw it as a highly problematic concept that planted the seeds of deep social conflict in the Hebrew polity. The source of the problem is, moreover, inseparable from theocracy for it is a function of the compact, which Spinoza claims is the institutional foundation of the regime. For Spinoza, the Hebrew polity rests on not one but two covenants. The first was a democratic compact whereby the entire community transferred "their right to no mortal man but rather to God alone," and the second is the following agreement according to which they "plainly abolished the first covenant and absolutely transferred their right to consult God and interpret his edicts to Moses" (17.7.213, 17.9.214). Herein Spinoza suggests that theocracy is a fluid concept adaptable in principle to both a democratic and a monarchical arrangement. The problem Spinoza identifies with these two concepts is not only the elevation of Moses to a quasi-monarchical position but also the inherent ambiguity relating to Moses' succession. The profoundly undemocratic character of the second covenant derives from the fact that the Hebrew people apparently did not retain any right to choose or limit the power of Moses' successors. Not only did Moses by this compact absorb the power of making and interpreting the laws solely on himself; he also reserved the authority to bequeath his office in radically altered form.

The central feature of the separation of powers established by Moses was the parceling out of power to a supreme military commander and twelve tribal chiefs, on the one hand, and to the Levites, a hereditary class of priests, on the other. While the supreme civil command assumed a decidedly ad hoc character after Moses' chosen successor, Joshua, the elevation of the Levites established an entrenched power that would for all intents and purposes dominate Hebrew theocracy. The Levites were also, according to Spinoza, a source of fatal instability in the commonwealth. He even goes so far as to suggest that the Hebrew republic "could have lasted forever," if it had not been for the introduction of religious and civil conflict by the Levites (17.30.229). What was it about the Levites that was so dangerous to the balanced government? Part of the problem is that the Levites sparked deep resentment from the other tribes, who were charged with supporting this nonlaboring priestly elite (17.26.226). It could hardly have helped matters that the Levites were also Moses' tribe and the first high priest was Moses' brother Aaron. Spinoza refers pointedly to the Korahide rebellion against Moses, fueled largely by the perceived favoritism for his own tribe, which was only suppressed after great loss and "terrible disaster" (17.28.227).[4] The more fundamental problem with the Levites, however, had to do with their role in the system of divided sovereignty whereby the high priests were "supreme interpreter of the divine laws" revealed to the people originally by Moses (17.11.216). Spinoza admits that the Levites were not given what he calls "the right to command"—that is, control over coercive power—but he insists that the Hebrew clergy were greatly empowered by the written Mosaic Law and the Jewish emphasis on ritualism. For as the Levites were supreme interpreters of the Mosaic Law, the separation of powers in the Hebrew theocracy could not help but slant the "greatest honour" in the regime toward the priestly class.

The Levite problem is inseparable from the specific properties of Mosaic Law, especially its reduction of divine law to written form. This is a function of the biblical narrative being designed to move the hearts of the "common people" to "obedience and devotion" (5.18.78). With a religion based on narratives and stories, Spinoza argues, necessarily comes "pastors or church ministers to explain these to them [the common people]" (5.18.78). Thus the power of the priesthood in theocracy differs in kind from the civil command with which it is paired. As Spinoza understands the Hebrew polity, the religious and civil leaders represent diverging tendencies: hereditary centralization with the Levites and a kind of meritocratic federalism embodied in the supreme military commanders and tribal chiefs. The conflict between the high priests and the supreme commanders reflects the fundamental incoherence of the notion of a prophet founder, for Moses could not establish a well-grounded balance of these powers because he did not possess them both himself. Moses, the legislator-priest, was not a military commander, and Spinoza suggests that he made a serious error by allowing the supreme command position to assume an ad hoc character after his death (17.14.217–18).[5] Constitutionally, the path to monarchy was laid by the Hebrew republic's inability to establish and maintain a unified and permanent office of supreme commander. In lieu of such a legal authority to counter the power of the priests, the Hebrew people, Spinoza argues, inevitably turned to monarchy. Thus the theocratic balance of power collapsed under the stress put on the governing structures by the weight of not only two different kinds of power—religious and civil—but also, and more important, very different principles of legitimacy. Divided sovereignty, then, could not avoid eventually producing the dreaded "government within a government" (17.29.228).

Spinoza's account of the defects in the Hebrew model of divided sovereignty did not, however, relate solely to explicating the conflict between the priests and the civil leadership. Rather, perhaps the peak of his analysis is his attribution of the root cause of the problem to an incident in biblical history predating the establishment of the Hebrew

Commonwealth per se. Spinoza identifies the event that gave rise to the power of the Levites as the infamous Golden Calf episode during the Exodus. As Spinoza interprets Scripture:

> The original intention was to entrust the sacred ministry to the first-born, and not to the Levites (see Numbers 8.17). But after everyone but the Levites had worshipped the Golden Calf, the first-born were rejected and declared unclean and the Levites chosen in their place (Deuteronomy 10.8). (17.26.226)

Spinoza presents the Golden Calf incident as a kind of second fall from innocence, which like the original Fall in Eden produced a punishment emerging from "much anger in the divine mind" (17.26.226). Remarkably he claims that scripture clearly indicates that God would not have instituted theocracy as it came to be if he had wished the Hebrew "state to last longer" (17.27.227). God at heart is not a theocrat! Indeed, if the Hebrews had retained the principle of every firstborn male constituting the sacred ministry, all the tribes would have been drawn closer together in "equal right" and "complete security" (17.27.227). This democratization of the priesthood would have had the effect of actually enhancing the bonds of civil union precisely because by privatizing the clergy the Hebrew state would have been freed of any religious authority possessing contestable claims to sovereignty.

As it was, however, the system of divided sovereignty perpetually threatened the coherence of the Hebrew polity. Not only was there the constant danger of one element of the government seeking to overturn the balance, but there was also the more insidious threat to Hebrew civic identity posed by the antagonism caused by the Levite hereditary priest class. With an oblique reference to the notoriously loose Dutch republic, Spinoza claims that the Hebrews were, like the Dutch, "not so much fellow citizens but confederates" (17.14.218). The ties of religion were more like treaty obligations among nations than the bonds of political union. Despite the symbolic connection provided by the Temple, the various tribes were practically strangers to each other (17.14.219). Given the hopelessly divided foundation of the Hebrew Commonwealth, it could hardly have been otherwise.

THE MORAL AND INTELLECTUAL PROBLEM OF THEOCRACY

Spinoza's detailed treatment of the separation of powers culminates in a portrait of the Hebrew Commonwealth as a kind of prototype of the "failed state." While their institutionalized system of divided sovereignty had some degree of success fending off absolutism and monarchy, this likely had more to do with the federal character of the polity and was nonetheless only temporary. With the establishment of the Levite monopoly over religious power, Spinoza argues, the decline of the Hebrew republic was inevitable. However, the specifically theocratic character of the Hebrew state requires us to probe beyond the bare outlines of the structures of government. Indeed, Spinoza affirmed that the core problem in Hebrew theocracy was the faults in their "laws or their morality" (17.26.225). It was essentially inadequate ideas about nature and the divine that grounded Hebrew moral and intellectual life. Beyond the problematic institutional structures of the Hebrew polity lay the deeper problem of theocracy: an incoherent principle of unity built on a fundamental contradiction.

The basic theoretical problem underlying the Hebrew theocracy has to do with the relationship between divine law and natural right. The notion of divine law is central to Spinoza's definition of theocracy for it is in the Hebrew Commonwealth that he identifies "by what means and by whose decision religion acquired the force of law" (Pref.14.11). Perhaps the most striking feature of Spinoza's treatment of divine law is the manner in which he employs the Hebrew polity to demonstrate the essentially historical character of divine law: "We must therefore admit unreservedly that divine law began from the time when men promised to obey God in all things by an explicit agreement" (16.19.205). In Spinoza's historicized account of divine law, the first compact among the Hebrews signifies the point in time prior to which no one was obligated to obey divine law.[6] In contrast to the historicism of divine law, Spinoza presents the state of nature as a reflection of the eternal principles of natural right. Divine law cannot be known prior to revelation, whereas natural right is in principle accessible to unassisted reason. Spinoza freely admits that the "state of nature" and the "state of religion" are different, even mutually exclusive conditions (16.19.205). However, does this mean that divine law repudiates or replaces natural right?

The status of divine law vis-à-vis natural right holds great political significance because, as we recall, democracy—Spinoza's best regime—is the form of government most like the state of nature. Democracy is most like the state of nature because it preserves the maximal degree of equality and freedom understood as rational action and free thought and expression (16.11.202, 16.10.201, 16.9.200–201, 20.14.257). Whereas divine law is characterized by "human agreement," democracy, at least in principle, according to Spinoza, is set in a realm of nature extending beyond the narrow confines of human convention. Spinoza does identify what he calls "natural divine law," but this is not a law strictly speaking because it does not depend on human artifice, and it amounts basically to a scientific understanding of natural necessity and material causality. The four main tenets of this natural divine law are (1) that it is universal to all human beings, (2) that it does not require "belief in any kind of historical narrative" (e.g., the Bible), (3) that it does not require ceremonies, and (4) that the supreme reward of the law is "to know God and to love him in true liberty" (4.6.61). Thus the universalism of natural divine law, indistinguishable from natural right, contrasts with the radical particularity and historicism of the divine law that established the Hebrew theocracy.

But was the divine law revealed to the Hebrews by Moses perhaps a rational deduction from natural right adapted to the particular circumstances of a specific people—an emanation from the universal, as it were? The key to answering this important question lies in understanding the role of Moses in the founding of the Hebrew polity. On the one hand, Spinoza insists that Moses tailored revelation to the capacity of the Hebrews, a people debased by centuries of slavery. As such, he did not speak as a philosopher teaching them to "live well, from liberty of mind," but rather "as a legislator obliging them to live well by command of law" (2.5.38). The relation of Moses to the people was as "parents teach their children prior to the age of reason" (2.15.38). On the other hand, Spinoza does not argue that Moses simply set the principles of natural right in rudimentary form suited to a backward people for, as we have seen, Spinoza detected serious limitations in Moses' conception of nature and the divine. While there are clear parallels to natural right in Scripture's teaching that God "reduced the visible world from chaos to order (see Genesis 1.2), and sowed the seeds of nature, and therefore has supreme jurisdiction and supreme power over all things," the idea that God "chose the Hebrew nation for himself alone . . . and left the other nations and territories to the care of other Gods" is difficult to square with natural right (2.14.37). Indeed, the culmination of Spinoza's treatment of Moses highlights the inadequacies of what he took to be the rather "commonplace notions of God and Nature among the Hebrews" (3.6.47).

According to Spinoza, divine law is inseparable from the personality and political skills of Moses. Moses is the central player in both the democratic and monarchical compacts founding the Hebrew state, for it is Moses who mediates between God and the people in both situations. And Spinoza is remarkably irreverent about the utilitarian motivation driving Moses; Moses "introduced religion into the commonwealth so that the people would do its duty more from devotion than from fear" (5.11.74). His goal clearly was to encourage loyalty by inculcating a habit of continual obedience in mild but intrusive daily rituals. The Mosaic Law is thus, in Spinoza's view, a reflection of an essentially unscientific perspective. It is in this sense that theocracy is the most narcissistic regime for, perhaps paradoxically, the regime supposedly founded on worshiping the glory of God constantly refers back to its own origins in the human agreement to obey God as the basis of its legitimacy. Unlike democracy, which humbles human pretensions to supersede or seek exemption from natural right, theocracy is a celebration of human pride or vanity, which places the whole of nature in an entirely unscientific way at the service of human identity formation through a people's relation to a providential deity. Theocracy is a "song of myself" casting nature and the divine in purely supporting roles.

The intellectual limitations of Moses need not, however, prove fatal to his capacity to institute a legal code that produces salutary moral effects among the Hebrews. Spinoza indicates that the only basis on which prophecy can be fairly judged is its impact on morality. Thus Moses could have been wise about political and moral matters while still lacking philosophic wisdom (Frankel 2001, 299–301; see also Bottici 2007, 167; Den Uyl 1983, 86). But did inadequate ideas about God and nature impair the moral capacity of the Hebrew state? On reflection, it is apparent that Spinoza believed the Hebrew theocracy failed gravely to do two things: create a coherent principle of political and moral obligation and encourage intellectual freedom.

On the vital issue of securing the obligation of its citizens the Hebrew republic failed badly because of the fundamental contradiction on which theocracy is built. This is the conflict between the notion of God as legislator and the idea of divine law as a product of human agreement. The main point of Spinoza's treatment of "natural divine law" is to demonstrate that the God of natural right—the God who is the totality of nature—is not a legislating force acting beyond or outside of the necessary physical laws of nature: "all God's decrees involve eternal truth and necessity, and God cannot be conceived as a prince or legislator enacting laws for men" (4.6.61, 19.8.241). Thus, to the extent that the Hebrew state was founded on a compact according to which all swore to obey God alone, then this compact could not explain the citizen's obligation to obey any written law putatively coming from this divine source. A second problem emerges from Spinoza's historicist account of divine law. Logically, if God vouchsafes the laws of the state, then they can never justifiably be broken. However, one of the central premises of Spinoza's natural right doctrine is that every compact or promise can be broken legitimately: "Any agreement can have force only if it is in our interest, and when it is not in our interest, the agreement fails and remains void" (16.7.199). It is this preservationist principle that "should play the most important role in the formation of a state," not pious devotion to holy writ. Here Spinoza presents one of the problems of theocracy as being the hyperextension of the logical fallacy animating the seventeenth-century idea of contractual absolutism. By natural right, any contract is breakable, even one presumably with God, although the God of natural right would never oblige anyone to a contract that did not allow for its own termination. Thus the central premise of the theocratic ideal of political obligation contradicts natural right.

One of the most important arguments in the *Theological-Political Treatise* is Spinoza's pathbreaking claim that intellectual freedom, especially freedom of thought and speech, is a vital element of a regime's political success. Spinoza herein seeks to reverse the long historical prejudice against freedom as being the cause of political instability and ruin.

Indeed, Spinoza identifies this defense of freedom as the "core thesis" of the entire work (Pref.8.6). Freedom is the central organizing principle of Spinoza's account of the true purpose of the state, and the "free state," which he associates unmistakably with democracy, enjoys "laws founded on sound reason" (20.6.252, 20.12.257, 16.10.201). Did the Hebrew theocracy encourage the civil and intellectual freedom Spinoza attributes to the best state?

What emerges from Spinoza's account of the Hebrew polity is his sense of the palpable lack of freedom in theocracy. First, there is the stultifying political impact of Mosaic Law. The law, Spinoza argues, was like a written constitution that people were encouraged to read and digest. The twin effects of having a written revealed law were that it empowered the reactionary tendencies of the priesthood given special power to interpret the law and seriously constrained Hebrew political leaders, who had to be very careful not to be seen to stray in the least from the prescribed laws for fear of generating "the most intense kind of hatred among their subjects, as intense as theological hatred tends to be" (17.17.220). While this particular lack of freedom on the actions of political elites could be seen as a healthy democratic suspicion of rulers, the extension of this intellectual rigidity and excessive formalism to a social principle could only result in the most intense theological patriotism. Thus the second instance of a lack of freedom is the xenophobia Spinoza attributes to the Hebrew Commonwealth: "The love of the Hebrews for their country was not simple love but piety, which along with hatred of other nations, was so nourished and inflamed by daily worship that it must have become second nature" (17.23.223). Spinoza implies that this fierce religious patriotism (or sectarianism) produced not only xenophobia among the Hebrews but also, unsurprisingly, the suppression of internal dissent. The manifold rituals and ceremonies of Mosaic Law only reinforced the broader culture of conformity by engraining the "continual practice of obedience" deep in the Hebrew psyche (17.25.224). Theocracy, in Spinoza's view, is thus indistinguishable from orthodoxy.

The general lessons about civil freedom that Spinoza draws from the example of the Hebrew theocracy are revealing. First, he distinguishes theocracy from the broader issue of religious freedom and toleration. Spinoza is not naive about the sovereign power's capacity to mold and shape people's thinking, especially when it has control over sacred matters: "I may say that whoever has this power has the greatest control over the people's minds" (19.16.245; see also 17.2.209–10). However, this does not mean that religion is incompatible with freedom. Rather, unlike public laws, religious belief "does not so much consist in external actions as in simplicity and truth of mind," and thus individual religious belief "does not belong to any public law or authority" (7.22.116). The legal character of Mosaic prophecy contradicts religion properly understood. Insofar as the goal of theocracy is to give religion "the force of law," it requires violating the very source of subjective intellectual freedom that Spinoza initially identified as the libertarian correction to theories of absolute sovereignty: "For simplicity and truth of mind are not instilled in men by the power of laws or by public authority, and absolutely no one can be compelled to be happy by force of law" (7.22.116). His reflections on the intellectual properties of religious belief lead Spinoza to the conclusion that theocracy, being based on preserving the prevailing religious prejudice, must eventually reduce to rule of force; that is to say, it will inevitably seek to compel individuals to be happy (Strauss 1997, 237). Such governments, Spinoza insists, cannot last long.

Second, Spinoza draws from the Hebrew theocracy a lesson relating to the dangers of referring "purely philosophical questions to divine law" and making "laws about opinions which men can or do dispute" (18.6.234). Steven Smith (1995, 1997) interprets this discussion to signify Spinoza's praise for the manner in which the Hebrew emphasis on works rather than faith helped avoid speculative controversy and suppression of heresy. For this reason, Smith sees Spinoza's account of the Hebrew polity as a model of protoliberal toleration and individual freedom (1995, 222–24; 1997, 147). However, the context of Spinoza's discussion suggests a rather different interpretation. Simply put, Spinoza claims that the Hebrew state was not adept at avoiding theological disputes, and given that it was a theocracy such a difficulty is hardly surprising. He reveals that the rise of sects within Judaism was a result of the high priests obtaining "authority to issue decrees and manage the business of government" in the later Hebrew Commonwealth (18.4.231). The original source of these clerical pretensions in politics was, as we have seen, the defective separation of powers established by Moses at the founding of the Hebrew state. Spinoza identifies the Pharisees—religious sectarians par excellence—as proof that the Mosaic republic did not adequately separate practical and speculative or moral and religious matters. The Pharisees are the legacy of Moses, much as every theocracy will require its own clerical champions, who will inevitably collapse moral and religious questions. Thus, far from being the progenitor of modern liberalism, the Hebrew theocracy stands as Spinoza's exemplar of the root causes of the kind of speculative controversy and theological conflict that so badly scarred the Christian states of his own time.

CONCLUSION

The unifying thread connecting the various defects of theocracy is, according to Spinoza, the fundamental misunderstanding of nature and divine on which theocracy rests. The lack of individual liberty and the incoherent principle of political obligation that Spinoza identifies in the Hebrew Commonwealth are problems deriving from the same mistaken belief that the civil laws are unchanging because God is the ultimate author of divine laws. Even if, as Spinoza admits, the moral qualities of Mosaic Law were often salutary, the political problem is that theocracy cannot restrict the role of religion to support for morality precisely because the logic of theocracy is to impose speculative ideas on the state, however defective they might be. Or perhaps better to say, the theological foundation of the theocratic state necessarily casts suspicion and hostility toward certain kinds of, in Spinoza's view, healthy speculative philosophy. Natural right philosophy contradicts theocracy, for given the dynamic character of Spinoza's account of nature, it is inevitable that the divine law will become gradually more brittle and eventually altogether obsolete under the strain of changing power relations in the actual world.

Spinoza's account of the Hebrew Commonwealth is, then, undoubtedly a cautionary tale, but the lessons he draws from Scripture extend beyond the particulars of biblical history, reaching rather a broader conclusion about the failure of theocracy as an approach to harmonizing the relation of politics and religion. While the principle of divided sovereignty and the idea of divine law are conceptually distinct, Spinoza reveals that theocracy involves the convergence of these two tendencies. The challenge of establishing a religion consistent with natural right—one of the central goals of Spinoza's political philosophy—required confronting the recurring attraction of theocracy as a regime that appeals to human vanity and desire to be the particular objects of divine attention. Spinoza's treatment of Hebrew theocracy is certainly, at least in part, about the religious conflicts in the Dutch republic of his time in which Christian sects and clerics threatened to tear apart the social fabric of the polity. Thus on one level Spinoza's treatment of the Hebrew Commonwealth is meant to be a lesson about how democracy, the "free state," must deal with religion. However, Spinoza's deeper impetus perhaps derives from his recognition that insofar as inadequate ideas about nature and the divine continue to plague humanity, then theocracy remains a perpetual political possibility even in modernity.

NOTES

1. Spinoza 2007, chap. 17, sec. 9, p. 214 (hereafter in notes and text simply chapter, section, and page). See also 19.6.240.

2. See, e.g., the classic Aristotelian typology at Aristotle 1995, 1279a25–1279b3.

3. As Feuer (1958, 120) and Balibar (1998, 45) observe, the term *theocracy* was originally coined by the ancient Jewish historian Josephus; however, Spinoza is the first thinker in modernity to try to give theocracy a distinct theoretical content.

4. Morgenstern (2009, 55) sees the Korahide incident as a democratic challenge to Moses' monarchical exclusivity, whereas McShea (1968, 99) sees it as an example of Moses' Machiavellianism as he put down an aristocratic revolt.

5. For this reason I disagree with McShea's presentation of Moses as a Machiavellian Hero-Founder (McShea 1968, 102). Indeed, Spinoza seems to suggest that if Moses had been more Machiavellian in some respects, such as establishing strong executive power, he would have been a better founder.

6. Here Spinoza's voluntarist conception of divine law most likely bears the influence of Thomas Hobbes, who famously defined divine law as "that which is declared to be so by the law of the commonwealth" (Hobbes 1994, chap. 6, sec. 36, p. 61; see also 26.40.188, 18.16.116). Gildin (1980, 168–69) shows how despite agreeing on the basic theologico-political problem, Hobbes and Spinoza took a dramatically different course on the issue of toleration.

REFERENCES

Aristotle. 1995. *The Politics.* Trans. Ernest Barker. Oxford: Oxford University Press.

Balibar, Etienne. 1998. *Spinoza and Politics.* Trans. Peter Snowdon. New York: Verso.

Bottici, Chiara. 2007. *A Philosophy of Political Myth.* Cambridge: Cambridge University Press.

Den Uyl, Douglas J. 1983. *Power, State and Freedom: An Interpretation of Spinoza's Political Thought.* Assen, Netherlands: Van Gorcum.

Feuer, Lewis S. 1958. *Spinoza and the Rise of Liberalism.* Boston: Beacon Press.

Frankel, Steven. 2001. "The Invention of Liberal Theology: Spinoza's Theological-Political Analysis of Moses and Jesus." *Review of Politics* 63, no. 2 (Spring): 287–315.

Gildin, Hilail. 1980. "Notes on Spinoza's Critique of Religion." In *The Philosophy of Baruch Spinoza,* ed. Richard Kennington, 155–71. Washington, DC: Catholic University of America Press.

Haitsma, G., and Eco O. Mulier. 1980. *Myth of Venice and Dutch Republican Thought in the Seventeenth Century.* Assen, Netherlands: Van Gorcum.

Hobbes, Thomas. 1994. *Leviathan.* Ed. Edwin Curley. Indianapolis: Hackett.

McShea, Robert J. 1968. *The Political Philosophy of Spinoza.* New York: Columbia University Press.

Morgenstern, Mira. 2009. *Conceiving a Nation: The Development of Political Discourse in the Hebrew Bible.* University Park: Pennsylvania State University Press.

Morrison, James C. 1980. "Spinoza and History." In *The Philosophy of Baruch Spinoza,* ed. Richard Kennington, 173–95. Washington, DC: Catholic University of America Press.

Negri, Antonio. 1981. *The Savage Anomaly: The Power of Spinoza's Metaphysics and Politics.* Trans. Michael Hardt. Minneapolis: University of Minnesota Press.

Rosenthal, Michael A. 1997. "Why Spinoza Chose the Hebrews: The Exemplary Function of Prophecy in the *Theological-Political Treatise.*" *History of Political Thought* 18, no. 2 (Summer): 207–41.

Smith, Steven B. 1995. "Spinoza's Paradox: Judaism and the Construction of Liberal Identity in the *Theologico-Political Treatise.*" *Journal of Jewish Thought and Philosophy* 4: 203–25.

———. 1997. *Spinoza, Liberalism, and the Question of Jewish Identity.* New Haven: Yale University Press.

Spinoza, Benedict. 2007. *Theologico-Political Treatise.* Ed. Jonathan Israel. Cambridge: Cambridge University Press.

Strauss, Leo. 1997. *Spinoza's Critique of Religion.* Trans. E. M. Sinclair. Chicago: University of Chicago Press.

Chapter Eight

Criminal Procedure as the Most Important Knowledge and the Distinction between Human and Divine Justice in Montesquieu's *Spirit of the Laws*

VICKIE B. SULLIVAN

Montesquieu is famous for his moderation in his consideration of the practices of the myriad regimes and cultures he discusses in *The Spirit of the Laws* (Carrithers 1977, 34–40; Durkheim 1960, 15–16). The author, who likens himself to a painter, presents these foreign practices in shades of gray rather than in bold declarations of praise or blame. He explains in his preface to the work: "I do not write to censure that which is established in any country whatsoever. Each nation will find here the reasons for its maxims" (xliv).[1]

This characteristic, among others, of Montesquieu's work immediately elicited the condemnation of the religious authorities. The failure of this French Catholic to readily admit the universal applicability of Christian teachings or to condemn such un-Christian practices as, for example, polygamy, was shocking (e.g., Plesse [1749] 1878, 105–7, 111; La Roche [1749] 1878, 117, 121, 126). So unorthodox were his views regarding Catholic teachings that the Abbé de La Roche ([1749] 1878, 117) accused him of both Spinozism and deism. The author responded to La Roche's criticism with his *Defense of the Spirit of the Laws;* eventually the Faculty of the Sorbonne voted to censure it, and the work was placed on the Papal Index of Forbidden Books (Shackleton 1961, 356–77; Lynch 1977).[2]

Given Montesquieu's own pronouncement as to his nonjudgmental approach to the political and social phenomena he examines, its evident application in the work itself, and the attention that this characteristic has generated among his commentators, the rare occasions when the judicious Montesquieu abandons this approach and recurs to superlatives are not only striking, but reveal his most deeply held principles. One topic that moves him to stark pronouncements is criminal procedure and punishment. In the second chapter of Book 12, titled "On the liberty of the citizen," he states, "The knowledge already acquired in some countries and yet to be acquired in others, concerning the surest rules one can observe in criminal judgments, is of more concern to mankind than anything else in the world" (12.2, 188). Montesquieu declares that criminal procedure is the most important knowledge for human beings to acquire (Carrithers 1998, 221–22; Carrithers 2001, 293–94; Pangle 1973, 139). An important reason for his pronouncement of the extreme value of this knowledge is that criminal procedure contributes directly to political liberty, which he defines as "that tranquillity of spirit which comes from the opinion each one has of his security" (11.6, 157). He explains, "This *security* is never more attacked than by public or private accusations. Therefore, the citizen's liberty depends principally on the goodness of the criminal laws" (12.2, 188; original emphasis). Without the protections afforded by a wise criminal procedure, magistrates and fellow citizens can arbitrarily deprive individuals of their property, their liberty, and even their lives (Zuckert 2004, 48–50). "When the innocence of the citizens is not secure, neither is liberty," intones Montesquieu (12.2, 188).

Moreover, human beings can be inexpressively cruel when dispensing criminal punishments, Montesquieu underscores. Indeed, Books 6 and 12 of *The Spirit of the Laws,* devoted to accusations and criminal judgments, are replete with examples from various cultures through the ages of extreme cruelties in punishment. The recounting of such offenses against human nature seems particularly trying for him as he also abandons his coolly objective approach when faced with treating especially terrible methods of torture or of putting the convicted to death, breaking off his discussion, unable to bring himself to describe such horrors (e.g., 6.17, 93; 12.4, 190). By contrast, he encourages gentleness and moderation. In speaking of the "power of penalties," Montesquieu declares that "men must not be led to extremes" (6.12, 84–85; see Pangle 1973, 95, 273).

Europe is not exempt from his censure on this score. Indeed, he finds the methods of papal and episcopal inquisitions both illegitimate and particularly cruel. His vehement condemnation of the cruelties resulting from trials for witchcraft implicates both Protestant and Catholic practices. This European divergence from a nondespotic criminal procedure arises from the fact that some Christians appropriate to themselves the very purposes and methods of the Christian God in their criminal judgments. In this work's deepest consideration of Christian doctrine, Montesquieu describes God as a judge and believers as sinners, whose thoughts and hearts the divine judge examines in the religion's pursuit of repentance for sin (24.13). These methods and this purpose are illegitimate, Montesquieu specifies, when human beings render criminal justice. He distinguishes, in fact, between "human justice, which sees only acts" in its pursuit of "innocence," and "divine justice, which sees thoughts" in its pursuit not only of innocence but also of "repentance" (26.12, 505). Tribunals in Europe have failed to maintain this fundamental distinction. Montesquieu's endeavor to render illegitimate this importation of the purposes and methods of the Christian God into human tribunals is a greater part of his treatment of criminal laws, accusations, and punishments than hitherto realized. His principles decree that the civil authority simply cannot punish religious crimes. He also warns repeatedly of the indignation that can fuel prosecutions for sacrilege and treason. When indignant, prosecutors are more likely both to search for hidden actions and to introduce as evidence the alleged thoughts of the accused. The latter form of evidence is never legitimate for human tribunals, according to Montesquieu, and the former are only a concern when the tranquillity and safety of the state, not the dignity of God, are at stake. When so agitated by indignation at the enormity of a crime, human judges must resist the impulse to attempt to descry intentions and to punish vengefully, he warns. Montesquieu's principles would offer freedom of conscience to human beings.

Montesquieu's extended focus on the deviation of Europe from proper criminal procedure is, indeed, a surprising result, as he initially points to the East—specifically, to Turkey—as the particular locus for a lamentable lack of understanding of proper criminal procedure (6.2, 74–75; 12.2, 188). He does, however, prepare his readers for the possibility of surprises in his examination of criminal procedure: "Criminal laws were not perfected all at once. In the very places one most sought liberty, one did not always find it" (12.2, 188). This link between criminal procedure and his concerns with human tribunals adopting illegitimately the purposes and methods of divine ones offers new insight as to why Montesquieu ascribes paramount importance to the "knowledge" of "the surest rules one can observe in criminal judgments" (12.2, 188; see also Pangle 2010, 89–90).

MONTESQUIEU'S ANALYSIS OF THE PURPOSES AND METHODS OF CHRISTIANITY AS A SEEKER AFTER DIVINE JUSTICE

In a chapter of Book 24, devoted to a consideration of "the religion established in each country," Montesquieu offers his deepest treatment of Christian teachings in *The Spirit of the Laws.* This discussion of Christianity is inserted in a chapter whose announced topic is "inexpiable crimes." He treats the religion as a type of criminal procedure, specifically referring to the Christian God as a "judge" and to the believer as a "criminal." It is no ordinary criminal procedure that he here describes, however, as he notes that the religion "leaves human injustice behind to begin another justice." He offers that this religion's judicial procedure pursues "love" and "repentance." He also reveals the methods by which it attains these purposes. In pursuing love and repentance, its divinity "is no more jealous of acts than of desires and thoughts" (24.13, 467). Elsewhere in the work, as I discuss below, Montesquieu refers to the injustice and cruelty that arise when human tribunals undertake these pursuits and these methods of divine justice.

There is no obvious sign that chapter 13 of Book 24 treats Montesquieu's understanding of the Christian religion, as it initially presents itself as a discussion of paganism as practiced by the Romans. Indeed, neither *Christianity* nor *Christian* appears in the chapter. Nevertheless, that this chapter contains Montesquieu's fundamental assessment of Christianity has not escaped prior commentators. Robert Shackleton, in fact, recognizes the significance and profundity of this passage, claiming that it establishes Montesquieu's "sympathetic comprehension of the Christian religion." Shackleton also mentions that the editor of the 1758 edition notes that the chapter contains "'a beautiful picture of the Christian religion'" ([1956] 1988, 113–14; my translations), and a more recent commentator declares that Montesquieu's "attitude towards the Redemption" that he displays in this chapter suggests that it would "not seem wrong to call him a Christian" (Waddicor 1970, 180). Finally, in disputing the charge of his ecclesiastical critics that the "author does not acknowledge the revealed religion," Montesquieu cites a series of passages from *The Spirit of the Laws* in which he refers to Christianity specifically, and within this series he quotes the entirety of this chapter's second paragraph, thus acknowledging that he does indeed speak of Christianity there (1949–51b, 1125–27; my translation).

Montesquieu begins the chapter by stating that "among the Romans there were inexpiable crimes." To corroborate this point, Montesquieu refers by name to two sources, Sozomen and Julian, both of whom discuss the motives for, in Montesquieu's words, "Constantine's conversion" (24.13, 467). Specifically, both of his named sources consider the possibility that Constantine converted from the pagan religion to Christianity in order to receive forgiveness for his prior crimes, including assenting to the murder of his son, an expiation that paganism denied him (Sozomen 1855, 15–16; Julian 1913, 413; see also Schaub 1999, 237). Montesquieu claims that Sozomen's account "so nicely poisons the motives" of that conversion, while Julian the Apostate makes a "bitter mockery" of it (24.13, 467). Through this cursory discussion of the role of paganism's inexpiable crimes in Constantine's conversion, Montesquieu establishes that Christianity itself is a fundamental theme in this chapter despite his not naming the religion of which he speaks.

After referring to this most famous conversion to Christianity, Montesquieu draws his conclusion about paganism. Because it "prohibited only some glaring crimes" and "checked the hand and abandoned the heart," paganism "could have inexpiable crimes." He turns to "a religion" that serves as his foil to paganism and offers what amounts to his account of the fundamental teaching of Christianity. The first portion of this account appears in one densely constructed passage:

> but a religion that envelops all the passions, that is no more jealous of acts than of desires and thoughts, that attaches us not by some few chains, but by innumerable threads, that leaves human injustice behind to begin another justice, that is made in order to lead constantly from repentance to love and from love to repentance, that puts a great mediator between the judge and the criminal, a great judge between the just man and the mediator: such a religion should not have inexpiable crimes. (24.13, 467–68)

Montesquieu comments that the religion itself is made to lead from repentance to love and then back again. The Christian apparently seeks repentance after having committed some error. Love follows this repentance, but that love leads back to repentance, apparently after the believer commits another error. In pursuing love and repentance, the divinity is "jealous" of "desires and thoughts" so that the religion "envelops all the passions" (24.13, 467). God not only witnesses the actions but also hears the prayers, uttered and unuttered alike, as well as the most inward and ineffable thoughts. This loving God offers forgiveness but scrutinizes the heart of the believer, ascertaining whether that devotion is true and complete (cf. Schaub 1995, 71–73).

Importantly, Montesquieu places this scrutiny in a judicial context, speaking here of justice, of a judge and a criminal, and of a just man and a great judge. Christianity is a seeker of justice, in his estimation, but not of human justice, as he specifies that this religion "leaves human injustice behind to begin another justice" (24.13, 467). In Montesquieu's description Christianity attaches the believer not by prohibiting merely a few grave crimes, which would produce the few chains of this metaphor, but rather by prohibiting innumerable crimes, as innumerable as the types of thoughts, desires, and passions that individuals are capable of entertaining, which produces the innumerable threads of the metaphor. Montesquieu describes Christianity as weaving a web from which there is no escape, not even within the solitude of the believer's mind. Being privy to all, Christianity's God judges all. Indeed, every thought is subject to judgment—every thought is actionable.

Montesquieu continues in this chapter to describe the character of Christianity's judging, specifying, for example, that this religion "puts a great mediator between the judge and the criminal" (24.13, 467). The criminal is clearly the believer, God the judge, and, as Shackleton's commentary suggests, Jesus Christ is the "great mediator" (Shackleton 1956, 113–14). Christian teaching, indeed, presents Christ in these very terms (1 Tim. 2:3–6 RSV). Montesquieu then returns to the characteristic of the religion that his sources at the beginning of the chapter highlight—forgiveness: "such a religion should not have inexpiable crimes" (24.13, 467–68). The mediator and the judge extend forgiveness for crimes.

Montesquieu's analysis in the remainder of the chapter actually undermines, however, the characterization of the religion offered by its pagan critic. Whereas Julian declares that Christianity offers easy forgiveness even to those who have committed the most heinous of crimes (Julian 1913, 413), Montesquieu highlights the burden for the believer of continual judgment and of the lack of assurance of ultimate forgiveness. His discussion continues: "But, though it gives fears and expectations to all, it makes them feel sufficiently that if there is no crime that is inexpiable by its nature, yet a whole life can be so; that it would be very dangerous to harry mercy constantly with new crimes and new expiations." Thus, according to Montesquieu's analysis of Christianity, whereas every type of crime can be expiable, the entire life of an individual can be inexpiable. The individual on trial is in jeopardy, Montesquieu states; there lurks the possibility that an individual life will be judged irredeemable and will be punished in the afterlife. Montesquieu puts the final clause in the first person and more clearly identifies the great judge as Our Lord: "that, troubled over old debts, never settled with the lord (*le Seigneur*), we (*nous*) should fear contracting new ones, overfilling the cup and reaching the point at which paternal goodness ends" (24.13, 468; 1949–51a, 723; capitalization in original). The Lord's paternal goodness can end. Love had been quite prominent in the first portion of this passage but is no longer the focus. Now the focus is on the individual's fear of God's retributive actions. Montesquieu and his fellow Christians live with the constant fear that their former sins will overwhelm the mercy of "le Seigneur." All their crimes and sins are subject to weighing and evaluation.

THE HUMAN USURPATION OF THE PURPOSES OF THE CHRISTIAN GOD IN CRIMINAL PROCEEDINGS

The Inquisition was not operative in eighteenth-century France, but both Spain and Portugal were undergoing inquisitions during that time. Montesquieu expresses disdain for these when he provides a "very humble remonstrance to the inquisitors of Spain and Portugal," dripping with irony, which he claims is written by a Jew on the occasion of an "eighteen-year-old Jewess" being "burned in Lisbon at the last auto-da-fe."[3] He quotes the Jew's letter as declaring, "'you have afflicted with iron and fire those who are in the quite pardonable error of believing that god still loves that which he loved'" (25.13, 490; Carrithers 1998, 227–28; Ehrard 1992, 336–38; Schaub 1999, 229–30). Montesquieu's treatment in *The Spirit of the Laws* of the purposes and the methods of the Inquisition far exceeds this explicit mention, however. Indeed, the manner in which some members of religions, including prominently those of Catholic Christianity, appropriate the purposes and methods of their divinity occupies him at several places in the work, including importantly in his discussion of criminal judgments and penalties. This section will examine Montesquieu's consideration of Christians who appropriate God's purposes to themselves—whether repentance for sinners or vengeance against those accused of denigrating the divinity—and who exact fearful corporal punishments in this world in an attempt to achieve them. By contrast, Montesquieu's own principles regarding criminal judgments would eradicate the very possibility of such inhumane punishments, because he propounds the principle that accusations of sacrilege, blasphemy, or heresy cannot be handled by the civil authorities; religious crimes can have only religious penalties, not corporal punishments, he teaches. He strictly separates divine justice from human justice, and thereby liberates the individual's conscience from inspection by human tribunals.[4]

Montesquieu also explicitly condemns the Inquisition in chapters 11 and 12 of Book 26.[5] Their title, "That human tribunals must not be ruled by the maxims of the tribunals that regard the next life," propounds his principle of the distinction between the two types of tribunals—human and divine. His first sentence condemns the Inquisition specifically: "The tribunal of the Inquisition, formed by Christian monks along the idea of the tribunal of penance, is contrary to all good police" (26.11, 504). The "tribunal of penance" is a reference to the Catholic sacrament of penance, in which a priest, as a representative of Christ, can offer forgiveness of sins and thereby remit the torments of the next life, when the Christian sincerely confesses and seeks absolution (Hanna 1911). Montesquieu ascertains that the purposes of a tribunal that regards the next life infect those of one that regards this life when the Inquisition "condemned to death" "the [accused] who denies" the charge while "the one who confesses it avoids punishment." Punishment rendered on this basis is one of the Inquisition's "abuses" and "is drawn from monastic ideas in which the one who denies appears to be unrepentant and damned and the one who confesses seems to be repentant and saved" (26.12, 505; Ehrard 1992, 339). Thus, in this way, he specifies that these human inquisitors exact a worldly punishment—death—for sins related to the next life, and in so rendering that punishment this tribunal appropriates the very end that their god seeks: "repentance" (cf. 24.13, 467).

Montesquieu also offers instances of human beings presiding over criminal inquiries that similarly usurp the purposes of the Christian God and that have decidedly this-worldly consequences for the accused in Book 12, which examines liberty in relation to the citizen as well as the most important knowledge available to human beings. He highlights the vengeance that fuels these inquiries and their subsequent punishment but insists that such vengeance should be God's alone. Further, he makes the prosecution of sacrilege and heresy an overriding concern of this book, as these crimes appear and reappear together in many contexts. For example, he links heresy to other hidden crimes that have in

Europe carried the extreme and cruel punishment of burning (12.6, 193). He advises caution in the pursuit of such crimes—including religious apostasy but not only religious apostasy—because their prosecution can eventuate in "infinite tyrannies" (12.5, 192). In this book he defines his essential principle that conviction for heresy and sacrilege cannot carry criminal penalties, which makes illegitimate corporal punishments for these infractions. Simultaneously, he denounces and renders illegitimate the various papal and episcopal inquisitions of the church as well as the civil authorities who were complicit in them.

In the fourth chapter of Book 12 Montesquieu defines four general categories of crimes: those against "religion"; those against "mores"; those against "tranquility"; and those against "the security of the citizens." He insists that the "penalties inflicted should derive from the nature of each." On his understanding, only the fourth category of crimes—those against the security of the citizens—would call for the application of the strongest punishments including the death penalty, which he calls punishments (*supplices*), as opposed to the softer penalties (*peines*), which he would impose for the other three categories (12.4, 189–91; 1949–51a, 435).

By contrast, Montesquieu specifies that "simple sacrilege" should be punished only by "the deprivation of all the advantages given by religion," such as "expulsion from the temples; deprivation of the society of the faithful for a time or forever; shunning the presence of the sacrilegious; execrations, detestations, and conjurations" (12.4, 189–90). Of course, although he speaks of religion in general terms, his words have an application to Christian Europe. "'Afflict[ion] with iron and fire'" (cf. 25.13, 490) is nowhere to be found among the penalties he here prescribes for such infractions, as his are considerably more mild than those applied in France and elsewhere in Europe before and during his lifetime (Carrithers 1998, 228–29; Carrithers 2001, 313–14; Waddicor 1970, 144–45). Indeed, his prescriptions have effectively given religion its own sphere, in which its jurisdiction is quite circumscribed.[6] Moreover, his proposed penalties contravene the typical historical practice of the various papal and episcopal inquisitions from the medieval period onward in which the inquisitors of the church would convict but then turn the condemned over to the secular authority for punishment. The punishments were determined by the prevailing criminal law of the locality and often entailed burning (Peters 1988, 59, 67, 94). Montesquieu's principles would eradicate the corporal punishments exacted by the various papal and episcopal inquisitions, as well as by the secular authorities who also undertook to punish religious crimes apart from these inquisitions.[7]

He reiterates his stand that sacrilege is not a criminal matter when he states later in the chapter that "in the things that disturb the tranquility or security of the state, hidden actions are a concern of human justice." By contrast, he notes that "those that wound the divinity (*blessent la Divinité*), where there is no public action, there is no criminal matter; it is all between the man and god (Dieu) who knows the measure and the time of his vengeance." God is a seeker after vengeance, he declares, but human beings should not arrogate to themselves God's "vengeance" (12.4, 190; 1949–51a, 433).

Montesquieu gives an arresting example of the cruelties that result when human beings do arrogate to themselves God's vengeance. He refers to an incident that took place in "Provence," in which a Jew was "condemned to be flayed" for being "accused of having blasphemed the Holy Virgin," but in this instance "the executioner" could not carry out the sentence because "masked knights with knives in their hands mounted the scaffold" "to avenge the honor of the Holy Virgin themselves" (12.4, 190).[8] The desire for vengeance of these knights was so intense that they undertook the punishment of this convicted blasphemer themselves. He warns of "what this idea of avenging the divinity can produce in weak spirits" (12.4, 190; Pangle 2010, 107). God's vengeance must be left to God, Montesquieu teaches.

That Montesquieu's teaching regarding the distinct spheres of religious and criminal matters challenged the teachings of his time is evidenced by the ecclesiastical criticism of the principles he expounds in 12.4. Machiavelli's declaration that one must never avenge "la Divinité" was in fact selected for censure by the Faculty of Theology of the University of Paris in 1752, which noted that this passage was "'scandalous, impious, erroneous, and heretical'" (Carrithers 1977, 394 n. 2).[9] The Jesuit Père Plesse also singled out this passage. Plesse writes, "one is never able to undertake to avenge the Divinity perfectly and totally, but there are circumstances where it is appropriate to punish the sacrilegious enterprises against God, because that is what serves to repair his supreme worship and to intimidate the wicked" ([1749] 1878, 103–4; my translation). Montesquieu's principles regarding the most important knowledge opposed the authoritative thinking and practices of Europe.

THE HUMAN USURPATION OF THE METHODS OF THE CHRISTIAN GOD IN CRIMINAL PROCEEDINGS

With its more than human powers, divine justice "is no more jealous of acts than of desires and thoughts" (24.13, 467). Not only the pursuit of repentance and love, but also of vengeance, when attempting to vindicate the honor of their God, drives human tribunals to attempt to employ these same methods against the accused. When in the hands of mortals these methods are faulty and thoroughly illegitimate, Montesquieu teaches. Indeed, in denouncing the "tribunal of the Inquisition" for "condemn[ing] to death" "the one who denies" and who thus "appears to be unrepentant and damned," he objects that "human justice" cannot proceed in this manner. Whereas "human justice, which sees only acts, has only one pact with men, that of innocence," "divine justice, which sees thoughts, has two pacts, that of innocence and that of repentance" (26.11–12, 504–5). Human justice sees only acts, Montesquieu here declares. In order to vindicate liberty, he propounds this principle throughout Book 12: only actions—not thoughts, desires, vague and inconclusive writing or speech, or dreams—can furnish evidence for criminal conviction. Human beings must be judged on their actions, but not all actions are overt and thus not readily judged, he concedes. "Hidden actions" are sometimes a concern of "human justice," he acknowledges, but only when "the tranquility or the security of the state" is at stake (12.4, 190). The pursuit of hidden actions in less serious cases or even in cases involving the security of the state when the indignation of the prosecutors is aroused poses a special threat to human liberty, a threat that he treats repeatedly in Book 12 when he considers the crimes of treason and sacrilege interchangeably (Pangle 1973, 141).

In 12.4, after Montesquieu delineates his principles that demand both that hidden actions be pursued only in cases concerning the tranquillity and safety of the state and that the civil authority not treat actions—whether hidden or not—that "wound the divinity," he declares, "For if the magistrate, confusing things, even searches out hidden sacrilege, he brings an inquisition (*il porte une inquisition*) to a kind of action where it is not necessary" (12.4, 190; 1949–51a, 433). Obviously, the term *inquisition* in this context is quite provocative given that magistrates did carry papal and episcopal inquisitions into their territory in order to search out hidden sacrilege—hidden away in the homes of the suspects or even in their hearts: "Inquisitors, like confessors, were trained to examine the mind and the soul" of the accused (Peters 1988, 87). He proceeds to ask rhetorically, if one were to proceed in such a manner, then "where would punishments end?" (12.4, 190). The magistrate's unnecessary—on the basis of Montesquieu's principles—action can issue in extreme and widely dispensed punishments (cf. Orwin 2010, 280).

In the next chapter Montesquieu examines the crime of heresy and links it to the crime of magic, noting that the "accusation of these two crimes can offend liberty in the extreme and be the source of infinite tyrannies if the legislator does not know how to limit it" (12.5, 192). The amount of resulting tyrannies is incalculable, he declares. Although trials for witchcraft were rampant in both Protestant and Catholic Europe in the sixteenth and seventeenth centuries, he does not refer in this chapter to any of these specific outbreaks but rather to the Byzantine Empire. His discussion of the combination of heresy and magic here emphasizes the fear and indignation that arise in the community as a whole and in the prosecutors; horrendous punishments result. "Now, by supposing a power in magic that can arm hell and by starting from this," Montesquieu explains, "he whom one calls a magician is considered the man in the world most likely to disturb and overthrow society, and one is drawn to punish him immeasurably." That is severe punishment indeed. He continues: "Indignation grows when one includes in magic the power to destroy religion" (12.5, 192). Severe punishments follow in this case as well.

In the following chapter Montesquieu continues his discussion of heresy and magic while he considers yet another crime, that "against nature." He notes, "It is singular that among ourselves three crimes, magic, heresy, and the crime against nature" "were all three punished by the penalty of burning." His remark underscores that this extreme penalty was inflicted in the lands of Europe. Moreover, his further comment suggests that so extreme a penalty for such nonexistent or petty crimes numbers among those "infinite tyrannies" to which he referred in the previous chapter: "it can be proved that the first does not exist, that the second is susceptible to infinite distinctions, interpretations and limitations, and that the third is often hidden" (12.6, 193).

He expresses particular concern that such accusations do "not bear directly on the actions of a citizen, but rather on the idea one has of his character." Because the accusation derives not from a specific action, Montesquieu explains, "a citizen is always in danger because the best conduct in the world, the purest morality, and the practice of all one's duties do not guarantee one from being suspected of these crimes" (12.5,192). Therefore, the innocence of the citizen is not assured, and "when the innocence of the citizens is not secure, neither is liberty" (12.2, 188).

Not only does the crime of sacrilege preoccupy Montesquieu throughout Book 12, but so too does that of high treason, and at several points in the book he refers to sacrilege and high treason interchangeably. Accusations of both crimes can arouse indignation, disgust, and fear in accusers and avengers, which makes the prosecution of them on the basis of thoughts all the more tempting. Moreover, sacrilege and treason are both crimes that can be perpetrated by means of conspiracies, and thus writings and speech are often called into evidence against the accused.

Montesquieu's collapsing of these two crimes becomes evident when a chapter titled "On the crime of high treason [Du crime de lèse-majesté]" is followed by three devoted to the subject, "On the wrong application of the name of crime of sacrilege and high treason (*lèse-majesté*)" (12.7–10; 1949–51a, 438). His first example of such a wrong application is that of a "law of the emperors" that "pursued as sacrilegious those who called the prince's judgment into question" (12.8, 195).[10] Perhaps the most striking instance of Montesquieu's own analysis collapsing these two types of crimes occurs in the chapter titled "On revealing conspiracies." Montesquieu begins this chapter not with an example of a turn against an earthly ruler but rather with a turn against a heavenly one, by speaking of the punishment of stoning that Deuteronomy 13:6–9 declares family members should themselves inflict on their kin who "'entice [them] secretly'" to leave the one true God to seek other gods. He here condemns this biblical approach to thwarting conspiracy, pronouncing that "this law of Deuteronomy cannot be a civil law among most of the peoples that we know because it would open the door to all crimes."[11] Montesquieu characterizes as "scarcely less harsh" another law, common in many states, that demands that individuals reveal conspiracies which they discover but of which they are not a party (12.17, 202).

By equating religious conspiracy with political conspiracy in this way, Montesquieu collapses his own approach to both. He advises extreme caution in pursuing such alleged crimes. Indeed, he offers the general admonition, "Vagueness in the crime of high treason is enough to make government degenerate into despotism" (12.7, 194). To treat these infractions too harshly is dangerous, dangerous for the citizen; and, to violate the life, liberty, and property in their pursuit can be despotic.

Montesquieu elaborates on the principle that only actions can provide the grounds for prosecution when he specifically objects to the use of thoughts as evidence in a case involving an attempt on a ruler. This discussion occurs in a very brief chapter in Book 12 titled "On thoughts," in which he recounts a story from Plutarch that tells of a man who dreamed that he had cut the throat of the despot. As a result of a mere dream, the despot, in reality, put the man to death. This punishment, declares Montesquieu, "was a great tyranny," and he explains that "even if [the man] had thought it, he had not attempted it" (12.11, 197). The story may derive from ancient times, but Montesquieu's conclusion has implications for modern times. Inquisitions investigate the same crime and also use thoughts illegitimately as evidence. Montesquieu concludes this chapter on thoughts with a forthright pronouncement against the use of thoughts as evidence in trials: "Laws are charged with punishing only external actions" (12.11, 197; Ehrard 1992, 339–40). The conscience is free.

In the immediately subsequent chapters, Montesquieu circumscribes the use of speech and writings in human tribunals. He notes, for example, that "speech does not form a *corpus delicti:* it remains only an idea." Referring to how "equivocal" its meaning can be, he says, "Silence sometimes expresses more than any speech." He then proceeds to delineate his rules of evidence:

> Actionable acts are not an everyday occurrence; they may be observed by many people: a false accusation over facts can easily be clarified. The

> words that are joined to an act take on the nature of that action. Thus a man who goes into the public square to exhort the subjects to revolt becomes guilty of high treason (*lèse-majesté*), because the speech is joined to the act and participates in it. It is not speech that is punished but an act committed in which speech is used. Speech becomes criminal only when it prepares, when it accompanies, or when it follows a criminal act. (12.12, 198–99; 1949–51a, 443)

In the following chapter, on writings, he notes that they "contain something more permanent than speech, but when they do not prepare the way for the crime of high treason (*lèse-majesté*), they are not material to the crime of high treason (*lèse-majesté*)" (12.13, 199; 1949–51a, 443; Carrithers 2001, 298).

Interestingly, when Montesquieu defended himself against the ecclesiastical critics he found them applying against him the very methods that he deemed impermissible in human tribunals. He writes in his *Defense* that although his accuser must admit that in some places the author of *The Spirit of the Laws* says some "'very fine things about the Christian religion,'" his accuser would assert that the author does so only to "'conceal [him]self.'" Montesquieu attributes to his accuser the assertions "'I know your heart, and I read your thoughts'"; "'I plumb the depths of all your thoughts'"; and "'I hear very well what you do not say'" (1949–51b, 1139; my translation). His accuser, Montesquieu charges, succumbs to the temptation to assume the powers of his divine exemplar and to read thoughts. But thoughts and desires and consciences are not the province of human tribunals, Montesquieu teaches.

CONCLUSION

For Montesquieu to assert that a specific type of knowledge "is of more concern to mankind than anything else in the world" should strike any reader as significant. The significance of the fact that he identifies criminal procedure as that most important knowledge, however, is greater than even his uncharacteristically forthright statement announces. In examining criminal procedure, he unmasks and condemns despotic and tyrannical practices wherever he finds them. Such practices include those of human beings who take their God as their model in attempting to read hearts rather than in judging actions and in seeking both the repentance that is the goal of their religion and vengeance against those who denigrate or otherwise rebel against the deity. His principles establish a strict separation between divine justice and human justice. Human beings should not endeavor to pursue divine justice on earth. If Montesquieu's principles were applied widely, citizens would not have to fear the suspicions of any prosecutorial authority that endeavors to pry into individuals' thoughts and desires in order to descry heresy. These very principles, articulated in a work that after publication was condemned by religious authorities in both Rome and France—authorities who sought the very purposes with the very methods that the work decried—also underscore Montesquieu's intrepidness in rooting out despotism and tyranny wherever he finds it.

NOTES

I would like to thank Nathaniel Gilmore, Lisa Gilson, Jennifer London, Dennis Rasmussen, Mark Somos, and Michael Zuckert for their comments on earlier drafts.

1. References to *The Spirit of the Laws* are by book and chapter number followed by the page number from Montesquieu 1989. I have occasionally corrected the translation or added the French using Montesquieu 1949–51a.

2. In addition to the original charges of heresy that were lodged against the work, scholars have long suspected that the author objected to aspects of Christian doctrine (e.g., Faguet 1890, 140, 169–70; Krause 2001, 252–53; Lowenthal 1959, 490–91; Orwin 2010; Pangle 1973, 258–59, 262–84; Pangle 2010; see also Rahe 2009, 151 and n. 7; Schaub 1995, 71–73, 144–49; Schaub 1999; Zuckert 2001, 234 n. 29). Other commentators, however, have sought to establish his sympathy with Christianity and even his personal faith (Cotta [1953] 1979, 9–67; Oake 1953, 548, 560; Shackleton [1956] 1988, 115; see also Samuel 2009, 317; Waddicor 1970, 177–81). As we will see below, Montesquieu objects to efforts to pry into his conscience on the basis of the perceived implications of his writings.

3. Shackleton (1988, 420) notes that in 1752 the Marquis d'Argenson wrote "with dismay that the Inquisition was gaining ground in France."

4. He also points to Christianity's jurisdiction in the next life: "Remarkably, the Christian religion, which seems to have no other object than the felicity of the other life, is also our happiness in this one!" The happiness to which he refers is Christianity's

effect of making princes less bloodthirsty (24.3, 461). See also *Mes pensées* 2172 (551) (Montesquieu 1949–51c, 1565).

5. The Congregation of the Index demanded that the entirety of chapter 11 be removed from the work (Shackleton 1961, 376).

6. In the words of one commentator, "Montesquieu effects nothing less than the separation of Church and State" "in a few masterful paragraphs" of this chapter (Bartlett 2001, 17; another commentator, on the basis of Montesquieu's distinction between the precepts of human law and the "counsels," or recommendations, of religion in 24.7, maintains that "state authority ought not to enforce religious law" (Mosher 2008, 10; see also Kingston 2001, 380–81). For discussions of the issue of the separation of church and state in Montesquieu's thought, see Ehrard 1992, 339; Kingston 2001, 385–87, 392; Samuel 2009, 317; Shklar 1987, 89–90.

7. Montesquieu notes that crimes against religion could in some cases eventuate in a disturbance of "tranquility," or in a threat to the "security of the citizens." These actions then would be tried by secular authorities and punished accordingly, with the harsher punishments befitting the nature of the crime. But those crimes warranting such punishment would not be sacrilege as such but rather crimes warranting the severest punishments, such as the crimes of robbery or murder (12.4, 189).

8. Montesquieu's reference to Provence calls to mind the very origin of the church's inquisitional procedure, which was formulated early in the thirteenth century to combat the heresy of the Cathars in southern France. After this heretical Christian sect had been quashed, the inquisitional procedure became notorious for its persecution of Jews in Provence during the latter part of the century (*Jewish Encyclopedia,* s.v. "inquisition").

9. Montesquieu responded that he would remove the passage (Montesquieu 1949–51d, 1175), but the deletion was not made in the edition of 1757 (Carrithers 1977, 394 n. 2).

10. This link between treason and sacrilege was also made by the papacy: Pope Innocent III, in 1199, fighting against the Cathar heresy, formalized the rules by which heresy and sacrilege would be prosecuted. Pope Innocent drew on the treatment of treason in Roman law, reinterpreting the political crime of *laesa majestatis* so as to encompass insults to God (Peters 1988, 48–49).

11. This chapter of Deuteronomy was used to justify the Inquisition's prosecutions of heresy. See the *Jewish Encyclopedia:* "Bellarmin says expressly, 'That heretics deserve the sentence is clearly seen, or at least is referred to in Deut. xiii.6 *et seq*' " (s.v. "auto da fé").

REFERENCES

Bartlett, Robert C. 2001. "On the Politics of Faith and Reason: The Project of Enlightenment in Pierre Bayle and Montesquieu." *Journal of Politics* 63 (1): 1–28.

Carrithers, David W., ed. 1977. *"The Spirit of Laws": A Compendium of the First English Edition.* Berkeley: University of California Press.

———. 1998. "Montesquieu's Philosophy of Punishment." *History of Political Thought* 19 (2): 213–40.

———. 2001. "Montesquieu and the Liberal Philosophy of Jurisprudence." In *Montesquieu's Science of Politics: Essays on "The Spirit of Laws,"* ed. David W. Carrithers, Michael A. Mosher, and Paul A. Rahe, 291–334. Lanham, MD: Rowman and Littlefield.

Cotta, Sergio. [1953] 1979. *Montesquieu e la scienza della società.* New York: Arno Press.

Durkheim, Émile. 1960. Trans. Ralph Manheim. *Montesquieu and Rousseau: Forerunners of Sociology.* Ann Arbor: University of Michigan Press.

Ehrard, Jean. 1992. "Montesquieu et l'Inquisition." *Dix-huitième siècle* 24: 333–44.

Faguet, Émile. 1890. *Dix-huitième siècle: Études littéraires.* Paris: H. Lecène et H. Oudin.

Hanna, Edward. 1911. "The Sacrament of Penance." In *The Catholic Encyclopedia.* New York: Robert Appleton Co. Retrieved Jan. 3, 2011, from www.newadvent.org/cathen/11618c.htm.

Jewish Encyclopedia: A Descriptive Record of the History, Religion, Literature, and Customs of the Jewish People from the Earliest Times to the Present Day. 1903. 12 vols. New York: Funk and Wagnalls.

Julian. 1913. *The Caesars.* In *The Works of the Emperor Julian,* trans. Wilmer Cave Wright, 2:345–415. Cambridge, MA: Harvard University Press.

Kingston, Rebecca E. 2001. "Montesquieu on Religion and on the Question of Toleration." In *Montesquieu's Science of Politics: Essays on "The Spirit of Laws,"* ed. David W. Carrithers, Michael A. Mosher, and Paul A. Rahe, 375–408. Lanham, MD: Rowman and Littlefield.

Krause, Sharon. 2001. "Despotism in *The Spirit of Laws.*" In *Montesquieu's Science of Politics: Essays on "The Spirit of Laws,"* ed. David W. Carrithers, Michael A. Mosher, and Paul A. Rahe, 231–71. Lanham, MD: Rowman and Littlefield.

La Roche, Jacques Fontaine, Abbé. [1749] 1878. "Examen critique de *l'Esprit des lois.*" Reprinted in *Oeuvres complètes de Montesquieu,* ed. Edouard Laboulaye, 6:115–37. Paris: Garnier Frères.

Lowenthal, David. 1959. "Book I of Montesquieu's *The Spirit of the Laws.*" *American Political Science Review* 53 (2): 485–98.

Lynch, Andrew J. 1977. "Montesquieu and the Ecclesiastical Critics of *'l'Esprit des lois.'*" *Journal of the History of Ideas* 38 (3): 487–500.

Montesquieu. 1949–51a. *De l'esprit des lois.* In *Oeuvres complètes,* ed. Roger Callois, 2:227–995. Paris: "Bibliothèque de la Pléiade," Librairie Gallimard.

———. 1949–51b. *Défense de l'esprit des lois.* In *Oeuvres complètes,* ed. Roger Callois, 2:1121–66. Paris:"Bibliothèque de la Pléiade," Librairie Gallimard.

———. 1949–51c. *Mes pensées.* In *Oeuvres complètes,* ed. Roger Callois, 1:973–1574. Paris: "Bibliothèque de la Pléiade," Librairie Gallimard.

———. 1949–51d. “Réponses et explications données à la Faculté de Théologie sur les 17 Propositions qu’elle a extradites du livre intitulé *l’Esprit des lois,* et qu’elle censurées. In *Oeuvres complètes,* ed. Roger Callois, 2:1172–95. Paris: “Bibliothèque de la Pléiade,” Librairie Gallimard.

———. 1989. *The Spirit of the Laws.* Trans. and ed. Anne M. Cohler, Basia Carolyn Miller, and Harold Samuel Stone. Cambridge: Cambridge University Press.

Mosher, Michael. 2008. “What Montesquieu Taught: ‘Perfection Does Not Concern Men or Things Universally.’” In *Montesquieu and His Legacy,* ed. Rebecca E. Kingston, 7–28. Albany: State University of New York Press.

Oake, Roger B. 1953. “Montesquieu’s Religious Ideas.” *Journal of the History of Ideas* 14 (4): 548–60.

Orwin, Clifford. 2010. “‘For Which Human Nature Can Never Be Too Grateful’: Montesquieu as the Heir of Christianity.” In *Recovering Reason: Essays in Honor of Thomas L. Pangle,* ed. Timothy Burns, 269–83. Lanham, MD: Lexington Books.

Pangle, Thomas L. 1973. *Montesquieu’s Philosophy of Liberalism: A Commentary on “The Spirit of the Laws.”* Chicago: University of Chicago Press.

———. 2010. *The Theological Basis of Liberal Modernity in Montesquieu’s “Spirit of the Laws.”* Chicago: University of Chicago Press.

Peters, Edward. 1988. *Inquisition.* New York: Free Press.

Plesse, Père. [1749] 1878. “Lettre au P.B.J. sur le livre intitulé: *L’Esprit des Lois.*” *Journal de Trévoux.* Reprinted in *Oeuvres complètes de Montesquieu,* ed. Edouard Laboulaye, 6: 101–13. Paris: Garnier Frères.

Rahe, Paul A. 2009. *Montesquieu and the Logic of Liberty: War, Religion, Commerce, Climate, Terrain, Technology, Uneasiness of Mind, the Spirit of Political Vigilance, and the Foundations of the Modern Republic.* New Haven: Yale University Press.

Samuel, Ana J. 2009. “The Design of Montesquieu’s *The Spirit of the Laws*: The Triumph of Freedom over Determinism.” *American Political Science Review* 103 (2): 305–21.

Schaub, Diana J. 1995. *Erotic Liberalism: Women and Revolution in Montesquieu’s “Persian Letters.”* Lanham, MD: Rowman and Littlefield.

———. 1999. “Of Believers and Barbarians: Montesquieu’s Enlightened Toleration.” In *Early Modern Skepticism and the Origins of Toleration,* ed. Alan Levine, 225–47. Lanham, MD: Lexington Books.

Shackleton, Robert. [1956] 1988. “La religion de Montesquieu.” In *Essays on Montesquieu and on the Enlightenment,* ed. David Gilson and Martin Smith, 109–16. Oxford: Voltaire Foundation at the Taylor Institution.

———. 1961. *Montesquieu: A Critical Biography.* London: Oxford University Press.

———. 1988. “Censure and Censorship: Impediments to Free Publication in the Age of Enlightenment.” In *Essays on Montesquieu and on the Enlightenment,* ed. David Gilson and Martin Smith, 405–20. Oxford: Voltaire Foundation at the Taylor Institution.

Shklar, Judith N. 1987. *Montesquieu.* Oxford: Oxford University Press.

Sozomen. 1855. *The Ecclesiastical History of Sozomen, Comprising a History of the Church from A.D. 324 to A.D. 440.* Trans. Edward Walford. London: H. G. Bohn.

Waddicor, Mark H. 1970. *Montesquieu and the Philosophy of Natural Law.* The Hague: Martinus Nijhoff.

Zuckert, Michael. 2001. "Natural Law, Natural Rights, and Classical Liberalism: On Montesquieu's Critique of Hobbes." *Social Philosophy and Policy* 18 (1): 227–51.

———. 2004. "Natural Rights and Modern Constitutionalism." *Northwestern University Journal of International Human Rights* 2 (Spring): 42–66.

Chapter Nine

Personhood and Ethical Commercial Life

Hegel's Transformation of Locke

JEFFREY CHURCH

John Locke, the enduring spokesman of liberalism and often its whipping boy, has suffered blow after blow from Marxists, communitarians, and multiculturalists. The charges are familiar: the political equality of the social contract obscures the deeper human inequalities lodged in our social interactions; the individualism of the social contract is too abstract, "atomistic," championing an "unencumbered self" far removed from the realities of human community; the abstract liberty of liberalism undermines traditional cultures and leaves individuals deracinated; and so forth. The problem with these criticisms of Locke is that they rely on a misreading of him. One of the main contributions of Michael Zuckert's sophisticated reading of Locke has been to show that Locke was hardly an "atomist" but rather keenly attuned to the social interactions and political conditions necessary for the shaping of rights-bearing citizens.

In this chapter I revisit G. W. F. Hegel's critique of Locke, as Hegel is the intellectual source of many of these criticisms and hence can provide us with a needed historical perspective "behind" Marx from which we can assess contemporary critiques of classical liberalism. However, the received wisdom is that Hegel himself leveled some of the same misguided charges against Locke that we see in contemporary critiques. My aim here is to challenge this received wisdom and argue that Hegel's debt to and critique of Locke is much deeper than is often considered. Zuckert's interpretation of Locke helps illuminate Hegel's debt to Locke. Like Locke, Hegel located the basis for moral "personhood" and private property in the structure of an autonomous human self-consciousness. He also followed the Lockean claim that a properly designed modern commercial society would increase the overall prosperity and liberty of a nation. Nonetheless, I argue, the crucial difference between the two consists in a disagreement about the nature of the human good. Hegel ultimately criticizes Locke on the ground that the latter fails to grasp the inescapably ethical and political nature of the self and civil society. In deepening this dispute between Hegel and Locke, I contribute to the literature on Hegel's critique of social contract theory. More important, my philosophical goal is to offer a moderate critique of Locke's natural rights liberalism, one derived from a sympathetic adversary of Lockean thought, in order to make a case for assessing the liberal self and commercial society in ethical rather than merely rights-based terms.

THE RECEIVED VIEW OF HEGEL ON LOCKE

Alan Patten's (2001) recent article is an insightful and well-documented account of Hegel's critique of social contract theory. It is also a good representative of the literature on the topic.[1] Patten enumerates and defends several criticisms of social contract theory, of which Locke is an important exemplar. Now it may be true that the criticisms are indeed damaging to some social contractarians. Hegel's targets were a rather diffuse group—theorists, citizens, revolutionaries—in the important sections in which he challenges social contract theory, including *PR* 75, 194, and 258.[2] However, my concern is whether or not these criticisms are effective against Locke in particular.

For Patten, Hegel's strongest criticism is that social contract theory excludes the very social and political conditions necessary for the cultivation of individual freedom stipulated in the state of nature. As Patten puts it, the state of nature is "not a state of freedom at all but of animal impulse and savagery" (172). Not in the state of nature "but only in the context of social institutions, including the rational state" can the "attitudes and capacities that make up free and rational agency" be developed (172). Social contract theory is hence incoherent or self-contradictory. Hegel's political theory provides a better alternative because he articulates the social and political institutions and mutual recognition among citizens necessary for the enjoyment of freedom and protection of individual rights.

However, this criticism fails to understand the nature of the state of nature in Locke. The state of nature is not (primarily) a historical state but a hypothetical situation that abstracts from empirical circumstance to reveal the principle of justice that ought to rule among human beings: natural rights. As Zuckert puts it, the state of nature is a "reconstruction of what rational human beings would agree to if they literally had come together to do this" (*LL* 230). Locke understands full well that as an empirical matter of fact human beings fail to be rational agents if they do not live within the right social and political conditions, with the right sort of education, family life, strong government, stable rule of law, and welfare. Zuckert argues that not only is Locke aware of the preconditions for individual freedom, but also that his normative theory guides a social science that would design a "rights infrastructure" in which these rights would find their empirical realization. As he puts it, "government must be concerned directly with the securing of [natural] rights and indirectly with the conditions for the securing of rights" (*LL* 328).

LOCKE AND HEGEL ON THE LABORING SELF

In emphasizing Hegel's critique of social contract theory, scholars overlook Hegel's debt to Locke. Hegel read Locke extensively as he was developing an interest in modern political economy in his youthful writings, but he maintained an avid interest in Locke's *Essay Concerning Human Understanding* throughout his career.[3] Hegel must have recognized the importance of engaging with Locke given the tremendous philosophical influence Hegel attributes to him: Locke's "philosophy itself is very well known. It is on the whole still the philosophy of the English and the French; in a certain sense it has also been the philosophy of the Germans and even today still is so in part" (*HP* 171). My argument in this section and the next is that Hegel appropriates and transforms two of Locke's central liberal arguments, arguments that are crucial to *The Philosophy of Right.* My aim in these sections is not so much to prove a textual or historical point that Hegel had Locke in mind when crafting his arguments but rather to demonstrate the deep Lockean influence on Hegel's thinking.[4]

Let us discuss first Hegel's debt to Locke on the concept of the self or "person." Famously, Locke argued that each individual by nature possesses rights to life, liberty, and property, and these rights entail a correlative duty on the part of all others not to infringe on my rights. The aim of government is to secure these preexisting natural rights, both by protecting them from infringement and by supplying the social and political preconditions for their enjoyment. Yet what is the foundation of the moral status of natural rights in Locke? Contrary to many Locke interpreters who try to harmonize or explain away the seeming conflict between Locke's two foundations in the *ST,* the "divine workmanship" and "self-ownership" arguments, Zuckert has persuasively argued that Locke distances himself from the Christian presuppositions of natural law and comes to defend a wholly "secular" view of natural rights, using reason as our "only star and compass" (*NRNR* chaps. 8–9; *LL* 138 ff., 188–90). For Zuckert's Locke, natural rights are based on "self-ownership," which in turn is based on a notion of the self defended in *ECHU* 2.27. The argument can be broken down into four steps, and we will see that Hegel follows Lockean logic in each step.

First, human beings are creatures distinct from animals and mere nature. Our distinctness consists not in a particular bodily trait, or in a mystical mental substance or innate principle.[5] Rather, our distinctness as "persons" comes from our self-consciousness, our ability to take up our perceptions and ideas in certain ways, to question them, reinforce them, abstract from them, and so forth (*NRNR* 281–82; *HD* 43–44). The "person" is a "thinking intelligent being, that has reason and reflection, and can consider it self as it self, the same thinking thing in different times and places" (*ECHU* 2.27.9). For Hegel, this principle of self-conscious subjectivity is the ground of "Abstract Right," derived from his lengthy analysis of the "I" in the *Subjective Logic.*[6] For Hegel, human beings are distinguished from the rest of nature in that we are (in principle) free from natural determinations. A cow or salmon has particular perceptions and "consciousness" of the world around it, but it is moved by its desires and its environment (*PR* 42A). Human beings experience the same desires and pressures from their environment, but yet all this experience is itself laden with normative content (*PR* 19–20). That is, the human subject always judges or takes up this or that experience within a certain normative framework. Our desires can lead us in a certain direction, but we can always step back and question whether I ought to act based on this desire or not. Each human being is a "person" in the sense that each of us is an "I," a subject detachable from every empirical experience, perception, desire, belief (*PR* 5). Each of us is "infinite" in our capacity to transcend any and all determinations of the natural world, and for Hegel, it is the "highest achievement of a human being . . . to be a person" (*PR* 35Z).

Second, this "I" is no passive ego receiving deliverances from an external world. For Hegel, the fault of Hume and Kant is that they fell into this trap and hence had to explain how a passive ego could connect to an external world, how thought and being could be unified (*PhG* 73–76). Rather, the subject is active, both in thought and action, always already bridging the gap between subject and object.[7] Hegel's joking proof against Kant's impenetrable "thing-in-itself" is the animal who consumes the thing and "thereby proves that [things-in-themselves] are not absolutely self-sufficient" (*PR* 44Z). Locke anticipated Hegel's joke on this count in arguing that one of the basic ways human beings remake the world is by ingesting it (*ST* 5.28). All subjects, whether human or animal, are active in that they transform the things of the world, turning them into the image of their own subjectivity. The core concept Locke and Hegel employ to understand the subject's native activity is labor. Labor is that archetypal human activity that transforms the structure of nature such that it comes to resemble the human laborer and serve his needs. In tilling a field or domesticating an animal (see *ST* 5.37; *PR* 56A), human beings "humanize" nature by shaping it to meet general human needs and to resemble particular individual identities (the house I have built bears my identity in certain crucial ways). Also, both Locke and Hegel envision education as a kind of shaping of the natural soul to form a more rational, human product (*TCE* 66; *VPR17* 21A). More fundamentally, Hegel extends this notion to encompass human thought itself in that human beings first approach the world as a place impenetrable to thought and fearsome; the development of human civilization brings with it the labor of thought, in the sense that coming to understand or "grasping" (*begreifen*) the world involves subjecting the world to our investigations, reshaping it, such that it resembles us and hence no longer appears alien.[8]

Third, Locke and Hegel do not just argue that human subjectivity labors on and transforms nature, but that the product of our labor is something we are entitled to by natural right, both in the face of nature and other human beings. Locke, challenging Grotius, claims that nature is unowned—that is, available to be appropriated by human beings (*ST* 5.25; *NRNR* 251). Hegel builds on this understanding of nature and argues that nature is "external to itself" (*PR* 42). That is, the interactions among animals and natural things are not mediated by self-conscious rational claims of right but rather consist of mere blind instinct. The blind thing is "external to itself" because "externality has no end in itself . . . but something external to itself" (*PR* 44Z). All external ends these natural things have are "relative," by which Hegel means that they are conditioned on further causes or determinations, which in turn are conditioned by further causes, and so forth, ad infinitum (*SL* 118–19). The human will, by contrast, is "infinite," in that it both sets and pursues its own ends. When I "give the living creature . . . a soul other than that which it previously had[,] I give it my soul" (*PR* 44Z), a soul that self-consciously, not instinctively, sets and pursues its ends.

Accordingly, when we labor on nature, Locke and Hegel claim, we gain an *exclusive* right to our product. Others have a moral duty to refrain from infringing on my property without my consent. Locke's justification for this claim lies in his famous statement on self-ownership: "every man has a property in his own person; this nobody has any right to but himself. The labor of his body and the work of his hands we may say are properly his" (*ST* 5.27). As Zuckert glosses the passage, "Human making, not divine making, is the primary moral fact. The chapter on property [*ST* 5] leads up to the suggestion that human beings are self-owners because they are makers of their selves and they own what they make" (*NRNR* 278). In addition to its laboring on the things of the earth, the personal "I" at once constitutes its personal identity or self. Locke argues that the unified identity of a human self over time is not due to some inner kernel of an immortal soul within me but rather is posited by the self that shapes a unified, coherent identity out of one's memory of the past and one's intended plans for the future (*ECHU* 2.27.10). Such positing of a unified self necessitates staking out this body as the "home base" for my identity. Yet it also forms the normative basis for private property beyond my body. Other objects that I invest with my labor become part and parcel of my identity. The house I built with my own hands, for instance, has become an integral part of my identity such that its seizure would involve a considerable distortion to the unity of my self. Zuckert helpfully alludes to the Beatles song "I Me Mine" to illustrate the self-owning self (*LL* 195). The abstract personal "I" is the basis for my unified identity, positing the confluence of things that make me "me," and it also extends its laboring transformation to the things of the world, turning object into subject, into what is "mine." As such, Locke's "self-ownership" justification of natural rights is not based on considerations of natural need or preservation but rather on property conditions for the person's self-making. As Zuckert argues, the right to self-ownership and private property is inalienable as they "inhere in the very structure of the self. There is no way they can be given away, for the self cannot deconstitute its own basic structure as self-owning consciousness" (*NRNR* 286).

Like Locke, Hegel argues that human identity is not "given" in some soul-substance but comes to be through the process of subjectivity positing a unified identity out of the often chaotic swirl of desires, drives, experiences, perceptions that make up our daily lives (*ES* 378Z; *PR* 11, 19). Yet this formation of identity cannot occur solely within our minds. We must first embody our personality, and our body shares a special relationship to our personality, as the seat of sensation and hence the immediate unity of soul and body (*ES* 389–90; *PR* 47–48). But for Hegel, subjectivity must be externalized because it is only in an external and public, shared world that anything takes on value or meaning, including my own identity, my projects and purposes (*SL* 523–28)—what "the subject is," Hegel argues, "is the series of its actions" (*PR* 124). For Hegel, subjects posit a unity of identity through the activity of negation, of differentiating or delineating the whole it constitutes from the other possible wholes it encounters (*ES* 413Z, 423Z). We "negate" and hence express our sovereignty over the animals and plants we eat, thereby investing them with our soul (*ES* 426–27). In our laboring activities as a farmer or a merchant or an artist, furthermore, we only come to constitute our identity as a member of this profession by externalizing our activity among them and differentiating myself from my fellows (*PR* 193, 253A). For Hegel, then, private property is not justified as an instrument for the satisfaction of natural need; other possible property arrangements could satisfy natural needs and preserve our lives. Rather, property serves as the external expression of my identity, the basis on which I can posit my allegiance with and difference from others.[9] Without an exclusive right to my property—in the case of commonly held property, say—I would no longer have a means of and basis for expressing my identity.

LOCKE AND HEGEL ON THE SELF LABORING

Labor plays an important role in the justification of natural rights, but it also is crucial in developing a commercial society that can provide the preconditions for the protection of such rights. The second crucial way Hegel is indebted to Locke, then, is in the latter's account of the creative power of human labor. According to Locke, human beings can enclose a portion of the earth from the commons so long as they leave "enough and as good" for others (*ST* 5.33). In primitive human settings nature provides us with enough to satisfy our meager needs while still leaving enough for everyone else. But, Locke argues, as human societies begin to form and grow, nature's bounty begins to seem more like niggardliness, as it is difficult to subsist on wild berries alone (*ST* 5.38, 43). Human labor on the earth corrects nature by transforming it through artifice, employing agricultural technology so that the earth will yield many times the goods bare nature does (*ST* 5.37). The task, then, of the statesman is to support the social and political institutions that will spur and defend the "honest industry on mankind" on the grounds that it produces far more material needs for everyone and hence creates a much more stable polity (*ST* 5.42). These institutions, then, in turn, provide the stable preconditions for the self-development of a free personality.

In his early work Hegel was fascinated by the problem Rousseau and Schelling posed in their work, which is how self-conscious human life emerged from natural, animal life. The Lockean view of labor helped Hegel find a solution, in that labor does not just augment nature but also ourselves. The labor of the slave, Hegel famously argues, frees the slave from nature by forcing him to hold his natural "desire . . . in check" for some higher purpose and to understand how nature works in order to master it for his master (*PhG* 195). The tool gives the slave an understanding of the abstract, as a tool can be used for multiple purposes without being used up (*SEL* 113). The slave develops self-consciousness in labor, that he can see his own "independence" in the stable product of my work (*PhG* 195). Hegel, following Locke, inverts the traditional valuation of aristocratic leisure over slavish labor: we have come to see that the master is dominated by his natural needs while the slave becomes increasingly liberated through the creativity of his labor. Labor creates a human world above the natural one and shapes human beings to live freely in it.

Labor, then, supplies the foundation for a distinctively modern social order that Hegel calls "civil society." We need not rely on the virtuous commitment of honorable individuals to sacrifice their own self-interest for the common good. For the early modern political theorists from Machiavelli through Locke, we moderns should not rely on such virtue as it requires tremendous sacrifice of individual liberty and hence is unduly demanding and rather rare. Instead of setting ourselves up for failure by "aiming high," we should found community on the more solid footing of self-interested human desires. Locke and his successors in Scotland helped Hegel see that this foundation is indeed solid. Nature is poor, but self-interested human labor "increases the common stock of mankind" (*ST* 5.37). The courage and honor of ancient societies drove societies apart and impoverished them in wars and wasteful expenditures, while the market exchange among individuals producing "surplus" goods in a system of divided labor drives human beings together in interdependence and cultivates in them a sense for strict justice and reciprocity (*SEL* 118–24; *PR* 198). Exchanging goods ultimately requires money to make objects commensurable according to an abstract standard, which gives human beings a sense of the abstract and provides a market mechanism for the satisfaction of particular needs. As Hegel sums up this element of modern political economy Locke initiated, "subjective selfishness turns into a contribution towards the satisfaction of the needs of everyone else" (*PR* 199).

HEGEL'S CRITIQUE OF LOCKE

Ultimately, however, Hegel is no Lockean, though it is not clear what Hegel's criticism of Locke is, since Hegel does not single him out for criticism in his writings. We can begin to reconstruct such a critique, however, by examining Hegel's explicit references to Locke in the *History of Philosophy*. In these lectures Hegel criticizes Locke's empiricist method of beginning with simple impressions in our experience and accounting for the origin and development of our ideas from these basic given materials. For Hegel, the "question whether these determinations of the infinite, of substance, and so forth are true in and for themselves gets completely lost from sight" (*HP* 173).[10] In other words, Locke's empiricism helps us understand what opinions and desires we have and where they came from, but, for Hegel, it does not admit of a priori justifications for the truth or goodness of these opinions or desires, as the a priori appeal to "innate principle" is ruled out of court in Locke's empiricist salvos in *ECHU* book 1. However, we cannot apply Hegel's argument here to Locke's political philosophy. As we have seen above, Locke clearly *does* appeal to a priori moral considerations based on the structure of the human person. At this point we must do a bit more reconstruction of the critique.

The fundamental difference between Hegel and Locke concerns the nature of the human good. As Zuckert makes clear, happiness is the good for Locke, implicitly related to a person's self-construction (*NRNR* 283–84). Following his predecessors' break from the ancients and Scholastics, Locke rejects the "function theory" of the human good associated above all with natural law thinking. According to this view, human beings possess a role or function assigned to them by nature, tradition, or God, and hence the human good consists in fulfilling our function, just as the goodness of a knife, say, derives from its ability to cut. For Locke, no such "objective" "Summum Bonum" exists for human beings, as human beings are the makers of our own selves and world through labor. The "philosophers of old did in vain enquire" into this good (*ECHU* 2.21.55). The good of the human self is not set objectively, but subjectively. Each of us constructs an "idea" of happiness and its opposite, misery, from the kinds of pleasures appealing to us. Each self has a different notion of happiness depending on the confluence of experiences and the manner of the self's positing of what is salient to its felicity and misery. As Locke puts it, the "variety of pursuits shews" that "every one does not place his happiness in the same thing, or chuse the same way to it." Hence, the "mind has a different relish, as well as the palate; and you will fruitlessly endeavor to delight all men with riches or glory . . . as you would to satisfy all men's hunger with cheese or lobsters; which, though very agreeable and delicious fare to some, are to others extremely nauseous and offensive" (*ECHU* 2.21.54–55). In short, "men may chuse different things, and yet all chuse right" (2.21.35 variant).

The basic problem with this view of happiness as the good is that it fails to liberate the human self fully to the activity of self-making. Hegel describes the person as "infinite" in part because it can abstract itself from every natural determination, desire, quirk, longing (*PR* 5). But also, it is infinite because it can call into question any and all of these determinations, ask "whether I ought" to follow this natural impulse or indulge in this pleasure. The infinite dignity of the human person requires that the answer to the "ought" question cannot be some "relative" claim, such as some deeper desire, pleasure, or belief, or else the human person does not "posit" its own identity, but rather it is fundamentally "posited" for it. Rather, the answer must come from the "infinite" claim of the subject's reason itself. As such, Locke's "empiricist" view of the good fails to live up to the dignity of the laboring self, because the "idea" of the good in Locke's view is a composite of natural pleasures. Indeed, Locke recognizes that reason ought to guide the human pursuit of happiness. In his *Thoughts Concerning Education* Locke argues that the pupil must be taught to control his passions in accordance with his reason (*TCE* 45, 107). Yet "reason" here is normative only in an instrumental sense.[11] Individuals can be better assured of pleasure and a closer approximation of happiness if they can learn better self-control. Locke's reason is akin to the helmsman in Socrates' image in the *Gorgias,* the man who can ferry individuals along to meet their needs but who does not improve their souls (511d ff.). Similarly, reason in Locke provides individuals with the instruments to succeed in commercial society but does not urge them to ethical improvement.[12] As such, the standard on which any individual action is performed will ultimately be based on some consideration of natural pleasure. From Hegel's perspective, then, Locke's view of the self-making self is an elaborate edifice based on natural, not distinctively human, ends.

For Hegel, the true human good is not "happiness" but "freedom," activity in accordance with substantive rational ends (*PR* 20–21; *ES* 479–82). The good of "freedom" differs from happiness in that it is ethical, concerned primarily with common goods. Hegel agrees with Locke that the human good is posited by the human self, but Locke's error lies in what Zuckert calls his "ontology of the self." As Zuckert puts it, the "self [that] is constituted around happiness and misery" is "decidedly self-interested" (*NRNR* 285). Only derivatively does it possess social and political aims. For Hegel, Locke's view fails to distinguish between selves who pursue ethical goals and those who pursue selfish goals. For human beings to be truly free, we must be free also from enslavement to our natural appetites. The human self can be truly self-realizing only by acting in such a way that transforms these natural desires, making them into our own. But in order to do this, Hegel argues, we must act based on an ethical principle that demonstrates our freedom from "selfish" actions, that we are able to set aside our natural desires and act for common human purposes (*ES* 428). Such an ethical principle is a standard that is established not by the conscious choice or agreement of individuals, but rather that emerges out of the common activities and history of a group, association, or nation (*ES* 436). Hegel's frequent examples of "communities" whose standards of the good transcend individual whim and which possess an implicit rationality are friendships, families, local communities, occupational associations, and, finally, states. Only through ethical activity can a human self incorporate those natural selfish desires into a larger set of common human purposes that we ourselves identify with and in so doing make these natural desires our own.

Hegel's critique of Locke's view of the good is not of mere private concern, but has consequences for political life. Happiness, understood as the satisfaction of "particular" desires, is the goal of commercial society (*PR* 124, 182). However, commercial society, Hegel argues, is structurally unstable and hence can undermine the very happiness sought therein.[13] Commercial society breaks up the family (*PR* 181), encourages and expands selfish desires beyond our capacity to fulfill them (*PR* 185Z), dehumanizes and mechanizes labor (*PR* 198; *HHS* 139), dissolves local communities as the source of esteem and recognition, and impoverishes a class of individuals (*PR* 241–45; *HHS* 140). An "ontology of the self" that is "decidedly self-interested" would only encourage the dissolution of the sources of ethical integration in civil society while at the same time driving individuals to insatiable, selfish natural desires. The task of ameliorating the problems of civil society must come, for Hegel, from a reformulation of its end in accordance with a better understanding of the good of human beings.

In order to satisfy the good of the human self, Hegel argues, we must aim higher than the "self-interested" goals of modern political theory and retrieve the ambitions of the ancient political theorists. The path to fulfilling this higher aim is emphatically not any kind of return to ancient or feudal regimes, which fail to recognize individual liberty and the "right of the subject's particularity to find satisfaction" (*PR* 124A). Hegel does not seek a wholesale transformation of modern political society. Instead, he thinks that we can aim higher by thinking through a bit more the logic of Locke's laboring self in relation to political society. As we will see, Hegel argues that ethical relationships, far from being foreign to modern commercial society, grow out of the solid basis of self-interested desire.[14] He argues that a proper political community will situate our individualist pursuit of happiness within our larger ethical vocation. The end of this community, then, is this: instead of political community being instrumental to the protection of natural rights, as in Locke's view, for Hegel, political community should be an expression of individual ethical self-realization.

For Hegel, these ethical relationships grow most fundamentally out of our economic associations—what he calls the estates and corporations—that structure the division of labor in civil society (*PR* 201).[15] By laboring together with others for common purposes, individuals come to regard their occupation not just as a job, but as a "calling" (*Bestimmung*), and hence they "endeavor to promote" the common good (*PR* 253). Hegel here extends the logic of the "laboring self" that he has developed from Lockean thought. Laboring with others in an economic association expands the self beyond my own embodied person and encourages me and my fellow laborers to identify with a common good and a collective identity that is the result of our labors. In shaping and contributing to common purposes, I make this common self my own, and hence I come to see the common as an extension of my own self and seek to promote its aims in ethical action and by garnering "honor in one's estate" (*Standesehre*) for such action (*PR* 253).

For Hegel, however, these associations must not take themselves to be self-sufficient (or else they will devolve into an irrational "miserable guild system" [*PR* 255Z]), because they can maintain their status and identity only as part of a rationally ordered political community. In the rational state, the economic associations must mediate the individual's relationship to the common good of the political community as a whole, so that individuals can act upon and embody in themselves principles of rational right. These associations do this by performing their functions related to local self-government and by electing representatives in the estates assembly (*PR* 288). Both tasks invest their individuals with a responsibility for and hence a sense of ownership over the common good of both local and national communities (*PR* 289A).[16] This political activity arising out of our economic associations expands our self beyond our local associations to the state as a whole where our "voice" can be heard and we can be self-legislating members of the political whole (*VPR*17 132A). The political community, like the economic association, hence becomes an expression of individual self-realization. I can thus craft my own self through my participation in these associations, as both association and state are shaped by, and hence bear the image of, my laboring self.

As such, Hegel's dispute with Locke over the nature of the human good has implications for the nature of political community and institutional design. Hegel's political philosophy hence seeks to realize, not just identify, the human good in contrast to Locke's. According to Hegel, the human self requires ethical communities in which to craft and express its identity. Modern commercial society, however, tends to undermine these very ethical communities. Further, the abstraction from such ethical claims as we see in Locke's rights philosophy fails to ground a theoretical and practical defense of such communities. By contrast, Hegel's philosophy provides a basis for the encouragement of such communities and a design of their structure and character on the nature of the laboring self. In short, Locke did not take his argument about the human self far enough. Finally, the Lockean need not worry that this ethical turn requires Romantic utopianism or state worship, since Hegel roots these ethical associations in a modern, Lockean basis of self-interested desire and maintains the internal differentiation and "subjective" freedoms of a modern commercial society.

This chapter does not aim to "settle" the dispute between Hegel and Locke in favor of Hegel. There are many rejoinders a Lockean would have to this Hegelian argument. Zuckert points toward one objection in his argument that the "ontology of the self" supports a "politics of the realist," one grounded on the firm foundation of securing property rights (*NRNR* 285). The reintroduction of "higher" ethical goals into politics might arouse conflict over how to interpret the standard of freedom as the good and sanction state-sponsored ethical judgments of economic activity. My main goal here has been to argue that Hegel owes much more to Locke than often considered, and hence that contemporary critiques of Locke deriving from Hegel would do well to engage with Locke more extensively. Yet Hegel's break from Locke on the ethical good of human beings nonetheless deserves emphasis because it has implications for liberal theory. Hegel makes a case for the inescapability of ethical aims of the self and of modern commercial society, that government policy and individual action should be justified ultimately not on their ability to defend natural rights but rather on their capacity to foster the good life for the modern citizen.

ABBREVIATIONS

ECHU John Locke, *Essay Concerning Human Understanding.* Ed. Peter H. Nidditch. Oxford: Clarendon Press, 1975. Cited by book, chapter, paragraph.

ES	G. W. F. Hegel, *Philosophy of Mind.* Trans. A. V. Miller. Oxford: Oxford University Press, 1971. Cited by paragraph number.
HD	Michael Zuckert, "Human Dignity and the Basis of Justice." *Hedgehog Review* (Fall 2007).
HHS	G. W. F. Hegel, *Lectures on the Philosophy of Spirit.* Trans. Leo Rauch. Detroit: Wayne State University Press, 1983. Cited by page number.
HP	G. W. F. Hegel, *Lectures on the History of Philosophy.* Trans. Robert F. Brown and J. Michael Stewart. Berkeley: University of California Press, 1990. Cited by page number.
LL	Michael Zuckert, *Launching Liberalism.* Lawrence: University Press of Kansas, 2002.
NRNR	Michael Zuckert, *Natural Rights and the New Republicanism.* Princeton: Princeton University Press, 1994.
PhG	G. W. F. Hegel, *Phenomenology of Spirit.* Trans. A. V. Miller. Oxford: Oxford University Press, 1977. Cited by paragraph number.
PR	G. W. F. Hegel, *Elements of the Philosophy of Right.* Trans. H. B. Nisbet. Cambridge: Cambridge University Press, 1991. Cited by paragraph number.
PW	G. W. F. Hegel, *Political Writings.* Trans. H. B. Nisbet. Cambridge: Cambridge University Press, 1999. Cited by page number.
SEL	G. W. F. Hegel, *System of Ethical Life.* Trans. H. S. Harris. Albany: State University of New York Press, 1979.
SL	G. W. F. Hegel, *Science of Logic.* Trans. A. V. Miller. New York: Humanity Books, 1969. Cited by page number.
ST	John Locke, *Second Treatise of Government.* Ed. C. B. Macpherson. Indianapolis: Hackett Press, 1980. Cited by chapter and paragraph.
TCE	John Locke, *Some Thoughts Concerning Education.* Ed. Ruth W. Grant and Nathan Tracov. Indianapolis: Hackett Press, 1996. Cited by paragraph number.
VPR17	G. W. F. Hegel, *Lectures on Natural Right and Political Science.* Trans. J. Michael Stewart and Peter C. Hodgson. Berkeley: University of California Press, 1995. Cited by paragraph number.

NOTES

Thanks to Paul Franco, Michael Gillespie, Andrew Buchwalter, and Jeremiah John for helpful comments on an earlier draft. This chapter would not have been conceived let alone executed without the many conversations over the past several years with Michael Zuckert about his "Hegelian Locke."

1. See also Gough 1957, chap. 11; Taylor 1985, "Atomism"; Knowles 2002, 309. Riley (1982, 168) and Haddock (1994) rightly point out that Hegel is much indebted

to social contract theory. Yet Haddock nonetheless claims that Hegel's concern with it is its inability to articulate the "social preconditions" for "individualism" (162). Riley makes much the same point, and claims that Hegel viewed "social contract theory only with loathing" (194–95).

2. Hegel singles out Rousseau, Kant, and Fichte for critique, but he notes that "in recent times, it has become very popular to regard the state as a contract of all with all" (*PR* 75Z), and that "the view that the state is a social contract between individual persons also had a great influence on the French Revolution" (*VPR17* 33A).

3. See Chamley 1965; and quote in Cullen 1979, 16. Cf. Lampert 1997 for Hegel's debt to Locke on the will as the basis of property rights. Other authors see Hegel as primarily critical of Locke on private property; see Thomas 2003; Stillman 1980, 133.

4. Locke's influence on Hegel was mediated by figures whose political philosophy he knew better—Jean-Jacques Rousseau, J. G. Fichte, Adam Smith, among others.

5. See *ECHU* 2.27.6–7 on the denial of bodily organization and unity of soul "substance" as the basis for human identity; see also Locke's claim that the substance of the self is unknowable (*ECHU* 2.27.27); finally, see his denial of innate principles in *ECHU* 1.

6. See *SL* 583–85 on the "I" as the basis of the subjective logic. Hegel has Kant in mind here, but see Allison 1977 for Locke's influence on Kant's transcendental unity of apperception.

7. See *ECHU* 2.21.2, 5 ff. on the will's "active power."

8. "When I think of an object, I make it into a thought and deprive it of its sensuous quality; I make it into something which is essentially and immediately mine" (*PR* 4Z).

9. See Waldron 1988, 373, for a helpful analysis of Hegel's view of moral action along these lines, along with a footnote on the "remarkable affinity to Locke's doctrine of personal identity" (373 n. 47).

10. Cf. also the similar point at *PW* 110, where the reference to Locke within "empiricism" is implied: "for pure empiricism, everything has equal rights with everything else, and it gives no precedence to any [one] determinacy, since each is as real as the other."

11. See *LL* 189: "reason . . . contains no substantive principles within it, not even such vague things as 'seek the good'; reason is merely a calculative power." Cf. *TCE* 143: "Virtue itself [is] valued only as conducing to our happiness," and "the happiness that all men so steadily pursue consisting in pleasure."

12. This was the main criticism Stoner (2004) leveled against Zuckert's Locke.

13. See Church 2010 for a further elaboration of this view.

14. Cf. Ross 2009, yet Ross emphasizes too heavily the state's intervention in civil society in cultivating an ethical politics. See, e.g., *VPR17* 132A: "the universal must be accomplished . . . in such a way that the individual, in accomplishing the universal, is working for himself. The particularity of the individual will must be maintained in the universal will."

15. Hegel of course thinks that a wide array of other institutions are necessary to sustain a flourishing ethical society, but he argues that the estates and corporations are the crucial pivots that turn the self-interested modern individual toward the common good based on the inner logic of his own activity (see *PR* 289A).

16. In this way, self-government has the same conceptual structure as the labor of the self. Hegel connects the two in an example from his fragmented Germany: "it is fundamental to human nature to be interested only in something which we can actively support, with which we can co-operate and share decisions, with which our will can identify itself. The provinces need to find some mode of joint action towards a universal end" (*PW* 98; cf. *VPR17* 132A).

REFERENCES

Allison, Henry. 1977. "Locke's Theory of Personal Identity: A Re-Examination." In *Locke on Human Understanding,* ed. I. C. Tipton, 105–22. Oxford: Oxford University Press.

Chamley, Paul. 1965. "Les origines de la pensée economique de Hegel." *Hegel Studien* 3.

Church, Jeffrey. 2010. "The Freedom of Desire: Hegel's Response to Rousseau on the Problem of Civil Society." *American Journal of Political Science* 54, no. 1 (January): 125–39.

Cullen, Bernard. 1979. *Hegel's Social and Political Thought: An Introduction.* New York: St. Martin's.

Gough, J. W. 1957. *The Social Contract.* Oxford: Oxford University Press.

Haddock, Bruce. 1994. "Hegel's Critique of the Social Contract." In *The Social Contract from Hobbes to Rawls,* ed. David Boucher and Paul Joseph Kelly. London: Routledge.

Knowles, Dudley. 2002. *Routledge Philosophy Guidebook to Hegel and the Philosophy of Right.* London: Routledge.

Lampert, Jay. 1997. "Locke, Fichte, and Hegel on the Right to Property." In *Hegel and the Tradition,* ed. Michael Baur and John Russon, 40–76. Toronto: University of Toronto Press.

Patten, Alan. 2001. "Social Contract Theory and the Politics of Recognition in Hegel's Political Philosophy." In *Beyond Liberalism and Communitarianism: Studies in Hegel's Philosophy of Right,* ed. Robert R. Williams, 167–84. Albany: State University of New York Press.

Riley, Patrick. 1982. *Will and Political Legitimacy.* Cambridge, MA: Harvard University Press.

Ross, Nathan. 2009. "The Mechanization of Labor and the Birth of Modern Ethicality in Hegel's Jena Political Writings." In *Hegel and History,* ed. Will Dudley, 177–94. Albany: State University of New York Press.

Stillman, Peter. 1980. "Property, Freedom, and Individuality in Hegel's and Marx's Political Thought." In *Property,* ed. J. R. Pennock and J. W. Chapman, 130–67. New York: New York University Press.

Stoner, James. 2004. "Was Leo Strauss Wrong about John Locke?" *Review of Politics* 66, no. 4 (Fall): 553–73.

Taylor, Charles. 1985. *Philosophy and the Human Sciences.* Cambridge: Cambridge University Press.

Thomas, Paul. 2003. "Property's Properties: From Hegel to Locke." *Representations* 84 (Autumn): 6–29.

Waldron, Jeremy. 1988. *The Right to Private Property.* Oxford: Oxford University Press.

Chapter Ten

Reflections on Faith and Reason

Leo Strauss and John Paul II

WALTER NICGORSKI

Relatively late in his life, in 1965, Leo Strauss wrote that the "theologico-political problem" had been "*the* theme" of his "investigations" (Strauss 1997a, 453; original emphasis).[1] Also in the 1960s and in the final sentence of *The City and Man,* Strauss stressed that "we [must] be open to the full impact of the all-important question which is coeval with philosophy although the philosophers do not frequently pronounce it—the question *quid sit deus*" (1964, 241). Early in the 1950s, in his most widely read book, *Natural Right and History,* Strauss wrote that "the fundamental question . . . is whether men can acquire that knowledge of the good without which they cannot guide their lives individually or collectively by the unaided efforts of their natural powers, or whether they are dependent for that knowledge on Divine Revelation" (1953, 74). In the same vein and in the same decade, Strauss spoke of philosophy and the Bible as "the alternatives, or the antagonists in the drama of the human soul. Each of the two antagonists claims to know or to hold the truth, the decisive truth. . . . Each of the two opponents has tried for millennia to refute the other. This effort is continuing in our day" (Strauss 1989, 260).[2]

One might speculate on how these three expressions of the bearing of the Divine on political philosophy relate. There is "the problem" that is the theme of Strauss's investigations, there is "an all-important question," and there is "the fundamental question" posed by seemingly uncompromising alternatives. These are not different expressions of essentially the same thing, but it appears that they highlight different aspects of a critical choice for the philosopher. Our speculation, informed by the writings of Catherine Zuckert and Michael Zuckert, as well as those of others, would not be unfounded if we were to say that Leo Strauss chooses Athens or philosophy as his response to the fundamental question, and that choice, and *perhaps* only that choice, allows the theologico-political problem to come into view. At the same time, that choice of the philosophical way of life brackets or sets aside the question about the nature of God while acknowledging its great importance. In this way, the philosopher Strauss acknowledges, as he has done explicitly and often, the theoretical basis for respecting the biblical alternative.

Those who have been attentive to Strauss and his teaching have been given a gift by his highlighting of these questions. It is a special benefit to those concerned with political phenomena and the tasks of social science, though it might be especially resisted in such circles. Needless to say, with a very way of life at stake, these are questions that tap into the deeply personal. So perhaps, even in a scholarly collection in honor of learning and scholarly distinction, long-standing and deeply felt personal engagement with such questions can be openly acknowledged without embarrassment. Strauss could not have intended otherwise, the Strauss who wrote of what is consequent to, yet conserving of, these questions, namely, his turn to "the political thought of classical antiquity," which he approaches with "passionate interest" unmarked by both "self-forgetting" antiquarianism and "self-forgetting" romanticism (1964, 1). The questions and the tension are, of course, ours. The self and its way of life is at stake. Steven Smith has properly and cautiously observed that the conflict between Jerusalem and Athens, "figuratively speaking," is "conceivably coeval with humanity itself" (2006, 10). Thomas Pangle, also explicating and writing on Strauss on these concerns, noted that what is "at stake is the ultimate source of our norms of justice or righteousness, the norms by which we guide our lives as citizens, ultimately citizens of the world, obligated to one another, and not merely concerned with and for our poor individual selves" (2006, 27).

The Zuckerts recall Strauss's essay "What Is Liberal Education," his taking his bearings from Plato, and declaring "philosophy is quest for wisdom or quest for knowledge regarding the most important, the highest, or the most comprehensive things; such knowledge, Plato suggested, is virtue and happiness. But wisdom is inaccessible to man, and hence virtue and happiness will always be imperfect" (Zuckert and Zuckert 2006, 46).[3] Shortly after citing this observation of Strauss, the Zuckerts draw attention to the tendency of his students to "continue to argue about whether he was a believer or, if not, exactly what his stance toward revealed religion was" (46).[4]

Before I came to know of John Paul II, I had encountered Leo Strauss. Yet when encountering Strauss, I was already well immersed in the tradition for which John Paul later came to speak. This makes understandable that I had all along a special interest in how Strauss came to terms with the claims of Revelation. I drew quite limited conclusions in a 1985 review essay which provided an initial public occasion to reflect on where Strauss stood on the question of reason and Revelation (Nicgorski 1985, 18–21). After cautioning that one should not underestimate the respect Strauss has for the life of faith or the tension he finds between the life of faith or piety and the life of philosophy or reason, I turned to Strauss's 1954 essay, "The Mutual Influence of Theology and Philosophy," where he argues that "the primary and necessary form of philosophy" is not to be identified with "a set of propositions, a teaching, or even a system" but with "a way of life" (Strauss 1979, 113).[5] My overall conclusion in interpreting Strauss at this time was the following:

> That way of life is not incompatible with what it strives to eliminate; namely, the apparent truth of ultimate mystery. Strauss chose the life of philosophy with an awareness that its best models, the ancient

> philosophers, gave witness to the elusiveness of the final object of that way of life. And so rigorous and self-critical was Strauss's devotion to this way of life that he observed that "the choice of philosophy is based on faith . . . the quest for evident knowledge rests itself on an unevident premise." Such considerations make clearer the ground of Strauss's deep respect for the life of faith and piety. (Nicgorski 1985, 21)[6]

Subsequent study, aided by the work of the Zuckerts, has made clear that it appears wrong to conclude or suggest that Strauss's own choice of the philosophic way of life rests on faith or an arbitrary act of the will. In the context of an examination of Stanley Rosen's critique of Strauss, the Zuckerts argue soundly that Strauss's statements on philosophy resting on faith or an unevident premise, such as that which I cited from "The Mutual Influence," do not apply to classical rationalism. Noting that Strauss makes similar statements "in the Weber chapter of *Natural Right and History* and with regard to the philosophy of Spinoza in his preface," they conclude that "in both cases he is speaking of the modern, not the Socratic conception of philosophy. The latter culminates in a natural and rational affirmation of philosophy; the former in the notion that the choice for philosophy is an arbitrary one, based on mere decision" (Zuckert and Zuckert 2006, 153–54). Confirmation of the Zuckerts' conclusion is right before one in "The Mutual Influence" piece, for after the very sentence in which Strauss writes that "the choice of philosophy is based on faith," he immediately states, "And it seems to me that this difficulty [so apparently it is a "difficulty" to have philosophy so feebly defended] underlies all present-day philosophizing" (Strauss 1979, 118; 1972, 271–72). Just before making the statement about philosophy resting on faith, Strauss relates that he is using the term *philosophy* in the "common and vague sense of the term where it includes any rational orientation in the world, including science and what have you, common sense" (1979, 117–18).

What is this "natural or rational affirmation of philosophy," this Socratic philosophy "in the original sense of the term," that appears to be the basis for Strauss's choice and perhaps elevation of the philosophic life. As the Zuckerts draw out of Strauss, it clearly is not a proof that the philosophic life is the superior way of life; rather it is assurance, in the words of Strauss, that "revelation cannot refute philosophy," for all arguments from Revelation "are conclusive only on the basis of faith" (Zuckert and Zuckert 2006, 150). So to inquire into all things including the intrusion of Revelation or alleged revelation and competing revelations into the world of experience can hardly be considered irrational. In a positive vein, the urgent question of how one should live must be addressed, and Strauss sees the question as "settled for Socrates by the fact that he is a philosopher. As a philosopher he knows he is ignorant of the most important things. The ignorance, the evident fact of this ignorance, evidently proves that quest for knowledge of the most important things is the most important thing for us." In the same paragraph Strauss comes again to speak of philosophy as a way of life. It is a life "animated by a peculiar passion, the philosophic desire or eros" (Zuckert and Zuckert 2006, 153; Strauss 1989, 259).

Such is Strauss's case for the philosophic way of life, and though it is clear that this philosophy embraced in a Socratic spirit is classical rationalism and aspects of that rationalism which appear in modernity, the opposition to and tension with Revelation are still present. This more compelling understanding of philosophy does not, in Strauss's understanding, rule out a life in the light of faith. It does not hold out, as modern philosophy often does, the prospect of overcoming and proving wrong the life taking its bearings from Revelation.

With Strauss's position clarified in the light of recent commentaries, among which is the work of the Zuckerts, there still remain perplexities about where Strauss leaves the topic of philosophy and the Bible. These have a persistence and an urgency noted earlier, and they came into sharper focus when the philosopher-pope, John Paul II, like Strauss shaped in part in the phenomenological tradition, issued the encyclical *Fides et Ratio* in autumn 1998.[7] These perplexities are here focused on two questions that compel our reflection. I state both at this point because it is perhaps only through the resolution of the second that we can make some headway with the first. It may then prove helpful to have the second in mind even as the first is explored. The first is whether Strauss's final position on reason and faith is one that emphasizes their irreconcilable conflict and endless antagonism. In the end, is he saying that this is a case of you must be on one side or the other? The second question or puzzle is about what it means for Strauss to say that the tension between Revelation and philosophy is "the secret of the vitality of the West" (1979, 113). What is particularly vital? In fact, what is useful about an apparent standoff between the way of reason and the way of Revelation? So what, then, does Strauss mean?

Strauss's description of the relationship between reason and Revelation as one of conflict, antagonism, opposition, and challenge precludes true harmonization and synthesis. In Strauss's view, harmonization and synthesis are never truly that but are always a mask for the triumph of one over the other, for the servility of philosophy to Revelation or vice versa.[8] It is important to understand where the conflict is rooted in order to understand Strauss's apparent insistence on the impossibility of synthesis and harmonization. Reason and Revelation represent different peaks, different understandings of the human good and happiness, thus, as noted, different ways of life, and in that difference is the basis for continuing conflict and tension. The fundamental tension at this point, at the peak as it were or at the very principle of human life, does not preclude, as Strauss often insisted, a substantial agreement on morality when the reason at issue is classical rationalism and the Revelation is biblical religion.

There is an apparent alternative to Strauss's way of viewing the relation of reason and Revelation. Consider viewing them as mutually supportive, in the sense that neither is able to attain its goal without the other. This seems to be the position of the philosopher-pope in *Fides et Ratio.* Eva Brann has captured in a simple sentence the essential character of John Paul II's teaching on our topic in *Fides et Ratio.* The pope, she writes, "distinguishes autonomy from self-sufficiency" (1999, 115). Philosophy and Revelation are autonomous but not self-sufficient. They are autonomous and thus in tension in that they answer to different first principles.

The encyclical unabashedly uses the language of synthesis and harmonization to describe the appropriate relationship between philosophy and Revelation. At one point, John Paul writes, "This is why I make this strong and insistent appeal—not, I trust, untimely—that faith and philosophy recover the profound unity which allows them to stand in harmony with their nature without compromising their mutual autonomy" (1998, #48).[9] At the same time, the encyclical bears out everywhere the truth of Strauss's observation about the nature of syntheses with respect to this question, namely, that one pole or principle is given superiority. The syntheses which John Paul holds up as he reviews the history of Western thought in the encyclical and the synthesis he endorses for our age are explicitly and decidedly on the ground of Revelation (#80). John Paul openly defends a ministerial or handmaid (*ancilla*) role for philosophy (#5, 77). Brann misses or obscures this dimension of the encyclical as she understandably marvels at the strength of its endorsement of philosophy and sees John Paul as proposing a "co-equality" of theology and philosophy (Brann 1999, 111, passim). She is drawn to that term *co-equality* by the memorable imagery with which the encyclical opens: "Faith and reason are like two wings on which the human spirit rises to the contemplation of truth" (epigraph/preface). We are reminded what Ernest Fortin has captured in his observation that "the best tradition of Catholic theology . . . has prized reason and looked upon it as an ally" (1996a, 302).

Overall in the encyclical, however, we have something less than co-equality and something more like the pseudosynthesis which Strauss said all syntheses of Revelation and reason must be. At the same time the endorsement of philosophy and its autonomy is forceful and repeated throughout the encyclical. Like Strauss, John Paul is wary of philosophic systems, especially such as proclaim completeness or totality. He sees philosophy as essentially "sapiential" inquiry, inquiry aimed at directing human life, inquiry that cannot be pointless and hence fruitless (#3–5, 81–82). The pope writes that "the Church cannot but set great value upon reason's drive to attain goals which render people's lives ever more worthy. She sees in philosophy the way to come to know fundamental truths about human life" (#5). At another point late in the encyclical, he writes, "I appeal also to philosophers and to all teachers of philosophy, asking them to have the courage to recover in the flow of an enduringly valid philosophical tradition, the range of authentic wisdom and truth—metaphysical truth included— which is proper to philosophical inquiry" (#106). At an earlier point John Paul cites approvingly a church council document from the nineteenth century:

> There exists a twofold order of knowledge, distinct not only as regards their source but also as regards their object. With regard to the source, because we know in one by natural reason, in the other by divine faith.

> With regard to the object, because besides those things which natural reason can attain, there are proposed for our belief mysteries hidden in God which, unless they are divinely revealed, cannot be known (#9).[10]

With regard to the strong distinction between faith and reason which he draws, Strauss appears to have thought his own view was in accord with the Catholic tradition. Eric Voegelin at one point objected to Strauss's distinction between Revelation and reason. Strauss defended himself in a letter to Voegelin saying that his distinction between Revelation and human knowledge "is in harmony with the Catholic teaching" (cited in Pangle 1994, 239). It is interesting to notice, though somewhat incidental to the main inquiry in this essay, that in the same letter Strauss appears to welcome and defend the principle of tradition in Catholicism (in effect, reason and Revelation co-developing knowledge) over against what he calls "the desert of Kierkegaard's subjectivism" (239). This can be seen to point readers to an objectivity that classical rationalism and a Bible-based tradition might seek to share. Both Strauss and John Paul explicitly defend the opening to transcendent objectivity against the confining claims of historicism (Strauss 1959, 64; John Paul II 1998, #95).[11]

Strauss repeatedly shows awareness of how reason and Revelation might work in tandem, though for him one is subordinate to the other.[12] He knows and seeks to draw attention to the ministerial or handmaid role of philosophy in the Catholic tradition, and there are indications, much remarked upon in the scholarship on Strauss, that Christian Revelation with its emphasis on the mystery and nature of reality is seen by Strauss as less subject to the tension with reason than the Judaic and Islamic Revelations with their emphases on law.[13] Strauss professes both amazement and concern about Christianity's favor of philosophy. His concern seems to be over the possible or likely loss of independence for philosophy when it is so embraced. In "Progress or Return?" he writes of philosophy's loss of its original character and its being "in the Christian Middle Ages deprived of its character as a way of life" and becoming "just a very important compartment" (Strauss 1989, 260).[14] Perhaps he emphasizes the difference and antagonism between philosophy and faith at least in part as a way of strengthening philosophy's autonomy, a concern of course not lost on John Paul, who writing of pre-Christian or ancient philosophy observes, "we see here philosophy's valid aspiration to be an *autonomous* enterprise, obeying its own rules and employing the powers of reason alone" (#75; original emphasis). Strauss was concerned not only that philosophy not be captured in an instrumental or servile role but also that it resist the temptation to be merely edifying.

Strauss, then, seems to have significant common ground with the Catholic tradition in the pointed distinction made by each between reason and Revelation and even in his concern for philosophy's autonomy. Yet is there not still a problem in reconciling Strauss to the Catholic tradition, a problem in the strength of the opposition that he sees between philosophy and Revelation? Would Strauss be able to accept the claim, to use Brann's apt formulation of John Paul's teaching, that philosophy and Revelation, while autonomous, are not self-sufficient? At least one formulation by Strauss of the struggle between faith and reason suggests that he could not. Strauss writes in "Progress or Return?" that each of the "two roots of the Western world sets forth one thing as the one thing needful" (1989, 245–46). What the Bible proclaims and what Greek philosophy proclaims as the one thing needful is incompatible: "The one thing needful according to Greek philosophy is the life of autonomous understanding. The one thing needful as spoken by the Bible is the life of obedient love." It appears, then, by this language of "the one thing needful," that Strauss understands the Bible and Greek philosophy as in contention because each proclaims its own self-sufficiency.

Let us turn to the second problem or perplexity, that concerning what Strauss means in the last paragraph of "Progress or Return?" when he says that the "unresolved conflict" between the Bible and Greek philosophy "is the secret of the vitality of Western civilization" (1989, 270). A secret source of vitality—what could this mean? In another formulation of this earlier in the same paragraph, Strauss writes, "The core, the nerve of Western intellectual history, Western spiritual history, one could almost say, is the conflict between the biblical and philosophic notions of the good life" (270).

Two other passages seem important to keep in mind in trying to understand how this conflict—this apparent standoff—can give vigor and vitality to the West, and do so secretly. First, Strauss says that "the whole history of the West presents itself at first glance as an attempt to harmonize, or to synthesize, the Bible and Greek philosophy. But a closer study shows what happened and has been happening in the West for many centuries, is not a harmonization but an attempt at harmonization" (1989, 245). Given the fundamental incompatibility of the Bible and philosophy, Strauss thinks such attempts are doomed to failure, yet he suggests in the very way he writes about the overall pattern of Western history that such attempts will continue, his observations notwithstanding. Seeming syntheses will be made, and then they will be unsettled, unraveled as we would say today, by the subordinated alternative in the false synthesis rising up. Is this macro picture of Western history, of recurrent syntheses making and then their undoing, is this the process of vitalizing the West? And it is secret because it is out of sight for most people most of the time for they would be living from the moral core shared by the two fundamentally incompatible sources of Western life. Recall that when Strauss speaks of Western civilization being invigorated, he means the intellectual and spiritual history of the West. So perhaps it is this macro picture of synthesis making and unmaking that is the very life of the West.

This solution to what he means gains plausibility and perhaps greater depth when it is joined to a micro or personal and individual picture that Strauss gives us in another passage found in the very closing lines of "Progress or Return?" Here Strauss claims that one can find comfort in Western civilization gaining and sustaining life through tensional conflict "only if we live that life, if we live that conflict." Then at once Strauss closes with his well-known words, "No one can be both a philosopher and a theologian. . . . But everyone of us can be and ought to be either one or the other, the philosopher open to the challenge of theology or the theologian open to the challenge of philosophy." So here, it seems, the secret of the vitality of the West is found, in the relatively few persons who recognize the basic incompatibility of philosophy and theology and commit to one or the other as one must do as an acting person, a political being—and who commit to one fully conscious of the powerful and irrefutable claims of the other. In addition, and perhaps more important, these few from each side participate in an orientation to the transcendent and are able to rise critically above their political community and its specific theology. This implies that for some revelations, not only for classical rationalism, the theologico-political problem can arise for the theologian.[15] This awareness of the fundamental choice, as well as the welcoming of the mutual challenge from overlapping transcendent grounds, seems to be the fullness of human life for Strauss and that life realized or approximated by the greatest thinkers of the West. This vitality would in some important respects proceed from an alliance of the contending parties, each arising from distinct principles.

I wonder whether, when this choice is faced, philosophy proves to be, as it might aspire to be, "the one thing needful." Likewise, can Revelation be lived without philosophy as "the one thing needful"? Is Strauss's asking each to be open to the challenge of the other an invitation to test the claim by each of exclusive adequacy? Most students of these texts of Strauss would say no; some would say that Strauss is pointing to the superiority of Athens or of Jerusalem, whichever might emerge from the test of life. It is here appropriate to be reminded that Strauss's title for his important and relatively late essay on our topic is "Jerusalem and Athens," not "Jerusalem or Athens."[16]

It is important to add at this point a word about an instance where Strauss himself apparently identifies with Athens. In "Jerusalem and Athens" Strauss writes that to examine the claims of Jerusalem against those of Athens is already to choose the side of Athens. But Strauss's precise words are important here. He writes, "By saying that we wish to hear first and then to act to decide, we have already decided in favor of Athens against Jerusalem" (Strauss 1995, 182). Strauss's phrasing does not preclude someone having decided, as in the instance of choosing Jerusalem, then, seeking understanding and reason's relationship to that choice. Perhaps one never comes at the choice with a wholly open mind, undisposed one way or the other, either ungraced by God or untouched by the prevailing culture. It is well that Strauss's phrasing does not simply preclude that kind of union between Revelation and reason, for Revelation in the West—notably Christianity—makes a place for "faith seeking understanding," to use the Augustinian formulation. This is picked up and emphasized in *Fides et Ratio* of John Paul (#8, 9, 55 ff., 73). This tradition of Revelation is not one of raw and simple obedience with no reasoning involved, nor is it requisite in this tradition of Revelation that it be embraced to the exclusion of reasoning. To say that, however, is not to deny the fundamental opposition in principle and in end or goal between reason and Revelation, though it suggests that each may not stand well alone or be simply adequate, one to the exclusion of the other, in a truly or authentically human life.

Finally, let us consider two observations about the interaction or dialectic between reason and Revelation. Such consideration seems especially appropriate as we further wonder what it means to live in the way Strauss called for, to live as a philosopher open to the challenge of theology or as a theologian open to the challenge of philosophy. The first of these observations from *Fides et Ratio* speaks to the large historical record or the macro level of our experience: "A survey of the history of thought, especially in the West, shows clearly that the encounter between philosophy and theology and the exchange of their respective insights have contributed richly to the progress of humanity" (#101). This was immediately preceded by John Paul recalling the church's long-standing conviction that "faith and reason 'mutually support each other'; each influences the other, as they offer to each other a purifying critique and a stimulus to pursue the search for a deeper understanding" (#100). And then with respect to the personal or micro level, John Paul writes that "without wonder, men and women could lapse into deadening routine and little by little would become incapable of a life which is genuinely personal" (#4).

Leo Strauss can be seen contributing to the Catholic tradition the purifying critique that John Paul invited from philosophy. He has exposed anew what the Catholic tradition has always known and has articulated well in its best moments, namely, that Catholic wisdom, belief, and teaching rest ultimately on Revelation, and that all must be understood and done in accord with an understanding of that Revelation. At the foundational or ultimate point of a framework of meaning and thus of a directive for action, for politics, is a distinct principle for Athens as well as one for Jerusalem or Rome. This distinctness is the basis for Strauss's insistence that synthesis and harmonization are never completely realized in the merging of the distinct claims of reason and Revelation, that synthesis always means subordination of the one to the other. In fact, in the Catholic or Christian tradition the "synthesis" must always be on the ground of faith and its objects, but the efforts at this kind of synthesis, as Strauss predicted and John Paul expected, are likely to be recurrent in accord with developments of both the theological and the philosophical understanding of reality.

Revelation's purifying critique of reason keeps it humble and above all from overextending its claims, the claims so characteristic of modern philosophy (#76). This might seem a critique unneeded by Socratic classical rationalism, with its self-formative respect for what philosophy cannot know. Yet contentment with the loving search that is philosophy, while proclaiming its object beyond us, can itself be seen as dogmatic and unconvincingly resistant to looking beyond the limits of philosophy and attending to the full satisfaction of the erotic pull that manifests itself in genuine philosophy.[17] Within the commitment of faith, reason continues to work and to exalt the human person. The commitment that is faith is not only assisted by reason but also calls on reason to understand more deeply its objects. This is the exalted role for reason that John Paul II returns to again and again in the encyclical. Why might not reason and faith work together to a full understanding of who we are and how we are to live. Strauss clearly does not object to this, but he seems to obscure it by his emphasis on the radical separation and mutual antagonism of the two sources of the intellectual and spiritual vitality of the West.

A Christian cannot end these reflections with a shred of fairness if he failed to acknowledge the greatest debt owed Strauss whose thought and teaching have brought a renewal of Socratic classical rationalism. That rationalism once served as the initial basis for the significant efforts in Christian history to aspire to the fullness of wisdom with the gifts of both reason and Revelation. What it can now become remains to be seen.[18]

NOTES

1. The "theologico-political problem" or "predicament" can be a somewhat elusive concept; it seems best understood in Strauss's work as the problem or predicament confronting a philosopher in his relationship to civic life when the political community including its good order rests on divine law, as has generally been the case. See Steven Smith's statement of the problem (2006, 10).

2. This essay, "Progress or Return?," is a compilation from lectures given by Strauss in the 1950s. Besides the formulation here as philosophy and the Bible, the alternatives of faith and reason (*fides et ratio*) are also expressed in the work of Strauss, and to a degree in the encyclical of John Paul II by that name considered here, in the terms of Revelation and reason, the Bible and reason, Jerusalem and Athens, theology and philosophy. Catherine Zuckert reports that Strauss's last book as projected and not completed was to contain seventeen chapters, the central one being his essay "Jerusalem and

Athens." The names of these cities for Strauss indicate "the broadest and deepest . . . of the experience of the past . . . [upon which a]ll the hopes that we entertain in the midst of the confusions and dangers of the present are founded" (Zuckert 1996, 169).

3. This essay by Strauss is based on a speech he gave in 1959 at the graduation exercises of the Basic Program of Liberal Education for Adults at the University of Chicago. A couple of years later it was reprinted from an official University of Chicago publication in Fletcher 1961. The Zuckerts quote here from the commonly accessible version: Strauss 1968, 6–7.

4. Note also the discussion of Strauss's alleged atheism in Colmo 1990, 147, passim.

5. This published lecture was in a very limited way incorporated in "Progress or Return?"; see Strauss 1989, 272 n. 17.

6. The quoted statement of Strauss is found in Strauss 1979, 118; see also Strauss 1997b, 30–31.

7. In the following, I use the official English translation of *Fides et Ratio* (John Paul II 1998). I have consulted quite often the bilingual edition of the encyclical containing an unofficial English translation as well as commentaries on the text (John Paul II 2003). All references to the encyclical are by paragraph numbers, which are the same in both sources.

8. Significant formulations of this by Strauss are as follows. "Syntheses always sacrifice the decisive claim of one of the two elements" (1981, 19). No one can live a life "which is beyond the conflict between philosophy and theology, or a synthesis of both" (1979, 111). See also Orr 1995, 24.

9. Earlier (#40) the encyclical described Saint Augustine's "synthesis" as one that has "remained for centuries the most exalted form of philosophical and theological speculation known to the West."

10. This teaching of the First Vatican Council was reaffirmed in the Second Vatican Council's *Pastoral Constitution on the Church in the Modern World* (*Fides,* #60).

11. Fortin comments, "By showing that modern science has not replaced God and that History has not replaced philosophy, or by showing as no one has done in four hundred years that the claims of Reason and Revelation are inherently untouched by modernity, Strauss may have performed as great a service for theology as he has for philosophy" (1996c, 295).

12. Smith notes that Strauss sometimes presents Jerusalem and Athens as "two limbs of the tree of knowledge that have mutually nourished and sustained one another" (2006, 10; also 126); and see Strauss 1989, 246.

13. E.g., Strauss 1952, 19–21. See the discussion of the likely Christian difference for Strauss in Smith 2006, 53, 73; Zuckert 1996, 110; Schall 1994, 212–13; and especially Guerra 2007, 53 ff., 66–67.

14. It appears that Strauss thought that Christian medieval philosophy betrayed or obscured the fundamental Catholic position about the difference and thus possibly the tension between faith and reason. In a letter to Karl Lowith (August 15, 1946), Strauss observes that "the greatest exponents of the ancients' side in the *querelle,* that is, Swift and Lessing, knew that the real theme of the quarrel is antiquity

and Christianity." By "Christianity" Strauss apparently means "Christian medieval philosophy," which in the previous paragraph he says has much that is essential in common with modern philosophy (Strauss 1983, 106).

15. See the comment on the transpolitical in Strauss (Zuckert 1996, 200). Consider Fortin's interesting observation that Christianity is transpolitical in contrast to other religions of the book and that "the philosopher is the man who comes closest to Christianity and at the same time the one who remains farthest away from it" (1996, 18).

16. Orr calls attention to this aspect of the essay's title (1995, 24). Delivered as a lecture at City College in New York in 1967, the essay was first published the following year. It is reprinted in the appendixes to the Orr book. Strauss still describes what he does here as "preliminary reflections."

17. Regarding this aspect of Strauss, Marc Guerra comments that "Strauss brackets all we know to be truly human about human life and exaggerates the degree to which the Socratic life is genuinely satisfying for embodied social beings" (2007, 75).

18. Beyond all those cited in the notes, there are others who in conversation and through their writings related to this topic have contributed to my thinking about Leo Strauss's thought on reason and Revelation. I wish especially to acknowledge Frederick Crosson, a conversation partner on this topic over many years, and the following: Harry Jaffa, James Stoner, Kim Sorensen, Heinrich Meier, Mary Keys, Peter Augustine Lawler, V. Bradley Lewis, and Derek Webb. Welcome contributions were made even, of course, when we had disagreements.

REFERENCES

Brann, Eva. 1999. "A Call to Thought." *St. John's Review* 45 (1): 109–18.

Colmo, Christopher A. 1990. "Reason and Revelation in the Thought of Leo Strauss." *Interpretation* 18 (Fall): 145–60.

Fletcher, Scott C., ed. 1961. *Education for Public Responsibility.* New York: Norton.

Fortin, Ernest. 1996a. "Faith and Reason in Contemporary Perspective." In *Classical Christianity and the Political Order,* ed. J. Brian Benestad, 297–316. Lanham, MD: Rowman and Littlefield.

———. 1996b. "The Political Thought of St. Augustine." In *Classical Christianity and the Political Order,* ed. J. Brian Benestad, 1–29. Lanham, MD: Rowman and Littlefield.

———. 1996c. "Rational Theologians and Irrational Philosophers: A Straussian Perspective." In *Classical Christianity and the Political Order,* ed. J. Brian Benestad, 287–96. Lanham, MD: Rowman and Littlefield.

Guerra, Marc D. 2007. "Leo Strauss and the Recovery of the Theologico-Political Problem." *Political Science Reviewer* 26: 47–80.

John Paul II. 1998. *Fides Et Ratio.* Boston: Pauline Books & Media.

———. 2003. *Restoring Faith in Reason.* Ed. Laurence Paul Hemming and Susan Frank Parsons, trans. Anthony Meredith, S.J., and Laurence Paul Hemming. Notre Dame: University of Notre Dame Press.

Nicgorski, Walter. 1985. "Reason, Politics and Christian Belief: A Review of Robert Sokolowski's *The God of Faith and Reason.*" *Claremont Review of Books* (Summer): 18–21.

Orr, Susan. 1995. *Jerusalem and Athens: Reason and Revelation in the Works of Leo Strauss.* Lanham, MD: Rowman and Littlefield.

Pangle, Thomas L. 1994. "On the Epistolary Dialogue between Leo Strauss and Eric Voegelin." In *Leo Strauss: Political Philosopher and Jewish Thinker,* ed. Kenneth L. Deutsch and Walter Nicgorski, 231–56. Lanham, MD: Rowman and Littlefield.

———. 2006. *Leo Strauss.* Baltimore: Johns Hopkins University Press.

Schall, James V., S.J. 1994. "A Latitude for Statesmanship? Strauss on St. Thomas." In *Leo Strauss: Political Philosopher and Jewish Thinker,* ed. Kenneth L. Deutsch and Walter Nicgorski, 211–30. Lanham, MD: Rowman and Littlefield.

Smith, Steven B. 2006. *Reading Leo Strauss.* Chicago: University of Chicago Press.

Strauss, Leo. 1952. *Persecution and the Art of Writing.* Glencoe, IL: Free Press.

———. 1953. *Natural Right and History.* Chicago: University of Chicago Press.

———. 1959. "Political Philosophy and History." In *What Is Political Philosophy?,* 56–77. Westport, CT: Greenwood Press.

———. 1964. *The City and Man.* Chicago: Rand McNally & Co.

———. [1961] 1968. "What Is Liberal Education?" In *Liberalism: Ancient and Modern,* 3–8. Chicago: University of Chicago Press.

———. 1972. "Niccolò Machiavelli." In *History of Political Philosophy,* ed. Leo Strauss and Joseph Cropsey, 271–92. Chicago: Rand McNally & Co.

———. 1979. "The Mutual Influence of Theology and Philosophy." *Independent Journal of Philosophy* 3: 111–18.

———. 1981. "On the Interpretation of Genesis." *L'Homme* 15 (1): 5–20.

———. 1983. "Correspondence Concerning Modernity: Karl Lowith and Leo Strauss." *Independent Journal of Philosophy* 4: 105–19.

———. 1989. "Progress or Return?" In *The Rebirth of Classical Political Rationalism,* ed. Thomas L. Pangle, 227–70. Chicago: University of Chicago Press.

———. 1995. "Jerusalem and Athens: Some Preliminary Reflections." In Susan Orr, *Jerusalem and Athens: Reason and Revelation in the Works of Leo Strauss,* Appendix, 179–207. Lanham, MD: Rowman and Littlefield.

———. 1997a. "Preface to Hobbes *Politische Wissenschaft.*" In *Jewish Philosophy and the Crisis of Modernity,* ed. Kenneth Hart Green, 453–56. Albany: State University of New York Press.

———. 1997b. *Spinoza's Critique of Religion.* Chicago: University of Chicago Press.

Zuckert, Catherine H. 1996. *Postmodern Platos.* Chicago: University of Chicago Press.

Zuckert, Catherine, and Michael Zuckert. 2006. *The Truth about Leo Strauss.* Chicago: University of Chicago Press.

PART III

American Political Thought and Practice

Chapter Eleven

Locke, the Puritans, and America

Reflections on the Christian Dimension of Our Personal Identities

PETER AUGUSTINE LAWLER

Provoked by the wonderfully lucid, penetrating, and pathbreaking work of Michael Zuckert and his excellent students, I've come closer than ever to figuring out what Americans owe the Puritans. I've been thinking, in other words, about the relationship between Locke and Christianity, coming to the conclusion that the Lockean conception of personal identity is unsustainable without some positive help from truthfully Christian conceptions of who we are and what we're supposed to do. With the help of Zuckert and Lee Ward, I think Locke might even have known that, although probably not well enough. For an articulation of the Christian or Puritan contribution to understanding who we are as free persons these days, I've gratefully relied on Alexis de Tocqueville and the self-described neo-Puritan novelist and essayist Marilynne Robinson, one of our country's best living writers. Let me begin with Michael Zuckert's Lockean America.

THE NATURAL RIGHTS REPUBLIC AND CHRISTIANITY

Better than anyone else, Michael Zuckert has displayed our country as "the natural rights republic," as *the* country most securely rooted in the secular, universalistic, and individualistic principles of John Locke. That's not to say, of course, that Zuckert is some kind of libertarian new atheist in favor of dispensing with religion altogether. Because the arguments that support the true principles of government, as Locke says, can be *known* only by a few, they must be *believed* by the many in any well-functioning free and democratic "regime." In Zuckert's astute interpretation of our Declaration of Independence, what's most important, politically, is that all citizens hold the truth of the Declaration to be self-evident, but they need not grasp the true foundation of their "cognitive or theoretical status." That means that "the highest kind of statesmanship is the cultivation of the necessary right opinion," and "right opinion"—as opposed to genuinely, self-evidently true opinion—is the necessary foundation of our political life (Zuckert 1996, 49, 54).

So in Zuckert's model American Christian preachers are the "Lockean Puritans" of the eighteenth century who transformed the puritanical view of Christianity to harmonize it with natural rights political doctrine—political life oriented around the self-interested individual and not republican or Christian idealism. He recommends those preachers to us, in effect, for following the example of Locke himself, for reconfiguring biblical doctrine in light of what we can know about ourselves through unassisted reason. They taught people to believe in the revolutionary doctrine of natural rights as flowing from what they believe to be true about the will of the Creator (Zuckert 1996, chap. 6).

When America works best, Zuckert claims, our devotion to our natural rights republic receives "salutary aid from deep-flowing religious impulses." *Salutary,* of course, is to be distinguished from *true.* Religious impulses and their theological articulation add nothing *real* to what we can know about who we are. America works best, in other words, when religious and secular, individualistic impulses and arguments, work "tensionlessly"—or don't compromise our basically secular devotion. When they are in "disharmony and tension," as they often seem to be today, America becomes disoriented and needlessly contentious (Zuckert 1996, 200–201, 8).

Christianity, so understood, ought to be our civil theology—or a way of getting God or the gods behind our "regime." Locke "affirms Christianity as a civil religion in Varro's sense . . . [and] attempts to reinterpret it as to be more civil" (Zuckert 2002, 162). But Locke, Zuckert observes, never really solved the problem that natural rights civil theology is somewhat of an oxymoron. His civil religion is in the service of "transforming the dominant understanding held by men of the human situation in the world for the sake of improving that situation physically, politically, and morally" (Zuckert 2002, 162). That means, among other things, leading them to think of themselves less as either citizens or creatures—as grateful to God or country or as part of wholes beyond themselves.

Locke, Zuckert shows us, both presented "a powerful case for the necessity of civil religion" in the modern world and "contributed to creating a climate of opinion in which civil religion . . . is most difficult, if not impossible, to maintain" (Zuckert 2002, 166). So we might criticize Locke for undermining even reformed Christianity's credibility by trying to civilize in a context in which civil religion has been rendered incredible and degrading by Christianity. The "Lockean Puritans," from Tocqueville's view, were actually on the way to becoming transcendentalist believers in the natural religion of pantheism—a religion with no place for either divine or human individuality, for neither Creator nor creature, not to mention citizen or statesman (Tocqueville [1835/1840] 2000, vol. 2, pt. 2, chap. 7).[1]

It's in defense of such an ambiguously Lockean transformation of Christianity that Zuckert dissents from Tocqueville's view that we Americans owe anything fundamental or deeply true to the Puritans. When he quotes what Tocqueville says about the Puritans with approval, it's the part when the Frenchman condemns their "ridiculous and tyrannical" laws. That just and severe criticism, in Zuckert's view, occurs in the midst of Tocqueville's abundant and unjustified praise of their political project on behalf of equality and liberty. Zuckert doesn't think

Tocqueville appreciates properly that Puritan legislative tyranny didn't flow from weaknesses in human nature but from "the specific character of Puritan principles and aspirations" (Zuckert 1996, 171).

Zuckert's bottom line here is that the Puritans had a "presumption against liberty," and that religious or Christian presumption explains why "their legislation . . . has earned the censure of mankind as Puritanical" (Zuckert 1996, 145). For Zuckert, the individualistic liberal, there's nothing positive about being a Puritan. So his polemical intention is to read anything distinctively Puritanical from our authoritative political tradition, from the core beliefs that identify us all as Americans. But is it really true that true Christianity is characterized by a presumption against liberty?

LOCKE AND THE GOD OF THE BIBLE

Zuckert presents Thomas Pangle's views of our natural rights republic's discontinuity with anything deeply Christian as more extreme or less nuanced than his own—and not, of course, without reason. But even Pangle admits, Zuckert reports, that "belief in the sanctity of all human beings as such" that somehow grounds natural rights philosophy "would seem to be a legacy of the biblical social and political tradition rather than the classical one" (Pangle 1992, quoted in Zuckert 1996, 120). That would seem to mean, from Pangle's view, that the insight into the unique irreplaceability of every human person *is* biblical—and so not reasonable. For Pangle far more than Zuckert, it would be historicism to believe that anything *that* essential or foundational and reasonable could not have been known to Plato (and Aristotle) (Pangle 1983).

The Lockean Zuckert, surely no historicist, sometimes emphasizes how much Locke actually discovered—or at least thought he discovered—that Plato and Aristotle didn't know. And Locke, he properly reminds us, holds that "the Bible in fact depicts the fundamentals of the human experience far better and to a far higher degree than any other premodern awareness"—including, of course, that of premodern or "pre-Cartesian" philosophy (Zuckert 2002, 142).

Locke denies, in fact, that any particular being can be reduced to or defined as essentially a member of the species. And we're the beings with enough self-consciousness or self-ownership to have a relatively stable and clear sense of who we are as particular, vulnerable, mortal (or embodied) beings. By thinking through all that is implied in self-ownership, Locke's best students, in particular Zuckert and Ward, show why Locke believed "he had discovered a new mental continent, a hitherto unexamined realm of subjectivity and interiority" (Ward 2010, 294; with Zuckert 1994, chap. 9). He had relocated being itself in the particular experiences of personal identity.

Locke, like the Bible, "sees man's differentia in terms of freedom." And at least it's unclear whether Descartes and Locke could have grasped that true insight about the true inwardness of each of us without knowledge of the Bible. According to Locke, it's freely creating man who created the freely creating God—or the opposite of what the Bible tells us. But the Bible—unlike other premodern texts—still shows *who* God should be if truly created in man's image. Man, alone among the animals, is partly and indefinitely free from nature (Zuckert 2002, 142). To say otherwise, Zuckert says in criticism of the Darwinian Larry Arnhart, is to succumb to "biologism" (Zuckert 1996, 255 n. 57).

Locke sides with the Christians against the classical thinkers and the Darwinians concerning free personal identity. From that personal view, even philosophy is not learning how to die; it's not forgetting about one's personal needs or personal contingency and mortality. For Locke, like the Christians, we might be able to say that our deepest longings are in some sense personal, for a sort of happiness compatible with the real experiences of personal identity. That's surely why Locke believed that his discovery of the "realm of subjectivity and interiority . . . surpassed in significance the discoveries" of the explorers, scientists, and so forth "in the terrestrial realm" (Ward 2010, 294).

LOCKE AS A POST-CHRISTIAN THINKER

Before Locke, according to Jefferson, there was tyrannical "monkish ignorance and superstition," and the despotic world of Christendom was a decline from the world of the classical Greeks and Romans. For a helpfully extreme corrective to that misleading view, we can turn to David Bentley Hart's *Atheistic Delusions* (2009). Hart describes a pre-Christian world that was cruel and capricious—reminding us forcefully of the torture and murder that ancient paganism tolerated as a matter of course, precisely because it regarded particular persons as unreal. The impersonal truth was best seen by the philosopher who became dead to himself, who resigned himself to the ephemeral insignificance of his particular existence. Christianity was, in a way, the slave revolt Nietzsche described: a cosmic rebellion against the enslavement of each of us to natural and political necessity. Christ, the Christians claimed, freed us from the limitations of our merely biological natures through his perfect reconciliation of God's nature and man's nature. He was, the Nicene fathers concluded, fully God and fully man, and his redemption was to divinize every man.

It is barely too strong to say that, for Hart, Christ transformed each of us from being nobody to being somebody—a somebody of infinite value. None of us is destined to be a slave, and death has been overcome. We are no longer defined by our merely biological natures, because our nature is now to be both human and divine. From one view, there is no empirical evidence that death has been overcome for each particular human being. From another, there's abundant evidence in the unprecedented virtue flowing from the unconditional love present among the early Christians and that virtue's indirect, historical transformation of the broader social and political world. The change in who we are is the result of a deepened human inwardness or self-consciousness: Christ made each of us irreducibly deeper by infusing divinity in every part of our natures. In our loving relationships with other persons and the personal God, we don't surrender what we know about our own irreducible personal identity.

Many of the features of the personal liberation praised by Lockeans, Hart even claims, came into the world in Christian communities. Even the Stoics didn't approach the Christians in their indifference to a person's social status. The Christians were the first to be completely opposed to slavery; the first for raising women to equality in marriage and elsewhere; the first for faithfulness in monogamous marriage; the first for the egalitarian brotherhood of all men. For the Christians, the community of personal love wasn't some otherworldly hope. Rather, that community was formed by obligations given to divinized beings here and now. Our divinization through Christ includes what is called life after death, but we can live lovingly liberated from death even before we die (Lawler 2010a).

The Lockean, from this view, is a kind of post-Christian who believes, without any belief in personal salvation, he was born to be free. He believes that all persons are equally not nothing, are equally not completely determined by the impersonal laws of nature. But the Lockean lacks any loving sense of a God who has freed us from death and necessity for love. So our freedom is to be used to win, by our own efforts, what the Christian God had promised to provide. Each of us is not nobody, but it's up to each of us to make himself into somebody, to create value and sustainability for his personal identity.

We are not, by nature, divine beings: there's no evidence for that without faith. But perhaps we can employ our freedom to make ourselves more and more divine—freer from the impersonal limits of our biological natures. The modern, Lockean thought is that faith in a personal Creator can be replaced by a more reasonable faith in the unprecedented historical future, faith in what I can do for myself in a world basically indifferent to my personal being. Locke and Lockeans, as Zuckert shows, tell tale after tale of our self-won or inventive, historical liberation from nature (Zuckert 1996, 128–29). Generally speaking, Lockean America is distinguished by a "progressive attitude toward politics and society," one "open to indefinite improvement" and regarding all limits to what we can do for ourselves as provisional (Zuckert 1996, 103). Those who contrast our Founders (good) with the Progressives (evil), in this view, are, to some extent, piously fooling themselves.

But the Lockean stands with the Christians against the later, or more rigorously, Historical—and so now opposed to individualistic or personal—faith. Free persons, for both the Lockean and the Christian, can't be reduced to merely part of History or anything else, and so my rights today can't be sacrificed for a better tomorrow for others. The future must be constructed with me—my personal identity—in mind. The Christians and Lockeans readily allied against the Marxists by being clear that not anything might be done in the name of progress, by remaining focused on what's best for the particular persons around these days. In that sense, the Lockeans and the Christians are united against the Progressive privileging of History (with a capital *H*) over the unique and irreplaceable person.

CAN LOCKE DISPENSE WITH CHRISTIAN TRUTH?

Still, without some Christian or loving help, modern thought, Tocqueville explains, morphs in the direction of individualistic indifference. I can recognize your equal freedom, but that recognition is, if anything, compromised by my loving or paternalistic care for you. The Lockean or "past-tense" God doesn't care or even know each of us in our personal identity, and each of us imitates him when it comes to other persons in pursuit of his or her personal freedom (Zuckert 2002, 165–66).[2] It's true that we know that each of us is equally not nothing, or equally distinguished from everything else that exists. We also know that personal identity—or avoiding not being—is somehow the bottom line of each of our existences.

Tocqueville was wrong to suggest that indifference could ever come to mean, in a Lockean world, indifference to *me* or my surrender of concern for my own, singular future (Tocqueville, 2.4.6). Lockeanism will never become nihilism because I will always know that I'm not nothing. Individualism means my surrendering any concern for *you,* based on the judgment that both love and hate are more trouble than their worth and get my mind off what's really important in life (Tocqueville, 2.2.2–3). From the beginning, as Sara Henary explains, the Lockean conception of self-ownership can't be expected to generate "an active, attentive concern for the other." So Henary concludes that even a Lockean defense of equality can't dispense with "a willingness to argue publicly from specifically Christian premises" (Henary 2010, 26). And a true defense of equality might defend those premises as being in some fundamental sense true.

THE DEPENDENCE OF THE PERSONAL IDENTITY ON THE CHURCHES' FREEDOM

Fortunately, with the help of Zuckert and especially Ward, we can see that Locke gives more independence to religion and the genuinely

Christian point of view than it first appears. Locke holds that it's Christianity that discredited the idea of civil theology. He observes that "prior to Christianity, political control of religion was the natural human condition." It was "the ancient pagans" who reduced religion to "simply the encouragement of superstition and empty rituals by priests who served their political masters by employing religion to serve civil law" (Ward 2010, 229). Locke stands with the Christians against politicized superstition and ritual.

Locke really means it when he holds that "it is only with the coming of Christ that the principle of separating of religion and politics first appeared" (Ward 2010, 229). So it's only with his coming, as Saint Augustine claimed, that popular religion can become something other than civil or political theology—or instrument of the "cave" or "regime" (Augustine, bks. 6, 7). It is, similarly, only with the coming of Christianity that religion also can't be reduced to natural theology—or a way of expressing the impersonal truth about nature discovered by the philosophers. Because the human difference is freedom, religion that does justice to who each of us is as a person must understand each of us as more than merely or even essentially a citizen or part of nature. Religion must do justice to what each of us can know about his or her irreducible interiority or personal identity. Religion must be in some sense personal.

Remi Brague, in *The Law of God,* explains better than anyone why the separation of church and state—or the separation of human law and divine law—necessarily depends on this Christian view of personal freedom (Brague 2007). If, according to the pre-Christian or classical philosophers, the truth about the impersonal *logos* of nature is equivalent to divinity truthfully understood, then human beings need illusions about providential divinity to sustain their illusions about their own freedom or personal significance. And then the task of the political philosopher is to protect the tension between the truth about impersonal divine "law" and the moral or political dogmas that support human law. That means that civil theology is indispensable but merely salutary, and true or natural religion is philosophical liberation from personal concerns. That understanding of civil theology, to repeat, couldn't be Lockean.

Insofar as our Darwinians share that view of the impersonal, species-oriented truth about the *logos* of nature, then religion still makes sense as a way of supporting those same beneficial communal illusions. Neither Aristotelians nor Darwinians can, however, make sense of the freedom from political/divine law that we all believe human beings to possess. Freedom from political/divine law must be for personal/divine law, for beings who are in some sense created in the image of a personal God. In that way, limited government must be for both personal freedom and freedom of the church (Lawler 2009).[3]

So it's easy to see why Locke can claim that "the notion of a national church is problematic both theologically and logically" (Ward 2010, 232). Some Christians, of course, have been for using the state to encourage true religion, but in that case the state is subordinate to the church. It's virtuous for Saint Augustine's Christian emperor to use his power to spread true religion, but that's in an idealized context where all political power is ministerial to virtue freed up from political utility (Augustine, bk. 5, chap. 17).

That's not to say, of course, that the nation's political life does not have its own goals—which, for the Augustinian Christian, are peace and religious liberty. The Christian is called to do his duty to his country—without the solace of sharing in its civil religious illusions. The Augustinian Christian, deeply unmoved by even the glory that was Rome, is most deeply an alien or pilgrim in his political home. The Christians and the Lockeans agree that we are not naturally political beings. The Christian even agrees with the Lockean that government is instituted in response to the neediness of free beings; it is one of the merely necessary consequences of sinful—or passionately self-interested and domineering—personal identity (Augustine, bk. 19, chaps. 14–17).

That's why at least the Augustinian Christian agrees with the Lockean that political goals—even political expansion—should be pursued through contract and consent and without war—which is good only for glory—whenever possible. And the Christians and the Lockeans agree that differences in forms of government are to be evaluated according to a standard of personal liberty that's not, most deeply, political liberty (Augustine, bk. 5, chap. 17). The form of government, in that sense, is not to be confused with some Platonic "regime." The personal Christian alien—in his apolitical, cosmopolitan detachment—is not so different from the Lockean person.

No Christian, Locke is right to say, sounds properly Christian when speaking of "religion established by law" (quoted in Ward 2010, 232). Locke's attack on using political coercion to enforce religious belief and practice is aimed both at pagan and premodern, Christian religious practice. Both, we might say, can be criticized as a violation of natural rights and genuinely biblical personal insight. Both Locke and true Christians are about articulating a universal ethics available to all free persons, and both agree that to be free—and moral—is not to be fundamentally political or deeply or merely philosophical (Ward 2010, 245–47).[4]

Ward emphasizes that "Locke's toleration argument presupposes that the churches are institutions with a vital role to play in a free society." He actually mentions two roles. The churches will provide "a support for the moral foundation of a free society," and they will be "a salutary counterweight to the potentially overweening claims of the state and political sovereignty." In neither case, of course, will the role of the church be civil theological. In order to be a "salutary counterweight," the church has to be an organized body of thought and action with the freedom to teach what it thinks best about who we are and what we're supposed to do, and on that score "Locke insists that churches enjoy complete autonomy" (Ward 2010, 249).

The solitary person can't resist the power of the state—either in thought or in action—alone. Inwardness or subjectivity, to be real and genuinely democratic, can't be too lonely. That means, of course, that Locke doesn't actually share the antiecclesiasticism of Madison's *Memorial and Remonstrance,* which is very extreme in portraying one's conscientious right to discovering one's duty to one's creator as a solitary or lonely activity. The true difference between the revolutionary American and French Constitutions, John Courtney Murray points out, is that our freedom for the exercise of religion is, in part, freedom of the church, an indispensable condition of the conscientious freedom of the more-than-political person (Lawler 2010b).[5] That's why Ward says that the "church is meant to assist the cause of freedom by serving as an independent source of moral authority to which the individual and larger community can refer on matters of conflicting principles" (Ward 2010, 258). It's the revolutionary French who, by denying the autonomy of the churches, made democracy "totalitarian" and religion merely civil theological.

"In the absence of the right of conscience," Ward goes on, "it is certainly possible to imagine a society directed to the Lockean goals of promoting economic industry and productivity that would allow such a massive system of coercion as to be unrecognizably liberal" (Ward 2010, 258). These days, we obviously don't have a massive system of political coercion, but times are still particularly bad for secure personal identity or the effective exercise of the right of conscience. Persons have a harder time than ever finding a secure point of view to resist impersonal public opinion or fashionable conformity and the reductionism of popularized science. We have a hard time defending genuine autonomy from the demands of productivity (Lawler 2010b). We also see, of course, that it's the religiously observant—or socially and morally "churched"—Americans who most readily resist fashionable conformism, as well as the aimless restlessness of an undirected pursuit of happiness (Tocqueville, 2.1.3).

We can conclude that Zuckert's and Ward's revelation of Locke's view of personal identity is far from free from Christian premises, and it depends on Christian support that's not merely salutary. The relationship between the indispensable churches and the secular state in even a Lockean regime shouldn't really be tensionless. The churches should be relatively counterweighty or countercultural proponents of a more deeply social and so more genuinely personal account of who we are, one that generates generous and charitable duties that go far beyond the domain of rights. Locke's attempt to turn God into a past-tense, unprovidential, unjudgmental, uncaring, basically impersonal being is at odds with his project of securing a free society based on secure personal identity. It's also at odds, perhaps, with what he recognizes as true about the free, willful, and caring biblical Creator—a "who," not some natural "what" (Delsol 2006, 194–95).

THE AMERICAN COMPROMISE

My view is that America at its best is a kind of genuine compromise between wholly Lockean and Christian (meaning Puritan, Calvinist, Augustinian, and/or Protestant) views of who we are. We can find one account of the magnificence of the American spirit of compromise in Tocqueville. Both the North and the South—New England and Virginia—began with extreme views of what human liberty is. Tocqueville could affirm neither as what's "true and just," although both have elements of truth and justice. America at its political best is a compromise between colonial North and South, between New England and Virginia, between meddlesome political idealists and vulgarly self-indulgent, morally indifferent pirates.

Virginia, Tocqueville reports, was founded by "gold seekers," "restless and turbulent spirits," solitary adventurers out to get rich quick. They were England's "lower classes," people "without resources" or virtuous habits, people incapable of being animated by "noble thought" or some "immaterial scheme." They had no sense of home and no sense of having the paternalistic, magnanimous responsibilities of class. They weren't even ennobled by any bourgeois devotion to the virtue of worthwhile work well done (Tocqueville, 1.1.2; Lawler 2011).[6] They, like the middle-class Americans Tocqueville elsewhere describes, loved money, but, unlike the properly middle class, they weren't at all devoted to the just principle that it should be the reward of one's own honest industry. The Virginians were in every crucial respect *uncivilized.*

Tocqueville goes on to observe that the Puritans established colonies without lords or masters—without, in fact, economic classes. They weren't out to get rich or even improve their economic condition; they were in no way driven by material necessity. They "belonged to the well-to-do-classes of the mother country" and would have been better off in the most obvious ways staying home. Their lives were structured by resources and by morality; they came to America as family men, bringing their wives and children. They were models of social virtue. They were also extremely educated men—on the cutting edge, in many ways, of European enlightenment. They were, Tocqueville observes, animated by "a purely intellectual need." They aimed "to make an *idea* triumph" (original emphasis) in this world. The Puritans were as civilized as the Virginians were not, and they devoted themselves to a kind of egalitarian idealism aimed at educating or elevating free beings with souls (Tocqueville, 1.1.2).

The Puritans can be criticized as hypermoralistic despots in some ways, but the Virginians were amoral despots in others. For the Virginian, in effect, every man is the despot, and his point of living is to make himself wealthy and powerful, even at the expense of others. That view, truth to tell, is even present in the Lockeanism of our founding Virginians, who regarded every man as a sovereign who consents to government only for his personal convenience (Brownson [1865] 2003; Lawler 2003).[7] And it's the individualism or emotional solitude that is the product of that Lockeanism that paves the way to the soft despotism he feared far more than any Puritan excess. The American religious and political, localist, familial, egalitarian, and intellectually idealistic ways of combating individualism, Tocqueville makes it quite clear, are our most fortunate Puritanical legacies, ones indispensable for combating individualism on behalf of civilization (Tocqueville, 2.2–3).

What was wrong with the Puritans, from Tocqueville's view, is that they weren't *civilized* enough. A Puritan enigma is how "the legislation of a rude and half-civilized people," that is, the people portrayed in "the texts of Deuteronomy, Exodus, and Leviticus," could have found its way "into the heart of a society whose spirit was enlightened and mores mild." The people of those books weren't much like the highly educated and civilized Puritans. That contradiction resulted in laws full of death as the penalty for violating all sorts of moral lapses, and severe penalties even for kissing, laziness, and the use of tobacco. But those barbarous penalties were, in fact, rarely enforced against the guilty, and the truth is that such legislation couldn't hope to be made effective for long among an enlightened and peaceful people (Tocqueville, 1.1.2).

The Puritans could have learned even from the Virginians and the Europeans of their time a lot about respecting the liberty of conscience. They eventually learned that respect, in part, from Locke, as Zuckert explains. But, for Tocqueville, they could have also learned it by being more consistently Christian. The Puritans weren't Christian enough! Jesus, in Tocqueville's view, showed little interest in enforcing religious morality through political legislation, and that's why Christianity, in fact, has been compatible with a variety of political arrangements. It's not the Gospels—which "speak only of the general relations of men to God and among themselves"—that were the inspiration of the Puritan dedication to criminalizing every sin (Tocqueville, 2.1.5). But it was the Gospels—more than anything in the books of the Old Testament—that devoted them so extremely to the equality of all moral creatures. The

Puritans' tyrannical idealism came from being inconsistently Christian; their dead-serious political utopianism came from attributing to the state what was properly the job of the church.

The truth, from both a Tocquevillian and a Christian view, is somewhere between Virginia and New England: The Virginians were uncivilized criminals; there was no order or direction to their freedom. But the Puritans criminalized sin. They didn't see the limits of political life as a source of civilization and personal elevation. But they were right to say that equality in freedom must be civilized, aiming to elevate every soul.

We see this spirit of compromise between Virginia and New England in our Declaration, in which the influence of the Virginian Jefferson was as much as a prudent statesmen as principled theorist. The Lockean theoretical core of the Declaration is all about inalienable rights and not about the personal God of the Bible. "Nature's God" is a past-tense Creator, and the guidance he provides men now is questionable, insofar as they institute government and many other inventions to move as far away from being governed by nature as possible. But thanks to the insistence of members of Congress who were more under the influence of Christian Calvinism than Jefferson and Franklin, God also became, near the Declaration's end, providential and judgmental, or present-tense and personal.

Zuckert acknowledges that the "appeals to God" found "at the very end of the Declaration . . . appear much closer to the biblical religions than to the natural theology dominant elsewhere in the document." And he acknowledges that "it is no accident" that these changes came from Congress, not the Lockean Jefferson or Franklin. They were part of a legislative compromise. Zuckert dismisses any claim that this compromise changed the essential teaching of the Declaration; the providential and judgmental God "acts to enforce the very order of the 'God of nature' affirmed in the Declaration" (Zuckert 2002, 215). But someone might respond that God coming to life as a personal being has to have huge consequences for understanding who we are. That change in our Declaration might even be thought of as removing a contradiction in Jefferson's Lockean draft: He incoherently attempts to ground personal identity in an impersonal or absent God. Chesterton, for one, was inspired by our Declaration precisely because it secures the equal personal significance of us all with a center of personal significance (Chesterton 1922).

Probably the most nuanced or balanced judgment on the significance of our Declaration comes from R. L. Bruckberger in *Images of America.* Bruckberger, another of our friendly French critics, took what Tocqueville said about our Puritans about as seriously as anyone, and maybe surpassed Tocqueville in seeing more clearly the connection between the Puritans and the Calvinist believers who helped to shape our founding documents. "The greatest luck of all for the Declaration," Bruckberger explains, "was precisely the divergence and the compromise between the Puritan tradition and what Jefferson wrote." A "strictly Puritan" Declaration, of course, "would probably not have managed to avoid an aftertaste of theocracy and religious fanaticism." But if it had "been written from the standpoint of the . . . philosophy of that day, it would have been a-religious, if not actually offensive to Christians" (Bruckberger 2009, 193–94).

The Declaration as a whole, Bruckberger concludes, might even be viewed "as a more profound accomplishment," one of "the great masterpieces of art, in which luck is strangely fused with genius." The combination of American Lockeanism and American Puritanism/Calvinism produced something like an accidental American Thomism. It's that fact that led the American Catholic John Courtney Murray in *We Hold These Truths* to praise our political Fathers for building better than they knew, although even Murray didn't acknowledge properly the Puritan contribution to what our political Fathers built (Murray 1960).

Arguably the Declaration as compromise is a better guide for Americans than the intentions of either of the parties to the compromise. God is personal, but that fact supports rather than negates the equal right to freedom all human beings have. Properly understood, in Tocqueville's eyes, that understanding of equality unites the teaching of Jesus and the teaching of Locke, while both Locke and Jesus distance religious idealism from the requirements of good government. But it's still the idealism of Jesus that turns equality into more than a principle of calculation or self-interested consent, into the Puritans' beautiful idea or an undeniable moral proposition that leads us to do good even at the risk of our lives. We can speculate that one reason Tocqueville doesn't discuss the Declaration as America's "creed" is that he regarded it as more Lockean and less Christian than it really is.

THE PURITAN/CHRISTIAN DEFENSE OF SUNDAY

Tocqueville singles out for special praise one particular residue of what might seem to be Puritan repression—the more or less compulsory cessation of all commercial activity on Sunday. This alleged repression he regards as liberation from the insane ardor of incessantly restless pursuit of an always-fugitive materialistic happiness for the secure and serene pleasures of the soul. On the Sabbath, on Sunday, Americans are confident that they're more than beings with interests, and the spirit of the seventh day elevates everything they think and do on the other six (Tocqueville, 2.2.15).

The Puritan defense of Sunday in our time has been taken up by Marilynne Robinson. The vulgarly Lockean absorption of the weekend into the busyness of commerce and recreation is at the expense of the time and discipline required to form humane and civilized being—of what's required to make our devotion to equality uncondescending. Our economists might tell us that we share nothing in common but the self-interested values that lead to productivity. For them, protecting Sunday from the market is an arbitrary deprivation of liberty.

Their choice, Robinson responds, is both "unpoetical" and "intolerant" (Robinson 1998, 98). It's unpoetical because it disrespects the loving and beautiful dimensions of inwardness—of the soul—that lead us to be poetic. It's intolerant because it dogmatically denies that there's any truth or goodness to the biblical understanding of our equal freedom. The surrender of Sunday to productivity and aimless recreation might be understood as a moment in our historical tale of Lockean liberation, but it's not, in truth, a victory for human interiority or secure personal identity.

Robinson's understanding of religion is, in fact, poetic. She observes, "If I were not myself a religious person, but wished to make an account of religion I would tend toward the Feuerbachian view that religion is a human projection of humanity's conceptions of beauty, goodness, power, and other valued things." That is, she would understand religion as "a humanizing of experience," thereby "dignify[ing]" religion as characteristic of "the mind as outwardly and imaginatively engaged in the world." Her understanding of religion is the opposite of our atheistic scientists today, who regard religion as mindless and infantile, something clever, scientific animals can get over, as if we should get over what distinguishes us—our truthful inwardness and responsible engagement with the world—as nothing but useless illusions. "It seems a little strange," Robinson adds, to regard religion as infantile but the mere indiscriminate desires for pleasure and power as somehow more responsible and truthfully scientific (Robinson 2010a, 128–29).

That scientific view about who we are suggests, of course, that any sense we have of personal significance is an illusion, and the truly scientific "assumptions about what we are and are not preclude not only religion but the whole enterprise of metaphysical thought"—thought about who we are as proud and humble beings capable of acting well or badly in response to what we really know. Robinson truthfully concludes that "the renunciation of religion in the name of science and progress has been strongly associated with a curtailment of the assumed capacities of the mind," especially the mental realms of interiority and subjectivity that Locke believed he discovered (Robinson 2010a, 75). Tocqueville says that the tendency of modern or technically scientific language to be emptied of metaphysical and theological distinctions is an offense against the soul or the true greatness of human individuality or personal identity. That emptying out is based on the false assumption that we are too much like the other animals in our material neediness to have the time for or be worthy of such magnanimous thought (Tocqueville, 2.1.10–20).

CHRISTIAN HUMANISM

According to Tocqueville, the Americans, on Sunday, stopped working in order to hear and think about the "delicate enjoyments" and "true happiness" that come from acting virtuously as beings made in the image of the great and eternal God. Even when they heard Christian sermons that enjoined them to be humble, they were exalted. They were always told that, as beings with souls destined for immortality, they were more than merely beings with interests. If people believe that everything perishes with the body and they're only fit for material enjoyments, they can't help but brutalize themselves. If they believe that nothing human endures, then they won't produce accomplishments—thoughts, writings, or deeds—that endure the test of time. So any religious teaching about the immortality of the soul, Tocqueville says, ought to be regarded as a precious inheritance, one that resists the arrogant efforts of democratic, materialistic, pop Cartesian theoretical experts to turn themselves into gods by brutalizing everyone else (Tocqueville, 2.2.15).

Tocqueville actually calls attention not to any distinctively Christian teaching but to Socrates and Plato, who taught that "the soul has nothing in common with the body and survives it" (Tocqueville, 2.2.15). The doctrine that we are in some sense immortal is indispensable to genuinely liberal education and great individuality, and it persists in America as a Puritan inheritance, although it isn't really distinctively Puritan at all.

Robinson, the Calvinist Christian, actually disagrees with Tocqueville on the purpose of Sunday as preserving a certain Platonism for the people. For Tocqueville, Sunday celebrates our immortality or connection with eternity; it is about our transcendence of our merely temporal being. For Robinson, "the concept of transcendence is based on a misreading of creation." The miracle we celebrate on Sunday is time, which is much more improbable or even "preposterous" than eternity (Robinson 1998, 243).

Tocqueville himself claims, "I have no need to travel through heaven and earth to discover a marvelous object, full of contrasts, of infinite greatness and pettiness, of profound obscurities and singular clarity, capable of giving birth at one to pity, admiration, scorn, and terror." That "marvelous object," he says, is "myself: man comes from nothing, traverses time, and is going to disappear forever in the bosom of God." Tocqueville understands something of himself but far from everything. As the being who lives between complete self-knowledge and "impenetrable darkness," the human being, Tocqueville and Robinson agree, is an inexhaustible source of poetry. Nothing is more strange and wonderful, even a Lockean must admit in opposition to, say, some Aristotelian or Darwinian, than the being with inwardness or subjectivity or personal identity. Nothing, Tocqueville himself admits, is more wonderful than the being with time with him, existing miraculously in this world for a moment between "two abysses" (Tocqueville, 2.2.17). There's no need to look beyond this world, Robinson claims, to honor the "great mystery," which, she reports, "is plainly before my eyes" (Robinson 1998, 243).

It's also true that death is an impenetrable mystery to us; both complete consciousness and complete love and complete nonbeing, the two obvious alternatives, elude even our imagination. So, Robinson concludes, "with all respect to heaven," Sunday doesn't depend for the genuinely attentive observer on faith in things unseen (Robinson 1998, 243). What we can really see about who we are, as Tocqueville explains, is what's denied or distorted—but can't be destroyed—by our survivalist and materialistic experts (Tocqueville, 2.2.12).

The Lockean American, as Tocqueville also explains, actually gets more restless as he gets more prosperous, and he seems to turn his life more and more over to pointless motion in pursuit of material goals that can't provide him any enduring satisfaction or happiness. He seems actually to make himself more miserable over time (Tocqueville, 2.2.13). As the Lockean Zuckert explains, our incessant pursuit of happiness is, in fact, evidence of "the human transcendence of mere survival as an end." But it also means, for a Lockean, we are "unalterably committed" to a pursuit that is "doomed to frustration" (Zuckert 1996, 84–85). The Americans stay feverishly in motion, in Tocqueville's eyes, to divert themselves from what they really know about the futility of their personal efforts and even the absurdity of their personal longings (Tocqueville, 2.2.13).

For the Calvinist, our restless discontent is a characteristic of a creature, or not a historical creation. It is an indispensable clue to the truth about our being. The "very discomfort" it causes "signifies a capacity for self-transcendence," which is not to be confused with a transcendence of this world. Because the cause of self-alienation lies within, all reform is fundamentally personal. We can—as did the Puritans—participate in generous and transformative political projects to display the ennobling truth about our own souls. "Feelings of guilt and obligation," Robinson contends, "dignify us rather than oppressing or frightening or humiliating us because they are assertions of a better—a surpassingly wonderful—self" (Robinson 2001, 79). And so Sunday is all about, paradoxically, restful reflection on the moral agency of the surpassingly wonderful, self defined by a narrative only possible in time.

We no longer believe in Sunday, Robinson goes on, for the same reason we don't believe in the true or highest purpose of words. We've lost touch with "the profoundly democratic idea" that every human being is "only incidentally the servant of his or her interests" (Robinson 1998, 9).

And so we've tended to forget that "there are rewards in experience" for thinking and acting generously or according to "our singular dignity as creatures who can act freely, outside the tedious limits of our own interests" (Robinson 1998, 69). Words are more than self-interested weapons; they're also in the service of the truthful dignity we share in common.

We still acknowledge that universal literacy is a precondition of our prosperity, and we're increasingly anxious that we're losing it. The radically egalitarian Puritans made provision for the education of everyone, not for political or economic reasons, but in order that everyone could read the Bible. Nobody is above or below what the Bible teaches. Nobody, for that reason, is exempt from work, especially for the practice of charity or generosity. But nobody is merely a being who works or a being with interests, and for no one is education to be merely technical or illiberal (Robinson 2008). Reading anything, if we think about it, is an undeniable manifestation of the inwardness or profound complexity characteristic of members of our species alone. Our respect for texts is really our respect for authors and readers, for persons singularly open to the mystery of being, especially their own being.

The more we respect persons, the more we respect texts. And it's part of the deep respect for who persons really are that we allow them time to read—maybe especially to read the Bible. Leisure, Robinson claims (against, say, Tocqueville's aristocrat), couldn't possibly be the basis of culture. The foundations of culture are personal responsibility and moral agency, and there should be no leisure class exempt from acting generously or charitably on behalf of others (Robinson 1998, 2008). But culture does depend on us thinking highly enough of ourselves that we have time enough to do a lot more than survive. For Tocqueville, the choice often seems to be the magnanimity connected with the unjust aristocratic leisure class or the vulgar, self-interested utility of the democratic middle class (Tocqueville, 2.1). But the Puritans, as he himself showed, presented a third alternative—one that's concerned with the soul and "attach[es] great importance to the day-to-day practical well-being of us all." And Robinson is Puritanical enough to say that "good works"—acts of charity and generosity—do more good when "assisted by means of government" (Robinson 2010b, 214).

We're no longer serious, Robinson complains, about the virtues or acts of discipline that are "the graces of personal and public life." There are, she observes, "too few uses for words like humor, pleasure, charm, courage, dignity, and graciousness, learnedness, fairmindedness, openhandedness, respect and good faith." Most of all, there's way too little use for the words *generosity* and *liberality,* the social virtue of the being who displays his freedom for the benefit of others. Robinson claims that for the Bible generosity, liberality, and nobility are synonyms, and they express even better than charity the virtue that best distinguishes who we are (Robinson 1998, 106–7).

Arguably what's disappeared from our society with Sunday is the respect and so the time for the reading and discipline required for us to practice the social, civilized virtues that are the true sources of our happiness. Anyone who looks at our country from outside right now should wonder "why we make so little of so much" (Robinson 1998, 106). One reason is we're not nearly as Puritanical as we used to and should be. "Just for the pleasure of it," Robinson complains, "I miss civilization, and I want it back" (Robinson 1998, 8).

Jefferson, Robinson observed, "was a civilized man." So it couldn't have been his intention "to lead us on a fool's errand." Because he was civilized he must have believed what Locke did not—that our pursuit of happiness would culminate in happiness itself. And so he must have thought we would privilege enjoyable activities (as he himself did) that were time-consuming and unproductive—time spent with and in the service of friends, children, our family, our country and its heritage, our books, and our Creator. Human happiness, we can learn from the Puritans, is only incidentally connected with our productivity or "nonfailure," and it involves activities and choices that are inexplicable to our Darwinians and weightless to our economists. Sunday, we can say, is for civilized human happiness, for the truest experiences of our inward personal identities. It's time, as Robinson says, "to enjoy *ourselves,*" who we really are (Robinson 1998, 107; original emphasis).

Americans are characteristically confused about their personal identities—about who they are. And the privileging of Sunday over other days might be criticized as part of the confusion. That's why a Lockean or progressively more individualistic history of America obliterates Sunday as nothing more than a lifestyle choice, one that can't be allowed to trump the requirements of productivity or personal preferences in pursuit of happiness. In my view, the privileging of Sunday has the character of a compromise that's meant to break our Lockean history or individualistic transformationalism over time. Sunday is for the churches making their indispensable and truthful contribution to understanding who we are and what we're supposed to do.

It's neither good nor truthful to believe Locke tells us all we need to know about who we are, and a tensionless America would, in fact, be a free but empty and so unsustainable one. Locke doesn't tell the whole truth about who we are as social, personal, erotic beings; the unique and irreplaceable person is a lot more than the being with rights. That doesn't mean that we shouldn't be grateful to Locke for the contributions our economic and political freedom make to our personal security and happiness. All in all, I'd rather be living in the natural rights republic, one in which we know why there's freedom for churches.

NOTES

1. Subsequent Tocqueville citations omit the abbreviations *vol., pt.,* and *chap.,* for example, 2.2.7.

2. Locke, of course, systematically, misquotes the Bible to turn the living, giving God into a God of the past who is, for all personal purposes, dead to us now. He wants to overcome any sense of creaturely love or gratitude, as well as creaturely guilt. See, for example, Zuckert 1996.

3. This paragraph and the preceding one are adapted from my "The Logos in Western Thought" (2009).

4. This is true even if Ward is right that Locke believes the Gospels add nothing to morality that might not be discovered through reason.

5. On Murray, see my *Modern and American Dignity* (2010b).

6. The account of the Virginians and the Puritans is found in this section of the book. It is developed at far greater length in my "Tocqueville on How to Praise the Puritans Today" (2011).

7. See the criticism of the Lockean theory of our leading Framers in Brownson [1865] 2003 and my long introduction to the ISI edition (2003).

REFERENCES

Augustine, Saint. 1993. *The City of God.* New York: Modern Library.

Brague, Remi. 2007. *The Law of God: The Philosophical History of an Idea.* Chicago: University of Chicago Press.

Brownson, Orestes. [1865] 2003. *The American Republic.* Wilmington, DE: ISI Books.

Bruckberger, R. L. 2009. *Images of America.* Trans. C. G. Paulding and Virginia Peterson. New Brunswick, NJ: Transaction.

Chesterton, G. K. 1922. *What I Saw in America.* New York: Dodd, Mead.

Delsol, Chantal. 2006. *The Unlearned Lessons of the Twentieth Century.* Ed. R. Dick. Wilmington, DE: ISI Books.

Hart, David Bentley. 2009. *Atheistic Delusions: The Christian Revolution and Its Fashionable Enemies.* New Haven: Yale University Press.

Henary, Sara. 2010. "The Problem of Human Equality in Locke's Political Philosophy: Responses to Jeremy Waldron and Michael Zuckert." Paper presented at the conference Stuck with Virtue, Berry College, Mount Berry, GA, November 4.

Lawler, Peter Augustine. 2003. Introduction to *The American Republic,* by Orestes Brownson, 1–123. Wilmington, DE: ISI Books.

———. 2009. "The Logos in Western Thought." *Modern Age* 50 (Winter): 42–46.

———. 2010a. "Equally Not Nothing." *Intercollegiate Review* 45: 49–52.

———. 2010b. *Modern and American Dignity.* Wilmington, DE: ISI Books.

———. 2011. "Tocqueville on How to Praise the Puritans Today." In *Alexis de Tocqueville and the Art of Democratic Statesmanship,* ed. B. Danoff and L. Herbert, 179–98. Lanham, MD: Lexington Books.

Locke, John. [1823] 2010. "A Third Letter Concerning Toleration." In *Locke on Toleration,* ed. Richard Vernon, 123–63. Cambridge: Cambridge University Press.

Murray, John Courtney. 1960. *We Hold These Truths.* New York: Sheed and Ward.

Pangle, Thomas L. 1983. Introduction to *Studies in Political Philosophy,* by Leo Strauss, 1–27. Chicago: University of Chicago Press.

———. 1992. *The Ennobling of Democracy: The Challenge of the Postmodern Era.* Baltimore: Johns Hopkins University Press, 1992.

Robinson, Marilynne. 1998. *The Death of Adam: Essays on Modern Thought.* Boston: Houghton Mifflin.

———. 2001. "'Americans.'" *Theology Today* 58: 72–81.

———. 2008. "A Great Amnesia." *Harper's* (May): 17–21.

———. 2010a. *Absence of Mind.* New Haven: Yale University Press, 2010.

———. 2010b. "Wondrous Love." *Christianity and Literature* 59: 202–15.

Tocqueville, Alexis de. [1835/1840] 2000. *Democracy in America.* Trans. Harvey Mansfield and Delba Winthrop. Chicago: University of Chicago Press.

Ward, Lee. 2010. *John Locke and Modern Life.* New York: Cambridge University Press.

Wolfe, Tom. 2006. *I Am Charlotte Simmons.* New York: Farrar, Straus and Giroux.

Zuckert, Michael P. 1994. *Natural Rights and the New Republicanism.* Princeton: Princeton University Press.

———. 1996. *The Natural Rights Republic: Studies in the Foundation of the American Political Tradition.* Notre Dame: University of Notre Dame Press.

———. 2002. *Launching Liberalism: On Lockean Political Philosophy.* Lawrence: University Press of Kansas.

Chapter Twelve

Thomas Jefferson, the First American Progressive?

JEAN M. YARBROUGH

Thomas Jefferson did not take part in the framing of the Constitution or in the drive to secure its ratification. These events he watched from afar, receiving regular briefings from James Madison while serving as minister to France from 1784 to 1789. At first he was part of a three-man delegation, but within a year Benjamin Franklin had returned to the United States and John Adams departed for London to serve as American minister there. During his stay in Paris, Jefferson became acquainted with the thought of many of the leading French philosophes, whose views on progress he readily absorbed. By the time of his arrival, French physiocrat and onetime finance minister to Louis XVI, Anne-Robert-Jacques Turgot, had been dead for three years, but his ideas, which were later collected and published by his friend and Jefferson's, DuPont deNemours, were well known in the intellectual circles in which Jefferson traveled. In his *Philosophical Review of the Successive Advances of the Human Mind,* delivered as a discourse at the Sorbonne in 1750, as well as in his more comprehensive *Universal History,* Turgot had traced the movement from barbarism to civilization through three stages, hunting, pastoral, and agricultural, each with its own language, laws, morals, arts, and thought. What made his account so influential was that he viewed this movement from one stage to another in terms of progress and perfectibility, spurred largely by natural causes, with only a thin religious veneer. To be sure, progress was frequently interrupted by periods of decline, but for Turgot the main point was that progress was inevitable (Meek 1973, 88).

Jefferson, whose political thought had been shaped by Lockean social compact theory and the more historically minded Scottish Enlightenment thinkers, saw no incompatibility between the two approaches. The movement from the abstract, ahistorical state of nature to civil society could readily be assimilated to the various stages of historical development that culminated in an agricultural society dedicated to the protection of individual rights. What this linear account did, however, was to underscore the possibility, and indeed in Turgot's argument the inevitability, of progress that Jefferson would find so compelling. The Virginian may very well have had Turgot in mind when he sketched his own "archeology" of progress in 1824:

> Let a philosophic observer commence a journey from the savages of the Rocky Mountains, eastwardly towards our sea-coast. There he would observe in the earliest stage of association living under no law but that of nature, subscribing and covering themselves with the flesh and skins of wild beasts. He would next find on our frontiers in the pastoral state, raising domestic animals to supply the defects of hunting. Then succeed our own semi-barbarous citizens, the pioneers of the advance of civilization, and so in his progress would he meet the gradual shades of improving man until he would reach his, as yet, most improved state in our seaport towns. This, in fact, is equivalent to a survey, in time, of the progress of man from the infancy of creation to the present day. (Peterson 1984, 1496–97)

More often than not, however, Jefferson was less interested in tracing the stages of American progress than he was in promoting its spread.

Accordingly, he began with the seacoast, or at least its agrarian fringes, and looked westward. Where this progress would stop, no one could say, but he expected that in time barbarism would disappear completely.

Although Jefferson knew Turgot only through his writings, he did meet Turgot's protégé and biographer, Marie-Jean-Antoine-Nicolas de Caritat, Marquis de Condorcet, the only philosophe to serve in the Revolutionary government and later one of its victims. The two did not always agree on practical politics. In his analysis of the revolutionary state constitutions in America, Condorcet, like Turgot, favored the unicameral legislature adopted by Pennsylvania over the bicameral models established in the other states, presumably because the Frenchmen were under the mistaken impression that Benjamin Franklin had drafted the Pennsylvania Constitution. Nor did they agree about the proper mode of government for France. Jefferson believed the French were not yet ready for republican government and recommended a limited monarchy, whereas Condorcet sided with the more moderate republicans and as a legislator prepared (unsuccessfully) reports on a permanent constitution for France. Finally, it is not clear that the two agreed on the equality of the black race. Although Jefferson forwarded to Condorcet Benjamin Banneker's *Almanac* as evidence that the degraded condition of blacks in America might be attributed to the circumstances under which they lived, his comments in *Notes on the State of Virginia* as well as letters to other correspondents suggest that he remained far more skeptical about the native abilities of the black race (Peterson 1984, 982–83).

But these differences aside, Jefferson and Condorcet were philosophical soul mates (McLean 2004, 13–30). Both were children of the Enlightenment who hoped that the spread of scientific knowledge would improve the lot of mankind by eradicating ignorance, superstition, and tyranny. Neither shared Rousseau's doubts about whether progress in the arts and sciences necessarily led to progress in politics and morality.

Ironically, Condorcet's most extravagant hope for progress, *Esquisse d'un tableau sur le progrès de l'esprit humain* (Sketch for a Historical Picture of the Progress of the Human Mind), was composed in 1794 while Condorcet was in hiding from the Jacobins. Shortly after its completion, he came out of seclusion and was immediately arrested as an enemy of the Revolution. He died the first night in prison, possibly by poison self-administered. His *Sketch* was published posthumously the following year. The main point of the *Sketch* was to demonstrate "by appeal to reason and fact that nature has set no term to the perfection of human faculties; that the perfectibility of man is truly indefinite; and that the progress of this perfectibility, from now onwards independent of any power that might wish to halt it, has no other limit than the duration of the globe upon which nature has cast us." Like Turgot, Condorcet acknowledged that this progress would vary in speed according to particular circumstances, but as long as the laws of nature obtained, it would "never be reversed" (Condorcet [1795] 1955, 4). Despite the desperate conditions under which Condorcet labored, he remained hopeful that, like the general laws that regulated all natural phenomena, the natural law of progress would continue to operate on man's intellectual and moral faculties, bringing them to an ever higher state of perfection. In particular, he expected in the coming tenth stage to see progress in three important areas: "the abolition of inequality between nations, the progress of equality within each nation, and the true perfection of mankind" (173).

It is ironic that Condorcet, who dismissed Christianity as an irrational superstition, and sought to ground his own philosophy of progress on science, in particular, the "calculus of combinations and probabilities," should in the end fall back on faith and hope in the perfectibility of human nature once it was freed from superstition and ignorance (Condorcet [1795] 1955, 190). As Karl Lowith (1949) has noted, there is something almost religious in Condorcet's irreligious faith in progress. When, in his final chapter, Condorcet speaks of his "hope that is almost a certainty" in the "absolute perfection of the human race," there is more than a little resemblance to the Christian hope of becoming perfect (Condorcet [1795] 1955, 184). Nor is this link accidental: the idea of progress is Christian in its origins, in the sense that for the first time the Bible treats history as the working out of God's plan for man on earth; however, insofar as this purpose comes to be understood by Enlightenment thinkers in secular terms, it is anti-Christian in its implications (Lowith 1949, 61). This is true of Turgot, who was the first to speak of progress in largely secular terms, and even more true of Condorcet, who transformed the theology of history into a secular philosophy of progress.

PROGRESS AND PERFECTIBILITY: TWO VIEWS

By the time Condorcet's *Sketch* was published in 1795, Jefferson had been back in America for six years, where he followed events in France closely, while serving as Washington's secretary of state from 1790 to 1793. Both he and John Adams, who had served briefly with Jefferson and Franklin in France and then as minister to England, obtained copies of the book and not surprisingly registered very different reactions to it. In a letter written to a young student seeking advice on whether to pursue the study of science, Jefferson moved seamlessly from specific recommendations to a more general statement of his philosophy: "I am among those who think well of the human character generally. I consider man as formed for society, and endowed by nature with those dispositions which fit him for society. I believe also, with Condorcet, as mentioned in your letter, that his mind is perfectible to a degree of which we cannot as yet form any conception." Jefferson then went on to discuss the state of knowledge among the different branches of science and ended, as was his wont, by agreeing with his correspondent: "I join you therefore in branding as cowardly the idea that the human mind is incapable of further advances."[1]

None of this was controversial. As any educated man or woman in Jefferson's day readily acknowledged, there had been enormous advances in modern science over the past few centuries. But Jefferson went further, suggesting that progress was also possible in "religion & politics." What especially annoyed him was the suggestion "'that it is not probable that any thing better will be discovered than what was known to our fathers.'" Jefferson did not cite the source of this remark (it was John Adams), but he did offer his own gloss, suggesting that the author meant "we are to look backwards then & not forwards for the improvement of science, & to find it amidst feudal barbarisms and the fires of Spital-fields" (Peterson 1984, 1064–65).

Writing to the English radical, Dr. Joseph Priestley, after the Republicans had swept to victory in 1800, Jefferson was even more pointed. He denounced his Federalist opponents as "barbarians" and "bigots in Politics & Religion," who strove to "bring back the times of Vandalism, when ignorance put everything into the hands of power and priestcraft."

In Jefferson's fevered imagination, his opponents sought to proscribe "all advances in science." Nor was it only science against which they warred. His opponents "pretended to praise and encourage education, but it was to be the education of our ancestors. We were to look backwards, not forwards, for improvement; the President himself [John Adams] declaring in one of his answers to addresses, that we were never expected to go beyond them in real science" (Peterson 1984, 1085, 1073).

John Adams could be excused for not recognizing himself in this caricature. And when, in 1812, Jefferson's private letters to Priestley appeared in print, Adams wrote to the Virginian demanding, in "the French sense of the word demand," proof of these charges and an explanation (Cappon 1959, 327). It was only in the previous year or so that the two had been reconciled, and the publication of the letters threatened to derail their renewed friendship. Jefferson did the best he could in this awkward situation, offering several explanations. The letters, he wrote, were confidential and never intended to be made public. Moreover, they were not really about Adams but about the high Tories in his cabinet, who were his secret enemies then and open ones now. Jefferson had only quoted Adams because once, in answer to an address, he had expressed "more pithily" one of the "mottos" of the Federalist Party. His letter was not meant as a personal attack but rather the expression of a principled difference: "One of the questions you know on which our parties took different sides was on the improvability of the human mind, in science, in ethics, in government etc. Those who advocated reformation of institutions, pari passu, with the progress of science, maintained that no definite limits could be assigned to that progress. The enemies of reform, on the other hand, denied improvement, and advocated steady adherence to the principles, practices and institutions of our fathers, which they represented as the consummation of wisdom, and *akme*[2] of excellence beyond which the human mind could never advance." But, Jefferson insisted, this could not be Adams's "deliberate opinion," for he was too much a man of science not to recognize that there was so much ahead of them, "unexplained and unexplored" (Cappon 1959, 331–32).

For the sake of their old friendship, Adams accepted the explanation, but he could not let the matter rest. He hunted down his answer to "The Address of the Young Men of Philadelphia," wanting to set the record straight, not only for Jefferson, but also for posterity. What Adams had said to his audience was, "I will hazard a prediction, that after all the most industrious and impartial Researches, the longest liver of you all will find no Principles, Institutions, or Systems of Education, more fit, IN GENERAL to be transmitted to your Posterity, than those you have received from you[r] Ancestors" (Cappon 1959, 339; uppercase in original). By "ancestors," Adams made it clear that he meant the two of them, and other revolutionary patriots, not the Goths and Vandals Jefferson had conjured up in his letter to Priestley. And the general principles to which he appealed were "the *general Principles* of Christianity," which united all the sects, and "the general Principles of English and American Liberty," stripped of their partisan character. Because the general principles of Christianity are "as eternal and immutable, as the Existence and Attributes of God" and the general principles of liberty "are as unalterable as human Nature and our terrestrial, mundane System," Adams doubted that there could ever be discoveries that would contradict them (Cappon 1959, 339–40).

That Adams doubted future generations would improve on these two general principles of the Founding did not, however, mean that he, and by extension his party, did not believe in progress. He ended the letter by reminding Jefferson that the very first sentence of the preface to his *Defense of the Constitutions of Government of the United States of America,* published in 1787 in response to the criticisms of Turgot and Condorcet, acknowledged that the "Arts and Sciences, in general, during the three or four last centuries, have had a regular course of *progressive* improvement. The Inventions in Mechanic Arts, the discoveries in natural Philosophy, navigation and commerce, and the Advancement of civilization and humanity, have occasioned Changes in the condition of the World and the human Character, which would have astonished the most refined Nations of Antiquity" (Cappon 1959, 340; original emphasis).

Perfectibility, however, was another matter. At one level, Adams could not deny it, since he saw clearly the link to the biblical injunction, "Be ye perfect" (Cappon 1959, 338). But in the secular sense in which the Enlightenment meant it, his hopes were more modest: "I am a Believer, in the probable improvability and Improvement, the Ameliorabi[li]ty and Amelioration in human Affairs; though I never could understand the

Doctrine of the Perfectibility of the human Mind" (435). Moreover, if progress were to be made, it would not be by following the recommendations of Turgot, Condorcet, and the rest of the French philosophes, who knew nothing about history and government and so favored concentrating all power in one center "and that Center the Nation" (356). As Adams had attempted to demonstrate in his *Defense,* progress required very different arrangements: "Checks and Ballances, Jefferson, however you and your Party may have ridiculed them, are our only Security, for the progress of Mind as well as the Security of Body. . . . Know thyself, human Nature!" (334).

Before the French Revolution, Adams believed, the nations of Europe had been making slow but steady progress in government, religion, and science. But, unlike Jefferson, who welcomed the Revolution and backed it enthusiastically even through the Reign of Terror, Adams predicted from the beginning that the "Troubles in France" would "not only arrest the progress of Improvement, but give it a retrograde course, for at least a Century, if not many Centuries." With the Napoleonic Wars raging in Europe and America again at war with England, Adams asked Jefferson, "very seriously my Friend, Where are now in 1813, the Perfection and perfectability [*sic*] of human Nature? Where is now, the progress of the human Mind? Where is the Amelioration of Society? Where the Augmentations of human Comforts? Where the diminutions of human Pains and Miseries?" (358).

It took Jefferson a long time to reply. When he did, he conceded that Adams's prophecies about the French Revolution had proved truer than his, though, oddly for one who believed in progress and perfectibility, he could not forebear pointing out that even Adams had underestimated the extent of the destruction. Instead of the one million Adams had predicted, the number of deaths was closer to eight or ten million. Nevertheless, Jefferson refused to give up hope. "Although your prophecy has proved true so far, I hope it does not preclude a better final result," he wrote (Cappon 1959, 459).

PROGRESS AND REPUBLICANISM

With this concession, the exchange between Jefferson and Adams about progress and perfectibility more or less came to an end, and the two moved on to more congenial subjects. About progress they clearly did not agree, and as Michael Zuckert has persuasively shown, Jefferson made it a point in his private writings to avoid arguing and, as far as he could, to agree with the recipients (Zuckert 1996, 87–89). He did, however, continue to sound these themes with other, more sympathetic correspondents. To his fellow Virginian Samuel Kercheval, who in 1816 was pushing for a new constitutional convention for the state, Jefferson revealed what he really thought about Adams's praise of the ancestors. "Some men," Jefferson observed, "look at constitutions with sanctimonious reverence, and deem them like the arc of the covenant, too sacred to be touched. They ascribe to the men of the preceding age a wisdom more than human, and suppose what they did to be beyond amendment." But even though Jefferson was part of that age, he refused to accept that it had a lock on practical wisdom. Much had been learned about politics in the forty years since the Declaration, and Jefferson was all for incorporating the knowledge gained from practical experience. Although he did not advocate "frequent and untried changes," he insisted that "laws and institutions must go hand in hand with the progress of the human mind. As that becomes more developed, more enlightened, as new discoveries are made, new truths disclosed, and manners and opinions change with circumstances, institutions must advance also, and keep pace with the times. We might as well require a man to wear still the coat which fitted him when a boy, as civilized society to remain ever under the regimen of their barbarous ancestors" (Peterson 1984, 1401).

Nor did Jefferson confine his views to private communications. When, in 1818, he drafted a report on behalf of the Commissioners of the University of Virginia, he once more returned to the themes he had first sounded privately more than twenty years earlier in his letters to Priestley. First was his faith in the power of education to transform human nature. The orthodox republican curriculum he drew up for the university would, he hoped, engraft "a new man on the native stock," changing his old vicious and perverse qualities into virtues. Second was his belief in the continuing progress of the human mind. He fully expected that each generation, by adding it own "acquisitions and discoveries," would "advance the knowledge and well-being of mankind, not *infinitely,* as some have said, but *indefinitely,* and to a term which no one can fix and foresee" (Peterson 1984, 461; original emphasis). But since even Condorcet had only spoken of indefinite advances, it is not clear from whom Jefferson wished to distance himself. As evidence for the "indefinite" progress he expected to continue, Jefferson cited the "wonderful advances in the sciences and the arts" that had been made even in the past fifty years.

Third, and more surprisingly, in view of Jefferson's excuse to Adams that his private communication to Priestley lacked the restraint one would expect in a statement intended for the public, Jefferson could not resist taking another stab at Adams's reverence for the ancestors. Yet, because it was a public document and because he and Adams had reconciled, Jefferson did not attack him and his Federalist allies openly but directed his ire against "our indigenous neighbors." What kept the Indians in a state of "barbarism and wretchedness" was their "bigotted veneration for the supposed superlative wisdom of their fathers, and the preposterous idea that they are to look backward for better things, and not forward, longing, as it should seem, to return to the days of eating acorns and roots, rather than indulge in the degeneracies of civilization." Jefferson went on to wonder whether the "desponding view" that the human condition "cannot be ameliorated, that what has been must ever be, and that to secure ourselves where we are, we must tread with awful reverence in the footsteps of our fathers" (whether held by the Indians or the here unnamed Federalists), was any more encouraging to the advance of science than the refusal to become civilized. Jefferson left no doubt that reverence for the fathers was the greater evil because at base it was nothing more than a defense of entrenched and corrupt interests: "This doctrine is the genuine fruit of the alliance between Church and State; the tenants of which, finding themselves but too well in their present condition, oppose all advances which might unmask their usurpations, and monopolies of honors, wealth, and power, and fear every change, as endangering the comforts they now hold" (Peterson 1984, 461–62).

Jefferson's faith in progress and his debt to Condorcet came out in other ways as well. On the eve of his departure from France in 1789, Jefferson penned a letter to Madison in which he attempted to think through the literal consequences of the idea that "the earth belongs in usufruct to the living." He took this to mean that one generation had no right to bind another with laws, constitutions, or debts. Jefferson was not content to draw out the obvious implication of this thought, namely, that future generations are free to revise or even overthrow their established conventions if they desire, but even recommended that they do so at regular intervals. Drawing on Condorcet's probabilism, he estimated that the length of a generation was thirty-four years, from which he concluded, "every constitution . . . and every law naturally expires at the end of thirty-four years" (Peterson 1984, 960; McLean 2004, 13–30). Madison, as is well known, did not think much of this suggestion, and as again was his wont, Jefferson pursued it no further with him. He did not, however, abandon the idea but found more congenial minds with which to pursue it.

Later, as Jefferson became acquainted with "the European tables of mortality," he revised the span of a generation downward to nineteen years. But he continued to insist that "each generation is as independent as the one preceding . . . [and] has then, like them, the right to choose for itself the form of government it believes most promotive of its own happiness" (Peterson 1984, 1402). Given his faith in the progress of the human mind, he no doubt expected each succeeding generation to make improvements in the original constitutional design. "The earth belongs to the living" was merely another way of putting the wisdom of the ancestors in its place. Constitutions and laws must keep pace with the times, though Jefferson insisted this be done by the people through constitutional amendments and conventions and emphatically not by an unelected judiciary. Only one thing was unchangeable and not open to revision: "the inherent and inalienable rights of man" (1494). Constitutions would of necessity change, but the truths of the Declaration would endure for all time.

As evidence of the progress that was possible in government, Jefferson could offer his own evolving view of republicanism. When, in his draft constitution for Virginia in 1776, Jefferson had expressed doubts about the capacity of the people for wise action, he hoped that experience might prove him wrong. And to his mind, it did. Reflecting on the lessons of experience in his retirement, Jefferson now conceded that at the time of the Revolution Americans were too much in thrall to European political thinkers for their understanding of republicanism. "We imagined everything was republican which was not monarchy," he wrote. "We had not yet penetrated to the mother principle that 'governments are republican only in proportion as they embody the will of the people, and execute it' " (Peterson 1984, 1396).

To another correspondent, Jefferson acknowledged that the term *republic* was admittedly vague, though he now thought it meant "purely and simply . . . government by its citizens in mass, acting directly and personally, according to rules established by the majority." Jefferson conceded that this definition, if strictly applied, would limit a republic to the size of a New England township, and so was unworkable. Happily, representation allowed the republic to expand over a larger area. But "the further the departure from the direct and constant control of the citizens," the less republican the government was. Applying this standard to the Virginia constitution, he now judged the lower house of the legislature the most republican; the Senate, equally so the first year but less so with each succeeding year; the executive, still less so because not chosen directly by the people; and the judiciary, "seriously anti-republican" because appointed for life. In addition, the county courts held office for life and exercised authority over nearly all the daily concerns of citizens, including "justice, the executive administration, the taxation, police, [and] the military appointments of the county." On top of this, nearly half the men who fought and paid taxes were excluded from the rights of representation, "as if society were instituted for the soil, and not for the men inhabiting it" (Peterson 1984, 1392–93). For forty years the citizens of Virginia had stumbled along with their first flawed constitution, and it was now past time to revise it to reflect the lessons of experience.

Nor were things much better at the national level. The House of Representatives was the most republican office, but the Senate was "scarcely so at all" because it was not chosen by the people directly. Unlike the Virginia governor, however, Jefferson considered the presidency more republican than the Senate because the term of office was shorter; the president was in practice elected by the people since they voted for electors on condition that they would vote for the people's choice; and an informal system of rotation prevailed, ensuring that no one would serve more than two terms. The judiciary, led by Jefferson's distant relation and archenemy, John Marshall, was not republican at all because it was "independent of the nation, their coercion by impeachment being found nugatory" (Peterson 1984, 1394). In short, at both the state and federal levels, the American governments were far less republican than they should have been, with the result that the people had far less control over their elected officials than their rights and interests demanded.

Jefferson did not accuse those who framed the state and federal constitutions of lacking in republican sympathies, but he did believe they tailored their republicanism to conform with "European authorities, to speculators on government, whose fears of the people have been inspired by the populace of their own great cities, and were unjustly entertained against the independent, the happy, and therefore orderly citizens of the United States." Although Jefferson here declined to identify these "speculators," his comments elsewhere suggest that Plato, Hobbes, Montesquieu, and Hume were prime candidates (Peterson 1984, 1228–30; Cappon 1959, 433). And much as he believed it was past time for the people to reform their first flawed experiments and reclaim the power that was rightfully theirs, he feared that the "golden moment" for reforming these "heresies" had passed" (Peterson 1984, 1394). But at least he could keep hope alive by refusing to venerate the Founders or their work.

JEFFERSONIAN LEGACIES

It is tempting to wonder what Jefferson would have made of the Progressive movement at the end of the nineteenth century and the beginning of the twentieth. Like the author of the Declaration, the Progressives were dismayed by the "superstitious awe" with which Americans continued to regard the Constitution, frustrating their reform efforts. Many of the practical changes they supported, such as the direct election of U.S. senators, direct primaries, and efforts to make state governments more responsive to the people through recall, initiative, and referendum, were precisely the kinds of alterations that Jefferson himself had either backed or likely would have supported had the occasion arisen. But beyond this the picture becomes more complicated, since many of the leading Progressives came out of the Republican Party and supported a strong national government in the tradition of Alexander Hamilton and Abraham Lincoln. They had little patience with the principles of federalism or the Jeffersonian understanding of limited government.

In *The Promise of American Life,* for example, Herbert Croly pointedly blamed Jefferson and his followers in the Democratic Party for most of the country's ills. Jefferson's suspicion of national power, combined with his attachment to equal rights, encouraged excessive individualism, mediocrity, and drift. The promise of American life surely meant more than the Jeffersonian vision of individuals pursuing their own selfish ends, taking for granted that everything would automatically turn out for the best. What the country needed was in fact a new Declaration of Independence that would free Americans from their bondage to the past so that they might chart their collective destiny as a sovereign people.

Even John Dewey, one of the few Progressives who admired Jefferson, regarded his attachment to natural rights as essentially outmoded. "Today," Dewey wrote, "we are wary of anything purporting to be self-evident truths; we are not given to associating politics with the plans of the Creator; the doctrine of natural rights . . . has been weakened by historic and philosophic criticism." But with some creative interpretation, Dewey was confident that the "spirit" of Jefferson's thought might be adapted to meet the needs of the twentieth century. Jefferson could be pardoned for referring to the laws of Nature and Nature's God as the ground of our rights, but after Darwin it made no sense to speak either of nature or of God as benevolent in intent. If instead of natural rights, which are based on empty abstractions, we substituted moral "ideals" rooted in "deep and indestructible" human "needs and demands," Jefferson's understanding of the purpose of government could be brought up to date, provided that we were prepared to rethink property rights. But Dewey believed that Jefferson had actually pointed the way. The substitution of the pursuit of happiness for property showed just how far Jefferson has traveled from Locke. Individuals have no inherent moral claim to property that governments are obliged to respect. "It is sheer perversion to hold that there is anything in Jeffersonian democracy that forbids political action to bring about the equalization of economic conditions in order that the equal right of all to free choice and free action be maintained" (Dewey 1939, 156–64).

Moreover, Dewey argued, Americans cling to a "distorted" idea of individualism, arising partly out of older (and now discredited) theological beliefs rooted in the idea of the soul and partly and more recently out of the idea that economic activity is for the sake of private profit. Changing historical and social conditions now required a new conception of individuality that would integrate the citizen into the community rather than pit him against it. Dewey's ideal was a democratic socialist community, in which the interests of the individual are at one with the interests of the whole. Here Dewey finds Jefferson's unjustly neglected ward system particularly suggestive, though he sees the wards more as functional than geographic units of self-government, facilitating "communication and cooperation" across the larger democratic community (Dewey 1939, 160).

How might Jefferson have responded to Dewey's proposed makeover? Although it is not completely inconceivable that Jefferson would have considered Progressivism the mark of progress, it would have required him to sacrifice his belief in natural rights, the one permanent principle on his political horizon. Whether Darwin would have caused him to rethink his belief in natural rights is unclear, since Jefferson conceived of Nature and Nature's God in an ethical rather than a naturalistic sense, and there was no necessity for him to abandon his approach.[3] Thinking of nature in the way that Jefferson did is arguably less abstract and more realistic that the "deep and indestructible . . . needs and demands of humankind."

Of special significance is that even though Jefferson declined to elevate property to a natural right in the Declaration, he staunchly defended the right of private property as a spur to greater industry and productivity, as well as a foundation for justice. In contrast to Dewey, justice for Jefferson lies on the side of rewarding individual industry and initiative rather than in the redistribution of wealth. Thus in his Second Inaugural Jefferson defends "that state of property, equal or unequal, which results to every man from his own industry or that of his father" (Peterson 1984, 522). And indeed, a decade later he made the same point even more emphatically, declaring the first principle of association "the *guarantee* to every one of his industry and fruits acquired by it."[4]

Whether Jefferson would recognize his ward system, separated from the larger federal "pyramid," and linked now with a new understanding of individualism, is also unclear. For although Dewey recognized Jefferson's devotion to states' rights and limited government, he passed over these quickly and without considering the full extent of Jefferson's attachment to these principles. For these reasons, Dewey's effort to find in Jefferson the seeds of his progressive politics remains unpersuasive. As a philosophical matter, Jefferson doubtless would have continued to affirm his belief in progress, but whether he would have regarded the Progressives as the political and moral fulfillment of this idea is a more difficult case to make.

NOTES

Exactly a quarter of a century ago, Michael Zuckert, along with several colleagues at Carleton College, prepared a nine-part radio drama, "Mr. Adams and Mr. Jefferson," based on the correspondence between the two Revolutionary heroes. Michael was generous enough to send the audiotape (how archaic that sounds today!) of the series, which charmed me for endless hours while chauffeuring my children around in the car. Those days are now long gone, but the tapes inspired me to read the Adams-Jefferson correspondence through in its entirety, affording me countless hours of pleasure. Over the years, I have had occasion to reflect on the letters in print, most recently in a Festschrift contribution on politics and friendship for Wilson Carey McWilliams. As I reread that essay, I noted with thanks that Michael had helped me with an earlier draft. Now that it is Michael's and Catherine's turn to be honored, I have to admit that I am flying solo. The theme is one that Michael first inspired, and it is offered in friendship and with admiration for them both.

1. Thomas Jefferson to William Green Munford, June 18, 1799, in Peterson 1984, 1064–65.

2. For Catherine.

3. Zuckert suggests that Jefferson viewed nature and human nature in both senses: 1996, 63–65, 68–71.

4. Thomas Jefferson to Thomas Milligan, April 6, 1816, in Bergh and Lipscomb 1907, 14:456–66.

REFERENCES

Bergh, Albert Ellery, and Andrew A. Lipscomb, eds. 1907. *The Writings of Thomas Jefferson.* 20 vols. Washington, D.C.: Thomas Jefferson Memorial Foundation.

Cappon, Lester J., ed. 1959. *The Adams-Jefferson Letters.* New York: Simon and Schuster.

Condorcet, Antoine-Nicolas de. 1955. *Sketch for a Historical Picture of the Progress of the Human Mind.* Trans. Judith Barraclough. New York: Noonday Press.

Croly, Herbert. 1909. *The Promise of American Life.* Boston: Northeastern University Press.

Dewey, John. 1939. *Freedom and Culture.* New York: G. P. Putnam's Sons.

Lowith, Karl. 1949. *Meaning in History.* Chicago: University of Chicago Press.

McLean, Iain. 2004. "Thomas Jefferson, John Adams, and the Declaration des Droits de l'Homme et du Citoyen." In *The Future of Liberal Democracy: Thomas Jefferson and the Contemporary World,* ed. R. Fatton Jr. and R. K. Ramazani, 13–30. New York: Palgrave.

Meek, Ronald L., ed. 1973. *Turgot on Progress, Sociology and Economics.* Cambridge: Cambridge University Press.

Peterson, Merrill D., ed. 1984. *Thomas Jefferson: Writings.* New York: Library of America.

Zuckert, Michael P. 1996. *The Natural Rights Republic: Studies in the Foundation of the American Political Tradition.* Notre Dame: University of Notre Dame Press.

Chapter Thirteen

Gouverneur Morris and the Creation of American Constitutionalism

DAVID K. NICHOLS

In recent years biographies of John Adams and Alexander Hamilton have led to a renewed appreciation of their contributions to the American founding, but five new biographies of Gouverneur Morris have done little to rescue him from relative obscurity (Adams 2003; Brookhiser 2003; Kirschke 2005; Miller 2005, 2008). He remains best known for his often colorful criticisms of democracy. Frequently quoted is his description of an anti-British protest held in New York in 1774: "The mob begin to think and reason. Poor reptiles! It is with them a vernal morning, they are struggling to cast off their winter's slough, they bask in the sunshine and before noon they will bite" (Sparks 1832, I:23). For defenders of the Constitution, the best course might well be to let the name Gouverneur Morris rest in peace. To resurrect his central role in the creation of the Constitution may only add fuel to contemporary criticisms of the founding.

If we are to understand the founding, however, it is difficult to ignore the major role Morris played in it. In 1775, at the age of twenty-three, Morris took a seat in New York's legislature and a year later helped to draft the state's new constitution. He was one of the youngest and most gifted of the delegates to the Continental Congress in 1777–79 and was asked by the Congress to write an account of the history of the Revolution. "Observations on the American Revolution" was published by the Congress in 1779 and widely circulated. From 1781 to 1785 Morris served as the principal assistant to Robert Morris, superintendent of finance for the United States. Not only did Gouverneur Morris play an important part in keeping the new country afloat financially, but he developed the initial plan for our decimal coinage system. His greatest contribution to the founding, however, was at the Constitutional Convention of 1787.

It is widely accepted that Morris wrote the final draft of the Constitution, but unlike Jefferson who gained lasting fame for his authorship of the Declaration of Independence, Morris's labors are barely recognized. The comparison to Jefferson is admittedly limited. Morris began with a series of propositions that had been decided in the course of extensive debates by the Convention delegates. Moreover, the Constitution was a legal document the purpose of which was to codify a system of government. It did not call for the lofty rhetoric needed to justify a revolution. Nonetheless, Morris's careful organization and rephrasing of the decisions of the Convention has had a major influence on the operation of the Constitution, and his preamble, though brief, rises to the level of Jefferson's clarity and eloquence.[1]

Morris was also deeply involved in the discussions that led to the Constitution. He spoke more often than any other member of the Convention, even though he was absent for the entire month of June. Nonetheless, scholars have often discounted his influence, complaining that he was fickle and inconsistent in debate (Brookhiser 2003, xvii). At one point he opposed impeachment and at another supported it, and at various times he supported life tenure for the president, a two-year term, and a four-year term. I argue, however, that Morris always kept his ultimate goals in mind, changing positions on particular issues in light of how those decisions would fit into a larger whole. Particularly in the debate on the presidency but also throughout the Convention, Morris in debate is like the master of a complex Rubik's cube. His positions appear random only to those who have no conception of the whole he envisions. Thus Morris deserves to be called the author of the Constitution in two senses: first, he shaped the language of the final draft; and second, he played a major role in the debates over its drafting.

Why has Morris not received more recognition? With the exception of a brief term in the Senate, Morris never held elective office under the Constitution. He played only a small part on the stage of honor he helped to build. In addition, Morris's relative anonymity may be indicative of a blind spot in both liberal and conservative constitutional scholarship. For liberals, his criticisms of democracy and defense of property are anathema, and conservatives recoil at his unabashed nationalism and support of a powerful and active government. Morris does not fit comfortably with the populist libertarianism that is today so influential at both ends of the political spectrum. Finally, Morris himself deserves some of the blame. His biting wit and penchant for stating arguments in the starkest possible terms was not a recipe for popularity then or now.[2] Many of Morris's criticisms of democratic politics were similar to those of James Madison, but whereas Madison spoke in the soothing language of a friend trying to calm one of whom he is obviously fond, Morris's rhetoric was often steeped in condescension or contempt.

As a result, even recent biographers who believe Morris is worthy of more attention do not fully appreciate his genius. For example, Richard Brookhiser's *Gentleman Revolutionary: Gouverneur Morris, the Rake Who Wrote the Constitution* delightfully describes Morris's iconoclastic politics, extensive sexual exploits, and financial speculation. Brookhiser's Morris should be irresistible to a contemporary popular audience, but even money, sex, and rebellion have proved inadequate to make Morris a best-seller. In part the reason may be that even though Brookhiser displays a genuine affection for his subject, it is affection for the eccentric uncle of the founding family rather than the respect one would have for one of the patriarchs of the clan. Brookhiser dismisses any claim Morris might make to be included in the ranks of Jefferson,

Madison, or Adams. He concludes: "If the founding of the state had rested on him, or men like him, it would not have happened" (Brookhiser 2003, 176).

William Howard Adams presents a more richly detailed portrait of Morris's life, as well as a defense of his commitment to republican government. As his title, *Gouverneur Morris: An Independent Life,* suggests, Adams fully appreciates his subject's unconventionality, but unlike Brookhiser, Adams places Morris "in the top rank of international nation builders" (2003, xi). Still, Adams's Morris remains more of a skilled craftsman than an architect. According to Adams, Morris understood the construction of the Constitution as an exercise of trial and error rather than the product of a coherent theoretical plan of government. Adams claims that "Morris knew that the Constitution was a 'bundle of compromises' without much logic to it" (2003, 165).

In *Gouverneur Morris: Author, Statesman, and Man of the World,* James Kirschke also praises Morris's literary and political skill. Kirschke claims that "those who characterize Morris as no more than a mere aristocrat have failed to measure the man accurately" (2005, 41). But Kirschke's defense of Morris on this score is not fully developed. He provides an extensive catalog of Morris's life and times, including a detailed account of his involvement in the Philadelphia Convention, but he does not provide a systematic account of Morris's political thought.

Unlike Adams and Kirschke, Melanie Randolph Miller in *An Incautious Man: The Life of Gouverneur Morris* finds consistency in Morris's arguments at the Constitutional Convention. Miller argues, "Throughout the Convention, Morris promoted a balanced governmental structure with three functions: moderating the influence of popular will, keeping the executive independent of the legislature, and ensuring the commitment of the rich to the scheme" (2008, 63). She provides a detailed account of the Convention that illustrates Morris's concern with these functions. Nonetheless, she fails to explain the way in which these three goals fit together into a coherent political theory or how they are related to other important issues addressed by Morris at the Convention. For example, Miller devotes a significant amount of time to Morris's opposition to slavery, but she never explains how that fits with Morris's commitment to moderating popular will and enhancing executive independence or his outreach efforts to the rich (2008, 73–79). Miller never endorses the simplistic view of Morris as a defender of aristocracy, but it is noteworthy that the three points on which she argues Morris had the most consistent impact on the Convention are those points in which Morris is most at odds with contemporary democratic theory.

For a more complete elucidation of Morris's political theory, however, we must go back to a single chapter of Jennifer Nedelsky's *Private Property and the Limits of American Constitutionalism* (1990). Nedelsky contends that Morris is moved by a coherent set of political principles, although in the end she is quite critical of those principles. She argues that "Morris was prepared to stake his entire political system on the hostility between rich and poor" (94) and concludes that his ultimate goal is "the clear subordination of liberty to property" (92).[3] There is ample evidence to support her thesis. At the Convention Morris proposed property qualifications for voters, a president for life, and a Senate representing the wealthy to be appointed by the president, also for life. But it is important to understand the context of these proposals. Morris's criticism of democracy and aristocracy can only be understood in light of the larger goals he articulated at the Convention. From the beginning, I argue, Morris's primary concern was not the protection of wealth but the creation of an effective, and essentially popular, national government, and he remained true to these goals throughout the Convention.

Morris was clearly influenced by the idea of a mixed regime that would use the interests of one class to check those of the other, but he was equally aware of the difficulty of instituting such a regime in America. A hereditary monarchy and a hereditary aristocracy were essential elements of the classical mixed regime, but Morris supported neither of them. He explicitly rejects any conception of monarchy, and while he speaks frequently of aristocracy, he uses the term in a number of different ways, and with varying degrees of admiration and distrust. Most often he appears to be referring to an economic interest or class that is found in all societies rather than the kind of titled nobility that characterized European aristocracy. His lack of precision in the use of the term may be the result of the attempt to describe innovative political institutions in terms of an anachronistic political language. In short, I contend that Morris is often more democratic than he sounds.

First and foremost Morris was one of the most committed nationalists at the Convention. He did not call for the abolition of the states, but he thought there was no alternative to their ultimate subordination. The failure of the articles was a direct result of the failure to establish national supremacy. Unless this mistake was corrected all other efforts would be in vain. Second, he wanted to structure the national government so that it would be an effective guarantor of the rights of the people. He knew that only a popular government would be acceptable, but like Madison he knew that friends of popular government must be willing to recognize its faults. Although Morris's expression of those faults never seemed to be an occasion for serious regret on his part, his greatest criticism of democracy was its tendency to degenerate into monarchy, aristocracy, or worse.

Morris hoped that the office of the presidency would be a crucial check on this tendency. He argued "that the way to keep out monarchical government was to establish such a republic as would make the people happy and prevent a desire of change" (Farrand 1967, II:35–36). He thought that the executive would be the primary instrument for effective government. Only a strong executive could hold the union together and protect it against internal and external threats. The executive must also serve as a counterweight to the legislature, according to Morris, not because it should check the democratic impulses of the legislature, but because the interests of the wealthy would inevitably dominate the legislature. The president, he argued, would defend the interests of the people as a whole against the oligarchic legislature. Thus the executive was the key to both effective and democratic government.

If there are any doubts of Morris's commitment to a popular government based on the foundation of individual rights, one need only turn to his antislavery speech at the Convention. It is one of the most eloquent condemnations of slavery ever written. Other delegates may have shared his sentiments, but none equaled his candor. Morris's caustic tongue served to bring to the fore, albeit briefly, the issue that lurked in the background of much of the Convention debates. He would not resolve that issue, but his speech demonstrates that he saw the tension between the principles of the Constitution he was helping to create and the institution of slavery.

In his later years Morris despaired that the Jeffersonians were undermining his handiwork, but after more than two hundred years it is his vision much more than Jefferson's that is reflected in the contemporary United States. The national government created by the Constitution has flourished and supported the growth of a dynamic commercial society. At the center of this successful national government is the powerful popular executive Morris fought so hard to create. By looking at his arguments at the Constitutional Convention, we may better understand the vision of constitutional democracy that moved one of our most influential and neglected founders. We may also come to see that despite language that is sometimes shocking to modern ears, we may find real insight into the forces that shape contemporary politics.

MODERN NATIONALISM AND THE MIXED REGIME

Morris made no extensive speeches in the early days of the Convention, but from the beginning he was on the side of the nationalists, seconding motions supporting a major revision of the articles and attacking equal representation of the states in the legislature. On May 30 he rose to explain "the distinction between a federal and national, supreme, Government; the former being a mere compact resting on the good faith of the parties; the latter having a complete and compulsive operation. He contended that in all communities there must be one supreme power, and one only" (Farrand 1967, I:34). This was the bedrock principle on which Morris thought a new government must be built. In a way it is fitting that after making this statement Morris left Philadelphia for over a month. Personal business took him to New York and thereby spared him a month of deadlock and debate over a point he considered to be beyond argument—the need for a new, truly national government.

In Morris's absence a compromise was proposed in which the House of Representatives would be apportioned on the basis of population and the Senate on the basis of the equal representation of the states, with senators to be appointed by state legislators, but this proposal did not gain immediate approval. When he returned on July 2 the Convention was stalemated on the question. Five states supported equal representation in the Senate, five opposed it, and one was divided. Morris immediately spoke against the proposal. Neither the mode of appointing the members of the Senate by the state legislators nor equal representation of the states would serve the purposes he favored for the Senate in the new government. Morris's opposition to the proposal first focused on the mode of appointment.

He argued that "the mode of appointing the 2nd branch tended he was sure to defeat the object of it" (Farrand 1967, I:511–12). The second branch was needed to check the "precipitation, changeableness, and excesses of the first branch," and Morris did not believe that a Senate appointed by state legislatures would provide an adequate check. Anticipating Madison's argument in *Federalist 51* Morris maintained that the members of the second branch "must have a personal interest in checking the other branch, one interest must be opposed to another interest. Vices as they exist must be turned against each other" (I:512). Looking back to the model of the mixed regime, Morris determined that the second branch must be made up of individuals who possessed a large amount of property and an "aristocratic spirit." Such individuals would be motivated by pride. "Pride is indeed the great principle that actuates both the poor and the rich. It is this principle in which the former resists and the latter abuses authority," he stated. Morris had no illusions about the virtue of the wealthy: "The rich will strive to establish their dominion and enslave the rest. They always did. They always will." Nonetheless, he believed that their vices could be put to good use: "By thus combining and setting apart the aristocratic interest, the popular interest will be combined against it. There will be a mutual check and mutual security" (I:512).

Morris rejected the idea of feudal aristocracy, based on the ownership of land. He looked forward to a dynamic commercial society. As Nedelsky explains, he wanted to "persuade people to think in terms of productivity rather than outmoded morality or mercantilist economics when making public policy" (1990, 72). For example, Morris contended that "a monopoly of the soil is pernicious or even destructive of society, let taxes, therefore compel the owner, either to cultivate it himself or sell it to those who would cultivate it."[4] Nedelsky elucidates: "A society in which taxes encouraged productivity and the investments of the wealthy created jobs, was a society of opportunity and fluidity. Men with talent would prosper unimpeded by those with entrenched advantages. Morris wanted a society which was not only prosperous, but open and free" (72).

Nedelsky describes Morris's political philosophy as "aristocratic capitalism" (1990, 67). The aristocratic aspect of Morris's capitalism is seen, according to Nedelsky, in his belief in the ongoing relevance of class conflict in American politics. "Unlike Madison," she writes, "he did not see the multiplicity of conflicts likely to develop in a large, diverse republic" (94). By institutionalizing class conflict in the two houses of Congress, Morris hoped to provide a basis for restraining the dangers of democratic envy. But one must ask if the term *aristocratic* retains much meaning in a system that rejects "entrenched advantages," a "monopoly of the soil," and "mercantilist economics" in favor of "opportunity," "fluidity," and "productivity."

Nedelsky herself is careful to note that Morris's view of the rich reflected a large degree of ambivalence. "On the one hand, they were a powerful class whose tyrannical designs had to be guarded against; on the other, the rich were the class from which men could be drawn who had the necessary qualifications to be guardians of the public interest" (Nedelsky 1990, 82). Moreover, she explains that Morris distinguished between the lower classes of America and those of Europe: "In America the division between rich and poor was not that between those with property and those with none. In 1787 Morris estimated that nine-tenths of the American people were freeholders" (77). But even if the American lower classes were not a European mob, she argues, he thought that their "envy and hostility toward the rich posed a serious problem" (78). She concludes that on balance Morris saw more danger from the poor and more potential good from the wealthy.

Nedelsky is correct that Morris "did not pay close attention to the gradations in the class structure of America" (1990, 78). His initial reaction was to look back to a mixed regime rather than forward to the pluralistic politics of a commercial republic. But Nedelsky may go too far when she argues that "Morris was prepared to stake his entire political system on the hostility between rich and poor." (92). Even in the debate over the Senate, Morris's political vision is more complex than Nedelsky acknowledges.

As early as July 5 Morris shifted the emphasis of his argument from class conflict to the effects of the proposed Senate apportionment on the national government. As Madison reports:

> He came here as a Representative of America; he flattered himself he came here in some degree as a representative of the whole human race; for the whole human race will be affected by the proceedings of this Convention. He wished gentlemen to extend their views beyond the present moment of time; beyond the narrow limits of place from which they derive their political origin. If he were to believe some things which he had heard, he should suppose that we were assembled to truck and bargain for our particular states. He cannot descend to think any gentlemen are really actuated by these views. We must look forward to the effects of what we do. (Farrand 1967, I:529)

Although it is impossible to ignore the sarcasm in Morris's comment, it would be a mistake to discount altogether his appeal to the nobler sentiments of the delegates. Morris believed that the future of America was dependent on a viable national union, and he wished to transfer the allegiance of the delegates from their states to that union. He was now willing to admit that a Senate elected by the states would have a distinct interest in checking the House, but it would be an interest antithetical to his nationalism. He wanted the Senate to check the House but not at the expense of the Union. "As the 2nd branch is now constituted," he stated, "there will be constant disputes and appeals to the states which will undermine the general government and control and annihilate the 1st branch" (Farrand 1967, I:530).

Again on July 7 Morris complained that no provision was being made "to protect the aggregate interests of the whole. Among the many provisions which had been urged, he had seen none for supporting the dignity and splendor of the American Empire. It had been one of our greatest misfortunes that the great objects of the nation had been sacrificed constantly to local views" (Farrand 1967, I:552). Morris went on to make one of his strongest denunciations of the states. He argued that as now constituted the Senate's only role would be "to keep the majority of the people from injuring particular states."

> But particular states ought to be injured for the sake of a majority of the people, in case their conduct should deserve it. Suppose they should insist on claims evidently unjust, and pursue them in a manner detrimental to the whole body. Suppose they should give themselves up to foreign influence. Ought they be protected in such cases? (I:552)

This was not the most politically sensitive way to state the issue, but Morris's point was to remind the delegates the reason they were there. The states, by themselves, were inadequate to the tasks of promoting justice and protecting against foreign influence.

Morris also called into question the principled basis of the Articles of Confederation. He contended that the only reason equality of the states had been accepted under the Articles was the pressing need to form some government in order to prevent anarchy. The large states went along because, in the midst of a war, they had no alternative. Morris argued, "[We] are at liberty now to consider what is right, rather than what may be expedient" (Farrand 1967, I:552). He left no doubt that what he thinks is right is a national government representing the people not the states. But at the same time he recognized that expediency may still require concessions from his notions of justice. He did not support the proposed compromise, but he "was ready to join in devising such an amendment of the plan, as will be most likely to secure our liberty and happiness" (I:553).

By July 13 Morris even provided a defense, albeit a grudging one, for equal representation of the states in the Senate. He complained of a widening division between the northern and southern states. "He had hitherto considered this doctrine as heretical. He still thought the distinction groundless. He sees however that it is persisted in; and that the Southern gentlemen will not be satisfied unless they see the way open to gaining a majority in the public Councils" (Farrand 1967, I:604). Morris was concerned that the southern and western states would come to dominate the House of Representatives. "The consequence of such a transfer of power from the maritime to the interior and landed interest will he foresees be such an oppression of commerce, that he shall be obliged to vote for ye vicious principle of equality in the 2nd branch in order to provide some defense for the Northern States against it" (I:604). When faced with the choice between southern agrarianism and a commercial republic, Morris unambiguously sided with commerce.

It is far from clear, however, at least at the Convention, that Morris's preference for a commercial republic was dictated, as Nedelsky argues, by a belief in the "subordination of liberty to property" (1990, 92). Morris's position can be better understood as a defense of liberty against the older feudal agrarian conceptions of property. His interest in a mixed regime should also be seen in this light. He was faced with a dilemma. He did not want a Senate that merely reflected the popular base of the House, nor did he want a Senate promoting the interests of the states at the expense of the Union. Morris may have underestimated the importance of institutional arrangements such as the longer terms, smaller size, and different responsibilities in maintaining a distinctive perspective, but if he did it is understandable. The mixed regime offered the only existing model for a bicameral legislature in which each house was independent of the other. Morris's advocacy of a mixed regime initially reflected his hope that the rich and poor would check one another in a bicameral legislature, but by the end of the debates his primary concern was that the Senate would have both institutional independence and a national perspective.

On July 17 Morris made one last attempt to have the Convention reconsider equal representation in the Senate. He suggested that the Convention had started from the wrong premise.

> It had been said, Let us know how the government is to be modeled, and then we can determine what powers can be properly given to it. He thought the most eligible course was, first to determine on the necessary powers, and then so modify the Government as that it might be justly and properly enabled to administer them. (Farrand 1967, II:25)

This undoubtedly was a rhetorical ploy on Morris's part. By redirecting the discussion to the question of the powers necessary for an effective national government, he hoped to lead the delegates through a more circuitous route to a reconsideration of the principle of equal representation. But this was not merely a rhetorical ploy. It was consistent with Morris's desire to establish an effective national government. He believed that the fears of various interests were thwarting the ability of the delegates to design an effective government. This concern, not a preoccupation with class conflict, animated his arguments.

Morris was unable to obtain any support for his proposal. The delegates had come to recognize that this concession to the interests of the states was a necessary precondition for any reform. Morris himself seemed content to drop the argument at this point.[5] His focus shifted from the attempt to create a classical mixed regime to the creation of the American presidency. It was here that Morris hoped to find a novel solution to the problems of class conflict and national unity.

THE POPULAR ENERGETIC EXECUTIVE

Scholars have long recognized Morris's important role in the creation of the American presidency, often citing him along with Alexander Hamilton, James Wilson, and James Madison as the principal proponents of a strong executive at the Constitutional Convention.[6] As noted above he was also one of the most vocal supporters of a popularly elected executive. On July 17 he made the case for election by the people, arguing, "If the people should elect they will never fail to prefer some man of distinguished character, or services; some man, if he might so speak, of continental reputation" (Farrand 1967, II:29). Morris was aware of the complaint that the people were too uninformed to choose a president, and one might well have expected him to subscribe to it, but he did not do so. The people might be led by a "few designing men" in a small district, but, he concluded, "it can never happen throughout the continent" (II:30).

Morris was particularly opposed to the proposed alternative—election by Congress. He claimed, "If the legislature elect, it will be the work of intrigue, cabal, and of faction: it will be like the election of a pope by a conclave of cardinals; real merit will rarely be the title to the appointment" (Farrand 1967, II:29). More important, Morris thought that legislative election would undercut presidential independence. If the president was not independent, Morris contended, "usurpation and tyranny on the part of the legislature will be the consequence" (II:31). Morris was willing to shift his position on specific provisions relating to the mode of election and the length of term, but he did so keeping in mind the goal of executive independence. For example, on the same day he proposed popular election Morris expressed his willingness to accept legislative election, if the president were allowed to serve for life. Today such a proposal would be unthinkable, but it is easy to forget that there were no models available for an effective popular executive. Morris was attempting to balance the concerns of popular legitimacy with the concerns for executive independence, energy, and stability.

Morris thought it was essential that the president be in a position to check the legislature. He maintained:

> The Legislature will continually seek to aggrandize and perpetuate themselves; and will seize those critical moments produced by war, invasion or convulsion for that purpose. It is necessary then that the Executive Magistrate should be the guardian of the people, even the lower classes, against Legislative tyranny, against the great and the wealthy who in the course of things will necessarily compose—the Legislative body. . . . The Executive therefore ought to be constituted as to be the great protector of the mass of the people. (Farrand 1967, II:52)

The legislature would represent the parts, the special interests of the nation. The wealthy would have the time to serve in the legislature or the money with which to influence those who did. Only the president could speak for the nation as a whole, because only he would have an institutional incentive to do so. He would be chosen by the people as a whole, and he would be suspicious of the power of the legislature. Thus he would have reasons to speak up for the "mass of people" whose voices might be drowned out by the clamor of special interests in the legislature. Morris had no doubt that "the love of fame is the great spring to noble and illustrious actions," and he thought and hoped that the office of the presidency would be the primary object of that passion (Farrand 1967, II:53).

The question of impeachment presented particular difficulty for Morris. On July 19 he said that the proposed plan for impeachment would hold the president "in such dependence that he will be no check on the Legislature, will not be a firm guardian of the people and of the public interest" (Farrand 1967, II:53). By July 20, however, he admitted that his "opinion had been changed by the arguments used in the discussion. He was now sensible of the necessity of impeachments, if the executive was to continue for any time" (II:68). He came to see that the desire for executive independence should not obliterate the desire for popular accountability.

Morris goes on to provide a succinct account of his understanding of the republican government he was helping to create. In recognition of the need for impeachment he explains, "The Magistrate is not the King but the prime-Minister. The people are the King. When we make him amenable to justice however we should take care to provide some mode that will not make him dependent on the legislature" (Farrand 1967, II:69). Morris may have failed to see that his analogy was increasingly inappropriate. In England the king was becoming a mere figurehead, and the prime minister would soon be the first minister of the king in name only. In reality the prime minister would be the first minister of Parliament. But Morris was looking forward, not backward. He was looking to a new form of government in which the executive rather than the parliament would be the primary representative of the public interest. The executive would not stand against the popular parliament but would instead draw strength and legitimacy from popular election. The danger in this new government would not come from a king—the people would be king; it would come instead from the legislature, which would try to usurp the authority of the people to promote the individual interests of its members. Thus Morris concludes that because the executive is not a king he should be impeachable, but because the primary threat to liberty will come from the legislature care should be taken in the creation of the mechanisms for impeachment to maintain the independence of the executive.

The centrality of executive independence to his vision of a new government is most evident in his dogged efforts to keep the election of the president out of the hands of the legislature. Whereas Morris eventually conceded to the political necessity of equal representation in the Senate, and in the closing days of the Convention proposed a provision preventing any state from being "deprived of its equal suffrage in the Senate,"[7] he never gave up in his pursuit of a popularly elected executive (Farrand 1967, II:631). As he said on July 24 he was "particularly anxious that the executive be properly constituted. The vice here would not, as in some other parts of the system, be curable" (II:105). But Morris was fighting an uphill battle. When the Committee of Detail made its report on August 6, presidential election remained in the hands of the legislature. As late as August 24, Morris's proposal for election by "electors chosen by the people of the several states" was rejected in favor of legislative appointment (II:404). It was not until the report of the Committee of Eleven on September 4 that it became likely that Morris would prevail.[8] The report recommended election by electors appointed in a manner determined by the legislatures in each state, with a backup election in the Senate if no candidate received a majority of the electoral votes (II:497–98).

The Convention accepted this proposal with one important change: the House, not the Senate, would conduct the backup election. Even this provision required a compromise, and in the House election each state delegation would have only one vote, a significant concession to state interests but one that removed the election from the control of senators chosen by state legislatures and placed it in the hands of popularly elected members of the House. Morris, however, thought that the backup election, whatever its form, would be less significant than many of the delegates suspected. Each elector would have two votes, one of which must go to someone outside the elector's home state. It was only necessary for a candidate to win a number of votes equal to a majority of the number of electors. Thus to be elected a candidate would need only one-fourth of the total votes plus one. Morris believed that in most cases "characters eminent and generally known" would achieve such a majority, and he proved to be correct (Farrand 1967, II:512). The advent of political parties did lead to practical difficulties, but Morris's main argument remained valid. The rise of parties itself pointed to the rise of national political candidates capable of garnering national majorities. Indeed Morris was uniquely prescient at the Convention in predicting the rise of national political parties centering on the election of the president.[9]

In removing the election of the president from the hands of the legislature and placing it in the hands of popular electors, Morris achieved his most significant victory at the Convention. He had ensured that the president would be independent of the legislature and able to stake a claim to popular legitimacy and authority. He sought to strengthen the presidency at every opportunity, supporting a strong role for the president in appointments and treaty making. When Franklin made his often-quoted argument in support of term limits for the president—"In free governments the rulers are the servants and the people their superiors and sovereigns. For the former therefore to return among the latter was not to degrade but to promote them"—Morris was ready with a reply (Farrand 1967, II:120).

> In answer to Dr. Franklin, that a return into the mass of the people would be a promotion instead of a degradation, he had no doubt that our Executive like most others would have too much patriotism to shrink from the burden of his office, and too much modesty not to be willing to decline the promotion. (II:120)

Morris understood that even in a free government love of honor would remain, and should be directed to the good of the nation. By the end of the Convention, Morris had come to see that it was the presidency and not the Senate that would be the primary object of that passion, and thus the primary mechanism for translating it into a concern for the public good.

MORRIS'S LIBERALISM

Morris explicitly argues that property is superior to liberty as an object of government: "The savage state was more favorable to liberty than the Civilized; and sufficiently so to life. It was preferred by all men who had not acquired a taste for property; it was only renounced for the sake of property which could only be secured by the restraints of regular government" (Farrand 1967, I:533). Given this statement, Nedelsky's claim that for Morris property had "an absolute primacy among the objects of government" seems undeniable (1990, 68).

It would be a mistake, however, to see this as evidence of Morris's preference for aristocracy, or his rejection of the fundamental rights of the people. Morris's conception of property is a modern one; it is based on the enjoyment of the fruits of one's labor rather than the protection of inherited property. Morris would undoubtedly accept Madison's formulation regarding the importance of property. As Madison argues in *Federalist 10* the protection of the "diversity in the faculties of men from which the rights of property originate" is "the first object of government" (Hamilton, Madison, and Jay 1961, 78). To be free was to be able to enjoy the fruits of one's labor without unnecessary government interference. For Morris individual rights and property rights are inextricably related. Property provides a security for the rights of the individual that is not found in the condition of absolute liberty of the state of nature.[10]

Morris believed that the closest thing to a traditional aristocracy in the United States was to be found in the plantation slavery of the South, and this was a model he clearly rejected. Slavery was in conflict with the fundamental principle of liberty, and he could not let that fact go without comment at the Convention. On August 8, in opposition to the South's insistence that the slave population should count for purposes of representation, Morris issued a forceful denunciation of slavery. As the *Records* of the Convention state:

> He would never concur in upholding domestic slavery. It was a nefarious institution. It was the curse of heaven on the states where it prevailed. Compare the free regions of the Middle States, where a rich and noble cultivation marks the prosperity and happiness of the people, with the misery and poverty which overspread the barren wastes of Virginia, Maryland and the other states having slaves. . . .
>
> The admission of slaves into representation when fairly explained comes to this: that the inhabitant of Georgia and South Carolina who goes to the coast of Africa, and in defiance of the most sacred law of humanity tears away his fellow creatures from their dearest connections and damns them to the most cruel bondages, shall have more votes in a government instituted for the protection of the rights of mankind, than the Citizen of Pennsylvania or New Jersey who views with laudable horror, so nefarious a practice. He would add that domestic slavery is the most prominent feature in the aristocratic countenance of the proposed Constitution. The vassalage of the poor has ever been the favorite offspring of Aristocracy. (Farrand 1967, II:221–22)

Morris's hostility to slavery could be explained by his economic interest in a capitalist economy, but whatever Morris's interests his arguments are directed to the inconsistency between the practice of slavery and the rights of mankind which governments are instituted to protect. He saw no principled basis on which the practice of slavery could be defended.

If Morris had believed that property rights were absolute, he could not so easily have rejected the claim of southern slaveholders to their property. The protection of the right of slaveholders to their property would by definition be the paramount aim of government. But in the end Morris concluded that the individual rights of the slaves trump the property rights of the slaveholders. It is liberal individualism rather than aristocracy or a defense of property that is the guiding principle of Morris's political thought.

Morris's liberalism, however, cannot be reduced to abstract individualism or the universalism of free market economics. In defending his proposal requiring senators to be citizens for fourteen years in order to be eligible for the office, Morris argued that political loyalty is a necessary support for good government.

> As to those philosophical gentlemen, those citizens of the world, as they called themselves, he owned he did not wish to see any of them in our public councils. He would not trust them. The men who can shake off their attachments to their own Country can never love any other. These attachments are the wholesome prejudices which uphold all governments. (Farrand 1967, II:239)

Economic calculation is no substitute for a love of one's own country. Political loyalty must supplement rational self-interest as a basis for politics. On this point Morris was a true conservative. He recognized the limits to enlightenment rationalism and the need for a kind of citizen virtue.

Finally, Morris was no libertarian. Nedelsky correctly notes that Morris saw the right to contract as a fundamental right and he feared legislative encroachment of that right. But unlike contemporary libertarians Morris understood that the free market he was championing required the support of a powerful government. He wanted a national government that was capable of protecting rights, including the right to contract, to provide a stable currency, promote commerce, and to resolve disputes between the states or with other nations. He even saw the need for government to undertake great projects of internal improvement. As early as 1777 he had proposed a canal connecting the Hudson River and Lake Erie, and in 1810 he was appointed head of the Erie Canal Commission (Mintz 1970, 236).

We can see his vision of government in his transformation of the Preamble to the Constitution. The preamble as reported to the Committee on Style read as follows:

> We the people of the states of New Hampshire, Massachusetts, Rhode Island and Providence Plantations, New York, New Jersey, Pennsylvania, Delaware, Maryland, Virginia, North Carolina, South Carolina, and Georgia, do ordain, and establish the following Constitution for the government of Ourselves and our Posterity. (Farrand 1967, II:565)

In this version of the preamble the states remained the primary political actors, and no mention is made of the purposes of the government to be established. Morris knew that as it stood the preamble was more in keeping with the Articles of Confederation than the government he hoped would grow out of the Constitution.

Morris revised the preamble in such a way as to provide a simple but expansive description of a powerful national government:

> We, the People of the United States, in order to form a more perfect union, to establish justice, provide for the common defense, promote the general welfare, and secure the blessings of liberty to ourselves and our posterity, do ordain and establish this Constitution of the United States of America. (Farrand 1967, II:590)

He makes clear that the Constitution creates a government of the people, not of the states, and moreover emphasizes that we are already one nation. The United States exists; the goal of the Constitution is to make it a "more perfect union." Morris understands that he is operating in a world where all reform is incomplete. A "more perfect union" is better than we now have, but he has no pretensions to absolute perfection. The goals he states for that union are broad, and some might complain, ambiguous, but they do provide a glimpse of his hopes for the new government. Everyone had agreed that common defense was a primary purpose of union, and for some it was the only reason to unite. But Morris thought the union should have a higher moral status—the establishment of justice was the first purpose that he lists. What does he mean by justice? Nedelsky claims that it is little more than the protection of contractual rights. She quotes Morris's statement that "Obedience to the moral Law" should be inculcated by making sure the laws "compel the Performance of Contracts, give redress for injuries, and punish crimes." Nedelsky remarks, "It is no accident that he cited the performance of contracts first. The values Morris wanted to protect were those of a market economy" (1990, 69).

This conclusion, however, is not altogether warranted by the quotation. Morris would rightly claim that a society that ignored contracts, gave no redress to injuries, and failed to punish crimes could hardly be considered just. Nedelsky is concerned that by emphasizing the right of contract, Morris will undermine the ability of government to act in the public interest. Morris would respond in two ways. First, as Nedelsky notes, the claim of the public interest is dangerous precisely because it can be so easily used to justify harming individuals. Property rights and the rights of contract serve to protect individuals against such injustice (Nedelsky 1990, 69).[11] Second, the preamble does not limit the government to the common defense and the establishment of justice; Morris also includes the function of promoting the general welfare. Morris understood the need to act for the common good. That was why he was so committed to the establishment of a national government. A strong national government was necessary in order to act for the good of the nation as a whole, to compel individuals in the states to look beyond their local interests to those of the larger community.

How did Morris understand those broader interests? Nedelsky may be correct that in other times and other places Morris spoke primarily of the protection of property, but at least at the Convention the closing line of the preamble is his last word on the ends of government. The ultimate goal of government is to "secure the blessings of liberty to ourselves and our posterity." Whatever Morris's personal views, he knew that the language in which he should speak to his fellow citizens was the language of liberty. It was their common ground, the common goal that would justify the establishment of a new Constitution.

RESURRECTING MORRIS

Morris's constitutional liberalism may have been a compromise between his most deeply held beliefs and the political beliefs of his fellow citizens.

But as Hamilton reminded us, one's motives are locked in the repository of his own breast. One's arguments are open to inspection by all, and by inspecting the arguments Morris made at the Convention both liberals and conservatives may be forced to rethink some of their most cherished assumptions about the character of constitutional government and its operation in the contemporary world. Are the state and local governments the natural home of liberty? Is the major battle of the modern world between property rights and human rights? Morris would say no to both propositions. He would remind conservatives that the national government has played an indispensable role in protecting the rights of individuals, just as he would remind liberals that the greatest conflict in human history has not been between property rights and human rights but between tyranny and freedom.

Morris's work in Philadelphia represents one of the great contributions to modern constitutional government. Morris was not always successful; he was not always right. Whatever his limitations, he nonetheless played an unparalleled role in the creation of the Constitution that survives to this day. Perhaps more than anyone at the Convention he saw the potential for a strong national government, a modern economy, the end of slavery, the rise of political parties, and the central role that the presidency would play in American political life. He might not mind that his name is not a household word, because he could see the marks of his efforts throughout the American political system. But if the recognition of his contributions would help to create a deeper and more complex understanding of the character of American constitutionalism, he would be too much of a patriot not to welcome it. And he would also be sufficiently modest to accept even the belated praise of the nation that owes so much to his work in summer 1787.

NOTES

1. Brookhiser's chapter on Morris's contribution to the Constitutional Convention focuses primarily on his job as stylist (2003, 78–93). In this he follows the biographer Max M. Mintz, who argues that the entire document is a tribute to Morris's literary skill: "We see the clear mark of Morris's gift for precision, vigor, and grace of expression. There is an elevating grandeur, an exhilarating tempo, and a rationality

of sentence structure which represents the best of eighteenth-century literary style" (1970, 199–200).

2. As Morris's biographer Mary Jo Kline explains, "His overriding misjudgment was an insistence on saying and writing exactly what he wished. . . . Morris fought a lifelong battle against this handicap, but his struggle was hopeless" (1978, 340).

3. In part my interpretation differs from Nedelsky's because my focus is more narrow. I am looking primarily at the Morris of the Convention debates and the way in which his participation shaped the debate as well as the political ideas he defended there.

4. *Pennsylvania Packet,* April 15, 1780, as quoted in Nedelsky 1990, 72.

5. The only other proposal that Morris would make at the Convention that could be interpreted as an attempt to institutionalize class conflict was his call for property qualifications for voters. Although this proposal indicated a distrust of the propertyless, it could hardly be seen as an institutionalized defense of the rich. The 90 percent of the people he believed to be property holders would hardly constitute an aristocratic class.

6. Mintz says, "Unquestionably the most penetrating and enduring contribution which Morris made during the Convention was in the deliberations on the formation of the executive" (1970, 192). Charles C. Thach Jr. claims that Morris was "the real floor leader of those attached to the idea of the independent executive. His speeches of July 19 and July 24 were, it is evident from Madison's notes, masterly analyses of the whole question" (Thach 1969, 99).

7. As Madison explains, Morris was attempting to preempt the criticisms of the small states that might undermine ratification.

8. As Thach has explained, prior to the end of August the issue of how the legislature would vote for the president had been avoided. When it became clear that the provision for election simply by the Senate would not be approved, the small states had hoped for a concurrent ballot, in which the House and the Senate would vote separately. Under such an arrangement, the power of the small states in the Senate would give them a virtual veto power over the choice of the president. The large states preferred a joint ballot, whereby the votes of the Senate would be diluted when added to the votes of the larger House. When the issue came to the forefront of the debate, it was obvious that the Convention was moving in the direction of a joint ballot rather than a concurrent ballot. The small states would no longer gain significantly from legislative election. Faced with this prospect the small states became open to a compromise. Gouverneur Morris and the Committee of Eleven were ready with such a compromise (Thach 1969, esp. 130–32).

9. Morris claimed, "In all public bodies there are two parties. The executive will necessarily be more connected with one than the other. There will be a personal interest in one of the parties to oppose as well as the other to support him" (Farrand 1967, II:104).

10. On this point Morris follows John Locke who says, "The reason why Men enter into Society is the preservation of their Property; and the end why they choose

and authorize a Legislative, is, that there may be Laws made, and Rules set, as Guards and Fences to the Properties of all the Members of the Society, to limit the Power and moderate the Dominion of every Part and Member of the Society. For since it can never be supposed to be the Will of the Society that the Legislative should have a Power to destroy that which every one designs to secure by entering into Society, and for which the People submitted themselves to Legislators of their own making: whenever the *Legislators endeavour to take away and destroy the Property of the People,* or to reduce them to Slavery under Arbitrary Power, they put themselves into a state of War with the People, who are thereupon absolved from any farther Obedience, and are left to the common Refuge which God hath provided for all Men against Force and Violence. Whensoever, therefore, the Legislative shall transgress this fundamental Rule of Society, and either by Ambition, Fear, Folly, or Corruption, endeavour to grasp themselves, or put into the hands of any other, an Absolute Power over the Lives, Liberties, and Estates of the People, by this breach of Trust they forfeit the Power the People had put into their hands for quite contrary ends, and it devolves to the People, who have a right to resume their original Liberty, and by the Establishment of a new Legislative (such as they shall think fit), provide for their own Safety and Security, which is the end for which they are in Society" (Locke 1960, 460–61; original emphasis).

11. It should also be noted that Morris opposed a provision that would have prohibited the states from interfering in private contracts. He argued that "within the state itself a majority must rule, whatever may be the mischief done among themselves" (Farrand 1967, II:439).

REFERENCES

Adams, William Howard. 2003. *Gouverneur Morris: An Independent Life.* New Haven: Yale University Press.

Brookhiser, Richard. 2003. *Gentleman Revolutionary: Gouverneur Morris, the Rake Who Wrote the Constitution.* New York: Free Press.

Farrand, Max, ed. 1967. *The Records of the Federal Convention of 1787.* Rev. ed. 4 vols. New Haven: Yale University Press.

Hamilton, Alexander, James Madison, and John Jay. 1961. *The Federalist Papers.* Ed. Clinton Rossiter. New York: New American Library.

Kirschke, James J. 2005. *Gouverneur Morris: Author, Statesman, and Man of the World.* New York: Thomas Dunne Books.

Kline, Mary Jo. 1978. *Gouverneur Morris and the New Nation: 1775–88.* New York: Arno Press.

Locke, John. 1960. *Two Treatises of Government.* Ed. Peter Laslett. New York: New American Library.

Miller, Melanie Randolph. 2005. *Envoy to Terror: Gouverneur Morris and the French Revolution.* Dulles, VA: Potomac Books.

———. 2008. *An Incautious Man: The Life of Gouverneur Morris.* Wilmington, DE: ISI Books.

Mintz, Max M. 1970. *Gouverneur Morris and the American Revolution.* Norman: University of Oklahoma Press.

Nedelsky, Jennifer. 1990. *Private Property and the Limits of American Constitutionalism.* Chicago: University of Chicago Press.

Sparks, Jared, ed. 1832. *The Life of Gouverneur Morris.* 3 vols. Boston: Gray and Bowen.

Thach, Charles C., Jr. 1969. *The Creation of the Presidency: 1775-89.* Baltimore: Johns Hopkins University Press.

Chapter Fourteen

The Presidency in the Constitutional Convention of 1787

DAVID ALVIS

Over the past few decades the field of political science has witnessed a substantial rehabilitation of the study of the American Founding and its contemporary relevance. Very few scholars have contributed as much to this development as Michael Zuckert. While Zuckert's scholarship ranges over a vast array of institutional and theoretical topics in American government, from the country's philosophic foundations in Locke to the doctrine of incorporation and the Fourteenth Amendment, there is a common theme that unifies all his writings: the novel ways in which statesmen and theorists in America have attempted to make the practice of democratic politics compatible with the doctrine of natural rights. For Zuckert, the Founders thought they discovered the happiest solution to these dilemmas in the form of what Madison called "a republican remedy for the diseases most incident to republican government" (*Federalist* 10).[1] In this chapter I hope to demonstrate how the creation of the American presidency also partakes of this solution and why a careful examination of its origins in the Constitutional Convention can inform our understanding of the institution today.

In the *Federalist Papers* Alexander Hamilton argues that the Convention adopted the electoral college system of presidential election because of a general reservation among the delegates about popular elections (*Federalist* 68). The system of electors, according to Hamilton, constituted a great achievement among the inventions of government ("if . . . not perfect, at least excellent") because, unlike popular elections, this method would separate the "sense of the people" from their baser interests and passions (*Federalist* 68, 458). Whereas popular elections had been the fuel that powered the engines of demagogues historically, they placed the choice in the hands of the few rather than the many, thereby guaranteeing the selection of a candidate that was head and shoulders above the common stock. According to Hamilton, the electoral college would offer a critical screening device that would bring to office the right kind of candidate.

> The process of election affords a moral certainty, that the office of President will never fall to the lot of any man who is not in an eminent degree endowed with the requisite qualifications. Talents for low intrigue, and the little arts of popularity, may alone suffice to elevate a man to the first honors in a single State; but it will require other talents, and a different kind of merit, to establish him in the esteem and confidence of the whole Union, or of so considerable a portion of it as would be necessary to make him a successful candidate for the distinguished office of President of the United States. It will not be too strong to say, that there will be a constant probability of seeing the station filled by characters pre-eminent for ability and virtue. (*Federalist* 68)

Seizing on Hamilton's argument here, many scholars of the presidency have concluded that the electoral college was part of a general design to limit democratic politics in the United States and to curb the dangerous tendencies inherent in popular government. As James W.

Ceaser summarizes this line of argument, "The most significant aspect of the indirect plan was . . . not the matter of who chose the electors, but the effect of an indirect selection on the character of the campaign. Since the people would not be choosing the president, aspirants to the office would have much less reason to cultivate popular favor" (Ceaser 1979, 72). By limiting the direct role of the public in the immediate choice of the executive, candidates would be more inclined to see their responsibilities in terms of constitutional duties rather than as plebiscitary mandates.

Judged in light of these standards for presidential selection, the evolution of the presidency during the twentieth century to the present would appear to mark a dramatic departure from the design of the Framers. Presidents no longer stand aloof from public opinion; rather, they now seem almost entirely reliant on popular tools (perhaps "little arts of popularity") that supposedly sit uneasily with the original intent of the Framer's constitutional scheme. In fact, one prominent book on the development of the modern presidency argues that the most significant challenge to presidential authority today stems from the tension between this original constitutional design of the office and the rise of popular expectations on presidential behavior (Tulis 1987). In *The Rhetorical Presidency* Jeffrey Tulis concludes:

> The modern presidency is buffeted by two "constitutions." Presidential action continues to be constrained and presidential behavior shaped by the original constitution. The core structures established in 1789 and debated during the founding remain essentially unchanged. . . . At the same time, contemporary presidential and public understanding of the character of the constitutional system and the president's place in it have changed. . . . Presidents work in a political system composed of elements in tension and, at times, in contradiction to one another. (1987, 17–18)

According to Tulis, the electoral college method of selection formed an important part of the "core structure" of the original Constitution in which each aspect of the national government's architectural apparatus was designed to mitigate the dangers implicit in majority rule. The electoral college's cumbersome legal requirements would remind presidents that their election was partly the result of a contrivance of law, not popular will. Such an arrangement, according to Tulis, neatly complemented the Framers' more general ideas about the role of the executive under Article II of the Constitution. Rather than look to popular mandates as a source of authority, presidential power was to be firmly rooted in and confined by the dictates of fundamental law (Nichols 1998).

While it is undeniable that presidents today devote more time to garnering popular support, seeking media attention, and publicizing their policy agendas than their predecessors in the period of the early republic, I believe that the evidence to support the claim that the electoral college system was designed to discourage these practices or to shelter the executive from public opinion is less compelling. Of course, there were members of the Convention who opposed a popular mode of election because they feared that a popularly elected executive would be tempted to act as a demagogue. For example, Elbridge Gerry argued, "A popular election in this case is radically vicious. The ignorance of the people would put it in the power of some one set of men dispersed through the Union, and acting in concert, to delude them into any appointment"; and George Mason stated, "The extent of the country renders it impossible, that the people can have the requisite capacity to judge of the respective pretensions of the candidates" (Koch 1984, 368 [Gerry]; 308–9 [Mason]). The problem with relying on quotes such as these from the Convention is that not one of the delegates who voiced such concerns about popular elections favored the electoral college system (Nichols 1994, 42).

In this chapter, I argue that, when we follow the debates of the Constitutional Convention chronologically, we discover that the choice of the electoral college system at the Convention was actually motivated by a desire to form a closer link between the president and the public. In fact, if seen in the context of the Framers' understanding of the purpose and duty of the chief executive, a popular presidential office was actually thought to be more complementary to the institution's purposes than the system imagined by Hamilton in *Federalist* 68.[2] Tulis and Ceaser are right to argue that for the Framers there were certain dangers in democratic government that need to be mitigated by fundamental law. But I think that these scholars fail to appreciate the degree to which the presidency, like many other features of the American Constitution, found a popular solution to the problems of popular sovereignty.

DEBATE IN THE CONSTITUTIONAL CONVENTION

Stage 1: The Executive Office

When the debates over the composition of the executive office began on June 2, the delegates were divided over what we would today regard as the most elementary features of the office, such as the number of people who should occupy it. Since the Articles of Confederation made no provision for an independent executive, any assumption about how this branch would be organized or even whether it would be independent of the legislature was unsettled. When Edmund Randolph proposed in the Virginia Plan that the executive be an independent branch of government, the ensuing debate indicated that delegates had embarked on entirely new ground for the organization of the federal government.[3] Under the Articles executive power was delegated to a select group of members appointed by Congress. Though John Dickenson's original draft of the Articles had proposed a council of state that would function as an independent executive, the final drafters rejected his proposal (Michaelsen 1987, 32). Instead, special committees were appointed ad hoc and were assigned certain executive powers that were to be exercised within the narrow guidelines established by Congress. The executive committees were even denied the ability to act when Congress was not in session (Burnett 1964, 216). By 1775 some of the special committees had been replaced with standing committees in the hope of achieving more uniform administration and to relieve members of Congress of the petty administrative details that were draining their time and resources. Nevertheless, even these newly created committees did not function independently of Congress since the legislature, conceiving of the executive office as merely an arm of the legislature, had created stringent reporting requirements. In a few areas Congress recognized the need to create an executive committee with some independence, which they did in the form of boards such as the Board of War (Burnett 1964, 118). Yet these boards were in no sense truly independent since they too reported to Congress, and their work was constantly subject to revision by the legislature (486–91). Furthermore, the fluctuation of membership both in Congress and in the executive committees had left a record of inconsistency and poor management. What was particularly lacking under the Articles was some truly independent, unified executive head that could consolidate these discordant parts of the administration and be held accountable for the myriad executive details that Congress had been attempting to manage (490–91).

The Virginia Plan's proposal for the national executive did depart in a few important ways from the model of executive power embodied in the Articles of Confederation. Most important, the plan made some provision for the independence of the executive. Though elected by the legislature, the executive would be ineligible for a second term, thus freeing him from considering the repercussions his decisions might incur among his congressional electors. But, as Charles Thach observes, the Virginia Plan still made the executive subordinate to Congress in one crucial respect. While the ineligibility provision guaranteed more independence than that enjoyed by the executive under the Articles of Confederation, any occupant of the office would still perceive of his tenure as a grant of legislative favor (Thach 1969, 84–85).

As the delegates debated the number of people who would occupy the executive office, the Convention came to confront the question of the very nature of the office that would be instituted in the Constitution. At stake was the issue of whether the executive office would be a strong and independent branch of government or perhaps a weak and dependent office that would operate under the thumb of the legislature. A plural executive would function as a weak executive, as did the office under the Articles of Confederation. An executive elected by the legislature would be dependent on Congress at least to some degree, depending on whether the executive would be partially shielded by an ineligibility provision. It is difficult to sketch a precise arrangement of the positions held by all the members of the Convention on the degree of strength and independence that ought to be incorporated into the executive office, but at least three combinations approximate the positions taken by the delegates at this point in the debate. A general outline of their respective positions is as follows: (1) weak and dependent executive, (2) weak but independent, (3) strong and independent.

The most vocal proponent of the first position—the weak and dependent executive—was Roger Sherman of Connecticut. According to

Madison's notes, Sherman stated his position on the constitution of executive power in the following terms:

> He considered the Executive Magistrate as nothing more than an institution for carrying the will of the legislature into effect that the person or persons ought to be appointed by and acceptable to the Legislature only, which was the depository of the supreme will of the Society. As they were the best judges of the business which ought to be done by the Executive department, and consequently of the number from time to time for doing it, he wished that the number might not be fixed but that the legislature should be at liberty to appoint one or more as experience might dictate. (Koch 1984, 46)

Sherman's model represents the most extreme version of executive weakness at the Convention. According to Sherman, the appointment of the executive would not only render him directly accountable to the legislature, but even the number of executive officers should be left to the discretion of the legislature. In Sherman's mind not only would the executive be deprived of the means of securing its independence in practice, but the executive could be weakened to a greater degree by Congress's power to appoint more members to frustrate its activity. While perhaps strange to us today, Sherman's position on executive power is really no different from that already embodied in the Articles of Confederation with its system of congressionally appointed executive committees. In fact, many state constitutions had been modeled on the same antipathy to executive power. As Thomas Jefferson explained, "Before the Revolution we were all good English Whigs, cordial in their free principles, and in theory jealous of executive Magistrates. These jealousies are very apparent in all our state constitutions."[4] As one of the oldest members of the Convention (besides Benjamin Franklin), Sherman probably still held the strong antipathy of the revolutionary generation to anything that smacked of monarchy (Lutz 1988).

Edmund Randolph offered a slightly different version of the constitution of the executive—one that would be plural (three members) and therefore weak *but* independent of the legislature. Unlike Sherman's model, Randolph's gave the executive office institutional protections against legislative interference by both fixing the number of members in the Constitution and instituting an ineligibility provision. But like Sherman's model, the executive in Randolph's model would also be weaker than the final version because the office would be filled by three officeholders rather than one.[5] A single-member office, explained Randolph, was "the foetus of monarchy." Randolph believed that most Americans regarded a single executive as unacceptable for the following reasons: (1) the people would never accept anything resembling monarchy and therefore could not stomach a single magistrate in the office, (2) unity was not among the critical ingredients of proper exercise of the powers of the executive, and (3) the people would never have confidence in a single magistrate. Randolph proposed that the three officeholders would represent the three sectional divisions of states: North, Middle, and South. Since one ostensible reason for convoking the Philadelphia Convention had been the publication of a proposal for the division of the country into three separate confederacies along these geographic lines, Randolph may have believed that his executive could better unite these regions under the newly proposed government without asking them to sacrifice much in the way of their provincial loyalties. According to Randolph's theoretical reasoning, the more diversified the representation of a particular branch of government, the more compatible it is with republican government (Koch 1984, 46). Like Sherman, Randolph reflects a common view of executive power in the early republic: political power is safest when it is vested in representative institutions. From this perspective, the legislature is the truly supreme institution in republican government and the model that other institutions must approximate to the degree possible.

The problem with Randolph's proposal is that, unlike in the legislature, a plurality of members in the executive office tends to perform its administrative tasks badly. We have already seen how this was true under the Articles of Confederation, but it was also true in many states that had a plural executive since the Revolutionary War.[6] In rejecting even the proposal of Randolph for an independent but plural executive, other delegates seemed to have come to the realization that the executive exercises distinct powers that differ from those of the legislature.[7] While legislation is best achieved by negotiation among a variety of narrow local interests, the execution of law requires a more single-minded effort in order to achieve consistency and in order to be rendered accountable for its failures. Consequently, the more the executive approximates the representative plurality of the legislature, the less it can carry out duties that require dispatch and the less it can be held accountable to those who are entrusted with its election.

As Sherman's and Randolph's proposals attest, the specter of the British monarchy still loomed large in the minds of the delegates. James Wilson of Pennsylvania was the first to speak on behalf of the idea of a single officer that would alone be vested with the powers of the executive. Explaining that only a single officer could exercise the requisite "dispatch and responsibility" required for the consistent execution of law, Wilson argued that the executive needed to be unified in order to have sufficient power to act (Koch 1984, 46). Wilson's comments again make clear what is at stake in the argument over a single or a plural executive: a single executive is strong; a plural executive is weak. If the executive is to carry out the laws, stated Wilson, only he alone can wield such powers. Furthermore, accountability for the office cannot be achieved if the office is divided among more than one person. A single executive, argued Wilson, is essential because executive strength relies on unity and accountability, a condition which, far from being a threat to republican government, is in fact "the best safeguard against tyranny" (Koch 1984, 47). Strength, therefore, not weakness, in the executive, according to Wilson, rendered the executive consistent with republican principles of government.

When the question of whether or not to have a single executive was originally raised, Madison reported in his notes that a silence engulfed the entire membership (Koch 1984, 47). In choosing a single member over plural membership for the executive office, the delegates had committed to a stronger executive in the new constitution. However, in order to wield this strength effectively, the executive would need a certain degree of independence from the legislature. There were only two choices for maintaining the executive's independence from Congress: either the executive would be elected by Congress but then made ineligible for a second term or there would have to be an independent mode of election.

Interestingly, it was also Wilson who first made the case that a popular election was the best means of guaranteeing that strength and independence in practice. Tulis cites the initial rejection of Wilson's proposal among the delegates as proof that the Convention was opposed to popular election.[8] However, the problem with a popular election, as

Wilson himself admitted, was how to design it in a country as large as America.[9] The next day Wilson did in fact suggest a method by which a popular election could have been feasibly instituted, one in which each state would be given a proportionate vote depending on its size. Though Wilson's proposal was rejected, the electoral college system operates in nearly the same fashion as the method he recommended. Why, then, did the delegates vote down Wilson's proposal? Since at this point the Convention had not even decided whether the new federal government would simply continue to be some sort of confederacy (as the New Jersey proposal would have rendered it) or a national government (as the Virginia Plan anticipated), it was simply too early to decide whether the executive should be elected by a popular vote.

What is interesting about Wilson's argument is its contrast to the arguments of Randolph and Sherman, both of whom claimed that what is not wanted in the executive is someone who feels himself above the legislature. Wilson, on the other hand, believed the executive must be someone of national repute whose vigor in the execution of his office would be sustained by a national mandate. In republican government strength and independence could be legitimated only by popular election. A popular executive, in Wilson's mind, was the solution to the historic tension between executive power and republicanism.

Stage 2: The Case for Popular Election

For nearly six weeks the Convention was absorbed in the debate over the distribution of representation in the legislature. Small states naturally preferred an arrangement like the New Jersey Plan in which every state would receive equal representation. The large states, by contrast, preferred the Virginia Plan's distribution of representation on the basis of population. Not until mid-July did the delegates arrive at compromise whereby the lower house would represent population and the states would receive an equal distribution of representatives in the Senate. Once the Connecticut Compromise had decided the issue of representation in the legislature, the delegates on July 16 again turned their attention to the method of election for the executive. At this point James Wilson renewed his earlier argument that a popular mode of election was necessary to counter the influence of the executive because only someone of "general notoriety" would feel sufficiently confident in a contest with the legislature over the exercise of executive power. But, as sympathetic as some delegates might have been to Wilson's argument, the majority of delegates felt that Wilson's objections to legislative election were best handled by the insertion of an ineligibility provision. In reply to Wilson, George Mason, Charles Pinckney, and Roger Sherman did in fact renew their earlier objection to popular election on the grounds that the people were not qualified to elect the executive. But the decisive objection at this point came from the coalition of state votes that had developed as a result of the Connecticut Compromise. In the compromise the small states had achieved a significant victory when they gained equal representation among all states in the national Senate. Moreover, in the wake of the Connecticut Compromise, the southernmost states (North Carolina, South Carolina, and Georgia) now joined the small-state voting coalition seeking to maximize protection for their slave interests. This coalition, therefore, believed that legislative election of the executive would be to their states' advantage (Slonim 1989, 41). Proponents of popular election would likely have been reminded by this victory of the small states in the compromise that there were limits to the degree to which they could push for institutions that represented purely popular interests. If the proponents of a popular executive hoped to persuade a majority of delegates to adopt an independent mode of election, they would have to find some way of palliating the small states.

For many weeks it seemed decided that the executive would be elected by the legislature, with some guarantee of independence through an ineligibility provision. However, on July 17 a proposal to remove the ineligibility provision brought all the questions about the status of the executive back to the floor. Proposed by Houston and seconded by Sherman, Gouverneur Morris of New York immediately came to the defense of this motion, forming a rather odd alliance with the most outspoken proponents of a weak and subservient executive. Morris was, besides Wilson, the Convention's leading advocate of popular election and eventually one of the primary drafters of the electoral college system. It was at this point that he took up the battle for an alternative mode of election where James Wilson had left off. "The ineligibility proposed by the clause as it stood," argued Morris, "tended to destroy the great motive to good behavior, the hope of being rewarded by a re-appointment" (Koch 1984, 310). But if reeligibility were to be permitted, then the executive would be rendered entirely dependent on the legislature. Morris seems to have inferred that even after the Connecticut Compromise a number of delegates harbored reservations about the idea of subordinating the executive to the caprice of the legislature. Morris must have thought that he could convince the delegates to assume the arduous task of designing an independent mode of election by making the issue impossible to circumvent. He could take advantage of two problems with the provision for ineligibility as a means of protecting the executive from legislative interference. First, depriving an elected officer of eligibility for another term appeared unrepublican because it deprived the public of freedom to choose any candidate. Second, ineligibility would be potentially harmful if it denied the country an opportunity to take advantage of experience, especially in time of great need. Instead of directly proposing popular election to the Convention, Morris appeared to have concluded that the best way to convince others of its merits would be to maneuver the delegates into a position in which they would forced to accept such a mode of election.

As Morris made his inroads against the ineligibility provision, the delegates scurried to find new props for executive independence from the legislature. When James McClurg of Virginia proposed replacing the seven-year term with lifetime tenure, Morris seconded it (Koch 1984, 310). Even the thought of an executive for life must have brought back the awful specter of monarchy, and it seems unlikely that the proposal could have been taken very seriously. Here, I think, we witness Morris's careful stage managing of the debate. If the delegates agreed that ineligibility was unrepublican and potentially harmful to the interests of the nation, then, without an independent mode of election, their only option was indefinite tenure or popular election. In the sweltering summer days of Philadelphia and the by now rancid air of the State House, Morris denied the weary delegates any place to retreat.

The tenure of good behavior was soon voted down, leaving the legislature in charge of selection and reeligibility still in question. Renewing his objections to legislative election in a lengthy speech on July 19, Morris explained to the delegates that there were only two options for guaranteeing executive independence: "give him his office for life, or make him eligible by the people" (Koch 1984, 325). At this point Morris perceived it was time to make a more substantive argument for the merits of popular election. A popular executive, he argued on July 19, was not merely a technical issue of checks and balances, but the most important feature of the new constitution's "efficacy and utility" for the Union.

> It is necessary to take into one view all that relates to the establishment of the Executive; on the due formation of which must depend the efficacy & utility of the Union among the present and future States. It has been a maxim in Political Science that Republican Government is not adapted to a large extent of Country, because the energy of the Executive Magistracy can not reach the extreme parts of it. Our Country is an extensive one. We must either then renounce the blessings of the Union, or provide an Executive with sufficient vigor to pervade every part of it. This subject was of so much importance that he hoped to be indulged in an extensive view of it. (Koch 1984, 322)

Republican government, it had been assumed, was impossible in a country of large extent. Without sufficient vigor in the executive office, claimed Morris, this assumption would prove accurate. The experiment of republican government in this country required a new conception of executive power—one that could utilize the extent of the country rather than be hindered by it (Koch 1984, 324).

An executive that conceived of himself as the "guardian of the people" would act with the necessary confidence to fulfill his duties as an independent and coequal branch of government, according to Morris (Koch 1984, 324). The president would serve as the people's protector from the great and wealthy whom Morris thought would most likely become concentrated in the national legislature of so extensive a nation.[10] In addition, Morris argued, the executive would not merely restrain the usurpation of powers by the legislature, but more important he would prevent the abuse of even legitimate legislative powers (Koch 1984, 328).

> One great object of the Executive is to control the Legislature. The Legislature will continually seek to aggrandize & perpetuate themselves; and will seize those critical moments produced by war, invasion or convulsion

> for that purpose. It is necessary then that the Executive Magistrate should be the guardian of the people, even of the lower classes, agst. Legislative tyranny, against the Great & the wealthy who in the course of things will necessarily compose the Legislative body. (Koch 1984, 328)

Morris's remarks provide some of the most important clues to understanding the purpose behind the final constitution of the office. Unlike previous arguments in favor of a strong and independent executive, which had been made on strictly defensive grounds, Morris believed that a strong executive (if popularly elected) could serve the positive function of supplying leadership for the government as a whole.[11]

While the delegates were unable to find a mode of election at this point that perfectly suited all their concerns, the substantial time they were willing to devote to considerations of an alternative mode of election attests to Morris's influence in moving the Convention toward this end. We must assume, then, that it was the argument for a popularly elected executive that had prevailed over the delegates' general reluctance to revisit legislative election. Furthermore, there is no evidence at this point in the debate that the delegates rejected popular election out of the fear that it might promote demagoguery or that the people are ill suited to judge presidential qualifications. On the contrary, Morris appears to have persuaded many of the delegates that a popular mode of election would be desirable for the kind of candidate it would produce. The only obstacle that stood in the way of adopting popular election was the interests of the small states and many southern states. In the case of the southern states, the three-fifths clause could not be incorporated into a popular mode of election. It was clear that the success of a popular election would require a method of selection that could satisfy the interests of the small states in maintaining a significant degree of influence in the election and a mode that could incorporate the three-fifths clause for the southern states.

Stage 3: Proposal by the Committee of Postponed Matters and Unfinished Business

Despite the significant progress that had been made in July toward the institution of a popular election, the Convention eventually retreated to the position of legislative election, where it remained during most of August. As before, legislative election functioned as the default position when the delegates could not find a compromise between those who favored the interests of their respective states and those who favored a popular national government. However, on August 24, when John Rutledge of South Carolina proposed that "joint" be inserted before "ballot," it became clear that even legislative election could not resolve the differences between the two. Advocates of state interests were quick to recognize that such a ballot would immediately undo what they thought they had gained by legislative election. The proposal for a joint ballot failed, with all small states voting against it. Jonathan Dayton of New Jersey then proposed a concurrent ballot between the House and the Senate. If adopted, a concurrent ballot would permit the small states to exercise a powerful veto power over the choice of the executive. Dayton's proposal also failed to win a majority.

With the delegates now divided over the method of legislative election itself, Morris sensed another opening for the introduction of an independent mode of election. However, rather than let the issue be engaged by the same procedure that had previously hindered its development, Morris motioned on August 31 to take the issue out of the Committee of the Whole and refer it to the smaller Committee of Postponed Matters and Unfinished Business. In committee, delegates could forge solutions to complex and intricate issues that could not be done in the larger body. Thus, even though alternative proposals to legislative election had been voted down numerous times, the delegates, by agreeing to Morris's motion, still appeared willing to entertain a proposal for an independent mode of election. As a member of the committee, Morris would be in a position to prevail over a small group of colleagues and thus fashion a method of election that suited his goals.[12]

On September 4 the committee presented a plan to the Convention for an alternative mode of election. First, each state would be entitled to as many electors for the office of the president as it possessed senators and representatives in the legislature. Given that the Connecticut Compromise had been agreed to by all the delegations to the Convention, advocates for state interests would have a difficult time arguing that such an arrangement for the election of the president was unfair. Furthermore, the plan incorporated the three-fifths compromise, so there was no need to raise the incendiary issue of representation for slaves again.[13]

The plan also alleviated fears of cabal or corruption in a small electoral body. The electors would now be appointed by the state legislatures to meet in their respective states rather than in some central location where as one body they might collude. While some have suggested that the provision was intended to supply defects in the public's capacity to choose well-qualified candidates and protect them from demagoguery, the chronology of events above indicates that the electoral college was actually the most feasible means of establishing popular election without completely diluting the influence of the small states. There appears to be little evidence that the delegates believed these electors would prove superior to the people in their knowledge and capacity to choose fit candidates for the office. In fact, Charles Pinckney argued that in his view the problem with the system of electors in the new mode is that it was too much like a popular election because these electors appointed by the state legislatures would not have sufficient knowledge to elect candidates of requisite qualifications for the office (Koch 1984, 582). Pinckney's comments are important because he was one of the more outspoken opponents of popular election on the grounds that it might create demagogues. Pinckney saw no distinction between the judgment of a handful of electors proportioned by population and a direct popular vote. Furthermore, no one at the Convention offered a defense of the electoral college as a screening device in response to Pinckney's criticism of the institution. Instead, the delegates must have thought that the system of electors was simply the most feasible means of registering a popular vote.

The case for the electoral college at the Convention is very different from the argument of Hamilton in the *Federalist Papers.* Whereas Hamilton's argument focuses on the special qualities of the electors that make them an august body, the spokesmen for the electoral college at the Convention, like Gouverneur Morris, argued that the merits of the scheme lay in the fact that they do *not* form an elite body and consequently do not deliberate on the choice of a candidate. Their dispersal during the election therefore implied that they would represent the general interests of the nation rather than act as a collective body. The electoral college was never conceived as a means of curbing the influence of direct democracy but only as a means of registering popular preference for a presidential candidate.

CONCLUSION

The greatest challenge facing the Founders was how to reconcile what they had learned from the experience of the Articles of Confederation—the need for a strong and independent executive—with the principles that had inspired the Revolution in the first place—a limited government that protects individual rights. Historically, successful nations have almost always possessed an executive sufficiently energetic to enforce the laws and to protect against external threats. But those great nations that have wielded this kind of executive power have rarely been remembered for their self-control and their respect for individual rights. The problem of executive power is particularly acute in a republic. Where law is the product of consent, its lax enforcement would call into question the very principles on which the nation is founded (*Federalist* 70). By the close of the Convention, the delegates had arrived at something genuinely new in the history of mankind: a solution to the modern "desideratum" of finding a government both capable of controlling the governed and capable of controlling itself (*Federalist* 51). Not persuaded that republican government can be better administered by anyone other than those who genuinely represent the will of the people, the popular presidency provided "a republican remedy for the diseases most incident to republican government" (*Federalist* 10).

NOTES

I am grateful to Michael Zuckert for the development of this chapter. While the faults are entirely my own, the chapter would not have been possible without his direction and thoughtful criticism.

1. All citations of *The Federalist* refer to Hamilton, Madison, and Jay, *The Federalist,* edited by Jacob E. Cooke (1961).

2. Among the most notable efforts to trace the development of the executive office chronologically over the course of the Convention are Thach 1969; Slonim 1989;

Roche 1961. My argument differs from Roche's in that I believe that the electoral college system embodied a more principled solution to the debates at the Convention, whereas he concludes that it was merely a "jerry-rigged improvisation" (Roche 1961, 811). My analysis is closer to that of Thach and Slonim, who think that the electoral college was a combination of principle and compromise among interests. However, I also believe that both understate the reasons in support of a popular election of the executive.

3. The concept of an independent executive office was not new of course since all the states, at least in theory, had one. But since the Articles of Confederation government had operated more like an international committee or league than the official organ of a state, the delegates did have to begin with first principles when it came to the constitution of any of the three branches of government. Thus what makes the debates particularly interesting is the opportunity to see how the different members of the Convention conceived of executive power in terms of its most fundamental ingredients and also how the delegates eventually developed a consensus about the constitution of executive power for the conduct of the national government.

4. Jefferson, *Writings*, ed. Ford, 1:112, cited in Thach 1969, 26.

5. Randolph understood quite well the incompetence of the Congress under the Articles and the need for an independent executive. He wrote to Washington before the Convention, "To you I need not press our present dangers. The inefficiency of Congress you have often felt in your official character; the increasing languor of our associated Republics you hourly see; and a dissolution would be, I know, to you a source of the deepest mortification" ("Randolph to Washington December 6 1786," in Conway 1888, 63).

6. See, e.g., Thach's treatment of the Pennsylvania plural executive (1969, 31–34). Those state constitutions that had a single executive often fettered them with a council by which the legislature could either frustrate the power of the office or limit the executive's chief tool of defense, the veto. See Thach on Virginia Council of State (1969, 29–31).

7. It is also important to note that the Convention eventually rejected even the suggestion of a council attached to the executive since in many states such a council tended to make the executive office plural in practice.

8. "Because independence from public opinion was the source of concern about the legislatures, the founders rejected James Wilson's arguments on behalf of popular election as a means of making the president independent of Congress" (Tulis 1987, 40).

9. On June 3 Wilson presented a formal account of a plan for popular election:

> That the States be divided into districts:& that the persons qualified to vote in each district for members of the first branch of the national legislature elect members for their respective districts to be electors of the executive magistracy, that the said electors of the Executive magistracy meet at and they or any of them so met shall proceed to elect by ballot, but not out of their own body person

> in whom the Executive authority of the national Government shall be vested. (Koch 1987, 306)

The method of election in the electoral college is not significantly different from that proposed by Wilson. Instead of creating new districts for proportional representation as Wilson proposed, it uses the preexisting district numbers (plus two Senate districts per state), which, in total, roughly approximate population.

10. Morris was not alone in this fear. When the backup plan was originally proposed, it designated the Senate as the selection body in cases where the electoral college did not produce a majority. Wilson argued that this would lend an aristocratic tinge to the election of the president and thereby undermine the president's role as guardian of the people.

11. As Nichols notes, it was Gouverneur Morris who was responsible for the requirement that presidents make legislative recommendations to Congress in what has come to be known today as the State of the Union Address (Nichols 1994, 56–57).

12. I agree with Thach's estimation at this point of the Convention: "Manifestly it was this committee that organized the executive, as it was the committee of detail that enumerated its powers. *If it could work out a compromise,* it was a foregone conclusion that the Convention would accept it" (1969, 132; emphasis mine).

13. I think it is true that although the plan put the small states at some disadvantage, many took consolation in the hope that if a majority could not be achieved the choice of the president was placed in the hands of the Senate (and, by later amendment, an equal vote of the states in the House). Nevertheless, proponents of popular election like Madison believed that the backup plan might actually spur the larger states to rally around a popular figure in order to avoid such a conclusion in an election.

REFERENCES

Burnett, Edmund Cody. 1964. *The Continental Congress.* New York: Norton.

Ceaser, James W. 1979. *Presidential Selection.* Princeton: Princeton University Press.

Conway, Moncure D. *Omitted Chapters in the History Disclosed in the Life and Papers of Edmund Randolph.* New York, 1888.

Hamilton, Alexander, James Madison, and John Jay. *The Federalist.* Edited by Jacob E. Cooke. Middletown, CT: Wesleyan University Press, 1961.

Koch, Adrienne, ed. 1984. *Notes of Debates in the Federal Convention of 1787 Reported by James Madison.* Athens: Ohio University Press.

Lutz, Donald S. 1988. *The Origins of American Constitutionalism.* Baton Rouge: Louisiana State University Press.

Michaelsen, William B. 1987. *Creating the American Presidency, 1775–1789.* Lanham, MD: University Press of America.

Nichols, David K. 1994. *Myth of the Modern Presidency.* University Park: Pennsylvania State University Press.

———. 1998. "A Marriage Made in Philadelphia." In *Speaking to the People: The Rhetorical Presidency in Historical Perspective,* ed. Richard J. Ellis, 16–34. Amherst: University of Massachusetts Press.

Roche, John P. 1961. "The Founding Fathers: A Reform Caucus in Action." *American Political Science Review* 55 (December): 799–816.

Slonim, Shlomo. 1989. "Designing the Electoral College." In *Inventing the American Presidency,* lst ed., ed. Thomas E. Cronin, 33–60. Lawrence: University Press of Kansas.

Thach, Charles C., Jr. 1969. *The Creation of the Presidency, 1775–1789: A Study in Constitutional History.* Baltimore: Johns Hopkins University Press.

Tulis, Jeffrey K. 1987. *The Rhetorical Presidency.* Princeton: Princeton University Press.

Chapter Fifteen

From Statesman to Secular Saint

Booker T. Washington on Abraham Lincoln

DIANA J. SCHAUB

In 1905 a white woman from California sent Booker T. Washington her design for a "Negro Flag": a portrait of Abraham Lincoln surrounded by thirty-six stars representing the states in the Union at the conclusion of the Civil War. It was apparently the custom of the day for various immigrant groups to display a heritage flag, such as the flag of their ancestral land, alongside the Stars and Stripes. A flag acknowledging Lincoln as the Moses of the Negro people in the United States would enable Afro-Americans to do something similar. In his response to Mrs. Colton, Washington, while courteously thanking her, makes plain that "the Negro needs no special insignia," having been "an integral part of the country" from the beginning: "as a consequence, Old Glory is his flag" (Harlan 1972–89, 8:299–300).

Directing his criticism at the very idea of a Negro flag (and its assumption of divided or dual loyalties), Washington says nothing about the specific design. We might note, however, that Mrs. Colton's proposed design is not in fact parallel to "other nationalities carrying their colors together with the Stars and Stripes" since it does not refer to a preexisting ethnic or national affiliation but instead commemorates the moment of emancipation *within* the United States. The flag asserts that Abraham Lincoln was the agent of black peoplehood and belonging. *He* put the hyphen in Afro-American. Washington may well dissent from that attribution also; his statement that blacks have "been identified in a most essential and important manner with the whole country's progress and development" applies to the era of black slavery as well as that of black freedom. As important as emancipation was, blacks had legitimate claims on, and attachments to, the land of their birth long before that most welcome revolution in their situation.

Washington, however, perhaps preferred not to say anything that might be construed as derogatory to Lincoln. Certainly, no black leader hosannaed Lincoln higher than Booker T. Washington did. *Hosanna* is from the Hebrew meaning "pray, save us!," and one of Washington's earliest memories was of his mother praying not *to* Lincoln but *for* him and for earthly salvation *through* him. Here is the story as told in the opening chapter of Washington's autobiography, *Up from Slavery:* "So far as I can now recall, the first knowledge that I got of the fact that we were slaves, and that freedom of the slaves was being discussed, was early one morning before day, when I was awakened by my mother kneeling over her children and fervently praying that Lincoln and his armies might be successful, and that one day she and her children might be free" (Washington 1986, 7). Washington's attitude toward Lincoln was thus fixed early in life. His adoration of Lincoln was by no means unusual. In a 1907 essay, "Early Problems of Freedom," Washington describes the joyous celebrations with which former slaves greeted the end result of the war: "No one who saw them could have any doubt whatever as to the Negro's appreciation of his freedom. It is a notable fact that in none of them was ever heard a word of hatred or revenge toward those who had been responsible for their long enslavement. Their gratitude was too great to leave room for resentment. God, Lincoln, and Freedom formed a mysterious trinity in the new awakening of these emancipated people" (Brotz 1992, 385). In this Trinitarian metaphor, Lincoln takes the person of Christ (rather than Moses), with Freedom as the Holy Spirit.

As a child born fatherless into slavery and freed at the age of nine, Washington experienced the "new birth of freedom" heralded in the Gettysburg Address. Not surprisingly, in later life he often described Lincoln as his "patron saint." The 1901 advertisement for *Up from Slavery* contained the following blurb:

> Booker T. Washington says biography is his favorite reading and Abraham Lincoln is his patron saint. He claims to have read every book written about Lincoln. Perhaps this is one reason why his own autobiography, just published by Doubleday, Page & Co., is so full of anecdotes and stories, and withal one of the more interesting, helpful and solid of American biographical writings. In his single-hearted devotion to a righteous cause he is not unlike the great President. (Harlan 1972–89, 6:365)

This comparison of Washington to Lincoln became common and not just in public relations boilerplate. The noted novelist and literary critic William Dean Howells, in an extended review of *Up from Slavery* (along with two biographies of Frederick Douglass), embraced the linkage: "His origin was not much more obscure, his circumstances not much more squalid, than Abraham Lincoln's, and his impulses and incentives to the making of himself were of much the same source and quality" (6:192). Belton Gilreath, a Birmingham coal and iron magnate of liberal sympathies, contacted Washington after reading his autobiography, having found it, he said, "more interesting than any book I have ever read with the single exception of part of the life of Abraham Lincoln. He too is my ideal Saint" (6:95). Gilreath became a strong supporter of Washington's and eventually a Tuskegee trustee. A humbler correspondent, a carpenter named Thomas A. Cooper, by his own description "an obscure atom of humanity," wrote a heart-felt letter in which he recurred to the Moses analogy, describing Lincoln and Washington as sequentially sharing the mission of Moses, with Lincoln conducting the black race out of Egypt and Washington leading them "out of the wilderness of enforced ignorance" toward the promised land of "education progress and agricultural commercial prosperity" (6:350).

GRAVEN IMAGES

This exact idea of Washington is embodied in a statue erected at Tuskegee two decades later, in 1922, some years after Washington's death. Titled "Lifting the Veil of Ignorance," it displays Washington standing behind the seated figure of a freedman, one arm outstretched as if offering the way, the other removing a veil that had draped the freedman's face. Bare-chested and bare-legged, the freedman (perched on a plow and anvil with an open book on his lap) joins the formally attired Washington in looking toward a point in the far distance. The composition of the figures is astonishingly like the Freedmen's Monument in Washington, D.C. That statue, "Emancipation," shows Lincoln standing beside a half-kneeling slave, with one hand holding the Emancipation Proclamation and the other outstretched above the manacled slave—again bare-chested and bare-legged—who is in the act of breaking his chains and rising. Commissioned and erected by "emancipated Citizens of the United States" (according to the plaque on the statue's pedestal), the Freedmen's Monument was dedicated in 1876 on the eleventh anniversary of Lincoln's assassination, with Frederick Douglass delivering his great "Oration in Memory of Lincoln." The two sculptures are strikingly similar; in both, the great benefactor stands with either a slave or a recently freed slave crouching at his feet. Lincoln and Washington are depicted realistically, in contemporary dress, while the slave/freedman is emblematic (his near-nudity an allegorical rendition of his material impoverishment). However, in neither statue is there intended to be anything of spiritual abasement in the lower figure. So, for instance, the slave does not look beseechingly to Lincoln; he is intent on his own rising, his head uplifted and his eyes forward. So, too, the freedman of the Washington statue is preparing himself, through labor and learning, for fuller freedom to come.

Nonetheless, despite the artists' intentions, viewers both then and especially now have expressed dissatisfaction with these "Mosaic" depictions. While the statesmanship of Lincoln and Washington was premised on the rights-based equality of all men (and furthermore was directed toward the political achievement of that equality), the depiction of their benefactions required a stark acknowledgment of the then-existing inequality of conditions. Moreover, both statues allude to a deeper and permanent form of natural inequality: there are characteristics of soul that distinguish a rare few from the vast majority. Our discomfort with these statues—only in part attributable to specifically racial sensitivities about black agency—indicates a profound democratic suspicion of greatness. I suspect we can admire a statue of a conquering hero on horseback more readily than we can an instantiation of gratitude that depicts both benefactor and beneficiary. Gratitude may be strongly felt in the moment, but reified gratefulness soon begins to grate on our egalitarian sensibilities. Viewing the figure on horseback, one can experience either a disinterested admiration of nobility or, alternatively, a self-referential delight from identification with the hero. By contrast, these statues of Lincoln and Washington compel one to identify with the beneficiaries. One has the experience that Alexander Pope described as "the inferiority which obligation implies." Absent an already felt sense of gratitude toward Lincoln and Washington, the statues themselves are unlikely to evoke or instill it. Indeed, they are just as likely to provoke ingratitude.

Missing from these graven images are the humility and humor with which both Lincoln and Washington tempered their grand statesmanship—and made it democratically palatable. Contemporary scholars have explored the degree to which Washington modeled his manner of speaking on Lincoln. A highly acclaimed recent biography of Washington notes that "his humility was reminiscent of that of Abraham Lincoln on the stump, and the presentation was undoubtedly deliberate. A student of rhetoric who observed Booker closely characterized it as having 'the quality of the sinking self . . . [which] takes attention away from the speaker and turns it to what he is saying'" (Norrell 2009, 138). Washington's deployment of humor also put his audiences at ease. As his biographer notes, "in his storytelling, there was again a strong similarity to Lincoln, with a rustic character always delivering the punch line" (139). At the same time, his use of dialect humor and "darky" stories could serve more sophisticated and critical purposes. Speech, particularly speech that involves irony, has layers of meaning that a plastic creation cannot achieve. The literary man William Dean Howells glimpsed something of the depths hidden by Washington's "unfailing sense of humor"—a trait that Howells regarded as characteristic of blacks who had risen to eminence:

> It enables them to use reason and the nimbler weapons of irony, and saves them from bitterness. By virtue of it Washington, and Dunbar and Chesnutt enjoy the negro's ludicrous side as the white observer enjoys it. . . . The fact is of all sorts of interesting implications; but I will draw from it, for the present, the sole suggestion that the problem of the colored race may be more complex than we have thought it. What if upon some large scale they should be subtler than we have supposed? What if their amiability should veil a sense of *our* absurdities, and there should be in our polite inferiors the potentiality of something like contempt for us? The notion is awful; but we may be sure they will be too kind, too wise, ever to do more than let us guess at the truth, if it is the truth. (Harlan 1972–89, 6:195–96)

LINCOLN: OUR MAN AND OUR MODEL

Monuments expressing gratitude to great men should not be scorned; nonetheless, speech is superior to sculpture (or any other fine art) as a vehicle of public gratitude and civic instruction.[1] Since Washington himself was both an admirer and emulator of Lincoln, it is worthwhile to examine those instances in which he reflected on Lincoln's life and work. They turn out to be central to an understanding of Washington's own life and work.

Washington's thoughts on Lincoln are of two main sorts: first, brief references to Lincoln in pedagogical and hortatory speeches delivered to black audiences; and second, a few speeches devoted explicitly and extensively to Lincoln, presented on ceremonial occasions to mainly white audiences. Most typical of the first are Washington's "Sunday Evening Talks"—a regular forum that Washington held for students at Tuskegee. In these homilies on character formation, Washington fairly often cited

Lincoln, counseling emulation of his virtues, especially honesty and simplicity. Four of the addresses in which Lincoln figures are "Reading a Means of Growth," "Self Denial," "Giving the Race a Reputation," and "Strength in Simplicity."

In the first, from 1890, Washington advises students to follow Lincoln's example of Bible reading. The recommendation is not so much for the sake of piety as proper self-development (which always has in view service to one's fellow man). Thus, "you never read in history of any great man whose influence has been lasting, who has not been a reader of the Bible" (Harlan 1972–89, 3:93). Washington is obviously aware of the world-altering impact of tyrants; but he is convinced that the power of good outlasts that of evil. The point about a life devoted to the good of others is sharpened in a talk a year later trumpeting the role of self-denial: "This is the secret of Abraham Lincoln's success in life. . . . He practiced this self-denial, and it gave him an element of strength which won for him the name of the 'first American'" (3:130–31). In 1898, while outlining the elements of a good reputation, Washington illustrates Lincoln's legendary honesty with a tale his students had obviously heard from him before:

> You recall that story of Abraham Lincoln, how when he was postmaster at a small village he had left on his hands $1.50 which the government did not call for. Carefully wrapping up this money in a handkerchief he kept it for ten years. Finally one day the government agent called for this amount and it was promptly handed over to him by Abraham Lincoln. . . . That trait of his character helped him along to the presidency. (4:514)

Finally, in a sermon on the value of simplicity as the outward expression of inner strength, Lincoln is offered as the model. Washington explores various ways in which one projects the self into the world. We utter or "outer" ourselves—whether through words or more superficial expressions like modes of address and dress. Washington urges simplicity in all three: neat and modest rather than attention-grabbing garb, no self-aggrandizing titles, and simple, direct speech. Lincoln is appealed to first with respect to naming: "Nobody would ever speak of Abraham Lincoln as LL.D., or anything of the kind. You could not add a single element of strength to his name by giving him all the titles you could conjure"

(10:11).[2] More importantly, Lincoln shows the great power of the simplest words. As a young man, while at Hampton Institute, Booker had studied the speeches of Lincoln. In turn, he recommended such study to the students at Tuskegee:

> If you will read, as I hope you will, . . . his speeches—especially that great speech, which will live longer than perhaps any other speech ever uttered in the English language, the speech at Gettysburg—read it for its simplicity of language, the shortness of its words and the directness of its sentences, the nobility and inspiring character of it, and you will see in it all and through it all, that Lincoln was great, that he was powerful, because in every movement, in every word, in every utterance, he was a simple, direct, natural human being.[3] (10:11)

The result of these lessons in rhetoric is confirmed by Howells, who says of Washington that "he has lived heroic poetry, and he can, therefore, afford to talk simple prose" (6:194). Greatness is a winnowing force. Howells concludes his review of Washington's life by crediting "the mild might of his adroit, his subtle statesmanship (in the highest sense it is not less than statesmanship)" (6:199). Simple prose is not incompatible with subtle statesmanship. It will not do to underestimate either Honest Abe or Uncle Booker.

THE SUBTLE STATESMANSHIP OF SIMPLE PROSE

Within a month of this Sunday Evening Talk, on February 12, 1909 (the centennial of Lincoln's birth), Washington delivered his most important speech about Lincoln before the Republican Club of New York City.[4] This "Address on Abraham Lincoln" deserves to be ranked with Frederick Douglass's "Oration in Memory of Abraham Lincoln." Moreover, it is a speech that serves as a precursor for two important later African American speeches with a connection to Lincoln: Robert Russa Moton's speech at the dedication of the Lincoln Memorial on the Mall in 1922 and Martin Luther King's "I Have a Dream" speech in front of the Lincoln Memorial in 1963 on the centennial of the Emancipation

Proclamation.[5] The tradition of black leaders reflecting on Lincoln, with a backdrop often provided by various Lincoln monuments and memorabilia, continues today: witness both Jesse Jackson Jr. (a member of the Lincoln Bicentennial Commission) and Barack Obama.[6]

Washington had to decline, with "keen regret," an invitation to speak in Springfield, Illinois, on Lincoln's birthday because of his long-standing New York commitment. In a letter to James R. B. Van Cleave, Washington states, "There is no spot in America where it would have given me greater satisfaction to have spoken my word than in Springfield," and not just because it was "the city that he loved and the city where his body rests," but because of "recent occurrences in this city" (Harlan 1972–89, 10:26–27). What Washington had in mind were the Springfield race riots of the previous summer. Those events (two days of intense rioting followed by weeks of sporadic attacks) were far from the first instance of antiblack mob action in a northern city, but they captured the attention of the press and the nation given both the location and the toll of the violence (two black businessmen lynched, four whites dead, more than forty black homes burned, extensive property damage to black businesses, threats against white establishments that employed or served blacks, and many injured residents).

In his letter to Van Cleave, Washington suggests that the context for these recent provocations is an increase in racial interaction. Population shifts mean that "many white people in the North who are now honoring the memory of Lincoln, are coming into contact with the race that Lincoln freed for the first time"—and behaving in very un-Lincolnian ways. Legend has it that the first black person to settle in Springfield was a Haitian named William Florville, who set up a barber shop in 1831 after benefiting from the assistance and advice of a young Abraham Lincoln in nearby New Salem. By 1908 the black population stood at 2,500 (of a total population of 47,000). In the rioting the first person lynched was a black barber. While the irony of that malicious act was doubtless not premeditated, the rioters were aware of the larger symbolic significance of their action, as some were heard to shout, "Lincoln freed you, now we'll show you where you belong!"[7]

In the wake of the attacks, Washington advises both groups on how they ought to handle themselves. The letter to Van Cleave gives a précis of his message: law-abidingness on all sides. Blacks must remain "patient, law-abiding and self-controlled as Lincoln was."[8] Whites must cease to "inflict injustice upon the Negro because he is a Negro or because he is weak. Every act of injustice, of law breaking, growing out of the presence of the Negro, seeks to pull down the great temple of justice and law and order which he [Lincoln] gave his life to make secure." The letter, obviously intended for publication, was printed in the Springfield *News* on February 13, 1909. It can be read as a reworking of the theme of Lincoln's "Lyceum Address" delivered in Springfield in 1838. That speech too was composed in response to the threat of mob rule; the rash of vigilante actions at that time included the lynching of gamblers, blacks suspected of crimes, and abolitionists. To counter the danger, Lincoln recommended a "political religion" of obedience to and reverence for the law. The solution may be a simple one, but it was no easier to effect in Washington's day than in Lincoln's. Both men summon the sentiment of gratitude to assist them. Lincoln calls for a national oath, sworn upon "the blood of the Revolution," to support the Constitution and laws; Washington presents his call for law-abidingness as fidelity to the memory of "the sainted Lincoln." These are names to conjure with. Lincoln closes the Lyceum Address by reminding his listeners of "our WASHINGTON"; George Washington's namesake (the fatherless Booker had chosen "Washington" as his surname when he first attended school lacking that appurtenance) closes his appeal by invoking the name of Lincoln. Moderation, which is always at risk of seeming tepid or mean, is ennobled by these great examples, and at the same time given firm roots in the soil of civic piety.

For a fuller account of what Washington means by—and expects from—the invocation and imitation of Lincoln, we turn to the "Address on Abraham Lincoln," noting first its careful construction.[9] The speech has twenty-seven paragraphs, which can be divided into four parts (see the outline below). Between the opening and concluding parts (each two paragraphs in length), there are two substantial parts of roughly equal length (thirteen and ten paragraphs respectively), one devoted to the legacy of the Emancipation Proclamation, the other to Lincoln's virtues. Each of these longer parts is in turn divided into four sections. The pattern of these two parts is identical: an introductory paragraph followed by sections addressing first blacks, then including whites, and finally expanding the message to the world at large.

I. Introduction: Slave Prayers (§§1–2)
II. Lincoln's Legacy "as chief executive of the nation" (§§3–15)
  A. "One composite nation" (§3)
  B. Black Citizens (§§4–6)
    1. Physical Freedom (§4)
    2. Educational and Economic Success (§5)
    3. Moral Aspiration (§6)
  C. All Citizens (§§7–11)
    1. Freedom of Soul (§§7–8)
    2. "Twenty-seven millions of Americans of another color" (§§9–11)
  D. The World (§§12–15)
    1. Free and Enlightened (§§12–13)
    2. From Slavery to Service (§§14–15)
III. Lincoln's Virtues "as a man" (§§16–25)
  A. The Risen Lincoln (§16)
  B. Black Imitation of Lincoln: Patience, Courage, and Service (§§17–20)
  C. "Brave and true white men of the South": Courage and Kindness (§§21–23)
  D. Gratitude and Progress (§§24–25)
IV. Conclusion: Freedom Oaths (§§26–27)

Washington's opening is humble. He stresses his slave origins, retelling the story of his mother's prayers for Lincoln and crediting Lincoln with turning "a piece of property" into "a free American citizen." In a curious way, however, Lincoln too is humbled, for he is presented as "the answer to that prayer." He was "an instrument used by Providence." To the extent that appeals to heaven are efficacious, slaves were not passive, nor were they without knowledge. In *Up from Slavery,* when Washington tells of his mother's prayers, he makes the point that slaves, although illiterate, were "accurately and completely informed about the great National questions that were agitating the country" (Washington 1986, 7). Thus the celebration of Lincoln is situated in the context of a dialogue initiated by freedom-seeking slaves with God. Despite Washington's initial claim that he is "not fitted by ancestry or training to be your teacher tonight," by the end of the introduction he has subtly insinuated a claim based on "knowledge of Abraham Lincoln."

The long second part is an explication of a Bible verse "as applied to our martyred President." The verse, Washington's paraphrase of John 11:25, reads, "Though a man die, yet shall he live." Washington finds that Lincoln still lives through his influence on the "complex American civilization"—which is described as "the moving story of men and women of nearly every race and color in their progress from slavery to freedom." Having begun with a national rather than narrowly racial focus, Washington is explicit about his intention to confound expectations: "Perhaps you expect me to confine my words of appreciation to the great boon which, through him, was conferred upon my race." While "undying gratitude" and "eternal fame" do come to Lincoln for freeing the slaves, "this is not the only claim that Lincoln has upon our sense of gratitude and appreciation." Washington aims to enlarge (or perhaps deepen) the ground for both black gratitude and the nation's gratitude.

He begins with his own race (§§4–6), asserting that "Lincoln lives today" in the visible educational and economic advancement of blacks. What he highlights is not the mere fact of freedom but rather the successful employment of freedom. He gives a quick survey of the record so far, citing data on such things as black property holdings and black schools staffed by black teachers. Five years earlier, on Lincoln's birthday, Washington had delivered a speech in Madison Square Garden entirely devoted to setting forth "the condition of my race." Filled with statistics and even polling data, that speech, titled "Negro Education not a Failure," mentioned Lincoln only once, in its opening sentence (Harlan 1972–89, 7:429). Now, however, he is in every paragraph and in some paragraphs, every sentence ("Lincoln" appears 33 times; "he" 25 times, along with other references such as "our martyred President," "our Emancipator," and "the Great Emancipator"). What Washington is tracking in this present speech is not what is seen but what is unseen, for "that which is unseen is eternal." Thus after only a paragraph on the tangible evidence of black accomplishment, Washington moves to its inward cause: "the steady and unalterable determination of ten millions of black citizens." It is through this moral aspiration toward self-perfection that "Lincoln lives."

Washington's analysis hinges on the distinction between inner and outer freedom. We learn, moreover, that this distinction applies "in every corner of the republic." With this phrase, Washington delicately begins to bring his message to bear on whites as well as blacks (§§7–11). He speaks in the first person again, expressing gratitude to Lincoln for "freedom of soul." His description of what it means to "live up in that atmosphere" is extremely interesting. Freedom, whether physical or spiritual, is a demanding activity. The man whose soul is free "refuses to permit sectional or racial hatred to drag down, to warp and narrow his soul." Spiritual freedom is ever vigilant, denying malice entrance. One is reminded of the closing lines of Lincoln's Second Inaugural. Washington took very literally the order of those famous clauses "with malice toward none; with charity for all," believing the first to be the precondition for the second. Washington does not say whether all or most blacks have experienced this highest form of emancipation. In speaking of spiritual freedom, he speaks "as an individual"; the gratitude he expresses to Lincoln is "my gratitude."

Having broached the theme of spiritual freedom, Washington now reveals its application to whites: "We who celebrate this anniversary should not forget that the same pen that gave freedom to four millions of African slaves at the same time struck the shackles from the souls of twenty-seven millions of Americans of another color." The end of slavery didn't just free blacks; it freed whites also. It freed them from participation and complicity in slavery. From this point forward, Washington charitably avoids racial modifiers (indeed, even the first reference to whites deployed the euphemism "Americans of another color"). However, in stating that "wherever people act upon the idea that the disadvantage of one man is the good of another, there slavery exists," the conclusion is inescapable: by enslaving blacks, whites enslaved themselves. (And by continuing to discriminate against blacks, whites prolong the self-inflicted harm on their own souls.) In antebellum America, blacks were physically enslaved, but it was whites who were spiritually enslaved. (Blacks may have been spiritually enslaved also but not inevitably so.) Washington agreed with

Saint Augustine who said that it was better by far to be the slave of a man than the slave of lust, especially the lust for dominion.

Washington, despite the misrepresentations of those who labeled him an "accommodationist," was a statesman of considerable moral audacity. He extends sympathy to whites from a position of moral superiority over them. Although whites sought to oppress blacks, "them it was their poison hurt" (to borrow a famous line from A. E. Housman). At the conclusion of an 1896 speech titled "Democracy and Education," Washington clearly expresses this insight about wrongdoing and its boomerang-like effect:

> The Negro can afford to be wronged; the white man cannot afford to wrong him. Unjust laws or customs that exist in many places regarding the races injure the white man and inconvenience the Negro. No race can wrong another race simply because it has the power to do so without being permanently injured in morals. The Negro can endure the temporary inconvenience, but the injury to the white man is permanent. It is for the white man to save himself from his degradation that I plead. (Brotz 1992, 370)

By abolishing slavery, Lincoln took the first step to release both races from their respective burdens: "He freed men's souls from spiritual bondage; he freed them to mutual helpfulness. Henceforth no man of any race, either in the North or in the South, need feel constrained to fear or hate his brother." With the shackles struck off, it remains to them to exercise their freedom. Given the recent events (and the longer-term advent and extension of disfranchisement, segregation, and discrimination), it is obvious enough that some of those brothers of another color have persisted in their malice. Washington's analysis has made plain that they do so *needlessly,* which is to say, willfully. Washington is precise in specifying what the Emancipation Proclamation achieved. It freed the physical slave and was "the symbol" of a more far-reaching spiritual emancipation. Lincoln "proclaimed the principle" that "the welfare of each is . . . the good of all," but the realization of this principle will depend on how whites and blacks behave. Do they move in the direction the new birth of freedom points them: "to mutual helpfulness"?

The scope of Washington's speech now expands to encompass the whole world (§§12–15). Just as the Gettysburg Address shifts its focal point from "this continent" (on which the new nation was conceived) to "this ground" (here where the battle was fought and the soldiers lie buried) and then finally to "the earth" (which has a stake in the fate of American liberty), so too Washington considers the global reach of the "Lincoln spirit of freedom and fair play." Lincoln himself, of course, in his 1857 speech on the Dred Scott decision, asserted that this transnational power belonged to the Declaration of Independence:

> [It] set up a standard maxim for free society, which should be familiar to all, and revered by all; constantly looked to, constantly labored for, and even though never perfectly attained, constantly approximated, and thereby constantly spreading and deepening its influence, and augmenting the happiness and value of life to all people of all colors everywhere. (Current 1967, 89)

Although Washington does not mention the Declaration in this speech, what he does say—namely, that Lincoln "*reestablished* the dignity of man as man" (original emphasis)—is compatible with Lincoln's view that the aim of his statesmanship was to return Americans to their ancient faith in the equality of all men (and further, that moral and political progress were contingent on that return). While Lincoln did not shy from the word *equality,* Washington never uses it in this speech (indeed, rarely uses it). When speaking of equality, Lincoln was careful to define exactly what he meant by the term, in part to stave off the misrepresentations of his political opponents. Thus he stated that the Declaration "did not mean to say all were equal in color, size, intellect, moral developments, or social capacity" but rather that all were equally entitled to their natural rights. I suspect that after slavery the term *equality* became even more contentious, particularly in the mouth of a black spokesman, inasmuch as it would imply civic equality (not just equality with respect to natural rights).

Lincoln's and Washington's respective strategies might be understood as an instance of rhetorical chiasmus: the white statesman appealed to *natural equality* in order to further the ultimate aim of *physical liberty* for the slaves, whereas the black statesman appealed to *spiritual liberty* in order to further the ultimate and unstated aim of *civic equality.*

In this section Washington adds the crucial ingredient of "enlightenment" to liberty. Because real freedom belongs to the soul, not the body, enlightenment is essential. The worst form of ignorance is a blinding race-consciousness: "One who goes through life with his eyes closed against all that is good in another race is weakened and circumscribed." There is, I think, a tacit acknowledgment in this sentence that the Springfield riots had indeed manifested white hostility toward the best elements in the black population. Although the rioters rampaged first in two impoverished downtown black neighborhoods (with commentators speculating that whites were responding to crime emanating from these areas, which also housed the city's red-light district), very quickly the rioters targeted working-class black neighborhoods and particularly more well-to-do blacks who owned homes and shops. If whites were intent on sabotaging black economic advancement, Washington's well-developed strategy of putting economics before politics might be derailed. And, indeed, the Springfield riots galvanized a more concerted effort to demand political rights; later the same year a conference was held leading to the founding of the NAACP. Although Washington was invited (very much against the wishes of some of the organizers), he declined, preferring to redouble his efforts to enlighten these white delinquents rather than turn to the politics of racial petition and protest. In this "global" section of the speech, Washington presents the lesson in a generalized and thereby more oblique form. So, for instance, he says "*The world* is fast learning" that "*one man* cannot hold *another man* down in the ditch without remaining down in the ditch with him" (emphasis added). Washington couches his argument in terms of an elevated self-interest: surely whites in the United States won't want to sentence themselves to such backwardness.

Part II of the speech concludes with a celebration of Lincoln as a model of spiritual self-emancipation. The Great Emancipator was first a great self-emancipator: "Lincoln was in the truest sense great because he unfettered himself." In breaking the enchainment of race hatred, he "climbed up out of the valley . . . unto the mountain top . . . which enabled him to rate all men at their true worth." Thus spiritual freedom conduces to equality in the sense that each individual is treated as an individual. It is "on such a mountain" that "the American people" should "strive to live." Half a century later, this mountaintop imagery was brilliantly elaborated by King in the "Let freedom ring" peroration of his "I Have a Dream" speech.

FROM GOOD CITIZEN TO GOOD MAN

Washington emphasizes that freedom abolishes slavery but not service. Indeed, in freedom, service to others becomes more possible and more powerful, since enlightened freedom enables individuals to render one another "the highest and most helpful form of service." We have seen that Part II of the speech presents Washington's assessment of the service Lincoln performed in signing the Emancipation Proclamation—how it benefited both blacks and whites; how it benefited both our nation and the world. Part III of the speech delineates a yet higher form of service rendered by Lincoln. It moves, we might say, from Lincoln's statesmanship to his saintliness (or in more Aristotelian terms, from Lincoln as a good citizen/ruler to Lincoln as a good man).

In keeping with his conviction that the personal is infinitely more important than the political, Washington here examines not Lincoln's actions as president but his rise to the presidency: "In fighting his own battle up from obscurity and squalor, he fought the battle of every other individual and race that is down, and so helped to pull up every other human who was down." In lifting oneself, one lifts others. Service to others isn't necessarily a matter of "giving back" or reaching out with a helping hand, as we tend to think today. Instead, individual example is itself uplifting. Lincoln spoke in these same terms of the system of free enterprise: "That some should be rich, shows that others may become rich, and hence is just encouragement to industry and enterprize" (Current 1967, 296). Washington generalizes and spiritualizes the lesson: Lincoln's struggle—"his ambition to do something and be something"—speaks to each of us "as individuals, no matter of what race or nation." The occasional passing references that Washington made to Lincoln (outside of either the Sunday Evening Talks or the Lincoln Day addresses) were almost invariably on this theme of Lincoln's rise "from the humble log cabin to the Presidency of the greatest republic on earth."[10]

Although Lincoln is a universal role model, Washington once again draws out specific messages for specific audiences. He begins as he did in Part II with his own race (§§17–20). The debt of gratitude toward Lincoln is paid by imitating him. The virtues that characterized Lincoln—or at least that subset of his virtues relevant to "my people"—were "patience, long suffering, sincerity, naturalness, dogged determination, and courage." When Washington restates Lincoln's virtues in §20, it is the first and last of these—patience and courage—that Lincoln is said to have "possessed in the highest degree."

Without retracting his earlier statement that the Proclamation "gave freedom to four millions of African slaves," Washington now asserts that "freedom, in the broadest and highest sense, has never been a bequest; it has been a conquest." The struggle, being first internal and second interpersonal, does not require militancy but instead the virtues of Lincoln: patience and courage, by which Washington means "moral courage." There are "new possibilities furnished by Lincoln's Proclamation," but only those individuals will succeed who meet the internal demands of freedom. Washington recaps some of what he had said in the Sunday Evening Talk at Tuskegee just the month before about the value of simplicity. It takes courage "to persistently seek the substance instead of the shadow." Expanding on his conception of service, Washington links it also to courage. A soul sovereign over itself can subordinate self to others. Fittingly, this section culminates in Washington's praise of black teachers, the "brave young souls who are erecting schoolhouses, creating school systems, prolonging school terms," "with little thought of salary, with little thought of personal welfare." Near the beginning of this section Washington had said "As a race we are learning . . . that the best way for us to honor the memory of our Emancipator is by seeking to imitate him." The end of the section reveals that this learning is owing to the guidance and example provided by Tuskegee-trained teachers, with the quite explicit intention "to lift up their fellows." This is courage "of the Lincoln kind."

The coin of Washington's realm is gratitude. He is attempting to establish what might be called a "service economy," driven by debts of gratitude, payable by the tribute of emulation. Praising Lincoln naturally leads to praising others whose gratitude to Lincoln led them to become Lincolnian. Benefactions fructify and propagate like seeds.

Whites too, even Southern whites, can be Lincolnian. The next section (§§21–23) praises the moral courage displayed by "brave and true white men of the South." Washington speaks of those who have "loyally accepted the results of the Civil War"—whatever their previous stance—and who are now working to "complete the emancipation that Lincoln began." He instances two former Confederate commanders, Robert E. Lee and John B. Gordon. In Part II Washington had appealed to white self-interest (with his argument that oppressors damage themselves by their oppressions). Now he appeals to what might be called "white pride." The noblest Southern whites are magnanimous. Washington points out that Lincoln himself "was a Southern man by birth." In the early twentieth century, white supremacists like Thomas Dixon, author of *The Clansman* (1905), were attempting to lay claim to Lincoln as one of their own.[11] Citing Lincoln's prewar disavowal of any intention to establish political and social equality, along with his support for colonization, Dixon sought to make Lincoln "the true prophet of white supremacy" (Peterson 1994, 168). Washington avoids any direct reference to the Jim Crow appropriation of Lincoln. Instead, he counters with a different conception of Anglo-Saxon superiority—one that does not rest on race hatred. Thus he says Lincoln "was one of those white men, of whom there is a large and growing class, who resented the idea that in order to assert and maintain the superiority of the Anglo-Saxon race it was necessary that another group of humanity should be kept in ignorance." This is an extraordinarily deft maneuver. Washington does not want any element of white opinion to feel alienated from Lincoln. If segregationists want to embrace Lincoln, so be it, since that embrace allows Washington to show that white dominance is not incompatible with treating others decently. Lincoln was confident enough in his own strength to be "just and kind." Washington throws down the gauntlet, challenging the proponents of white pride to be chivalrous and to disdain fear. In essence, he accuses the vicious breed of white supremacists of cowardice: "it requires no courage for a strong man to kick a weak one down." Like a jujitsu master, Washington tells whites, if you really had pride, you wouldn't be without pity. Moreover, the pitiless are truly pitiful. Thus, I, Booker T. Washington, pity you.

Recognizing that race pride is not so easily dismantled, Washington appeals to race pride of a better sort to vanquish the nastier versions of race pride and perhaps to lay the groundwork for the disappearance of race pride. Washington does what he can to convince white Americans that their proper pride lies in dedication to "the Lincoln spirit of freedom and fair play."

The final section of Part III (§§24–25) summarizes Washington's this-worldly answer to the biblically inspired question with which he began: "If a man die, shall he live?" According to Washington, "Lincoln lives today" because he attained the peak of virtue. The amalgam of moral courage and patience, to which Washington now adds "foresight," enabled Lincoln "to suffer in silence, to be misunderstood, to be abused, to refuse to revile when reviled." Washington here accounts for Lincoln's persistence in the face of a very large measure of public incomprehension and ingratitude. This section might be read as a gloss on the closing lines of Lincoln's Cooper Union address: "Let us have faith that right makes might, and in that faith, let us, to the end, dare to do our duty as we understand it." Once again, there is a startling element of moral reproof in what Washington is willing to say to white Americans. Citizens are inclined to believe that the outpourings of gratitude, occasioned by the centennial of Lincoln's birth, honor not only Lincoln but also themselves in a certain sense. There is an element of self-satisfaction in linking oneself and one's nation to past greatness. Washington works against this national complacency. He reminds the celebrants that they can receive credit only for hindsight and not, as with Lincoln, for foresight. Here is how Washington drops his hint that a dose of democratic contrition should figure in our remembrance of Lincoln:

> He knew, too, that at some time in the distant future our nation would repent of the folly of cursing our public servants while they live and blessing them only when they die. In this connection I cannot refrain from suggesting the question to the millions of voices raised today in his praise: "Why did you not say it yesterday?" Yesterday, when one word of

approval and gratitude would have meant so much to him in strengthening his hand and heart.

The statesman acted for the good of all, North and South. But he had to proceed without gratitude. One can't help but hear Washington's own lament. He too was a public servant who was much abused and whose aims and policies were misrepresented (often by those whom Washington called, with some derision, "The Intellectuals"—a group of northern black leaders that included W. E. B. DuBois). While Washington believed that the virtues of patience and courage may be found even in ordinary men, "foresight" is rare, and those blessed with it need perhaps a double share of patience and courage for they will have to press forward alone. Washington points to the role that public support could play in strengthening the democratic statesman's "hand and heart." Note he exempts the "head" from this (a significant omission given that Washington was well known for his definition of education as involving the "head, hand, and heart"). The statesman's "head"—his knowledge of right and his foresight—is an independent capacity. The attitude of the public may well affect his efficacy—restricting what his hands can achieve—but it will not alter his principles.

The final paragraph of Part III (§25) looks ahead. Because of Lincoln's example (especially now that the audience has been properly chastened by the reminder of its own past failures), "faith in the future" is strengthened. The recollection of Lincoln sustains the faith in moral progress. Despite the backsliding that appears "for a little season," righteousness will prevail—not only among us, but throughout the world.

The conclusion of the speech (§§26–27) proposes a dramatic act in the present moment: a mutual oath-taking by whites and blacks that will bridge past and future. Declaring whites and blacks "brothers all," Washington asks ("may I not ask") that his audience ("the worthy representatives of seventy millions of white Americans") join with black Americans (all "ten millions") and "swear eternal fealty to the memory and the traditions of the sainted Lincoln." Washington's formulation of the oath indicates a key difference between blacks and whites. His invitation highlights the distance between these "worthy representatives" of white America (who may be inclined to extend themselves "heart and hand" across the color line) and the unworthy sort. Blacks are, on the whole, frankly better, for they "have never lifted their voices or hands except in defense of their country's honor and their country's flag." The same cannot be said of whites. Perhaps that is why he repeats the invitation with a telling modification: "I repeat, may we not join with your race." Although both versions are formulated with a deferential negative ("may I not ask that you join" and "may we not join"), they are not precisely reciprocal. In the first formulation he had asked "worthy" whites to join with blacks; in the second, although still asking something of whites (acceptance rather than outreach), the initiative shifts to blacks. After all, the condescension, if there is any among brothers, would be on the black side. They, in their loyalty, are willing to reach out to the whole white world, even though so many white Americans have so often traduced the nation's founding principles. If kept, this oath of brotherhood sworn on the blood of Lincoln could heal both the sectional and racial divides, thereby ensuring that Lincoln "shall not have lived and died in vain." This is what we must "here highly resolve."

Washington's language deliberately echoes the Gettysburg Address, although the idea of a sacred oath as a political instrument for securing our national freedom is more reminiscent of the Lyceum Address. Despite these resonances and parallels, Washington's Address has a different overall arc than either the Lyceum or Gettysburg Addresses, both of which begin with praise of the Founding Fathers who bequeathed to us "a political edifice of liberty" (as the Lyceum Address puts it) or "brought forth . . . a new nation, conceived in Liberty" (as the Gettysburg Address has it). Washington, however, did not begin either his speech or his life in that way. He takes his initial conception from slavery: "I was born a slave." He moves from a slave's prayers to a free man's promises.

In the final paragraph, Washington offers his own pledge on behalf of his race. I believe he intends this pledge to be kept regardless of the success or failure of the mutual black/white justice oath. This pledge transcends politics, although it is not without political ramifications:

> And, finally, gathering inspiration and encouragement from this hour and Lincoln's life, I pledge to you and to the nation that my race, in so

> far as I can speak for it, which in the past, whether in ignorance or intelligence, whether in slavery or in freedom, has always been true to the Stars and Stripes and to the highest and best interests of this country, will strive to so deport itself that it shall reflect nothing but the highest credit upon the whole people in the North and in the South.

Washington does not call for blacks to behave in ways that will be (as the saying once went) "a credit to their race." His aspiration is much higher and more redemptive. What he pledges is that his race will be a credit to America. Blacks have it within their power to manifest the highest possibilities of citizenship and humanity. That power, being spiritual, does not depend on whites making good on their oath to "justice, good will, and peace." Washington acknowledges through the qualifying phrase "in so far as I can speak for [my race]" that he cannot in fact guarantee black deportment. Thus the firmest pledge here is for himself alone. Even if either whites or blacks collectively fail in their respective pledges, the individual possibility of abiding with Lincoln would remain. Booker T. Washington, through times of great trouble in American race relations, did remain true to Lincoln, "for he knew that, if he was right, the ridicule of today would be the applause of tomorrow." The time will come when Booker T. Washington will be generally acknowledged as an American statesman and secular saint.

NOTES

1. The phrase is from Frederick Douglass's "Oration in Memory of Abraham Lincoln." In that speech Douglass began by asserting that Lincoln, as a white man, was not "either our man or our model." Over the course of the speech, Douglass considerably revised that assessment. For interpretations of the Douglass speech, see Schaub n.d. See also Morel 2003, 2005; Myers 2010.

2. Lincoln is not appealed to as a model for proper dress. Far from overdressing, he may rather have erred on the side of underdressing. There are stories of Lincoln greeting visitors at his home in Springfield with bare feet, and his suits were notoriously ill fitting.

3. Frederick Douglass always spoke of Lincoln's Second Inaugural as his greatest speech. This difference in their judgments might reveal interesting differences in their temperaments and teachings.

4. Ten years earlier Washington had given another Lincoln birthday address, "An Abraham Lincoln Memorial Address in Philadelphia" (Harlan 1972–89, 5:32–38). Some of its themes are similar.

5. Moton was Washington's successor at Tuskegee Institute.

6. See Jackson's May 9, 2009, Lincoln College commencement address and his September 3, 2008, column, "The Power of Forgiveness and Reconciliation," and his December 3, 2007, column, "Jesse Jr. to Jesse Sr.: You're wrong on Obama, dad." Obama announced his candidacy for the presidency in Springfield and took the oath of office on the Lincoln Bible (now known as the Lincoln-Obama Bible). Obama's 2005 essay in *Time* magazine, "What I See in Lincoln's Eyes," is his most sustained reflection on the meaning of Abraham Lincoln.

7. Available at http://sangamon.ilgenweb.net/1881/florville.htm (last accessed May 2011).

8. Washington essentially repeats the kernel of the lesson about simplicity from the Sunday Evening Talk, which was delivered during the time he was preparing the "Address on Lincoln."

9. Since my exposition follows the order of the speech paragraph by paragraph, I will not provide page citations beyond this first mention: Harlan 1972–89, 10:33–39.

10. See Letter to the Editor of the Charleston *West Virginia* (Harlan 1972–89, 2:73). See also "An Interview in the Chicago *Inter Ocean*," where Washington speaks of the need for black role models for black youth (4:355).

11. Dixon's novel was the inspiration for the D.W. Griffith film *The Birth of a Nation* (1915), which led to the second founding of the Ku Klux Klan.

REFERENCES

Brotz, Howard, ed. 1992. *African-American Social and Political Thought, 1850–1920.* New Brunswick, NJ: Transaction.

Current, Richard N., ed. 1967. *The Political Thought of Abraham Lincoln.* New York: Macmillan.

Harlan, Louis R., ed., with various coeditors. 1972–89. *The Booker T. Washington Papers.* 14 vols. Urbana: University of Illinois Press.

Morel, Lucas E. 2003. "America's First Black President? Lincoln's Legacy of Political Transcendence." In *Lincoln Reshapes the Presidency,* ed. Charles M. Hubbard, 120–52. Macon, GA: Mercer University Press.

———. 2005. "Frederick Douglass's Emancipation of Abraham Lincoln." Unpublished manuscript.

Myers, Peter C. 2010. "'A Good Work for Our Race To-Day': Interests, Virtues, and the Achievement of Justice in Frederick Douglass' Freedmen's Monument Speech." *American Political Science Review* 104, no. 2 (May): 209–25.

Norrell, Robert J. 2009. *Up from History: The Life of Booker T. Washington.* Cambridge, MA: Harvard University Press.

Peterson, Merrill D. 1994. *Lincoln in American Memory.* New York: Oxford University Press.

Schaub, Diana. n.d. "Learning to Love Lincoln: Frederick Douglass's Journey from Grievance to Gratitude." Unpublished manuscript.

Washington, Booker T. 1986. *Up from Slavery.* New York: Viking Penguin.

Chapter Sixteen

Theodore Roosevelt on Statesmanship and Constitutionalism

KIRK EMMERT

Even before he embarked on his political career, and long before he described the presidency as a bully pulpit, Theodore Roosevelt became an educator of the American people. Most politicians might be said to be educators, more or less, as they seek to persuade by means of their political and largely partisan advocacy, written or spoken. But in his prolific writings—histories, essays, political biographies—Roosevelt provides a political education that is broader, less direct, and more disinterested than is found in common political advocacy. Similarly, Roosevelt's efforts at political education should be distinguished from political propaganda or indoctrination: His account of American history and its leaders is not meant to promote a specific political agenda; rather, his books promote the political understanding and moral character that, he argues, are the necessary foundation of a healthy constitutional democracy.

This chapter focuses on Roosevelt's political education as found in his biographies of Oliver Cromwell, Thomas Hart Benton, and Gouverneur Morris. The literary form historical biography facilitated the conveying of this political teaching. Writing on historical leaders enabled Roosevelt to illustrate with actual historical individuals and events his general point that the American Constitution was the outgrowth of several centuries of progressive developments in England and France. Further, the need to treat his biographical subjects in their historical contexts allowed Roosevelt to make general reflections more accessible to a wider readership by tying them to specific historical events, by comparing, for example, Cromwell's action in 1648 to the American and French Revolutions, as well to the statesmanship of Washington and Lincoln. Similarly, the biographical form expanded the audience for Roosevelt's broader reflections by allowing them to emerge from the engaging, dramatic personal lives of the subjects of his biographies. Simultaneously, it facilitated addressing more thoughtful citizens by presenting specific opportunities to illustrate the complex nature of statesmanship and its problematic existence in a popular government. To explore this subject Roosevelt needed to illuminate the moral and intellectual excellence and failings of the leaders he discusses, a matter more properly explored and understood by consideration of individual statesmen embedded in their political context, as against a more ahistorical, theoretical account. Biography was the proper or natural way to get at the truth of his subject and at the same time educate American citizens about the kind of leaders—what qualities of character, intellect, judgment, and political outlook—they should admire and promote.

Repeatedly, Roosevelt stresses the moral qualities of the leaders he discusses, in particular, their courage, moderation, and public-spiritedness. He presents these virtues as the indispensable foundation of sound leadership and thus as signposts for a citizen's assessment of present and aspiring statesmen. More thoughtful readers are also invited to consider the problematic aspects of these virtues and their relation to qualities of mind and political judgment.

Roosevelt's biographies present courage as indispensable to sound political leadership, to say nothing of statesmanship. He relates the legendary battlefield courage of Cromwell and his Ironsides, but the biographies stress personal and political, not military, courage. Benton was a "faithful friend and a bitter foe"; his "courage was proof against all fear, and he shrank from no contest, personal or political" (Roosevelt 1926, 7:232–33).[1] He was "utterly fearless" and his unyielding "tenacity, . . . unflinching will and stern strength of character" enabled him "to stand out against any section of the country, even his own, if it was wrong" (7:232, 145, 70). Roosevelt recounts Morris's "gallant and fearless" conduct and "generous daring" as ambassador to France during the French Revolution (7:469, 237). Reflecting this character and outlook, Morris did not have "the least regard" for the "mere amiability and good intentions" of Louis XVI "when unaccompanied by any of the ruder, manlier virtues. . . . He very soon began to despise him for his weakness." Earlier, Morris had been one of the "men of 1787" whom Roosevelt describes as "great men"; "but it was less the greatness of mere genius," he continues, "than that springing from the union of strong, virile qualities with steadfast devotion to a high ideal" (7:376, 325).

Courage is admirable in itself—Roosevelt was impressed by the reckless "wild love of fighting for fighting's sake" of the Highland Scots (10:245)—but courage should be understood primarily as a means, not as an end in itself: The most admirable courage serves sound military and political purposes. Benton, whom Roosevelt most frequently praises for his tenacious courage, exemplifies its problematic nature. As an ardent Jacksonian, Benton made "irrelevant and abusive" attacks on the "'money power'" and gave dogmatic "obedience to the spirit of Democracy" (10:145, 179). But the more courageously he fought for these objects, the greater the potential damage to the nation. Thus Roosevelt reserved his highest praise for Benton's tenacity when he fought for purposes Roosevelt strongly supported, purposes such as defense of the Union, western expansion, and opposition to the expansion of slavery. Benton's "tenacity and his pertinacious refusal to abandon any contest no matter what the odds were against him, and no matter how often he had to return to the charge, formed two of his most invaluable qualities, and when called into play on behalf of such an object as the preservation of the Union, cannot receive too high praise at our hands, for they did the country services so great and lasting that they should never be forgotten" (7:145). Benton was at this best when important national purposes were most endangered: "He always rose to meet a really great emergency, and his services to the nation rose steadily in importance to the very close of his life," when he lost his Senate seat due to his firm defense of the Union (7:217). No statesmanship without courage, but courage is subordinate to the political purposes it serves.

Further, since courage is, Roosevelt suggests, frequently associated with excessive self-assertion and aggressiveness, it must often be restrained or moderated. To be militarily effective, courage must be disciplined: The wild courage of the Highlanders was "formidable" in a battle, but it could not sustain an extended military "campaign" (10:245). The "gallant and fearless" Morris needed, Roosevelt observed, "more steadiness and self-control." He had a "proud, almost hasty temper, and was quick to resent an insult." Similarly, Roosevelt suggested that Benton's "fearless, aggressive courage" inclined him to be a "faithful friend and a bitter foe" who was "rather quarrelsome and revengeful in character" (7:409, 145, 232, 230). In time, however, Morris advocated and displayed more restraint: In revolutionary Paris he "soon learned to combine courage and caution"; and when speaking with republican revolutionaries in Paris, Morris reported that he "preach[ed] above all moderation, not only in the object, but also in the pursuit of it" (7:402, 353). Roosevelt makes this broader case for political moderation directly by comparing the Puritan Revolution of 1648 to the Glorious Revolution of 1688. The "men of the second Revolution," he contends, "had learned the moderation which the men of the first had lacked. . . . The men of 1688 were, as a whole, actuated by far less lofty motives than the men of 1648; but they possess the inestimable advantages of common sense, of moderation, of readiness to accept compromises. They made no attempt to realize the reign of the saints upon the earth; and therefore they were able to work a permanent betterment in mundane affairs, and to avoid provoking a violent reaction" (10:333).

The valuable courage of the political leader tends to become too aggressive and imperious when not restrained and understood as instrumental. Possessing or cultivating moderation enables statesmen to avoid these excesses. They cannot, however, be unfailingly moderate. In his discussions in the Benton biography of the annexation of Texas and of the northern border disputes with Great Britain, Roosevelt also teaches that statesmen should on occasion support and employ aggressive spiritedness in domestic politics and, more robustly, in foreign relations. Thus in the political struggles over annexation of Texas as a slave state, "the iron Westerner['s] . . . stern, defiant, almost prophetic warning" of threats to the Union "did more to help the Union cause than volumes of elaborate constitutional argument" (7:195). Benton personified the assertive spiritedness which fueled western expansion. For Roosevelt, Benton's support of the policy of manifest destiny ranked second only to his support of the Union in his service to the nation. At "the root of the doctrine of 'manifest destiny'" was the "belligerent, or more properly speaking, piratical way of looking at neighboring territory." The westerners had "very little more idea of there being any right or wrong in the matter than so many Norse Vikings might have felt" (7:13, 36–37). Roosevelt contrasts "the domineering, masterful spirit" of the frontiersmen with the decline in the "militant spirit" of the northeasterners. He observes that the "richer and more educated classes of the Northeast . . . have always been more cautious and timid . . . and have never felt much of the spirit which made the West stretch out impatiently for new lands" (7:114, 37, 172). Benton lived in "the heroic age of the Southwest," but as in "every other heroic age," Roosevelt acknowledges, "there were plenty of failings, vices and weaknesses." The Texans were "brave, . . . warlike, resolute, and enterprising, . . . with the pride of strength and self-confidence. On the other hand they showed again and again the barbaric vices of boastfulness, ignorance, and cruelty; and they were utterly careless of the rights of others, looking upon the possessions of all weaker races as simply their natural prey." Yet, despite his awareness of the vices and "raw, crude immaturity" associated with this militant spirit, Roosevelt observes that the decline of this spirit in the Northeast was "sincerely to be regretted" (7:118, 115, 117, 37, 172).

Individual statesmen, and the nations they lead, need to be courageous, but why does Roosevelt move beyond his defense of restrained courage to endorse the aggressive spiritedness of Benton and the westerners, particularly when he is aware that it is semibarbaric? In part, he feared that in his own time, as commerce, wealth, and education migrated westward, the "cautious and timid" ethos of the easterners of Benton's time was spreading throughout the country. The emphasis on courage in the Benton and Morris biographies and on aggressive spiritedness in his account of Benton reflect Roosevelt's early efforts—continued in subsequent years in his accounts of his adventures in the West and in his dramatization of the Rough Riders—to sustain and reawaken spiritedness in the American soul. More fundamentally, robust spiritedness was so important for him because of his view of how individuals and nations act when unrestrained by domestic law or clear claims of right and because of his aspiration for America.

Roosevelt's accounts of boundary disputes with Mexico in the south and Great Britain in the north suggest that military strength and national assertiveness, not moral principle, usually decide international disputes. Nations have

> at times proved themselves capable of acting with great disinterestedness and generosity toward other peoples; but such conduct is not very common at the best, and although it often may be desirable, it certainly is not always so. If the matter in dispute is of great importance, and if there is a doubt as to which side is right, then the strongest party to the controversy is pretty sure to give itself the benefit of that doubt; and international morality will have to take tremendous strides in advance before this ceases to be the case. (7:168–69)

These general principles were reflected in the border disputes Roosevelt discusses. Due to poor mapping in the West, "ownership . . . could with great difficulty be decided on grounds of absolute and abstract right," with the result that the "comparative might of the different nations, and not the comparative righteousness of their several causes, was the determining factor in the settlement" (7:167). Disputes between nations are often decided not by considerations of justice but by superior might. Statesmen understand that an assertive foreign policy is required to deal with the world as it is, not as they might like it to be. But Roosevelt goes one step further: Adapting successfully to the world as it is should be understood as an energizing opportunity, not a regretful, perhaps even degrading necessity. Benton's "intense Americanism, and his pride and confidence in his country and in her unlimited capacity for growth of every sort" led him aggressively to promote a nation of sufficient size to accommodate and reflect that capacity. "More clearly than almost any other statesman," Roosevelt observes, Benton "beheld the grandeur of the nation loom up, vast and shadowy, through the advancing years." His "violent and aggressive patriotism" was "very repugnant to the quiet, peaceable, [and] order-loving." Still, "the arrogant attitude he assumed was more than justified by the destiny of the great Republic." And, Roosevelt continues, "it would have been well for all America if we had insisted even more than we did upon extension northward of our boundaries" (7:34, 170).

Roosevelt's praise of Benton for his statesmanlike support of the Union and of national expansion unites in his endorsement of Benton's aspiration for national grandeur. This endorsement appears, however, to be in tension with, if not to contradict, his close association of statesmanship with moderation. As an educator his teaching might appear, therefore, to be both confusing and harmful. Perhaps the tension between assertive courage and moderation cannot be overcome, but it is reduced by Roosevelt's explicit effort to limit his support for national expansion to the unique historical circumstances present in mid-nineteenth-century America: no clear individual or national titles to a vast expanse of largely unpopulated or unsettled land. "Of course no one," he observed, "would wish to see . . . settled communities, now added to our domain by force; we want no unwilling citizens to enter our Union; the time to have taken the lands was before settlers came into them." America has been "wiser" than European nations that have warred over "possession of thickly settled districts which, if conquered, will for centuries remain alien and hostile to the conquerors." We Americans, in contrast, "have seized the waste solitudes that lay near us, the limitless forests and never-ending plains[,] . . . and have thrust our own sons into them to take possession," with the result that "we see the conquered land teeming with a people that is one with ourselves" (7:171).

Roosevelt teaches that robust national expansion was necessary, morally defensible, and politically beneficial; Americans should be grateful for aggressively courageous leaders such as Benton who supported manifest destiny. The time for continental expansion has passed but not, however, the need for the assertive courage that supported it. Since military power rather than moral principle is usually the decisive factor in the relation of nations, American statesmen must be prepared to respond courageously to internal and external dangers, and to do this they need to find support for their responses in the character of the American people. Occasionally they will need to draw on the aggressive courage displayed by Benton; and at all times they need sufficient personal courage so that their own judgment is not undermined by timidity. But, unlike Benton, they should be sufficiently disciplined and moderate so that they can actually choose whether to be more assertive or restrained. Above all, they need the robust common sense to determine which approach to follow.

Politics is a practical endeavor. Statesmen should be judged by whether they actually better "mundane affairs." To accomplish this, Roosevelt stresses, they must possess good judgment or common sense. Elizabeth I "possessed that shrewd good sense which, if not the noblest, is perhaps on the whole the most useful of qualities in the actual workaday world" (10:333, 193). Cromwell was saved from some of the zealotry and the "worst eccentricities" of his fellow Puritans "by his hard common sense." A leader can do "nothing of permanence," Roosevelt observes, "save by joining his zeal to sound judgment, moderation, and the desire to accomplish practical results" (10:217, 306). In the biographies Roosevelt presents Morris, particularly during his ambassadorship in revolutionary Paris, as an exemplar of common sense. As a result of both "natural ability" and previous "training," Morris had "wonderful insight into the motives and characters" of French revolutionary leaders; he had a "capacity for striking straight at the root of things." Roosevelt quotes extensively from Morris's letters from Paris to President Washington and praised him for his "incisive truthfulness" and "clear and sound judgments of those [revolutionary] years" (7:237, 418, 301, 354).

The common sense required to make good judgments rests on a moral foundation—courage and moderation especially—but it is largely an intellectual capacity, a kind of knowing. Morris's capacity for truthful observation and insight reflected a form of rationality—a kind of rational intuition—but Morris himself observed that the statesman must also possess a more complete rationality: "The gush of sentiment will not," he noted, "alter the nature of things, and the business of the statesman is more to reason than to feel." The mercurial Mirabeau was "'venal, shameless,'" often dominated by "'the whim of the moment.'" Yet when pushed by a "'prevailing impulse,'" he could also be "'greatly virtuous . . . but never truly virtuous, because never under the steady control of reason, nor the firm authority of principle.'" In revolutionary Paris, Morris witnessed the failure of this reason to control "extreme licentiousness." His letters indicate "his abiding distrust and fear of the French character, as it was at that time, volatile, debauched, ferocious, and incapable of self-restraint" (7:312, 380, 357).

Morris also experienced the failure of reason, in its less repressive, more positive form of common sense, to control the moral and religious zealotry that resides at the opposite extreme of the moral spectrum from licentiousness. In the Cromwell biography Roosevelt notes that the earnest Puritans endeavored "to shape the whole course of individual existence in accordance with the . . . law of perfect righteousness." Even Cromwell's "hard common sense" was overwhelmed on occasion by his religious zealotry. In their indifference to results and impatience of limitations, the Puritan Barebones Parliament adopted a high moral posture toward politics similar to that of the Abolitionists. The Puritans' proposals were "excellent in point of moral purpose, just as it would have been absolutely right, from the abstract ethical standpoint if the Constitution of 1789, or the republican Convention of 1860, had declared the abolition of slavery in all the states." But the "abstract ethical standpoint" should not be, Roosevelt suggests, the standard of political right or justice: If the Abolitionists had carried the day, the Constitution would not have been ratified, Lincoln would not have been elected, and slavery would have been perpetuated. As for the Puritans, Roosevelt contrasts efforts "to realize the reign of the saints upon earth" with the politics of the leaders of the Glorious Revolution (1688) who were "activated by far less lofty motives." The statesmen of 1688, however, "possessed the inestimable advantages of common sense, of moderation, of readiness to accept compromises." As a result, unlike the Puritans, "they were able to work a permanent betterment in mundane affairs, and to avoid provoking a violent reaction" (10:215, 307, 333).

Commonsense reasoning is threatened by ungovernable passions and by moral and religious righteousness, but perhaps the most dangerous threat, the Morris biography suggests, comes from an extreme form of reason itself: abstract, speculative reason. Advocates of religious or moral excesses tend to seek out political ideas or rationalizations to justify their positions. Political views regarding the good political order, although often difficult to distinguish from these derivative justifications, can also spring directly from abstract reasoning. "The men who live in the world are very different," Morris wrote from Paris to President Washington, "from those who dwell in the heads of philosophers. . . . The systems taken out of books are fit for nothing but to be put back into books again." The philosophers and the legislators who absorbed their views had, Morris continued, "all those romantic ideas of government, which, happily for America, we were cured of before it was too late" (7:356). The "wisdom" derived from political experience cured Morris of any romantic, speculative ideas: "Educated in the intensely practical school of American political life, . . . [he had] utter contempt for the wordy futility and wild theories of the French legislators," Roosevelt writes. Explicitly agreeing with Morris, he observes that Morris "knew that a pure theorist may often do as much damage to a country as the most corrupt traitor; and very properly considered that in politics the fool is quite as obnoxious as the knave" (7:356, 359, 355–56). Political theory abstracted from political experience is the enemy of common sense, the necessary foundation of the statesman's sound political judgments. But might the school of political experience teach that while common sense is indispensable, it is not sufficient, that the statesman needs some kind of political wisdom or more general knowledge to supplement common sense?

Roosevelt acknowledges the need for such a rational understanding beyond common sense in his criticism of Cromwell for his failure to constitutionalize his rule: More "interested in righting specific cases of oppression than in advancing the great principles of constitutional government," Cromwell failed to understand that constitutional government "alone make[s] possible that orderly liberty which is the bar to . . . individual acts of wrong-doing." Similar to "many a so-called 'practical' man," Cromwell "would have done better work if he had followed a more clearly defined theory; for though the practical man is better than the mere theorist, he cannot do the highest work unless he is a theorist also." Cromwell was "no theorist; in fact, he was altogether too little of one. . . . He failed to see that questions of form—that is, of law—in securing liberty might be themselves essential" (10:215, 254). Roosevelt admired Cromwell's common sense and shared his wariness of visionary schemes, but he stresses that his singular focus on "concrete acts" and immediate problems reflected the mind of an "administrator rather than a constructive statesman" because of his "inability to appreciate the necessity of theories to a practical man who wishes to do good work" (10:307, 309). Statesmen wed common sense to reflection or practical "theories" regarding political forms, the most important of which is the rule of law supported by a fundamental law or constitution. Roosevelt criticizes Cromwell's failure to constitutionalize his personal rule by persevering with Parliament to seek agreement on a new constitution. His growing "love of power," his unquestioning "righteousness," and his "acquired . . . dictatorial habits of mind" all contributed to this failure, but these might have been retarded or overcome had Cromwell reflected on, and subsequently understood, the importance of constitutional forms to the support and restraint of personal rule. Roosevelt brings home the lesson of Cromwell's failure by contrasting it with the deliberate commitments of Presidents Washington and Lincoln to constitutional rule, as seen in Washington's forbearance in his dealings with the Continental Congress and Lincoln's commitment to following the Constitution by allowing the election of 1864 to occur. When Cromwell rejected constitutional rule, he "lost the right to stand with men like Washington and Lincoln" (10:315–16).

If Cromwell's failure as a founder teaches that statesmen need to be reflective about political forms, Benton's counterexample shows that academic learning is no substitute for a lack of sound political reflection or, incidentally, for "a total lack of the sense of humor." A pompous man of "much erudition," Benton "took a most justifiable pride in his wide reading and especially in his full acquaintance with history, both ancient and modern." He was a "learned man," but his studies did not issue in political wisdom; rather, they were somewhat pedantically employed to defend political positions, both sound and mistaken in Roosevelt's view, which he adopted and rigidly adhered to without sufficient reflection (7:146, 131). In Morris, however, Roosevelt found, particularly during his stay in Paris, someone whose reflections on his political experiences, supplemented by study, issued in the kind of political knowledge most useful to statesmen: constitutional understanding in the broader sense. Such knowledge is required especially when statesmen address significant constitutional changes or the founding of a new constitution, the situation Morris observed in Paris. To arrive, in these demanding situations, at sound, commonsense judgments, statesmen must accurately discern the particular circumstances that confront them, the most important being the character and abilities of the people to be governed. In this regard, Roosevelt observes that Morris stood "alone . . . in his time" as a "penetrating observer and recorder of contemporary events." Because statesmen necessarily govern in particular circumstances, they need a sharp, accurate eye for those circumstances, a "keen . . . intellectual vision," in order to make sound political judgments and undertake prudent actions (7:346–47). Equally important, to guide their judgments and actions they require some broader political principles grounded in an understanding of the different forms of constitutions and in what is required to support a particular form.

Roosevelt presents Morris as an exemplar of this political knowledge. An "eminently practical—that is, useful—statesman," Morris thought "that each people must have a government suited to their own individual character, and to the stage of political and social development it had reached. He realized that a nation must be governed according to the actual needs and capacities of its citizens, not according to any abstract theory or seeming ideal principles." Thus, disagreeing with the Lafayettes, Morris predicted that the "popular party was going straight to destruction, . . . for their views respecting the nation were totally inconsistent with the materials of which it was composed" (7:322, 353). He saw that the French were "not fitted to use liberty aright" because "'republican virtues were not of Gallic growth.'" Both Morris and Washington "called for moderation among the friends of republican freedom" in France, since liberty "could only be gained and kept by self-restraint" (7:347, 420, 360). But moderation and the other republican virtues do not grow up overnight; they are the product of habituation and prior education. A "previous education is necessary," Morris wrote, "to fit a people for a republic, as for any other form of government." Concurring with Morris, Roosevelt observes that there "can be no absolute answer" to the question of how to choose the "best" men to rule: "No mode will invariably give the best result. . . . Where the people are enlightened and moral they are the ones themselves to choose their rulers, . . . but if they are corrupt and degraded, they are unfit for republicanism." Based on his knowledge of the available "materials" and of the forms of government, Roosevelt thought that the statesman should advocate the best form of government that a people is capable of supporting, erring, if he must, on the side of adapting to their capacities. Thus he observes that "sounder and truer maxims never were uttered" than when Morris noted that "'every kind of government was liable to evil; that the best was that which had fewest faults; that the excellence even of that best depended more on its fitness for the nation where it was established than on intrinsic perfection'" (7:349–50, 360, 457).

Roosevelt's account of statesmanship has general application—all statesmen must be courageous and have good judgment—but his discussion is also constitution- or regime-specific. The focus is on statesmanship in a constitutional context and, more specifically, informed by the American Constitution. Statesmen should be guided by the purpose of the constitutional order in which they govern, assuming a minimally decent purpose. The "distinguishing feature" of the American Constitution is "the freedom of the individual" (7:80), a guiding purpose unquestioned by Morris, Benton, or Roosevelt himself, and repeatedly advocated, if finally abandoned, by Cromwell. But if Roosevelt's own presentation in the biographies suggests that the statesman does not question the purpose of his constitution, it also makes clear that American statesmen must think about the nature of freedom, its preconditions and necessary supports.

Statesmen understand that like other good political purposes liberty can become destructive when carried to an extreme and when unrestrained tends in that direction. The aggressive courage of the westerners of Benton's time, which Roosevelt admired, also had a darker side: "their lawless and arrogant freedom" stemming from "their lack of self-restraint" and their giving "free rein to their passions." The growing "separatist feeling" in the South and West, which Roosevelt viewed as a "dangerous failing and weakness," was a "perversion and distortion of the defiant and self-reliant independence of spirit" which is "one of the chief" American "virtues" (7:15, 12, 33). Similarly, the "very follies" of the citizens of postrevolutionary America, particularly their resistance to "being ruled, . . . sprang from their virtues, from their inborn love of freedom, and their impatience of the control of outsiders." Beyond these historical examples, Roosevelt denounced more intellectualized versions of uncivil liberty held by "extreme doctrinaires, who are fiercest in declaiming in favor of freedom" and who are, "in reality, its worst foes, far more dangerous than any absolute monarch ever can be" to a free people, for "when liberty becomes license, some form of one-man power is not far distant" (7:291, 322).

Even if freedom is the highest political good under a liberal, democratic constitution, it is still one of several important goods, most of which are also preconditions for personal and civic freedom. The men of the revolution were "taught . . . only by the grinding logic of an imperial necessity, that it was no surrender of their freedom to submit to rulers chosen by themselves, through whom alone that freedom could be won." They had to learn the "right"—their rights—"could be enforced only by might" and that "union was to the full as important as liberty, because it was the prerequisite condition for the establishment and preservation of liberty" (7:291). Morris, "like every other patriot and statesman," opposed the "extreme particularistic bent" of "ultra States'-rights men or separatists" because he understood that government should be "strong and responsible as well as free" (7:291, 321–22). And free government rests on the opinions and character of the citizenry. Republican citizens need to possess self-restraint to enable them to control their excesses, such as that for liberty, and to be capable of acting "in concert with their fellows." And they must have commonsense opinions like the "shrewd, thrifty, independent" New Englanders who were "fully aware to the fact that honesty and order are the prerequisites of liberty." America has "succeeded as no other people ever has," Roosevelt observes, because of "that common sense which has enabled us to preserve the largest possible individual freedom, while showing an equally remarkable capacity for combination on the other" (7:12, 444, 323). Roosevelt's account of the citizen opinion and character that sustained the free American republic suggests that a republican statesman needs to draw on, and at the same time reconcile, the more sober, orderly, combining character of the New Englanders with the more unruly, assertive spiritedness of the westerners, favoring one or the other as needed.

The American Constitution is dedicated to liberty and grounded in majority rule. "To Americans of today," Roosevelt observes, "the rule of the majority seems part of the natural order of things," just as earlier Englishmen considered "hereditary kingship . . . the only natural government" (10:202). In fact, however, this is not a matter of "divine or natural law . . . at all; how large a portion of the population should be trusted with control of government is a question of expediency merely," as is the question of the breadth of the franchise in a majority-rule constitution. The statesman is guided by prudential judgments rather than considerations of abstract right in addressing questions of majority rule because he knows that some communities "are totally unfit for its exercise"; majority rule requires a citizenry possessed of enlightenment, common sense, and morality (7:156, 334). Given this dependence, majority rule constitutions are not the only just "form of government." They are, however, "unquestionably the highest of any [form], and the only one that a high spirited and really free nation will tolerate." The "people make mistakes when governing themselves," but majority rule is best because it enjoys the greatest coincidence of the governing power's interest and the public interest. The people's "self-interest is on the side of good government." Thus when the "interests of the whole community are at stake, it is found best in the long run to let them be managed in accordance with the wishes of the majority of those presumably concerned" (7:360, 157).

This does not mean, however, that statesmen should simply adhere to majority will or that, following Benton, the majority is "always right" or that the average voter possesses "moral perfection." Benton was careless about protecting individual liberty. He did not understand that it "is quite as important to prevent" an individual from "being oppressed by many men as it is to save him from the tyranny of one" or a few. Benton's thoughtless majoritarianism was the foundation of his, and his fellow Jacksonians', readiness to bow "down before the mob" and to make demagogic political appeals to "caste prejudices" (7:79, 80, 87, 78). The Jacksonians "perpetually kept themselves" in a "wholly irrational state of mind. . . . Every canvass on Jackson's behalf was one of sound, fury, excitement, of appeal to the passions, prejudices and feelings, but never the reason of the people" (7:88).

In contrast to Benton, Morris correctly emphasized the limitations of majority rule: Referring to Parisian ultra-democrats, "he denounced, with a fierce scorn that they richly merit, the despicable demagogues and witless fools who teach that in all cases the voice of the majority must be implicitly obeyed" (7:457). Morris thought that since the majority may err statesmen need some detachment from its immediate desires so that, on occasion, they may restrain it and try to persuade it otherwise. But Morris, though he understood the constitutional foundation of politics and had a "keen, masterful mind, . . . never rose to the first rank of statesman," because his "far-sightedness" and reasoning were "marred by his incurable cynicism and deep-rooted distrust of mankind," especially westerners, who lacked the "refinement" of his eastern associates (7:328, 238). Roosevelt points out that Morris shared excessive distrust of the people with other prominent Federalist leaders, with the exception of James Madison. This distrust led Morris to favor a "strong national government, wherein he was right," but also a system of "class representation, leaning toward aristocracy, in which he was wrong" (7:328).

Roosevelt does not suggest that the Constitution of 1787 was itself excessively aristocratic, but he does attribute the decline of the Federalists to their subsequent failure to interpret the new Constitution in a more democratic manner: "Hamilton and the Federalists . . . could not learn the one great truth taught by Jefferson—that in America a statesman should trust the people, and should . . . secure to each man . . . liberty, confident that he will use it aright." Jefferson, on the other hand, could not have governed successfully without acquiescing "thoroughly in some of the fundamental principles" of the Federalists. Despite their insufficient trust of the people, Roosevelt holds that the Constitution "was good chiefly insofar as it followed the theories of the Hamiltonians," particularly in its support for a strong national government and president.

Roosevelt concludes by holding up President Lincoln as the "true successor of the Federalist leaders" in that he married their Constitution to a more Jeffersonian trust in the people: "Lincoln was the first who showed how a strong people might have a strong government and yet remain the freest on the earth. He seized . . . all that was best and wisest in the tradition of Federalism; . . . but he grafted on their system a profound belief that the great heart of the nation beat for truth, honor, and liberty" (7:326–27).

Roosevelt teaches that American statesmen should trust the people but not simply acquiesce in, to say nothing of deifying, majority rule for it can be unjust, mistaken, and even tyrannical. The apparent tension in this view is reduced by the qualifications that trust should be bestowed only on a "people sufficiently high in the scale to be fit for self-government" (Roosevelt, 10:334) and that trust should be in the "long run" soundness of the "bulk of the people," not in every more immediate majority desire (7:464). This basic trust is the necessary foundation for adherence to the wholly popular government established by the American Constitution, which, in turn, establishes various restraints on majority will. The people are trusted in the long run to support policies that enhance liberty and justice; but more fundamentally they are trusted to support the Constitution that establishes a government capable of promoting and protecting these guiding purposes. Popular support of the Constitution will be enhanced if the citizenry understands why it needs its institutions, such as a strong presidency, including accepting the perhaps unwelcome truth that some of that need stems from their own shortcomings. Roosevelt seeks to promote this understanding in the school of his political biographies.

To this end, he presents a high-toned view of the kind of statesmanship that would provide the greatest support to the American Constitution and its purposes. The subjects of the three biographies all fall short, some more, some less, of this standard of statesmanship that was fully attained, Roosevelt repeatedly stresses, only by Presidents Washington and Lincoln. In addition to having constitutional understanding, good judgment grounded in common sense, courage, and moderation, the exemplary presidents are praised for being "disinterested," and so in varying degrees are Cromwell, Benton, and Morris, particularly the latter for his "generous daring and lofty disinterestedness" (Roosevelt also describes Charles Pinckney as "one of the most high-minded and disinterested statesmen we have ever had") (7:237, 447). A disinterested statesman is able to do justice in specific situations and to focus on the common good because he is not unduly influenced by external interests or his own ambition, personal well-being, or inflexible political commitments. Disinterestedness is closely associated with public-spirited intent, but good intent when unaccompanied by political understanding and good judgment does not excuse bad results. Lafayette "acted with such unselfish purity of motive," but he lacked political understanding and common sense and was "without the great abilities necessary to grapple with the tumult of French affairs" (7:412). John Calhoun, a far less admirable man, is ascribed "purposes [that] seem to have been, in the main, pure." "But few criminals have worked as much harm to their country as he did. The plea of good intentions is not one that can be allowed to have much weight in passing historical judgment upon a man whose wrong-headedness . . . produced, or helped to produce, such unwelcome evil" (7:72). In contrast, "the men of 1787 were earnestly patriotic. They unselfishly desired the welfare of their countrymen." But they were also "cool . . . hard-headed men of common sense, . . . emphatically practical men" who accommodated their new Constitution to "the shortcomings of the average citizen." Morris was "perfectly right" when, despite his principled opposition to slavery, he supported the three-fifths and related constitutional compromises: "Wise and high-minded statesmen . . . had to accomplish their purposes by yielding somewhat to the prejudices of their more foolish and less disinterested colleagues" (7:325, 342).

Although emphatic that disinterestedness or good intent is but one and not the most important excellence of the statesman, Roosevelt, unlike the Federalists, does not endorse the institutional channeling of self-interest so as to promote the common good. Morris spoke with "more cynicism than common sense," Roosevelt contends, when he told Lafayette that when men "'go into an administration, . . . they are prompted by ambition and avarice, and that therefore the only way to secure the most virtuous is by making it in their interest to act rightly.'" Given his mistaken "disbelief in all generous and unselfish motives," Roosevelt suggests, Morris could not give an account of his own "lofty disinterestedness" and "generous daring" (7:380). Roosevelt acknowledges that nations act from selfish motives but is very reluctant to recognize self-serving motives as a legitimate source of statesmanship. His reluctance may be in the service of his educative effort to elevate the aspirations of prospective American statesmen, and of the citizenry who elect them, by reminding them of the highest form of republican statesmanship. And this could be part of a more general effort to counter what Roosevelt seems to view as a too great reliance under the Constitution to seek good outcomes from self-interested motives. Finally, his reluctance also suggests a more sanguine view than that of the Founders of the possibilities, through education and habituation, of elevating the character and opinion of the citizenry and their leaders.

Roosevelt's thematic emphasis on statesmanship in the biographies suggests its importance, in his view, to the governance of a free people, but his account also emphasizes the statesman's limited power to direct public affairs. The American and other constitutions empower public offices but also place limits on their power. More fundamentally, the way a people are constituted—their character, opinions, and aspirations—determines their aptitude for free government and thus the kind of constitution and leadership they will support. Confronted in revolutionary France with a "people who made-up in fickle ferocity what they lacked in self-restraint, . . . the French statesmen, even had they been as wise as they were foolish, would hardly have been able to arrest or alter the march of events" (7:392). Statesmanlike leadership cannot preserve free government in a nation that "loses the capacity for self-government, loses the spirit of sobriety and of orderly liberty." On the other hand, a "nation struggling out of darkness may be able to take its first steps only by the help of a master hand" such as that provided by Peter the Great. However, "a really great people, a people really capable of freedom and doing mighty deeds in the world, must work out its own destiny." Still, they also need assistance: This people "must find men who will be its leaders—not its masters" (10:335). Roosevelt's biographies are meant to assist the American people to identify and elevate such leaders. Within the boundaries of regime opportunities and restraints, the examples of the Founders and, above all, of Washington and Lincoln, exemplify that statesmanship and demonstrate that it can make a decisive difference to a free people.

NOTE

1. All citations in this chapter refer to Roosevelt 1926. Subsequent citations are given in the text by volume and page number.

REFERENCE

Roosevelt, Theodore. 1926. *The Works of Theodore Roosevelt: National Edition.* 20 vols. New York: Charles Scribner's Sons.

PART IV

Politics and Literature

Chapter Seventeen

Of "Demagogic Apes"

Euripides' Democratic Critique of Democratic Athens

ARLENE W. SAXONHOUSE

> Sophocles represented people as better than they are, whereas Euripides represented them just as they are.
>
> —Aristotle, *Poetics* 1460b33

Euripides does not fare well in Aristophanes' plays; in this, he is no different from most of the characters, human or divine, who walk on Aristophanes' stage. Mostly, though, the scurrilous portraits (with the notable exception of Socrates) attack political actors pursuing political power for their self-interested purposes. Like Socrates, Euripides may not be politically ambitious, eager to win glory for himself by controlling the decisions of the demos in the assembly, but he, like Socrates again, earns Aristophanes' ridicule for his impact on the life of the city. Aristophanes, as a playwright himself, understands only too well (or, perhaps we should say, very much hopes for) the impact that speaking from the stage can have on the understanding of the political world that the Athenian audience has. In his several presentations of Euripides, Aristophanes suggests how Euripides' democratic principle of equality affects the city, whereas Euripides, democratic egalitarian that he may be in Aristophanes' eyes and in the speeches of a number of his characters, also suggests in his own plays certain self-undermining aspects of democratic equality. In the first part of this chapter I look at the equalizing Euripides who appears in Aristophanes' comedies. In the second part, I briefly sketch how the Aristophanic portrait of Euripides plays itself out in two of Euripides' works. I conclude with the understanding of the democratic perspective that emerges from considering the relationship between Aristophanes' portrait of Euripides and the performance of Euripides' tragedies.

ARISTOPHANES' DEMOCRATIC EURIPIDES

Already in Aristophanes' earliest play, *Acharnians,* Euripides appears as distinct from the tragic poets who elevate their characters, capturing in their plays examples of tragic nobility. Euripides' appearance in the *Acharnians* is momentary but telling. It is to Euripides that Dikaeopolis, a man eager to make his own peace with Sparta during the Peloponnesian War, appeals when he is in need of rags, of a beggarly appearance, in order to speak incognito to a chorus of angry Acharnians. Though Euripides is sitting high above the stage when Dikaeopolis arrives at his abode, Dikaeopolis remarks that Euripides might as well be sitting on the ground, such lowly creatures does he introduce into his tragedies (414–18). It is from these characters that Dikaeopolis hopes to get his disguise, and there follow references to a number of plays no longer available in which Euripides places onstage his poverty-stricken characters wrapped in rags. Dikaeopolis's requests for more and more demeaning cloaks and accoutrements—a pitcher plugged with a sponge, withered herbs—continue until Euripides finally complains that all his plays are disappearing. Instead of writing of lofty things from his lofty perch, Euripides appears as one who populates the stage with the lowliest of the low, the poorest of the poor, with the petty objects of everyday life. Such characters and their meager possessions—like the befuddled husbands and chamber pots of the *Ecclesiazusae*—are usually the property of Aristophanic comedy, not tragedy. By bringing them to the tragic stage, Euripides has democratized the most exalted of the poetic arts. As such, he can be a resource for poor Dikaeopolis, who is weary of a world that looks to the fame and glory attending noble actions; all he wants is the end of soldiering so he can enjoy his cups full of sweet wine.

Euripides plays a more central role in two other comedies, the *Thesmophoriazusae* and the *Frogs,* and Aristophanes' mockery of him and his poetry is more focused in those plays. In the former Euripides enters the stage soliciting the help of his cousin Mnesilochus. The women of Athens have gathered at the secret festival of the Thesmophoria and, angered by the things Euripides says about them in his plays (he "makes tragedy of them and slanders them," 85),[1] they plot his destruction. Euripides is right to worry. We eventually see the women in their assembly and hear them deliberate about how Euripides is to suffer for the injustices he has perpetrated on them and specifically for how he has besmirched them onstage, calling them "lover-keepers," "man-chasers" and "wine-oglers," "traitors" and "chatterboxes" (392–94). Their anger is fueled not only because he has thrown offensive names at them; he has also revealed their misdeeds and peccadilloes to their husbands, causing the women to be imprisoned in their houses without access to the wine cellars or their lovers. They do not contest the accuracy of these depictions, but the consequences of such portrayals dismay them. Mnesilochus, having disguised himself as a woman in order to participate in the women's festival and assembly, defends Euripides not by denying that Euripides does all that the women claim he does but by arguing that there are so many more things that Euripides could have revealed but chose not to. The defense rests on Euripides' restraint, on what Euripides does not say. It could have been so much worse. This defensive strategy, though, is not particularly effective. The women condemn Euripides to death.

Though the comedy concludes happily (after many threats and disguises) with Euripides managing the release of Mnesilochus and escaping his own execution on the condition that he will no longer speak ill of the women, once again Aristophanes shows Euripides as appropriating the comic art, using tragedy to speak to the lowliest everyday passions—the desires for wine and fornication—and reducing the noble to the ignoble.[2]

Tragic characters on Euripides' stage are no more than your average housewife chafing at the restraints placed on her. The hierarchies of nobility dissolve under Euripides' direction; the noble appears as no more worthy than the lowly. The problem is that Euripides has presented his women onstage as they are—no better than you or me—not as characters worthy of our awe for their majesty and proximity to the divine. It is Euripides' "realism" that the women at the Thesmophoria resent, for that realism has led, they claim, to changes in their actual lives. Aristophanes (with an eye to his own art) is, for sure, affirming the status of the poet as more than an entertainer; he is the social transformer. And the transformation that Euripides effects comes from his presentation of an egalitarian world so that his audience sees the noble heroes of old in the shape and language of themselves.

Whereas Aristophanes is consciously mocking the men and women whom he puts onstage before the city, showing their foibles and unheroic stature so that he may (as he makes clear when he speaks directly to the audience) earn their laughter and their prizes, Euripides, continuing the legacy of Aeschylus and Sophocles, pretends to offer grand works of tragedy. The effect of Euripides' plays, though, is not to teach justice through laughter as Aristophanes claims to do but simply to turn the noble into ignoble. Euripides appears as full of pretense as the democratic leaders filling all of Aristophanes' comedies. Under the cover of a noble art, Euripides is the practitioner of a democratic art that reduces all to equals, to the lowliest common denominator. Aristophanes pursues this point most powerfully in the brilliant trial of the *Frogs* where Euripides and Aeschylus vie for the tragedian's chair in Hades. This comedy initially finds Dionysus dressed in the lion skin of Heracles. As the god of theater and thus the Dionysian festivals, he claims to have a longing for the recently deceased Euripides. The lion skin, he tells his servant Xanthius, will give him the courage to make the descent into Hades to bring Euripides back to the theater. Of course, in comedy things never go as planned, and when Dionysus eventually arrives at Pluto's house, he finds the two playwrights Aeschylus and Euripides engaged in a contest about who deserves to be honored as the greatest, most skillful, and best technician of his art (762–63). With the appearance of Euripides in Hades, Aeschylus's claim to the "throne of tragedy" had been challenged (769). As the slave of Pluto explains to Dionysus's servant, "When Euripides came down here, he started giving recitals for the muggers and purse-snatchers and father beaters and burglars . . . and when they heard his disputations and twists and dodges, they went crazy for him and considered him the best (*sophōtaton*)" (772–76).[3] The collection of ne'er-do-wells who favor Euripides reflects the people who populate his plays—and, we should note, the *dēmos* at large. Indeed, it was the *dēmos* in Hades who in true democratic fashion "clamored to hold a trial of who's best (*sophōteros*)" (779–80).[4] When Xanthius asks whether there were not some who sided with Aeschylus, the response is, "The good are the minority (*oligon to chrēston*), just like up here [i.e., in the theater]" (783). It was *panourgoi* (781), the knavish, cunning types, Pluto's slave tells Xanthius, who clamored for Euripides; his tragedies appeal to the democratic many, not the aristocratic few.

And so we are witness to the contest between the two tragedians. It begins, in true Aristophanic fashion, with invectives. Euripides calling Aeschylus a "big bombastolocutor" is met with "you scion of the greenery goddess[,] . . . you babble collector, you creator of beggars, you rag stitcher" (839–43). When the argument moves beyond name calling and Dionysus has established himself as the judge, the language is no less vitriolic, but both Euripides and Aeschylus get into the specifics of content and style that differentiate the tragic art practiced by each. Those differences are framed, as the initial invectives foreshadow, in the language of aristocratic nobility versus democratic baseness. After Euripides complains about the topics as well as the characters that make it into Aeschylus's plays, Aeschylus responds by asking, "And you, you enemy of the gods, what subjects did you write on?" To which Euripides responds, "Certainly not horse cocks or goatstags, like you, the sort of things they embroider on Persian tapestries" (936–37). While Aeschylus's plays resonate of Eastern luxuries, Euripides remains a man of the people, leaving the embroidered linens to the high-talking characters who populate Aeschylus's plays. As we saw in the *Acharnians,* Euripides hands out rags, not elegance.

Avoiding the "bloated" language with which Aeschylus invested his art, Euripides claims that he put his plays on a "diet," reducing Aeschylean bombast, using an economy of language appropriate to the characters he introduces: "From the very first lines I wouldn't leave any character idle; I'd have the wife (*hē gunē*) speak, and the slave just as much, and the master and the maiden and the old lady" (948–49). Euripides praises his openness, his inclusion of all popular types, his willingness to treat even the women as equal participants in his performances. For this Aeschylus (ignoring the fact that this contest is taking place in Hades) proclaims that Euripides ought to die. It is to this remark that Euripides defends himself: "No, by Apollo: it was a democratic act (*dēmokratikon*)" (950). Jeffrey Henderson in his paperback edition of his *Frogs* translation adds this footnote to this startling exclamation: "That women and slaves should have any kind of equality with adult male citizens was in fact a radical idea" (2008, 76 n. 119). It is not clear that one can conclude that Euripides is suggesting such a radical idea in these lines, but Aristophanes does portray him as recognizing that the way he presents women and slaves onstage captures the egalitarian sympathies and tendencies of democratic regimes.[5] To be clear: of course, women, very powerful ones at that (think of Clytemnestra and Atossa), appear in Aeschylus's tragedies, but Euripides' women who may be princesses and queens appear here simply as *gunē,* women or wives and old ladies, without regard to status.

Euripides proudly continues to defend his portrayal of the *panourgoi* and begins to elaborate on the social consequences of doing so: "I taught these people how to talk . . . and how to apply subtle rules and square off their words. To think, to see, to understand, to be quick on their feet, to scheme, to see the bad in others, to think of all aspects of everything" (951–58). Aristophanes, thus, has the tragedian Euripides present himself as the educator of the *dēmos,* giving them skills by which they could participate in the decision-making processes of the city, speak in the assembly and in the law courts, defend themselves against those who had more wealth and training. He did so, according to Aristophanes' Euripides, "by staging everyday scenes, things we're used to, things we live with, that I wouldn't have got away with falsifying, because these spectators knew them as well as I and could have exposed my faulty art" (959–60).

By presenting to the Athenian audience people like themselves, "bringing them onstage," and using language that they use and can understand, not the "bombastic bluster" of Aeschylus (962), Aristophanes' Euripides reiterates and reemphasizes the point he made before about teaching them how to participate in their political lives: "I encouraged these people to think (*phronein*), by putting rationality and critical thinking (*logismon*) into my art, so that now they grasp and really understand everything, especially how to run their households better than they used to and how to keep an eye on things" (971–78). The democratic playwright educates in reasoning and teaches them to ask, "Where'd that get to?" and "Who took that?" (978–79). He hands them skills and attitudes that enable them to protect themselves against the "few best" who are busy managing the polis for their own, not the city's, benefit. Notably, it is the foolish Dionysus who sees the flip side of this "education": "Heavens yes, these days each and every Athenian comes home yelling at his slaves" (980). Whereas previously, Dionysus notes, they used to "sit there like dummies, gaping boobies, Simple Simon," now they are a demanding lot, insisting on knowing "Where's the garlic from yesterday? Who's been nibbling the olives?" (984–92). The examples belong to comedy, but the suggestion is that Euripides has taught the many to demand explanations, to assert their own interests and not foolishly accept the pillaging of their resources whether by their own slaves or those who have power in the city. Whether Euripides has indeed had this effect is unclear, but according to the comedy Athens has become more democratic, more egalitarian because of his plays. The causal connection seems clear at least to Aristophanes.

After Euripides has had his turn, the chorus calls upon Aeschylus—he (they say) who was "the first of the Greeks to rear towers of majestic utterance and adorn tragic rant" (1004–5)—to respond. In defense of his throne, Aeschylus asks, "For what qualities should a poet be admired?" (1008), to which Euripides, following up on his previous claims about his success teaching people to think and his articulation of the didactic role of poetry, responds, "Skill and good counsel, and because we make people better members of their communities (*beltious te poioumen tous anthrōpous entais polesin*)" (1009–10). Against these claims, Aeschylus complains that Euripides has instead turned "good upstanding people (*chrēstōn kai gennaiōn*) into scoundrels (*mochthērous*)" (1011) and transformed his own "noble six-footers" into "the civic shirkers (*mē diadrasipolitas*), vulgarians, imps, and criminals that they are now." The characters in Aeschylus's plays, in contrast, have an "aura of spears, lances, white-crested helmets, green berets, greaves, and seven-ply oxhide hearts" (1014–17). The echo of the Homeric hero in Aeschylus's tragedies contrasts sharply with the average Athenian citizen; such heroes, Aeschylus asserts, encouraged men to yearn for victory (1027); his "profiles in courage" (1040) push the Athenians to emulate such godlike characters. Scornful of Euripides' tragedies, he scoffs, "I certainly created no whores like Phaedra and Stheneboea, and [ignoring Clytemnestra] no one can find a lustful woman in anything I ever composed" (1043–44). In this comedy Aeschylus is the poet of war; Euripides is the poet of Aphrodite, leading the Athenians to long for the softer, less noble pleasures.

Aeschylus continues to explain his own role as the educator, elevating the members of the audience, reiterating his point that the poet has "a special duty (*chrē*) to conceal what is wicked (*ponēron*) and not stage it or teach it. . . . [G]rownups have the poet [who instructs]. It's very important that we tell them things that are good (*panu . . . chrēsta*)" (1053–56). Euripides rejects this: "It is necessary to speak in human language (*anthrōpeis*)" (1058), but Aeschylus returns to his demands that the poet speak in the lofty language appropriate to the demigods—"just as they wear much more impressive clothing than we do" (1061). And so we are back to Euripides' rags. As Dionysus had identified the consequences of teaching the many to "think" on social relations within the household, so now Aeschylus explains the harm of dressing "royals in rags" (1063): it makes the rich man unwilling to command a warship since he is happy to wrap himself in rags and claim to be poor. Euripides' heroes dressed in rags inhibit men's desires to be heroes. "To cultivate chitchat and gab, which has emptied the wrestling schools and worn down the butts of young men as they gab away," as Euripides has done, Aeschylus complains, has "prompted the crew of the *Paralus* to talk back to their officers." Those who watch Aeschylus' tragedies know how to show respect, ask only for their rations, and are eager for the ship to sail (1069–73). Those who watch Euripides' are garrulous and insolent. Dionysus intervenes here on the side of Aeschylus, complaining that because of Euripides' plays, "Now they talk back and refuse to row, and the ship sails this way and that" (1076–77). The lofty language and the gloriously attired kings of Aeschylus teach obedience and respect. The rag-infested egalitarian world where poetry is reduced to colloquialisms in Euripides' plays fosters resistance to authority as everyone sees himself or herself as the equal of all others. The consequence is the sailing "this way and that," the loss of guidelines of what ought to be, of the direction the ship (or city) ought to follow. Without the hierarchies of the past, the city as a whole is a morass, in this view, of indecision and moral decline. Indeed, Aeschylus asks what evils *cannot* be attributed to Euripides: "Pimps he brings on in defiance of laws / A woman in a temple becoming a mother, / A woman lying with her own brother / . . . Filling it [the city] with clowns of diverse shapes, / Half-educated demagogue apes, / Whose study it is the people to debauch" (1079–86).[6]

The connection between the women of the Thesmophoria who express their fury at Euripides for his portrayal of them as sex-mad wine guzzlers and Aeschylus's criticism of Euripides' tragedies for their failure to portray the noble stature of his characters highlights Euripides' democratic tendencies. As the Aristotelian epigraph to this chapter suggests, Euripides presents men as they are, not as they ought to be. Anachronistically, we might refer to these as Machiavellian resonances; Machiavelli's work smashed the old hierarchies that set princes above their subjects, men over women, human over animal, and even God over human. Euripides' tragedies likewise undermine the hierarchical world of the ancient myths. Euripides does reduce his heroes to cowering wimps we so often see in Aristophanes' plays;[7] he does dress his princesses and kings in rags. In doing this, Euripides picks up the fundamental tenets underlying the democratic regime of ancient Athens. That world depended on the principle of equality (of course, it was an equality among the citizens of Athens, those born of citizen parents) and interchangeability where all citizens not only participated in the assembly voting on the actions of the city, but where they also took turns performing the various offices, sometimes ruling and being ruled at other times. Aristophanes in bringing Euripides so often into his comedies focused on the tragedian who was most similar to himself, turning heroic characters—not to mention the gods—into trembling cowards, making them appear just like all of us.

THE DEMOCRACY OF EURIPIDEAN TRAGEDY, THE TRAGEDY OF EURIPIDEAN DEMOCRACY

Though scholars are always eager to note that Euripides ends his life as a guest of the Macedonian king Archelaus (of *Gorgias* notoriety),

Euripides' plays were performed before a democratic audience and spoke to the issues that democracies, experimenting with a radically new political regime based on equality, confronted. The portrait he offers of his characters is indeed "democratic," as Euripides claims and Aeschylus complains in the *Frogs,* but by uncovering the equality that undermines false pretenses to hierarchy, Euripides also forces his audience to confront the challenges of democratic equality. In particular, equality raised the challenge of how choices between the noble and the base were to be made and how to identify who is equal and who is not. Below I explore Euripides' democratic tragedies—works filled with just those themes for which Aristophanes and Aeschylus mock him—and then his implicit critique of Athenian democracy (any democracy) that must in the end articulate the difference between the high and the low, the equal and the unequal. In the fantasy world of Aristophanes' *Ecclesiazusae* the women take over the political machinery of Athens and decree an equality that destroys the difference between attractive and vile, between mine and thine. At the same time that the comedy points to the artificial nature and harmful effects of many of the inequalities in the society, it also illustrates the consequences of an overattachment to equality in the absurd and repulsive efforts to create a sexual equality that requires young men and women to satisfy the longings of the old and ugly. Aristophanes who had so much fun mocking Euripides' egalitarianism raises his questions about democratic equality through comedy. Euripides does the same through his tragedies, which, while sympathetic to the principles of equality by which the Athenian democracy functions, also identify the limits of that equality. Euripides manages to bring to light in several of his plays the complex consequences of any efforts—past or present—to apply principles of equality in a political regime.

The rags with which Euripides dresses his heroic mythical characters and which so offended Aristophanes' Aeschylus are perhaps nowhere more vivid than in the opening scenes of *Electra* when Electra in what she herself describes as "filthy locks and robes all torn into slavish rags "(184–85)[8] is mistaken by her brother for a slave girl (106–10) as he watches her carry a jug of water on her razor-cropped head (241). Prior to Electra's appearance, her farmer husband introduces the play. His engaging modesty, his complete lack of pretension, sets him in a hierarchical world readily acknowledging his inferior status: "I was born of Mycenean / family, on this ground I have nothing to be ashamed of, / in breeding they shone bright enough. But in their fortune / they ranked as paupers, which blots out all decent blood" (34–48). The play makes a mockery of his shame; Electra describes him as "decent by nature" (261) and "a poor man, but well born" (253), making ambiguous the language of "blood" and "decent." The farmer informs the audience that he has not "violated" his wife: "I would feel ugly holding down the gentle daughter / of a king in violence, I was not bred to such an honor" (45–46). And yet, in the very portrayal of this man—humble, honest, restrained—Euripides dismantles the aristocratic world of wealth and the bloodlines of those "shining bright enough" where wives kill their husbands and kings cruelly abuse the children of their wives. It is the lowly farmer lacking "all decent blood" who exhibits the nobility of character lacking in those who rule over him. When Electra enters bearing the water jug on her head, she reinforces the audience's sense of the generous spirit of her farmer husband when she addresses him, "I think you equal to the gods in kindliness" (67). It is the farmer who is like the gods, not those who claim political and social power.

The beginning moments of the play unsettle hierarchies based on blood rather than on virtue, but it is Orestes' speech after he meets this noble farmer that most powerfully undermines the traditional inegalitarian notions of worth.

> We look for good on earth and cannot recognize it
> When met, since all our human heritage runs mongrel.
> At times I have seen descendants of the noble family
> Grow worthless though the cowards had courageous sons;
> Inside the souls of wealthy men bleak famine lives
> While minds of stature struggle trapped in starving bodies. (367–72)

So much for the hierarchies of old. So much for those fine embroidered linens that dressed Aeschylus's heroes. So much for the language of bloodlines. Orestes continues speaking in this vein for many more lines, asking:

> How then can man distinguish man, what test can he use?
> The test of wealth? That measure means poverty of mind;
> . . .

By nerve in war? Yet who, when a spear is cast across
His face, will stand to witness his companions' courage?
We can only toss our judgments random on the wind. (373–79)

Nothing seems to enable us to establish by nature the hierarchical ordering among men. We create those hierarchies in opposition to nature. Looking at the lowly farmer, Orestes now exalts the man who is without any noble blood to his name: "This fellow here is no great man among the Argives, / Not dignified by family in the eyes of the world— / He is a face in the crowd (*en tois pollois*), and yet we choose him champion (*aristos 'ēurethē*)" (380–83).

Orestes, though, veers slightly to suggest that there may be something that enables us to distinguish men, though it is not based on the criteria of earlier times. "Can you not come to understand, you empty-minded, / Opinion-stuffed people, a man is judged by grace / Among his fellows, manners are nobility's touchstone? Such men of manners can control our cities best, / And homes" (384–87). It is he, this "face in the crowd" (in Wyckoff's translation), marked only by grace and not by birth, who understands best how to rule in the city—so says the scion of Agamemnon. No wonder the ire of Aeschylus was roused and the comic wit of Aristophanes warned of the demagogic apes of Euripides' plays. Though the farmer will later say, "A small crumb of gold will buy / our daily bread, and when a man has eaten that, / you cannot really tell the rich and poor apart" (429–31), and the old man later in the play will remark, "Often a noble face hides filthy ways" (551), it is Orestes, the son of a king, who is conveying the same point that makes the play such a powerful expression of democratic egalitarian principles. Electra, not happy (to say the least) with the shameful position to which she has been reduced, nevertheless says to the corpse of Aegisthus, "Wealth stays with us a little moment if at all; / Only our characters are steadfast, not our gold (*hē gar phusis bebaios, ou ta chrēmata*), / For character stays with us to the end" (940–44). The external, the observed, obscures what makes men good, and the old hierarchies have lost their grounding in nature. We cannot tell the good from the bad by relying on the language of wealth or birth. The traditional visual cues are lost, and we find good character may attend poverty.

The challenge of making this move—and thus the challenge that faces democracy—is that these words are spoken by the siblings who cannot remove themselves from those old models. Despite their speeches which resonate so powerfully in the modern world of democratic equality, they are tied to the hierarchical aristocratic life. Though both Orestes and Electra give eloquent speeches articulating the inadequacy of relying on the cues of blood and wealth as defining worth, though such speeches encourage welcoming the man in rags into the assembly, teaching the sailors to thumb their noses at their commanders, the two still find themselves attached to, indeed bound by, the old symbols. Despite their grand speeches, tradition has not yielded to a new world. At the end of the play, under the direction of the gods, Electra abandons her farmer husband and marries Pylades. Euripides does not let the inadequacy of distinctions identified by his characters lead to their rejection in an explosion of social and sexual equality. Nor does Euripides leave us to blame the gods who through the literal deus ex machina reassert the status of wealth and birth against the egalitarian momentum of Athenian democracy. Is it that humans do not have the insight to judge worth when they cannot rely on the external signs? Must the gods reestablish not only justice, but hierarchy?

While *Electra* raises the questions of who it is we call noble, of what "decent blood" might be in a world in which the rulers are vicious and the subjects are filled with kind virtues, let me explore how this issue plays out in another Euripidean tragedy. The *Phoenician Women* tells the story of Polyneices returning to take his turn ruling over Thebes after his brother Eteocles has ruled for his allotted time. Though Thebes is not a city of assemblies and courts, the Athenian political system in which citizens fill an office for an allotted time before others take their place lies securely behind the premise of each ruling in turn. The exchange of offices recognizes each citizen as equally equipped to perform the functions to which he has been assigned. The lottery system used to assign offices denies the hierarchy entailed in identifying one rather than another as fit for a particular office. In the Thebes of the *Phoenician Women,* though, unlike in Athens, the transition of power from one to the other does not proceed smoothly. Eteocles' refusal to yield power to his brother leads to the invasion of Thebes by the Argives and the death of both brothers.

In Sophocles' more famous version, the focus is on Antigone's desire/need to bury Polyneices' body. Euripides' play is much more complex (too complex to even begin to summarize). Near the beginning, a slave, Antigone's Pedagogus, remarks that women are by nature (*ephu*) "lovers of censure" (198) and that they find a certain pleasure in speaking "what is not sound (*mēden hugies*) about one another" (200–201). Reminiscences of the women of the *Thesmophoriazusae* surface, but in fact the rest of the play is one in which the courage and wisdom of the women shine, in which Antigone changes from a timid maiden to an active and daring participant in the life of her city.[9] While the elevation of Antigone and to some extent Jocasta undermines Pedagogus's misogynist statement and accentuates Euripides' tendencies to undercut the traditional hierarchical world, the challenges that egalitarianism poses appear in a debate between the brothers. Polyneices, defending his claim to power in Thebes, explains, "So willingly myself I left this land, / leaving the rule to him for a year's cycle, / so that I myself might take the rule in turn. / Thus we should not fall into hate and envy / doing and suffering evil—but that has happened" (475–78). Eteocles, Polyneices says, may have sworn to abide by the agreement to take turns ruling, but he "did nothing of what he promised and still holds / the tyranny" (482–83). Eteocles in his turn responds, "I'll speak . . . without concealment: / I'd go to the stars and beyond the eastern sky / or under earth, if I could do one thing, / seize tyranny, the greatest of the gods. / I will not choose to give this good thing up / to any other, rather than keep it myself" (502–7).

As noted above, the Athenian model of all taking turns filling the various offices in the city is echoed in the proposed exchange between the brothers, and it captures as well the egalitarian principle underlying the sharing of rule. Neither is better qualified to rule or has a higher claim to rule. Rule comes from chance, not virtue. Yet that egalitarian principle that denies a natural superiority for rule and that Euripides expresses in such plays as *Electra* must confront the passionate drive for power expressed by Eteocles. Such a drive imposes an inequality that, though the plays may reveal such inequality as false, intrudes on any regime that builds on visions of equality. The battle against inequality, the imagining a world where the decent farmer and the female can be as noble and brave—even nobler and more brave—than those born as kings may be lost because of individuals like Eteocles who assert, "It's cowardice to let the big thing go / and settle for the smaller" (509–10). He concludes his speech, "If one must do a wrong, it's best to do it / pursuing power—otherwise, let's have virtue" (524–25). Missing from Wyckoff's translation is the shocking *kalliston adikein,* beautiful injustice, that begins line 525. So long as men like Eteocles can call doing injustice beautiful, appeals to equality are endangered. Euripides' plays show us both sides of the democratic impulse: the leveling of kings, the elevating of the humble, as well as the human passions that resist the democratic sharing that accompanies the institution of equality.

CONCLUSION

Euripides boasted in Aristophanes' *Frogs* that his characters in rags and their language, freed from the bloated bombast of Aeschylus, are democratic. In his own tragedies he speaks from the stage to the democratic audience, highlighting just those democratic principles that Aristophanes ascribes to him, but in so doing he uncovers some of the unpleasant consequences and inherent contradictions that surface with the rejection of the heroic past. The democratic principle of equality suffers under its own weight. This is the weight Aristotle expresses philosophically when he agrees that justice is a certain equality but recognizes the political difficulty of identifying who is equal. It is the weight Thucydides identifies when an Alcibiades bred in the democratic world of Athens fundamentally rejects that equality. Euripides' plays do not answer these challenges, but through the power of his works he forces us to confront difficult truths about our politics. Aristophanes' comedies can make us laugh at the absurdities of Euripides' infatuation with rags and sponge-stuffed buckets, but they also alert us to the need to understand Euripides' plays as reflections on the democratic world of ancient Athens. We could read Euripides running off to Archelaus in Macedonia as his throwing his hands up at the problem, but I would rather focus on how the playwright left the Athenians—and us—with an awareness of the difficulty of trying to incorporate principles of equality into political communities.

NOTES

Catherine Zuckert and Michael Zuckert have throughout their careers understood the power of literary texts to convey the theoretical understanding of political life and aspirations. Their engagement with a variety of literary forms has been an inspiration; this chapter is offered in appreciation of their efforts to legitimize the study of literary texts as valuable resources for the pursuit of political philosophy.

1. For the *Thesmophoriazusae* and the *Frogs* I use the translations of Henderson (2000; 2002), except where noted.

2. Indeed, as the comedy proceeds, Aristophanes shows that women conform to just those portraits of them for which they condemn Euripides.

3. Henderson (2002, line 776) has "best" for *sophōtaton.*

4. Henderson translates *dēmos* as "the public" (2002, line 779), which misses the democratic implications of the appeal of Euripides' plays.

5. This, of course, is not fair to Aeschylus, who has sympathetic portraits of the watchman in the *Agamemnon* and the nurse in the *Libation Bearers,* but we should not ask for scholarly precision from Aristophanic comedy.

6. Here I use the translation of R. H. Webb (2006, 465). What Webb translates as "demagogue apes," Henderson renders as "clownish monkeys." The Greek is *bōmolochon dēmopithēkōn* (1085).

7. Witness Heracles' performance at the end of the *Birds.*

8. I use the translation by Emily Townsend Vermuele (1959).

9. For elaboration of this see Saxonhouse 2005. There I focus on the role of Antigone; here I limit my attention only to lines 476–525. Translations are those of Wyckoff (1959).

REFERENCES

Henderson, Jeffrey, ed. and trans. 2000. *Aristophanes' Thesmophoria.* Loeb Classical Library. Cambridge, MA: Harvard University Press.

———. 2002. *Aristophanes' Frogs.* Loeb Classical Library. Cambridge, MA: Harvard University Press.

———. 2008. *Aristophanes' Frogs.* Newburyport, MA: Focus/R. Pullins.

Saxonhouse, Arlene W. 2005. "Another Antigone: The Emergence of the Female Political Actor in Euripides' *Phoenician Women.*" *Political Theory* 33 (4): 472–94.

Vermuele, Emily Townsend. 1959. *Electra.* In *Euripides V,* ed. David Grene and Richmond Lattimore, 7–66. Chicago: University of Chicago Press.

Webb, R. H., trans. 2006. *Frogs.* In *The Complete Plays of Aristophanes,* ed. Moses Hadas, 422–78. New York: Bantam Classics.

Wyckoff, Elizabeth. 1959. *The Phoenician Women.* In *Euripides V,* ed. David Grene and Richmond Lattimore, 67–140. Chicago: University of Chicago Press.

Chapter Eighteen

The Inevitable Monarchy

Shakespeare's Julius Caesar

TIMOTHY SPIEKERMAN

Julius Caesar has always been one of my favorite Shakespeare plays. I tend to attribute this to the way Shakespeare draws us inside a political conspiracy, allowing us to experience in a very intimate way the tension, danger, and exhilaration of playing politics, at the very highest level, for keeps. For much the same reasons, I've always liked *Macbeth,* which is also about a conspiracy and is perhaps more intense and more psychologically rich and revealing. I've changed my mind about the latter point: *Julius Caesar* reveals as much about the political psyche as *Macbeth* does and, in fact, the plays share more in common (ghosts, for example) than the starkly different settings might at first suggest. And while I still think *Macbeth* is a better thriller, I find myself caring more about the outcome of the conspiracy in *Julius Caesar* and in that sense am more deeply involved in the plot. For what's at stake here is not whether a good or bad man becomes king but whether a kingdom will replace a republic. The political scope of *Julius Caesar* is grander; and insofar as one has an opinion about the relative merits of republics and monarchies, the play engages us more intensely, as I will argue Shakespeare himself intended.[1]

Which brings me to the question that has long perplexed me: why is Shakespeare so interested in involving us in a conspiracy that will not only fail, but must fail? Why does he seem to want us to sympathize with a doomed effort to save a republic that is already on life support and speeding toward death? Why, in other words, does Shakespeare appear to celebrate a great republic when history, as he knew firsthand, had decided on monarchy? It was only when I turned this question around, asking myself if the Roman republic was indeed doomed and if Brutus and Cassius had to fail, that the play opened up for me. What if Shakespeare thought the monarchy that Julius and then Octavius Caesar established was not in fact inevitable? That's the question I consider in this chapter.

Of course, Shakespeare couldn't rewrite history—Brutus *did* fail—but if that failure were not necessary, history *might* be written differently in the future. Since Shakespeare is usually thought to have written *Julius Caesar* (1599) immediately after *Henry V* (1598) and Parts 1 and 2 of *Henry IV* (1597), the relationship between monarchy and republic must have been very much on his mind. And since the Roman monarchy might plausibly be thought to bear some relation to the great European monarchies that followed it, the fate of the Roman republic and the nature of its failure might have greater historical resonance. It might be a mistake, in other words, to treat *Julius Caesar* primarily as a "period drama." As we shall see, Shakespeare gives lines to Brutus and Cassius, lines that appear nowhere in Plutarch, in which they speak to posterity in an effort to keep the republican cause alive.

MACHIAVELLI, PLUTARCH, AND SHAKESPEARE

The death of the Roman republic is typically thought to have been the natural and necessary outcome of its extraordinary imperial success. As the empire expanded, Rome became richer and richer, which fed the popular appetite for further expansion; it also allowed wealthy generals to use the money they gained in conquest abroad to influence elections at home.[2] And because of the long duration of their commands and the size of their armies, Roman generals themselves became political contenders and rivals, capable of influencing behavior at the center and eventually threatening Rome itself with their armed supporters. So we have, on the one hand, a Roman people who care more and more about acquiring wealth and, on the other, powerful and popular Roman generals who contemplate seizing sole power. The competition between various armed factions (led by Marius, Sulla, Pompey, Caesar) embroiled Rome in constant conflict, and according to Plutarch, this led to a popular acceptance of "monarchy as a respite from the evils of the civil wars" (*Caesar,* 57; see also 28). Machiavelli concentrates the problem on the adoption of the Agrarian Law, which provided that "fields taken from enemies should be divided among the Roman people" and "which in the end was the cause of the destruction of the republic."[3] The appetite for conquest lured Roman armies farther and farther from home, which necessitated the prolongation of command. And "when a citizen remained commander of an army for a very long time, he would win it over to himself and make it partisan to him." "Because of this," Machiavelli continues, "Sulla and Marius could find soldiers to follow them against the public good" and "Caesar could seize the fatherland" (*Discourses,* III.24). The combination of ambitious generals, partisan armies, and a corrupt and eventually war-weary public proved too much for the republic.

We don't know if Shakespeare read Machiavelli's *Discourses* (he probably did read his *Prince*), but we do know he was a careful reader of Plutarch, his primary source for *Julius Caesar.* Plutarch says many of the same things Machiavelli does about the fate of the republic, though he is less clear, to me at least, about the *inevitability* of its demise. Plutarch does emphasize the long history of tyrannical ambition to be sole ruler of Rome, describing Caesar as a more talented and fortunate contender for a prize many men sought:

> For no one had expected that Pompey the Great, if he overthrew Caesar, would insist on dismissing his forces in obedience to the laws, but all thought that he would continue to retain his power, appeasing the people

> by using the name of consulship or dictatorship or some other less obnoxious form of government. And now it was thought that Cassius, vehement and passionate man that he was, and often swept from the path of justice by his passion for gain, was incurring the perils of wars and wanderings principally to establish some great power for himself, and not liberty for his countrymen. For the men of a still earlier time than Pompey and Cassius, men like Cinna and Marius and Carbo, made their country the booty or prize round which they fought, and they all but confessed that they waged war to establish a tyranny. (*Brutus,* 30)[4]

At one point, Plutarch attributes the fact that "the government of Rome could no longer be a democracy" to an act of "Heaven," and he compares the flight of the senators from Rome on Caesar's approach to "the sweep of a great tide" (*Brutus,* 47; *Caesar,* 34).[5] But Plutarch also contends that "the most open and deadly hatred towards [Caesar] was produced by his passion for royal power" and that the success of the conspiracy against him was an act of "destiny" or "the work of some heavenly power" (*Caesar,* 60, 63, 66). And if Plutarch sometimes employs the language of cosmic necessity, albeit on both sides of the struggle, more often his accounts emphasize the talents, intentions, and mistakes of particular individuals, and the effects of ordinary accidents. Julius Caesar, for example, is treated as a traditional historical actor motivated by extreme ambition: what "led him to war against all mankind, as it had led Alexander before him, and Cyrus of old, was an insatiable love of power and a mad desire to be first and greatest" (*Antony,* 6).[6] And while Plutarch calls Octavius's victory over Antony "destined," he elsewhere describes how Octavius, sick in his tent and not expecting an attack by Brutus's army, "barely succeeded" in escaping. He "was thought to have been slain," along with the thousands of his soldiers captured and then slaughtered by Brutus (*Antony,* 56; *Brutus,* 41).

But what about Shakespeare? His account of the republic's demise shares more of the ambiguity and nuance of Plutarch than the decisive clarity of Machiavelli. As with Plutarch, the evidence seems to cut both ways. Consider the following two statements, both spoken by Cassius:

> Men at some time are masters of their fates:
> The fault, dear Brutus, is not in our stars,
> But in ourselves, that we are underlings. (I.ii.139–41)[7]

And why should Caesar be a tyrant then?
Poor man, I know he would not be a wolf
But that he sees the Romans are but sheep;
He were no lion, were not the Romans hinds. (I.iii.103–6)

In his first remarks Cassius insists that men are free to enact their destiny and so free to either oppose or submit to Caesar. Allowing Caesar to seize sole power would be an act of cowardice, not a dictate of heaven or an unavoidable fate. In his second statement, however, Cassius seems to attribute Caesar's ever-increasing success to the corruption of the common Roman people, suggesting that they are more responsible than Caesar for the looming monarchy and that the conditions favoring single rule may be more important that the courage of elite actors. (Of course, if Cassius were simply resigned to Caesar's triumph, he wouldn't be organizing his assassination.) Shakespeare devotes a number of striking scenes to the Roman people, who sometimes support the republic but are mostly fickle—the picture, I think it is fair to say, is critical to the point of being hostile. When Antony contrives to crown Caesar king, the people resist until a surprised Caesar actually faints, and is later forced to ascribe his overreaching misjudgment to his medical condition; it was the epilepsy talking, not me! According to Casca, many in the crowd then "forgave him with all their hearts" (I.ii.273). Plutarch remarks that "this was strange, too, that while the people were willing to conduct themselves like the subjects of a king, they shunned the name of king as though it meant the abolition of their freedom" (*Antony,* 12). After the conspirators kill Caesar and Brutus explains to the crowd why Roman freedom required it, one enthusiastic plebian shouts, "Let *him* be Caesar," and another, "Caesar's better parts / Shall be crowned in Brutus" (III.ii.52–53; emphasis mine). Soon after, Antony sways the people against the conspirators by reminding them how much they loved Caesar, and an angry mob kills a man whose only crime is sharing the name "Cinna" with one of the conspirators. "I am Cinna the poet! . . . I am not Cinna the conspirator," he cries. "It is no matter," one plebeian responds; "Tear him, tear him," says another, "Come, brands, ho! Firebrands! To Brutus', to Cassius'! Burn all!" (III.iii.29, 31, 36–38). Shakespeare is even harsher on the mob than Plutarch is, adding the "it is no matter" in order to further emphasize, I suppose, that the people are not only pliable and fickle, but lawless and tyrannical. Earlier reports that Caesar had exiled (or executed) the Tribunes for opposing his campaign to be king appear to meet no popular objection.[8]

But if Shakespeare thinks the people are corrupt beyond repair, that republican virtue can no longer inspire or restrain them, then it's odd that he devotes so much attention to the conspirators' mistakes. If they could not have succeeded, why dwell in such detail on their errors? Following Plutarch, Shakespeare seems to blame Brutus for wrongly overruling Cassius on three crucial decisions: not to kill Antony along with Caesar, allowing the celebration of a public funeral for Caesar—with Marc Antony as the featured speaker!—and fighting too early at Philippi. In addition, Shakespeare draws more attention than Plutarch does to Brutus's quarrel with Cassius over allowing corruption in the army, implying that Brutus is too morally delicate under the circumstances.[9] On a related point, and again following Plutarch, Shakespeare implies that Brutus may be too "intellectual" to effectively defend the republic. Finally, and in my mind most important, Shakespeare suggests that Brutus and Cassius fail because they are too superstitious. Interestingly, Shakespeare never suggests, as Machiavelli does, that the conspiracy itself was ill-advised, and that the better course would have been waiting for Caesar's popularity to wane.[10]

THE CONSPIRATORS' ERRORS

Shakespeare seems to lay most of the blame for the failure of the conspiracy on Brutus, who as I noted above rejects what seems to be the superior advice of Cassius on several crucial occasions. But Brutus's decisions are not as obviously stupid as critics sometimes maintain and seem reasonable enough at the time. He is, in my view, the hero of the play, a flawed and unsuccessful hero to be sure but one from whom we can learn a lot about the nature of conspiracy in general. By inviting us to think through Brutus's decisions, Shakespeare seems to be providing a kind of primer on conspiracy. What kind of character lends itself to good decision making in real time? What kind of character lends the greatest luster to a cause over the long haul? Cassius may be superior at the first,

Brutus at the second. Of course, both conspirators succumb to superstition, which may be the ultimate reason for their defeat and the ultimate lesson to be learned by future students of conspiracy.

Brutus rejects Cassius's advice that they kill Marc Antony along with Caesar on the grounds that it "will seem too bloody." "Let's be sacrificers," he argues, "but not butchers" (II.i.162, 166). Compared to the reign of terror unleashed by Antony and Octavius when they seize power—they kill one hundred senators, some of whom are their own relatives—Brutus's course seems humane and decent. But insofar as his primary concern is with appearances, Brutus's decision is motivated by political prudence rather than an aversion to bloodshed or moral delicacy.[11] After giving it a great deal of anguished thought, Brutus is confident that his cause is just,[12] so here, I think, his concern is tactical rather than moral.[13] And Brutus couples his thoughts about appearances with the judgment that Antony is not dangerous, a judgment that turns out to be wrong but which is remarkably similar to Caesar's view of Antony as an ultimately harmless sensualist.[14] *If* Antony is harmless, Brutus's judgment that a surgical strike will seem more palatable than a bloodbath seems sensible, though one wonders if killing two rather than one would count as "too bloody." And of course no one contemplates killing Octavius, who proves to be the most dangerous and effective politician in Rome. Killing Antony would not solve *that* problem. According to Machiavelli, the root of the problem isn't this or that individual but Caesar's popularity: "the conspirators do not have any remedy for this since they can *never* secure themselves against it . . . because he had the people of Rome as his friend, [Caesar] was avenged by it" (*Discourses,* III.6.18; emphasis mine). More puzzling to me than Brutus's decision to spare Antony is his later decision that the conspirators should bathe themselves in Caesar's blood and parade themselves before the people. *That* seems too bloody; and it leaves nothing to the imagination. Was that the point? Did Brutus intend to terrify the crowds? It doesn't seem so, for immediately before addressing them he reassures an old senator, "There is no harm intended to your person, / Nor to no Roman else" (III.i.89–91). And immediately after inviting his comrades to bathe their hands and swords in blood, he says, "Let's all cry 'Peace, freedom, and liberty!' " (III.i.110), as if to emphasize the positive and to treat the event as an occasion for celebration.

Initially this works, but using the same props—Caesar's blood—Antony is able to turn the celebration into a frenzied desire for vengeance against the conspirators.

For this, Brutus is to blame, though his reasoning isn't without some merit. Consistent with his earlier decision to limit the violence in order to stress that the conspiracy was motivated and governed by principle rather than power, Brutus thinks showing generosity toward Caesar in allowing a public funeral is the best course. In this, he may have been following Caesar's own example, for Caesar showed extraordinary generosity to his opponents after his victory over Pompey. Pompey's supporters, including Brutus and Cassius, were not only spared, but rewarded, and his toppled statues were ordered set up again (which is ironic, considering the site of Caesar's assassination). "After the civil wars were over," Plutarch concludes, "[Caesar] showed himself blameless; and certainly it is thought not inappropriate that the temple of Clemency was decreed as a thank-offering in view of his mildness" (*Caesar,* 57). Allowing an unescorted Antony to speak at the funeral, however, proved disastrous. Antony's speech is so cynical and slimy that I always dread reading it; but it was terribly effective and causes Cassius and Brutus to flee the city and to regroup in the Eastern portion of the empire. Allan Bloom suggests that Brutus made another error in not inviting Cicero into the conspiracy, whose powerful reputation and skills as an orator would have enhanced their cause at this crucial moment (Bloom, 98 and n. 42). Brutus dismissed the idea, arguing that Cicero was too prickly and unreliable, which seems to be borne out by his decision to remain in Rome and support Octavius, which Plutarch contends was motivated by "his hatred of Antony." For this, "Brutus rebuked him severely, writing that Cicero did not object to a despot as such, but only a despot who hated him" (*Brutus,* 22).[15]

Brutus overrules Cassius a third time when he decides to engage Antony and Octavius at Philippi instead of biding his time, taking advantage of his superior wealth and supplies, and wearing down their army. Brutus worries that the patience of his Eastern hosts, who "stand but in forced affection," is fraying—"we have tried the utmost of our friends"—and fears defections to Octavius's camp (IV.iii.204, 213). According to Plutarch, "sundry desertions to the enemy, and suspicions and assertions that others would follow, brought many of the friends of Cassius in the council over to the side of Brutus" (*Brutus,* 39). While Shakespeare alludes to these worries, he does not dwell on them, instead giving Brutus a speech not present in his source where Brutus justifies his timing in the most grandiose way, almost as a matter of cosmic necessity:

> There is a tide in the affairs of men
> Which, taken at the flood, leads on to fortune;
> Omitted, all the voyage of their life
> Is bound in shallows and miseries.
> On such a full sea are we now afloat,
> And we must take the current when it serves,
> Or lose our ventures. (IV.iii.217–23)

Perhaps because he cannot imagine how one might rebut such a statement—would it help to remind Brutus it's (largely) a land battle?—Cassius, as usual, defers to Brutus. And Brutus wins, his troops handily defeating Octavius's and ravaging his camp. Cassius's army quickly falls apart and suffers a devastating loss to Antony. Though it's impossible to know what might have happened had they postponed engagement and prolonged the war, both Shakespeare and Plutarch attribute their failure at Philippi to misunderstandings and false interpretations: Brutus fails to rescue Cassius because he's unaware of his defeat; Cassius commits suicide because he thinks Brutus has lost. "One thing alone brought ruin to their cause," Plutarch says, "namely, that Brutus thought Cassius victorious and did not go to his aid, while Cassius thought Brutus dead and did not wait for his aid" (*Brutus,* 42). Thus the "one thing alone" that caused their defeat was not the timing of the battle but the way it was conducted. Things might have turned out differently had Brutus and Cassius understood their respective situations more clearly. Their failure is in some sense self-inflicted—Brutus will also commit suicide in his next and final engagement with the enemy—and unnecessary, at least if their misunderstanding and lack of clarity were avoidable. Shakespeare gives us some reason to think that they were, which I will explain shortly.

Immediately prior to the battle at Philippi, Brutus and Cassius have a falling out over corruption in the army. In short, Cassius allows it and

Brutus does not. The quarrel arises when Brutus punishes a soldier for taking bribes, despite Cassius's pleas that he overlook the offense. Brutus then accuses Cassius himself of corruption—"you yourself . . . have an itching palm" (IV.iii.9–10)—and blames him for failing to share his ill-gotten gains with Brutus's army. "I can raise no money by vile means," Brutus says (IV.iii.71). This is Brutus at his least attractive, imprudently self-righteous and hypocritical at once. But Shakespeare makes clear that Brutus's moralism has a political purpose: the assassins of an aspiring tyrant must themselves appear beyond reproach. And as Plutarch points out, while Caesar himself was not corrupt, he tolerated abuses among his friends (notably Antony), who "brought [him] into odium" (*Antony,* 6; see also *Brutus,* 35).

This is not to say that Brutus's moral inclinations are always at bottom prudential, that he is only concerned with appearances. But I have tried to show that in his disagreements with Cassius, Brutus cannot persuasively be cast as an inflexible moralist who for this reason is blind to what might seem the superior prudence and political judgment of his friend. Shakespeare did not intend for us to simply disparage Brutus, or even, I think, to admire his stern virtue while lamenting its incompatibility with political reality; for Brutus's reputation for virtue is a great political strength. He may indeed have been wrong about Antony, Caesar's funeral, and Philippi, but in each instance he makes a political case for his decisions. In the quarrel over corruption I just discussed, he may also be wrong, for had he been more liberal and tolerant with his soldiers, they might not have so quickly "fell to spoil" (V.iii.7) after defeating Octavius, and so might sooner have perceived the danger Cassius was in. But as I indicated above, Shakespeare seems intent on exposing a deeper and more fundamental reason for the conspirators' failure. As this reason touches *both* Brutus and Cassius, their disagreements may be less important than their similarities.

SUPERSTITION

Caesar, Brutus, and Cassius share an interesting quality: all are highly rational men who eventually become superstitious. According to Plutarch,

Antony and Octavius were also influenced by dreams and visions, but Shakespeare does not emphasize this, and does not present them as men who undergo a fundamental change. Antony, of course, will succumb to another irrational power in his disastrous love for Cleopatra, but that's another story—and another play. Besides, Antony is characterized as a sensualist from the beginning, so his love for Cleopatra is less surprising than Brutus's belief in ghosts and Cassius's belief in bird signs.

While assessing the danger an increasingly ambitious Caesar poses to the republic, Brutus admits to himself that Caesar has always been highly rational: "I have not known when his affections swayed / More than his reason" (II.i.20–21). Cassius, however, notes that Caesar "is superstitious grown of late," and seems to have abandoned the critical or dismissive "opinion he held once / Of fantasy, of dreams, and ceremonies" (II.i.195–97). Cassius tries to connect Caesar's new irrationality to tyrannical ambition—"this man is now become a God"—and Caesar's own words seem to confirm the connection. In an effort to "explain" a decision, Caesar announces that "the cause is in my will," and in reply to a plea that he change his mind about a man he's exiled, Caesar shouts, "Wilt thou lift up Olympus?" (II.ii.71; III.i.73). The tendency of both Brutus's and Cassius's remarks is to associate reason with republican self-rule and lack of reason or irrationality with tyrannical ambition. But this neat formula does not hold up, for the republicans will eventually succumb to superstition themselves, and the ultimate victor and Rome's first emperor, Octavius Caesar, will prove a model of cool rationality. The simpler explanation for Caesar's turn to superstition, an explanation that may also apply to Brutus's and Cassius's later turn in the same direction, is guilt. As Caesar once experienced trepidation as he contemplated crossing the Rubicon,[16] he now experiences trepidation as he contemplates destroying the republic. Responding to his wife's ominous dream that he will be murdered at the Senate and to her reports of miraculous disturbances in the streets of Rome, Caesar is at first his old, rational self, insisting that nature is impersonal and so cannot be speaking of him: "Caesar shall go forth; for these predictions / Are to the world in general as to Caesar." But after hearing from his augurs, Caesar quickly changes his mind—"I will stay at home"—only to again change his mind when Calpurnia's dream is interpreted (by one of the conspirators) in a favorable light (II.ii.28–29, 56, 83–91). The man who conquered the world and is poised to take a great republic for himself now makes decisions based on dreams!

The miraculous events reported on the eve of Caesar's second effort to crown himself—the skies alight, men on fire walking down the street, a lion roaming through the capital, an owl seen in broad daylight in the marketplace[17]—also precede the day of the planned assassination of Caesar. One of the conspirators, a frightened and no doubt guilt-stricken Casca, is certain the heavens are speaking to him: "When these prodigies / Do so conjointly meet, let not men say, 'These are their reasons, they are natural,' / for I believe they are portentous things" (I.iii.28–31). Responding to Casca's reports of "a tempest dropping fire," Cicero says, "Why, saw you anything more wonderful?" And to Casca's insistence that the events are unnatural, he remarks that "men may construe things after their fashion, / Clean from the purpose of the things themselves" (I.iii.14, 34–35). Cicero, who has not been invited into the plot and so cannot know the true source of Casca's terror, doesn't provide the needed comfort. Cassius, who appears next on the scene, does, convincing Casca that the (supposedly—it's clear enough that Cassius is making the best use of Casca's superstition without sharing it himself) miraculous signs show heaven's disapproval of Caesar. Brutus isn't around for these exchanges, but later we see him at home late at night, pleased that the bright meteors allow him to read (II.i.44–45). Later, Brutus gives us another indication of his view on divine intervention when he rejects the proposal that the conspirators should swear an oath of allegiance before the gods. "Priests" and "cowards" may need divine assistance; honorable Romans do not (II.i.114–140).

Soon enough, however, Brutus is seeing ghosts. Shortly before the battle at Philippi, an "evil spirit" that Brutus later identifies as Caesar (V.v.18–19) appears to him late at night while he is reading and announces that he will see Brutus again at Philippi. Brutus does not seem frightened, and his response is funny enough to be played for laughs: "Why, I will see thee at Philippi then" (IV.iii.285). But Brutus is clearly disturbed by his vision and immediately wakes his three companions to ask if they saw or heard anything. They didn't, but Brutus does not as a consequence doubt his experience, or assume, as Hobbes does, that he was dreaming:

> For sitting in his tent, pensive and troubled with the horror of his rash act, it was not hard for him, slumbering in the cold, to dream of that which most affrighted him; which feare, as by degrees it made him wake; so also it must needs make the Apparition by degrees to vanish; And having no assurance that he slept, he could have no cause to think it a Dream, or any thing but a Vision. And this is no very rare Accident: for even they that be perfectly awake, if they be timorous, and superstitious, possessed with fearfull tales, and alone in the dark are subject to the like fancies, and believe they see spirits and dead mens Ghosts walking in Churchyards. (*Leviathan,* I.2)

Brutus's behavior here contrasts strikingly with the uncanny calm he showed moments before the assassination. When a senator not involved in the conspiracy makes a suggestive comment to Cassius—"I wish your enterprise today may thrive" (III.i.13)—and is then seen talking to Caesar, Cassius is certain they've been exposed and advises immediate action. Brutus, however, advises patience, and observing the nature of the conversation between Caesar and Popilius, correctly concludes that it is harmless.[18] Commenting on this passage in Plutarch, Machiavelli explains the source of the "false imaginations" that grip Cassius: "For whoever has a stained conscience easily believes that one speaks of him; one can hear a word, said for another end, that perturbs your spirit and makes you believe it was said about your case" (*Discourses,* III.6.16). Later, in an interesting reversal, Cassius will try to rein in Brutus's imagination. In a long account in Plutarch that Shakespeare chose not to dramatize, Cassius, who like Hobbes is a materialist, attempts to talk Brutus out of his vision of Caesar's ghost, which he chalks up as a dream: "The imagination is by nature in perpetual motion. . . . In thy case, too, the body is worn with hardships and this condition naturally excites and perverts the intelligence" (*Brutus,* 37). Since the ghost or spirit does not identify himself, Brutus's certainty that he is Caesar is an interpretation, as is his later assumption that Caesar's second appearance means his cause is lost.

After the inconclusive first battle at Philippi and the defeat of Cassius, Plutarch reports that Brutus's position was still strong. And were it not for an accident ("some chance"), he might well have ultimately prevailed:

> For a large force which was being brought from Italy by command of Octavius was attacked by the ships of Brutus and destroyed, and the small remnant of them that escaped their enemies were driven by hunger to subsist on the sails and tackle of their ships. On hearing of this, they were eager to have the issue decided by battle before Brutus learned what great good fortune had come to him. But by some chance, rather than by the fault of his naval commanders, Brutus was ignorant of their success until twenty days afterwards. Otherwise he would not have proceeded to a second battle, since his army was supplied with provisions for a long time, and he was posted in an advantageous position, so that his camp did not suffer from wintry weather, and on the side towards the enemy was almost impregnable, while his secure mastery of the sea and the victory of the land forces under his own command had put him in high hopes and spirits. (*Brutus,* 47)

Plutarch continues that "since, *as it would seem,* the government of Rome could no longer be a democracy, and a monarchy was necessary, Heaven, wishing to remove from the scene the only man who stood in the way of him who was able to be sole master, cut off from Brutus the knowledge of that good fortune, although it very nearly reached him in time" (*Brutus,* 47, emphasis mine). It's hard to know how to take Plutarch's remarks here: was this an accident, or an act of Heavenly necessity? I'm inclined to stress Plutarch's qualification—"it would seem"—as his narrative gives the powerful impression that this was a very close call and that Brutus and the republic might have prevailed. Shakespeare says very little about the circumstances surrounding the second battle and compresses events so that Brutus almost immediately determines his cause is lost, and attributes it not to any accident or military misfortune but to a second visit from Caesar's ghost:

> The ghost of Caesar hath appeared to me
> Two several times by night; at Sardis once,
> And this last night here at Philippi fields.
> I know my hour is come. (V.v.18–21)

In fact, Brutus seems to predict his suicide and Caesar's role in it even earlier. Standing over Cassius's dead body, he says, "O Julius Caesar, thou art mighty yet! / Thy spirit walks abroad, and turns our swords / In our own proper entrails" (V.iii.94–96). On Shakespeare's account, what stands between victory and defeat for the Roman republic is a "stained conscience" and a ghost. Brutus's *belief* that his cause is hopeless, the victim of irresistible cosmic forces, is what finally defeats him.

Shakespeare makes exactly the same point with respect to Cassius. Having reluctantly deferred to Brutus's decision to stake their cause on an immediate battle at Philippi, Cassius confides his worries to Messala:

> Be thou my witness that against my will
> (As Pompey was) am I compelled to set
> Upon one battle all our liberties.
> You know that I held Epicurus strong,
> And his opinion; now I change my mind,
> And partly credit things that do presage.
> Coming from Sardis, on our former ensign
> Two mighty eagles fell, and there they perched,
> Gorging and feeding from our soldiers' hands,
> Who to Philippi here consorted us.
> This morning are they fled away and gone,
> And in their steads do ravens, crows, and kites
> Fly o'er our heads and downward look on us
> As we were sickly prey; their shadows seem
> A canopy most fatal, under which
> Our army lies, ready to give up the ghost. (V.i.73–88)

Like Brutus, Cassius's confidence in his ability to prevail over the monarchists is affected by seemingly ominous signs. And at least according to Plutarch, he could not as a consequence still the fears of his own troops: "the superstitious fears which were gradually carrying even Cassius himself away from his Epicurean doctrines . . . had altogether subjugated his soldiers" (*Brutus,* 39). Many of those soldiers, as Shakespeare shows us, turn to flee when confronted by Antony's army (III.i.1–4). In the run-up to the assassination, Cassius himself interprets supposed signs for the benefit of his cause and Decius reinterprets Calpurnia's dream in order to coax Caesar to the Senate. In Xenophon's *Education of Cyrus,* Cyrus's father tells his son, who is about to leave home at the head of an army, that the most important advice he can give him is to always be his own augur.[19] Of course, one also needs the ability to interpret "signs" in a politically useful way. By calling Cassius's fears "superstitious," Plutarch at least implies that they were unwarranted. And in another context, he makes the same connection between the sharing of ominous signs and the poor spirit and performance of the army. When Caesar unexpectedly attacked a formidable German army, Ariovistus's troops were alarmed. "Still more, too," Plutarch continues, "was the spirit of the Germans blunted by the prophecies of their holy women, who used to foretell the future by observing eddies in the rivers and by finding signs in the whirlings and splashings of the waters, and now forbade joining battle before a new moon gave its light" (*Julius Caesar,* 19). When Cassius and a few of his aides escape Antony's rout and retreat to a hill above the battlefield, Cassius, who is nearsighted, asks Titinius to ride back down to determine how badly they're faring. He then asks Pindarus to move farther up the hill and to follow and report on his progress. Pindarus proceeds to misinterpret what he sees, explaining to Cassius that Titinius was captured by the enemy when he was actually being greeted by Brutus's troops. Cassius then commits suicide and like Brutus gives credit to Caesar: "Caesar, thou art revenged, / Even with the sword that killed thee" (V.iii.45–46). But if Cassius had not been shortsighted, if he had been able to see clearly what was truly happening, as opposed to what he imagined was happening, on the battlefield, Caesar might not have been avenged. Standing over Cassius's dead body, Titinius and Messala provide a revealing commentary. "The sun of Rome is set," says Titinius. "Mistrust of my success hath done this deed." "O hateful Error," says Messala, "Why dost thou show to the apt thoughts of men / The things that are not?" (V.iii.63, 65, 67–69). I think Messala's comments could apply both to the birds that vex Cassius and his troops and to his misunderstanding of the state of the battle: his false belief that he was doomed was the cause of his defeat.

"Cassius and Brutus," Montaigne argues, "demolished the last remnants of Roman liberty, of which they were the protectors, by the rash haste with which they killed themselves before the proper time and occasion."[20] They gave up too early. And as I have argued, their suicidal surrender is caused in large part by the belief that fate opposes them. But why are they so ready to believe this? Shakespeare suggests it is due to guilt over murdering Caesar, but he also hints at a more general answer: Brutus and Cassius think too much. In this he follows Plutarch, who opens his *Life of Brutus* with a revealing comparison between Marcus and Junius Brutus:

> Marcus Brutus was a descendant of that Junius Brutus whose bronze statue, with a drawn sword in its hand, was erected by the ancient Romans on the Capitol among those of the kings, in token that he was most resolute in dethroning the Tarquins. But that Brutus, like the tempered steel of swords, had a disposition which was hard by nature and not softened by letters, so that his wrath against tyrants drove him upon the dreadful act of slaying his sons; whereas this Brutus, of whom I now write, modified his disposition by means of the training and culture which philosophy gives, and stimulated a nature which was sedate and mild by active enterprises, and thus seems to have been most harmoniously attempered for the practice of virtue. (*Brutus,* 1)

As Shakespeare indicates, Brutus prefers reading to political scheming and generalship, and he cares deeply about his reputation for virtue. Had he cared less about reading philosophy deep into the night, he might not have fallen asleep and dreamed that Caesar was haunting him; had he cared less about his reputation for virtue, he might have sided with Cassius on killing Antony. Both Brutus and Cassius were members of a philosophical circle led by the Greek rhetorician Artemidorus, who was aware of their scheming and attempted to warn Caesar. In addition to thinking too much, they apparently talked too much. And if Cassius had not been such a doctrinaire materialist, he might not have been so open to a conversion. Furthermore, if he had cared less about being paraded before the Romans by a victorious Antony, he might not have ended his life prematurely (see the discussion of suicide between Cassius and Brutus at V.i.92–125). I don't want to make too much of the connection between philosophizing and political weakness, but Shakespeare does go out of his way to emphasize that Brutus and Cassius are no ordinary men of action, and to suggest that they are perhaps softer, more refined, and more impressionable or imaginative because of their intellectual leanings.

I don't think one can conclude, on the basis of Shakespeare's play, that he was convinced that Brutus and Cassius could have ultimately prevailed, that the structural forces aligned against the survival of the Roman republic were finally beatable. But he certainly does want to emphasize that it was a close call, that Brutus and Cassius made unnecessary mistakes, and that their belief in providence or cosmic necessity influenced their behavior to the detriment of their cause. To use Brutus's words against his precise intention, his belief that "there is a tide in the affairs of men / Which . . . leads on to fortune," is perhaps the most fundamental explanation for his failure. As I suggested at the very beginning of this chapter, Shakespeare is not only looking backward, but forward in this play: he very much wants to keep the republican dream alive. In some of the most memorable lines in a memorable play, Shakespeare invents speeches for Cassius and Brutus that appear nowhere in Plutarch and which celebrate their bloody defense of liberty as an act worthy of emulation anywhere and anytime:

> Cassius: Stoop then, and wash. How many ages hence
> Shall this our lofty scene be acted over
> In states unborn and accents yet unknown!
>
> Brutus: How many times shall Caesar bleed in sport,
> That now on Pompey's basis lies along
> No worthier than the dust?
>
> Cassius: So oft as that shall be,
> So often shall the knot of us be called
> The men that gave their country liberty. (III.i.111–17)

As Brutus's lines especially imply, Shakespeare considers the performance of his play a political act. In another addition to his source, Shakespeare's Brutus, who is about to kill himself, looks forward with confidence to his ultimate triumph: "I shall have glory by this losing day / More than Octavius and Marc Antony / By this vile conquest shall attain unto" (V.v.36–38). That may be a stretch with respect to Augustus Caesar, and of course it depends on who one reads or listens to (Virgil and Dante don't help . . .), but Shakespeare certainly did his part to memorialize and celebrate Brutus. At the very end of the play, even Marc Antony bows to Brutus, graciously and sincerely calling him "the noblest Roman of them all" (V.v.68). But celebrating Brutus turns out to be a rather difficult task, for Shakespeare must make him attractive enough to inspire admiration among the friends of liberty while also pointing out his dangerous shortcomings. And he must make a loser, who had all sorts of historical currents running against him, attractive to those who want to win. In asking us to consider exactly how powerful those currents were, Shakespeare seems to want us to question the power of providence or fate. And even if we were finally to conclude that Brutus's cause was hopeless, we need not also conclude that fate is equally powerful at all times or that all causes which appear hopeless are truly so. Shakespeare directs our attention to other times, times when divine power also seems to authorize and necessitate absolute rule, by subtly comparing Caesar's death to Christ's, adding ten wounds to the twenty-three reported by Plutarch and so alluding to Christ's age at his death. To what extent are the supernatural powers which legitimate absolute monarchy in modern Europe, Shakespeare seems to ask, dependent on beliefs that are subject to doubt?

NOTES

1. It is important to remember that the Roman republic was aristocratic, governed by senators of noble birth, and that the monarchy established by Octavius was absolute, and so might usefully be distinguished from limited or constitutional monarchies.

2. Plutarch, *The Life of Julius Caesar,* par. 28. I will be referring to and quoting from the Loeb Classical Library editions of *Brutus* (1918), *Caesar* (1919), and *Antony* (1920), trans. Bernadotte Perrin, all of which are in the public domain and available on the Internet. In addition to being accessible, the Loeb translations are more modern and readable than the North translation (which uses a French translation of the Latin as its source) that Shakespeare used. When the meaning seems slightly different, I will quote the North edition as well. Future references to Plutarch include the title followed by the paragraph number. Note that the Loeb paragraph numbers differ from North's.

3. Machiavelli, *Discourses on Livy,* 1.37.

4. Plutarch defends Cassius from the charge that his hatred of tyranny arose out of a personal grudge against Caesar. "For from the outset there was in the nature of Cassius great hostility and bitterness towards the whole race of tyrants, as he showed when he was still a boy" (*Brutus,* 9).

5. For "democracy" North writes "governed by many Lords" (which better captures the actual character of the Roman republic); for "Heaven," he writes "God" (*Shakespeare's Plutarch,* 147).

6. "Do you not think," Caesar reportedly said after reading a history of Alexander the Great, "it is a matter for sorrow what while Alexander, at my age [presumably 33], was already king of so many peoples, I have as yet achieved no brilliant successes?" (*Caesar,* 11).

7. I will be referring throughout to the Signet edition of Shakespeare's *Tragedy of Julius Caesar,* ed. William and Barbara Rosen (New York: Signet Classic, 1963).

8. Caesar is using the festival of Lupercal to celebrate his recent victory over the sons of Pompey in Spain, which also calls up his victory over Pompey himself. Plutarch notes that "the triumph that was celebrated . . . vexed the Romans as nothing else had done. For it commemorated no victory over foreign commanders or barbarian kings, but the utter annihilation of the sons and the family of the mightiest of the Romans, who had fallen upon misfortune; and it was not meet for Caesar to celebrate a triumph for the calamities of his country" (*Caesar,* 56). Pompey, it should be noted, restored the Tribunate in 70 B.C.E.

9. See the discussion in Bloom, *Shakespeare's Politics,* 100.

10. See Machiavelli on "temporizing," *Discourses on Livy,* I.33.5. Plutarch also suggests that patience might have been the better course for Brutus personally, if not for the republic: "And verily it appears that Brutus might have been first in the city with none to dispute him, could he have endured for a little while to be second to Caesar, suffering his power to wane and the fame of his successes to wither" (*Brutus,* 8).

11. As Plutarch reports, Brutus was capable of great violence and brutality. After capturing Octavius's camp, the prisoners "were slaughtered, and two thousand Lacedaemonians who had recently come as auxiliaries were cut to pieces along with them." Before the second battle at Philippi, Brutus promised his soldiers that "if they now fought well, he would turn over to them two cities for plunder and booty, Thessalonica and Lacedaemon." Plutarch notes that "this is the only accusation in the life of Brutus against which no defense can be made," thus implying that the slaughter of Antony's prisoners and auxiliaries could be defended (*Brutus,* 41, 46).

12. See, e.g., II.i.10–34; as for Brutus's anguish, Plutarch reports that Caesar may have been his father (*Brutus,* 5). If he knew or suspected as much, Brutus's fratricide imitates in reverse the horrible yet patriotic act of Junius Brutus, who killed his sons to protect the recently restored republic. Junius, unlike Marcus, feels no guilt. See the quotation from Plutarch toward the end of this chapter, which compares the two figures.

13. Earlier, both Casca and Cassius discussed the political utility of Brutus's moral reputation: "that which would appear offense in us, / His countenance . . . / Will change to virtue and to worthiness" (I.iii.157–60).

14. cf. II.i.185–189 with I.ii.192–210; note that Antony misjudges Cassius: "Fear him not, Caesar, he's not dangerous" (I.ii.196).

15. See also *Antony,* 17–20: Octavius turned against Cicero and after he "had been butchered, Antony ordered his head to be cut off, and that right hand with which Cicero had written speeches against him" (20).

16. "When he came to the river which separates Cisalpine Gaul from the rest of Italy . . . and began to reflect, now that he drew nearer to the fearful step and was agitated by the magnitude of his venture, he checked his speed. Then, halting in his course, he communed with himself for a long time in silence as his resolution wavered back and forth, and his purpose then suffered change after change. For a long time, too, he discussed his perplexities with his friends . . . estimating the great evils for all mankind which would follow their passage of the river, and the wide fame of it which they would leave to posterity" (*Caesar,* 32).

17. Plutarch's source here, interestingly enough, is "the philosopher Strabo" (*Caesar,* 63).

18. Plutarch writes that Brutus received a report—later revealed as false—that his wife had just died; he proceeded with the assassination as planned (*Brutus,* 15). Shakespeare does not show us this Brutus, almost inhuman in his self-possession. Later, in reaction to the actual death of his wife, Shakespeare's Brutus shows some emotion: "O Cassius, I am sick of many griefs . . . Portia is dead" (IV.iii.143, 146).

19. Xenophon, *The Education of Cyrus,* I.6.2; note also that priests were public officials in Rome: Julius Caesar and later Marc Antony served as Pontifex Maximus (Plutarch, *Antony,* 33).

20. Montaigne, "A Custom of the Isle of Cea," in *The Complete Works,* 310.

REFERENCES

Bloom, Allan. "The Morality of the Pagan Hero: *Julius Caesar.*" In *Shakespeare's Politics,* by Allan Bloom with Harry V. Jaffa, 75–112. Chicago: University of Chicago Press, 1964.

Hobbes, Thomas. *Leviathan.* Ed. C. B. MacPherson. London: Penguin Books, 1985. [Reprint of 1651 edition.]

Machiavelli, Niccolò. *Discourses on Livy.* Trans. Harvey C. Mansfield and Nathan Tarcov. Chicago: University of Chicago Press, 1996.

Montaigne, Michel. "A Custom of the Island of Cea." In *The Complete Works,* trans. Donald M. Frame, 305–18. New York: Knopf, 2003. [Essay written in 1573–74.]

Plutarch. *The Parallel Lives,* "The Life of Brutus," "The Life of Julius Caesar," and "The Life of Antony." Trans. Bernadotte Perrin. Loeb Classical Library edition, Vols. VI, VII, and IX, 1918, 1919, 1920. [In the public domain.]

———. *Shakespeare's Plutarch: Being a Selection from the Lives in North's Plutarch Which Illustrate Shakespeare's Plays.* Trans. Sir Thomas North, ed. Rev. Walter W. Skeat. London: Macmillan, 1875. [First edition of North's translation appeared in 1579.]

Shakespeare, William. *The Tragedy of Julius Caesar.* Ed. William Rosen and Barbara Rosen. New York: Signet Classic, 1963.

Xenophon. *The Education of Cyrus.* Trans. Wayne Ambler. Ithaca, NY: Cornell University Press, 2001.

Chapter Nineteen

Preliminary Observations on the Theologico-Political Dimension of Cervantes' *Don Quixote*

THOMAS L. PANGLE

> Those who guide their morals by the examples drawn from the old books, their histories, their fables, are subject to falling into the extravagances of the knights-errant of our novels, and conceiving designs that surpass their powers.
>
> —Descartes, *Discourse on Method* (1637)

Among the many playfully provocative, enigmatic features of Cervantes' masterpiece, none is so basic as the puzzle posed by the bewilderingly manifold authorial voice and perspective through which the tale is delivered to us. In the first two sentences of the prologue to the first volume (published in 1605), Cervantes emphatically avows his "parentage" of "this book" as his "offspring." But he adds that though he may have engendered the book—"my offspring," as he again calls it—the same cannot be said of the book's eponymous hero: "although I pass for the father, I am the stepfather of Don Quixote." What this means becomes clearer as soon as we begin to read the body of the book.

At the outset, our author presents himself as having assembled his account from the writings of others—from the "veracious history" found in "the annals of La Mancha" (25, 28, 31 = 28, 32, 36).[1] But at the end of the "First Part" (chap. 8) we learn from our "second author" (as he now calls himself) that "the author of this history" abruptly broke off, leaving the reader in suspense as to the outcome of the battle being narrated, and excusing himself on the grounds that he was unable to find any more writings about Don Quixote (64 = 83).

Our "second author" opens the Second Part (chap. 9) by telling us that he felt that it was "impossible, and contrary to all good custom, that such a good knight should have lacked some sage (*sabio*) to undertake to write of his wonderful adventures." He reports that his laborious searches for further record were finally rewarded: "with the help of heaven, chance, and fortune," our compiler discovered in the marketplace of Toledo a *"History of Don Quixote of la Mancha,"* written in Arabic, by one "Cide Hamete Benengeli, an Arab historian." This work the narrator was able to get translated, over the course of a month and a half, by a Morisco[2] whom he found "by luck." It is this translation that constitutes all the rest of the book (including the interspersed "novellas"), except for occasional remarks, and some paraphrases or summaries of omitted matter, by the translator—as well as a few comments of our compiler or "second author."

Our "second author"-now-become-conduit concedes that an objection could be raised as to the truth of the account that follows, given that it was written by an Arab—"since lying is very common among those of that nation." But he counters this with the observation that "they are such enemies of ours" that the Arab historian "is more likely to have erred by diminishing rather than by overstating the case." Such indeed, in the opinion of our conduit, is what "this cur of an author" has done: he has obviously kept silent at key points when he ought to have praised Don Quixote (68 = 88).

We are not surprised to see that the Morisco translator is more favorably disposed to the Arab historian. The translator opens the Third Part (chap. 15) by characterizing Cide Hamete Benengeli as a "sage" (*sabio*). Soon thereafter, he judges that "Cide Mahamete [as he now calls him] Benengeli was a historian very curious and scrupulous in all things," whose example ought to be followed by "serious historians." The translator deduces that Benengeli, though an Arab, must be a "Manchegan," or from La Mancha, since he evinces close personal acquaintance with some of the persons whose deeds he recounts (107 and 151 = 141 and 199), and eventually offers eyewitness reports of having seen Sancho Panza regularly (618 = 815). So it would seem that Cide Hamete (or is it Mahamete?) Benengeli, "the Arab and Manchegan author," lived or is living in Spain under a disguise.[3] Could he be a Morisco? Another possibility is that he is a Christian Manchegan who wishes to ascribe his writing to an Arab; but why would a son of Christian Spain wish to appear in his writing as one of the enemies of Spain and of the true religion? The answer is obvious: given the omnipresence of the frightful Inquisition, whose burning of books and heretics looms over the entire work,[4] it is only prudent to wear as many veils as possible when one appears in print with anything other than orthodox expressions.

In light of the ambiguity in the preceding clues as to the identity of the true author or "father" of Don Quixote, we are not totally dumbfounded when the first volume ends with a brief passage that momentarily verges on collapsing the distinction between the compiler-conduit (Cervantes), the Morisco translator, and the Arab historian Cide Hamete: the narrator suddenly identifies himself as "the trustworthy author of this new and never before seen history." But even here the narrator continues to insist that he is no more than a compiler, who "brought the history to light by searching the Manchegan archives" (402 = 529).

In the beginning of the second volume (published in 1615), Cervantes slips back under the mask of Cide Hamete (now designated "the first author": 558 and 641 = 734 and 848). We are soon made aware that the first volume has been published, to acclaim. For Don Quixote runs into one of his admiring readers, who so informs the hero, and who is quoted as saying to him, "a blessing on Cide Hamete Benengeli, who has written the history of your great deeds, and a double blessing on that curious fellow who took the trouble of having it translated out of Arabic"— "the Moor in his language, and the Christian in his." Don Quixote, for his part, reacts to this with "uneasiness at the thought that the author was a Moor," since "no truth was to be expected from Moors" (439 = 566–67). The Moorishness of the author is certainly now made more prominent by the Morisco translator: "'Blessed be Allah the powerful (*el poderoso Alá*)!,' says Hamete Benengeli in beginning this eighth chapter: 'Blessed be Allah!' he repeats three times" (462 = 601). Oddly, however, the Moor is thus quoted as blasphemously failing to ascribe *omnipotence* to Allah.[5] What kind of Muslim is Cide Hamete? At the beginning of the twenty-seventh chapter, we are told by the compiler-conduit, in an editorial comment, that "Cide Hamete begins this chapter with the words, 'I swear as a Catholic Christian'"—and that the translator, in his editorial comment, tried to explain this away as follows: Cide Hamete, "since he was a Moor without a doubt" (see also 665 = 882), "only meant that he was telling the truth" and thus writing as a good Christian *would* write (577 = 759–60). It appears that if one were to suspect that the story of Don Quixote might be fiction, one might well suspect that it was not written by a good Christian.

But subsequently we are jarred to discover, through the compiler-conduit, that in a passage omitted by the translator from the forty-fourth chapter of the second volume but reported by unnamed other sources, Cide Hamete betrayed his very great lack of respect for Don Quixote as well as for Sancho Panza. Indeed, the historian is said to have "complained against himself" for having undertaken to write the "history" of the "mad antics of Don Quixote and the nonsense of Sancho Panza," when he "has ability, capacity, and understanding to discuss the whole universe" (662 = 878). This report, if true, shows that in the original Arabic version Cide Hamete impatiently revealed, even earlier than now appears in the Spanish translation (810 = 1077), how heavy was the irony of his previous, apparently enthusiastic, praise of the crazy knight and his babbling squire (e.g., at 515 = 674–75). Cide Hamete's indication that his inclination and capacity direct him toward discussion of "the whole universe"—from which the telling of the story of Don Quixote is an (eventually irritating) digression—prepares us for the subsequent revelation of the true character and outlook of the authorial voice responsible for Don Quixote.

Chapter 53 of the second volume commences (718 = 953) with the sole quotation expressing the conception of existence held by "our author" (*nuestro autor*), who is identified finally, by our compiler-conduit, as a "Mohammedan philosopher (*filósofo mahométtico*)." As such, "our author" is "guided without the fiery light of faith (*sin lumbre de fe*) but by the natural light (*con la luz natural*)." On that basis, our "Mohammedan philosopher" declares that "to think that in this life the things belonging to it endure always in one state is to think erroneously; on the contrary, it appears that it goes in a complete cycle—I say, in a circular fashion: spring gives way to summer, summer to fall, fall to autumn, autumn to winter"; and "thus, time turns in this wheel continuously." Our "Mohammedan philosopher" manifestly conceives of the visible universe as eternally in cyclical motion, following Aristotle, and sees no evidence of a creation in time or of a "Creator of all things (*Criador de todas las cosas*)" (71 = 93)—such as Don Quixote has been led to believe in, by "the fiery light of faith." Our "Mohammedan philosopher" may then be best characterized as an Averroist[6]—a disciple of the most influential philosopher ever produced by Spain and Spanish culture and a follower of "the ancient philosophers, who were without true understanding of God" (508 = 665). In the Averroist framework, individual human existence, as self-consciously mortal, is to be conceived as the agonized exception that emerges out of the eternally cyclical universe: "only human life" (our "Mohammedan philosopher" is quoted as teaching) "runs to its end faster than the wind, without hope of renewing itself, unless in the other [life], which has no termination that limits it." For there "are many," adds our conduit-compiler in an editorial remark, "who without the light of faith, but by the natural light, understand the swiftness and instability of the present life, and the duration of the eternal life that is hoped for." To understand that there is an eternal life hoped for after death of course does not require revelation or faith but only reason and philosophy, according to Cervantes (after all, Plato's Socrates demonstrates in the *Phaedo* the existence of the afterlife, without any reliance on revelation or faith). Yet it is not at all evident from the Mohammedan philosopher's words that he, as a philosopher, shares with the "many" in such a "hope"—though one surmises that the philosopher as philosopher "understands" fully what that hope means and what it consists in, and why it is so deeply embedded in human nature (see also 825 = 1099: "the human things are not eternal").

But why in the world would an Averroist philosopher expend such enormous time and energy narrating the "mad antics of Don Quixote and the nonsense of Sancho Panza?" Why would he turn aside from his investigations into the unchanging nature of the universe? The Muslim philosopher's purpose, as stated in his (or his "pen's") closing words, is "no other than to cause real men (*los hombres*) to abhor the false and foolish tales of the books of chivalry/knighthood (*la cabelleria*)" (830 = 1106). Now why is this a task worthy of a philosopher, or for that matter, a great comic artist informed by philosophy? What is so important about "the false and foolish tales" of these books? In one of the wise speeches that Cervantes has put in the mouth of Don Quixote, a speech whose theme is the nature of poetry and poets, Cervantes has his "ingenious" knight declare that "sprightly and artful comedies" must "not be touched by the buffoons or the ignorant vulgar (*ignorante vulgo*), incapable of understanding or valuing the treasures that Poetry hides within herself"—"and do not think, sir" (adds Don Quixote), "that I apply the term 'vulgar' here merely to plebians and the lower orders; for everyone who is not wise, be he lord or prince, may and should be included in the number of the vulgar" (509 = 667; see also 376 and 442 = 493–94 and 572). So what are the principal "hidden treasures" that wise readers—in contrast to "the ignorant vulgar"—are supposed to grasp in the comic poetry that is the book *Don Quixote*? What is it that the books of chivalry represent? What is their power and evil, as expressed in the effect these books have in driving poor Don Quixote into the peculiarly inspired insanity that he exhibits?

Very early in the work, Don Quixote declares, "I know who I am"—and proceeds to assert that he is the reincarnation, not only of the twelve peers of Charlemagne, but of the "Nine of Fame (*los nueve de la Fama*)," who include three biblical figures—Joshua, David, and Judas Maccabeus—along with three pagan heroes and three Christian knights. Two pages later a priest, who identifies himself as a personal friend of Cervantes, familiar with his writings, says that the very first book of chivalry—the book, not the author(s)—is "something mysterious," on account of its influence; and he pronounces that first book itself to be the "dogmatist of a very wicked sect (*dogmatizador de una secta tan mala*)." Much later, a learned clerical canon tells Don Quixote that the books of chivalry are themselves equivalent to "inventors of new sects," whereas the Book of Judges, in the Bible, is *the* book of *true* chivalry; to this Don Quixote replies that the canon's remarks disparaging the *other* books of chivalry constitute "blasphemy" (*blasfemia*), deserving of condign punishment (383–84 = 504–5; we often hear Don Quixote accusing people who doubt the truth of the books of chivalry of "blasphemy").

In the vision by which Don Quixote guides his life, there is a continuum from the books of chivalry back to both classical antiquity and, above all, the Bible, conceived as itself the preeminent and original book of chivalry (with Catholicism considered part of this chivalry: 71, 130, 432 = 93, 173, 558). Saint Paul, in Don Quixote's view, was a very great knight-errant—along with Saints George, Martin, and James "the Muslim-slayer." These were all, Don Quixote says, "of the same profession as myself, which is the calling of arms. Only there is this difference between them and me, that they were saints, and fought in the divine manner (*a lo divino*), and I am a sinner and fight in the human manner (*a lo humano*)" (743 = 987; Don Quixote here quotes Matthew 11:12 and refers twice to "Christ"). Or as Don Quixote says near the outset, "we are God's ministers on earth and the arms by means of which is executed His justice" (85 = 112). When Sancho Panza listens to Don Quixote discourse on divine providence, he gratifies his master by judging that Don Quixote "would make a better preacher than a knight-errant" (124 = 164). Above all, when Sancho suggests at one point that he and his master should pursue the calling of Christian saints rather than that of knights-errant, Don Quixote insists and teaches that this is a totally false dichotomy or choice: "*knighthood is religion;* there are sainted knights in glory (*religión es la cabelleria, caballeros santos hay en la gloria*)" (467 = 608; emphasis added). In accordance with this sacred standard of true knight-errantry, Don Quixote is by no means an indiscriminate admirer of the conventional books of chivalry; in fact, he sees his mission as one that will "consign to oblivion the whole herd of famous knights-errant of yore," by obscuring their deeds with his own—and thereby bringing back the superior, "golden" age of the Bible and the classical era as well as Charlemagne and the pious knights of the Round Table (132 = 175). In his most rigorous defense of the meaning of his life (299–303 = 392–97), Don Quixote justifies the superiority of the life of arms to the life of just rule or of judging by appealing to the New Testament teaching that peace rather than justice is the greatest good; for the peace commanded by the New Testament is a universal "peace on earth" (quoting Luke 2:13–14); and such a peace cannot be achieved except through conquest of the entire earth, by Christian men of war. This interpretation of the true meaning of the Christian elevation of peace over justice is ratified as correct by the priest, "a man of letters and a university graduate" (304 = 398). *The* "duty" or calling of Don Quixote is to "undo force" (*desfacer fuerzas*)—which requires the most extreme use of force, in a kind of pious dialectic (151 = 200). Accordingly, the explicit long-range political project of Don Quixote from the outset and repeated throughout is Christian *imperialism.*

Don Quixote is a noble, intelligent, highly imaginative and articulate but fanatically moralistic and pious gentleman who has become inebriated to the point of insanity by the idea of devoting his life to the imperial religious heroism and chaste love he finds commanded by sacred Scripture tinctured by classical moral philosophy. In other words, the figure and the deeds and the animating beliefs of Don Quixote represent a grotesquely caricatured, and thus appropriately veiled, portrait of the fanaticism to which militant "modern" religion can lead. Writing in an era of intensifying religious warfare and persecution—expressed most immediately in the brutal expulsion of the Moriscos from Spain in the years intervening between the publication of volumes 1 and 2 of *Don Quixote*—the poet holds the febrile knight up as a kind of mirror image that will arrest, alarm, and chasten thoughtful readers who inhabit modern (primarily Spanish) Christian culture.

But through his portrait of Don Quixote, Cervantes satirizes more than simply the militant tendencies or temptations of modern religion. It is evident from the start, and becomes plainer when we learn of the religious orientations of the translator and the "first author," that what Don Quixote personifies is an infatuation that combines "gentile" and Muslim as well as Talmudic elements together with Protestant and Catholic Christianity (see esp. 30, 44–45, 79, 86 = 35, 55–57, 103, 113). In the tale of Don Quixote, we venture to say, we are given a preposterously exaggerated but thus safely revealing representation of how the great monotheistic religions, taken together, appear to "a philosopher." Once we begin to catch on to the fact that this is the deepest meaning of the figure of Don Quixote and his infatuation with "books of chivalry," we are in a position to discern manifold dimensions of Cervantes' Averroist satirical caricature of the mentality that subordinates guidance by the "the natural light (*la luz natural*)" to guidance by the "fiery light of faith (*lumbre de fe*)." And we begin to see how this satire illuminates, by contrast, the outlook of the satirical poet temporarily assuming the mask of "Mohammedan philosopher."

As the saga draws to its close, Don Quixote, discouraged by defeat, laments that "*fortuna* made me the victim of its twists and turns" (792 = 1054–55; see also 729 = 969). Sancho tries to comfort his master by remarking that he has heard it said that what people call Fortuna is really a drunken, fickle, blind woman, whose judgments ought not to be taken seriously. Don Quixote declares that in speaking thus, Sancho shows himself to be "very philosophical (*muy filósofo*)"; indeed, Don Quixote is so impressed by Sancho's expression of this "philosophical" outlook that he exclaims, "I don't know who taught you that!" Yet Don Quixote insists that this philosophic outlook, however sensible and comforting it may be—or precisely because it appears so sensible—is not in conformity with reality: "I say to you that there is no *fortuna* in the world (*no hay fortuna in el mundo*), nor do the things that happen in the world, be they good or evil, come about by chance." In reality, Don Quixote insists, everything occurs by "particular providence of heaven (*particular providencia de los cielos*)." Much earlier, Don Quixote had eloquently preached to Sancho that providence extends even to each mosquito of the air, each worm in the earth, and each tadpole in the water (124 = 164). Yet this does not relieve humans of personal responsibility: "each is the artisan of his own happenings" (792 = 969; see also 154 = 203).

Don Quixote has difficulty, however, clinging to this belief in all-encompassing particular providence. He finds himself impelled to contrast the agency of "heaven" with the agency of "Fortuna"—viewed as heaven's rival.[7] Precisely because he sees everywhere the effects of superhuman will, he confesses his bewilderment at the manifestations of *competing* wills: "God help it, this world is all machinations and appearances" (590 = 777).

The most radically antiphilosophic, and complex or perplexingly thought-provoking, dimension of Don Quixote's outlook is his belief in the enchanted character of what is given to us in ordinary experience. Through this massive aspect of Don Quixote's lunacy, Cervantes depicts or explores, in comic and unforgettable fashion, what it means to try to live conceiving of reality after having jettisoned, in the name of belief in divine omnipotence, the notion of natural necessity. As I have emphasized, Cide Hamete invokes Allah as the "Powerful"—*not* the "All-powerful"; in contrast, Don Quixote "swears by the omnipotent God (*por el omnipotente Dios juro*)."[8] Don Quixote does refer to a "natural order (*orden natural*)" on one occasion. This occurs when he believes he is being conveyed through space in a way that violates the ordinary course of things (652 = 864): that is, when he thinks he is in the grip of what one is tempted to call a "miracle." But, in contrast to other characters in the book, Don Quixote tends not to speak or think in terms of "miracles."[9] The concept of the miraculous presupposes a fixity in the world of our ordinary experience that is *interrupted* by the miraculous; but Don Quixote conceives the world of our ordinary experience as rife with illusions woven by enchanters "from the other world" (130 = 173), who are usually hostile to the human saints like Don Quixote who have the capacity to see through their enchantments. Don Quixote may be said to take to the end the road pointed to by C. S. Lewis in his famous characterization of the given world as "shadowlands." Don Quixote's "usual practice" is to characterize "all inns" that he approaches as castles, enchanted so as to appear, especially to others, as if they were merely inns (751 and 816 = 998 and 1087). When Don Quixote encounters herds, he usually interprets them to be armies engaged in (sometimes religious) war but which have been "enchanted" to *appear,* especially to others, as herds of goats and pigs. As Don Quixote makes clear in major general pronouncements on reality as he conceives it (180, 590, 607 = 237, 777–78, 800), he sees the given world as in large part a cover for a dramatically mysterious reality in which superhuman agents engage in a struggle of good and evil, into which are drawn the saints and religious heroes. This deeper reality is revealed in sacred books, to such an extent that Don Quixote understands himself, from early on, to be a persona in a book of knight-errantry that is in the process of being written or that has been already written by an invisible "sage" (30, 129–30 = 35, 173).[10] Not only are certain books the key to the secret of existence; existence is a book, being written or having already been written by an invisible wisdom.

It would seem, then, that the deeper reality, or "the other world," and its "sage," causes and controls while being uncontrolled and unaffected by the shadowy world of our ordinary experience. It would seem that there is an ultimate nature of things underlying the mutable apparent world of our ordinary experience. Thus when Sancho challenges Don Quixote's claim that certain water mills which they are approaching are castles, Don Quixote replies as follows: "though they look like mills, they are not; . . . enchantments transform things and change their natural shapes. I do not mean to say that they *really* (*realmente*) change them, from one form into another, but that it *seems* (*parece*) as though they did, as experience proved (*como lo monstró la experienca*) in the case of Dulcinea" (588 = 776; emphasis added). Just as Don Quixote can see Mambrino's helmet for what it "*really* and *truly is*" (*real y verdaderamente es*), while "enchantment" makes the helmet *seem* to be a mere basin to everybody else (180 = 237; emphasis added), so enchantment cannot alter the true, divine essence of Dulcinea; enchantment can only make her *appear,* to various humans, to be part of the everyday world.

Dulcinea is indeed the supreme case. For, in her "beauty superhuman (*hermosura subrehumana*)" Dulcinea is for Don Quixote divinity incarnate in human flesh. "Sole refuge of my hopes," she is divinity to whom Don Quixote offers prayers and from whom he experiences intimate inspiration: "she fights in me and conquers in me and I live and breathe in her and owe my life and being to her" (paraphrasing Acts 17:28 and Galatians 2:20).[11] When Don Quixote sees Dulcinea looking like a coarse peasant girl, he insists that it is enchantment that makes her appear so, to him; on this occasion it is Sancho whose report proves that he is privileged with correct vision of the true, superhumanly beautiful Dulcinea who persists behind all enchantments that make her appear altered; whether other knights will also, like Don Quixote, see her in the disgusting veil of enchantment or whether they will, like Sancho, see her in her unchanging essence is a question to be tested by empirical experimentation (476 ff., 608 = 620 ff., 802).

But Don Quixote cannot unwaveringly maintain this faith in the independent status and unchanging essence of the incarnate divinity.

Precisely because divinity as Dulcinea is so intimately involved with his human existence and suffering, Don Quixote is driven to conceiving of his divine Dulcinea as having been in herself, at least temporarily, "enchanted, offended, changed, altered, transformed" by his wizard-enemies; Don Quixote is driven to conceive of his divinity as having undergone a degradation from which she herself actually suffers (608 = 802). What remains unclear is whether this degradation reaches to the divine Dulcinea's very core.[12]

But does or can Don Quixote believe wholeheartedly in Dulcinea or in his faith-based vision of reality? That Don Quixote's faith cannot be equated with sheer insanity, that he embodies a faith that wavers, becomes evident from the occasional indications the author gives of Don Quixote's doubts. It is only when Don Quixote is being fooled by the Duke and Duchess that "*for the first time* he thoroughly knew and believed (*conoció y creyó*) himself to be a *real* knight-errant and not an imaginary one (*fantástico*)" (595 = 784; emphasis added); but two pages later he is confessing to Sancho his anxiety lest their hosts think him "an imposter or swindler" (597 = 787; see also 178 = 235). When Sancho challenges Don Quixote's faith in the existence of Dulcinea as divine, on the grounds that Sancho knows the actual peasant girl Aldonza Lorenzo to whom Don Quixote is referring, Don Quixote confesses that the divine Dulcinea is a product of his "imagination," like the creations of the poets (184–85 = 243–44); in this context Don Quixote makes his sole reference to Aristotle by name, in the course of telling what is—for our chaste and bashful knight—a strikingly uncharacteristic comic story combining obscenity with blasphemy (for just one instant, under the influence of recalling Aristotle, Don Quixote sounds like Cervantes). Much later, Don Quixote is highly evasive in replying to the Duchess's suggestion that Dulcinea is "not in the world except as an imaginary lady that you begot and gave birth to in your understanding and adorned with whatever graces and perfections you chose" (606 = 800). The "fiery light of faith" manifests itself as sometimes flickering.

Don Quixote, as Cervantes' archetypical zealot, is without doubt a kind of noble soul; and his squire, Sancho Panza, is an amiable and shrewdly sensible if shallow fellow (whose longing for prestige, wealth, and power renders him susceptible, in some measure, to the contagion of

Don Quixote's "delusion"—372, 473, 501 = 489, 616–17, 656). We are *not* led by Cervantes to hate the knight; we even develop a certain indulgent fondness for him, and even more for his squire; but we are never allowed to forget that Don Quixote is a dangerously pestilent troublemaker. Don Quixote regards himself as authorized by heaven to commit as many "homicides" as he thinks fit, without ever having to answer in a court of law (70 = 91). He ruthlessly seeks to murder or to maim, and succeeds in crippling, numerous innocent people whom he conceives to be evil and magical; he even twice tries to murder poor Sancho (140, 233 = 184–85, 306). Indeed, today's reader cannot help but be reminded at times of certain contemporary religious terrorists—though it must be stressed that Don Quixote loathes artillery and explosives because they are too indiscriminate and preclude single combat (303 = 397). The unease or guilt we may naturally begin to feel at the delight we find ourselves induced to take in the hilarious tales of the knight's sufferings (as we watch him repeatedly humiliated, ridiculed, gulled, imprisoned, terrified, beaten to a pulp with countless bones broken) becomes alleviated when we finally learn that in the long run these cruel sufferings, especially the worst spiritual sufferings, and our hero's very "unhappiness" (see the title of 2.64) can lead to his recovery of his senses—which is the happy ending, though it entails the zealot's death.

Cervantes paints in vivid colors two forms of human ambition or passion that stand as major alternatives to the religious lunacy of Don Quixote—one of which is more prominent in the first volume, the other in the second. The first volume is distinguished by the romantic novellas interpolated into the main narrative. That these interrupt, and are in some sense alien to—but thereby illuminate by way of contrast—the tale and character of Don Quixote is made plain by the fact that our ascetic hero sleeps through the drama of the most elaborate love story (293 = 384). And when, at the start of the second volume, Don Quixote learns that the first is interrupted with a long extraneous story, he complains bitterly that this proves that "the author of my history was not some sage but some ignorant chatterer" (441 = 571). Don Quixote, we may say, experiences love in a form so chastely exalted in its devotion that it exists on a plane above and beyond what we may call "natural" romance; and Sancho Panza, for his part, is so little animated by the devotional (241,

292 = 316, 382–83) that his faithfulness to his fat peasant wife exists on a level below the possibility of such romance. Like Cervantes' *Exemplary Novellas,* the novellas within the first volume of *Don Quixote* show romantic love flaming up at the margins and in the interstices of ordinary life, where sectarian and ethnic strife, differences of rank and nation, arranged marriages, the seclusion of women are temporarily overcome or broken through.[13] The fugitive character of romantic love is linked with its terrible, simultaneous, strength-and-weakness, or its contradictory character: Cervantes shows such love inspiring those whom it bewitches to seek and to demand unbreakable, reciprocal, devoted fidelity; yet this passion is unstable in both its strength and its objects—waxing and waning, attaching to and then abandoning successively different "beloveds"—unless or until it is restrained, confined, and in large measure repressed by artificial constraint and convention. As is highlighted by the famous antierotic speech of Marcella, romantic love appears as another kind of infatuation, though one whose irrationality is much more attractive, gentle, natural, and beautiful than Don Quixote's.

In the second volume we are made witnesses to Sancho Panza's unexpectedly effective governance of a village he is deceived into supposing is a semi-independent island community. Sancho rules without any reliance on chivalry, or indeed religion (one of his innovative laws restricts claims of miracles). While he seems to profit from at least one teaching in a long and pretty sound lecture on governance given to him by his master, Don Quixote, Sancho confesses that he forgot most of the lecture as soon as he heard it. Sancho as legislator and judge is guided by a shrewd, peasant common sense and humanity. Ruling on this simple, equitable basis he arouses everyone's admiration; Spanish governance, we conclude, is "normally" pretty bad. But the decisive defect of Sancho as governor, the failing that leads to the voluntary termination of his rule after a few days, is his cowardice and petty selfishness or self-indulgence. It is precisely the contrary virtues that are Don Quixote's strong suits; when Sancho as governor is asked to take up arms to defend his realm, he replies, "Better leave all that to my master" (719 = 954)—and soon abdicates. Sancho Panza embodies, and presents as a standard by which heroism is ridiculed but in a degree vindicated, what we may term a peasant version of a protobourgeois or proto-Hobbesian mentality.

There seems to be a pointer to a nonclownish or more serious version of his down-to-earth, nonheroic ethos in the alternative to knight-errantry that is developed in the major speech of Don Quixote (299–301= 390–94). There we hear of the life of the judge, devoted not to war (or to Quixotic "peace") but to justice; and such a life we then witness embodied in the judge of the Supreme Court of Mexico who soon thereafter makes a cameo appearance (336 = 440–41). When Sancho is given his island to govern, the Duke declares that such rule requires a combination of arms and letters (654 = 866). Could Cervantes be inviting us to imagine, as exemplary of true manly virtue, a well-orchestrated synthesis of Sancho and Don Quixote, elevating the former and bringing down to earth the latter—a ruler who combined legislative and judicial common sense with warrior courage and a nonfanatic capacity for devotion to ruling? We are explicitly encouraged to "unite in one individual all the faculties that serve to make an illustrious gentleman perfect" by gathering and judiciously combining the virtues distributed among multiple heroes of legend (375 = 492). In this connection, we note that in the prologue to the second volume Cervantes identifies himself as, not a warrior-ruler, but a warrior-poet.

NOTES

Catherine Zuckert and Michael Zuckert have been leaders in advancing and encouraging serious scholarly study of the political-philosophic implications of great works of literature. As one of those who have been encouraged in this regard by their work, I offer this essay as a tribute to them.

1. In quotations from *Don Quixote* I have made use of Cervantes 1981, modified for the sake of greater accuracy. Numbers in parentheses refer to pages of this translation, followed after an equals sign by page numbers in the Real Academia Espanola edition (2004). I have been helped by Higuera 1995 and by Leo Strauss's letter to Jacob Klein of August 18, 1939, in Strauss 2001, 578–79.

2. The name given to Spanish Muslims who accepted baptism, and also to their descendants. From 1609 to 1614 they were expelled from Spain with great cruelty, involving over three hundred thousand individuals.

3. Not unlike principal characters in Cervantes' "exemplary novella" titled "The Spanish-English Lady." And consider Mahmoud in "The Generous Lover."

4. 47, 53, 334, 568, 775, 805 = 59, 67, 438, 748, 1030, 1070–71.

5. Contrast 365 = 478 where Don Quixote swears by "the omnipotent God (*el omnipotente Dios*)"; and see 535 = 703, where the god Cupid boasts of himself as "the powerful god (*el dios poderoso*)"; Cupid's boast is disputed by the god Wealth, who claims to be a still more powerful divinity. For Cupid's power, see also the closing words of Cervantes' exemplary novella "The Two Damsels."

6. See *Condemnation of the 219 Propositions*, #110–12, 137–39 (in Lerner and Mahdi, 347–48); and Mandonnet, 1.170 ff. and 2.186; also Marsilius of Padua, *Defensor Pacis* 1.17.10.

7. See e.g., 389, 476, 506, 590, 654–55 = 511–12, 620, 662, 777, 867–88.

8. 365 = 478; Cervantes, for his part, appeals to "the natural order" in the second sentence of the prologue. The wisest character ever to appear in the novel, Marcela, says she relies on the "*natural* understanding God gave me" (94 = 125); one suspects Cide Hamete would put it the same way as regards himself. Averroes remarks (1954, 1.97, 273), "The philosophers only call the world eternal in order to safeguard themselves against the kind of creation . . . in time, and after a state of non-existence"; for "then anything whatever might proceed from anything whatever, and there would be no congruity between causes and effects."

9. See the references to "miracles" at 58, 66, 113, 133, 161, 162, 232, 258, 287, 302, 333, 338, 377–78, 392, 412, 441, 467, 471, 507, 542, 561, 631, 712, 746, 763, 815 = 74, 85, 150, 176, 212, 214, 305, 339, 377, 395, 437, 444, 496, 516, 539, 571, 608, 613, 664, 703, 712, 739, 834, 897, 945, 990, 1014, 1085 (see also the exemplary novella "The Dialogue of the Dogs"); for Don Quixote's occasional mention of miracles, see 227, 522, 607, 677 = 298, 683, 801.

10. Don Quixote thus divines that the true "wise enchanters" are the poets such as Cervantes.

11. 234 = 307; also 240–41, 548, 588 = 314–16, 720–21, 776.

12. We cannot help but be reminded of the profound Christological controversy that haunts Christianity, and that came to a peak in the age of the Apollinarian and Nestorian heresies, leading finally to Justinian's (Christian imperialist) authoritarian settlement. For an orientation, see Pelikan, *The Christian Tradition,* 1: chap. 5, "The Person of the God-Man"; and chap. 7, "The Orthodox Consensus." "The critical problem was his suffering, crucifixion, and death. Who 'cried with a loud voice—Eli, Eli Lama sabachthani?' " (245). The Council of Chalcedon with its Augustinian doctrine of two simultaneous natures in Christ was an unsuccessful "agreement to disagree" (266). See Thomas Aquinas, *Summa Contra Gentiles* 4.34–35, 39.

13. Of Cervantes' twelve *Exemplary Novellas,* only the last contains discussion of theology, as well as the only speech by someone (a witch) who with some irony calls herself a "theologian (*téologa*)." This same story contains the sole thematic discussion of "philosophy." In the penultimate novella, titled "The Deceitful Marriage," a pious soldier-swindler tells an old pious friend how he tried, through marriage, to swindle an attractive and apparently wealthy woman—who turned the tables on him (it turned out that the pious soldier-swindler was himself amazingly gullible). The pious

swindler claims to his somewhat incredulous friend that, as he was being treated in a religious charity hospital for the syphilis with which his whoring and thieving wife infected him, one night he witnessed a miracle: a long private conversation between two pious dogs who had that very day been supernaturally granted rational speech (it transpires that, according to the witch-"theologian," this miracle probably had its source in the devil or in one of his witches). In the course of the pious dogs' long conversation about their life experience—a conversation reported verbatim in the final novella, "The Dialogue of the Dogs"—the canines agree that "humility is the basis and foundation of all virtues, without which there is none," and they articulate and embrace the doctrine of original sin as explaining and justifying God's permission of evil. They warn one another that "this urge to philosophize (*"esa gana de filosofar"*) may be a "temptation of the devil," inasmuch as philosophizing serves as an excuse for engaging in the sin of gossip or satire (as if "exposing the defects of our fellows is a worthy and conscientious act")—a sin which the two pious dogs strive earnestly, but with comic lack of success, to avoid throughout their Cervantian-satirical dialogue.

REFERENCES

Averroes. 1954. *The Incoherence of the Incoherence.* 2 vols. Trans. Simon Van den Bergh. London: Luzac.

Cervantes, Miguel de. 1980. *Novelas ejemplares.* 2 vols. Ed. Harry Siebert. Madrid: Catédra.

———. 1981. *Don Quixote: The Ormsby Translation, Revised, Backgrounds and Sources, Criticism.* Ed. Joseph R. Jones and Kenneth Douglas. New York: Norton.

———. 2004. *Don Quijote de la Mancha.* Ed. Francisco Rico. Madrid: Real Academia Espanola.

Higuera, Henry. 1995. *Eros and Empire: Politics and Christianity in "Don Quixote."* Lanham, MD: Rowman and Littlefield.

Lerner, Ralph, and Muhsin Mahdi, eds. 1963. *Medieval Political Philosophy: A Sourcebook.* Glencoe, IL: Free Press.

Mandonnet, P. 1911. *Siger de Brabant et l'averroisme latin au XIIIe siècle.* 2nd ed. 2 vols. Louvain: Institut supérieur de philosophie.

Pelikan, Jaroslav. 1973. *The Christian Tradition: A History of the Development of Doctrine.* Vol. 1. Chicago: University of Chicago Press.

Strauss, Leo. 2001. *Gesammelte Schriften.* Vol. 3. Ed. Heinrich Meier and Wiebke Meier. Stuttgart: J. B. Metzler.

Chapter Twenty

Custom, Change, and Character in Edith Wharton's *The Age of Innocence*

CHRISTINE DUNN HENDERSON

Edith Wharton's *The Age of Innocence* is partly a sociological study, a detailed portrait of the manners and mores of the society in which Wharton herself grew up, the old New York of the 1870s. It is also, of course, a dramatic tale, depicting the ill-fated love between Newland Archer and Ellen Olenska. Both Newland and Ellen are members of the families who dominated old New York society in the 1870s, but Ellen has lived the better part of her life abroad, distant from the cultural dictates which govern Archer's world. On the eve of Archer's engagement to Ellen's cousin, Ellen returns to New York, having fled her dissolute husband. The two meet, with mutual attraction following. Their story is one of desire thwarted by the protagonists' loyalty and sense of duty to the moral codes of their society. Commentary has emphasized the subordination of the individual's desires—particularly the female individual's desires—to the "desires" of society as embodied in its moral codes, and critical literature is rife with terms such as *strictures* and *confinement*.[1] Much has also been made of the autobiographical dimension of this theme and of Wharton's struggle to free herself from the very society recalled with such detail in *The Age of Innocence*.[2] The tension between individual desires and society's mandates is surely at the heart of Wharton's novel, and Millicent Bell's observation that "it is New York society itself, the organism of the tribe, that is her chief actor" is shrewdly made (Bell 1995, 6). But the novel is more than a treatment of New York's rigid upper class: it is a study in how the conventions of that society interact with change and with character, and it is the interplay of these three forces that gives the novel its power.

Laws and explicit rules are far from the only factors governing societal and individual behavior. Beyond these codified guides are the implicit standards of custom, convention, even taste—those unwritten rules which can be grouped together under the heading "mores." America's most penetrating observer, Alexis de Tocqueville, understood mores very broadly, not merely "habits of the heart," but also "the whole moral and intellectual state of a people," including a people's general character, disposition, and degree of "enlightenment, habits, knowledge" (Tocqueville 2010, 466–67). Tocqueville understood the power of mores as superior to the power of laws, noting that "mores form the only resistant and enduring power among a people" (447).

Regimes—or societies—are most stable when laws and mores reinforce each other. But mores and laws are not always in harmony. When they are opposed or in tension, one or the other must eventually be modified to bring them into harmony. Despite the fact that Tocqueville believed mores possess greater strength than laws, he suggests that either can give way to the other: laws may modify mores, or mores may modify laws.[3] Wharton's novels follow the Tocquevillian distinction between mores and laws—the very title *The Custom of the Country* nods in this direction—but her dominant line on the relationship between mores and laws seems to be an assertion of convention's greater power when laws and mores conflict.[4] Enlightening Ellen on old New York's unwritten rules, Archer notes that "in spite of appearances" (of individual freedom), their society is ruled by "a few people with—well, rather old-fashioned ideas," and there are things which "our legislation favours" but "our social customs don't."[5]

From the opening pages of *The Age of Innocence,* convention and mores dominate the narrative. The reader quickly learns that "what was or was not 'the thing' played a part as important in Newland Archer's New York as the inscrutable totem terrors that had ruled the destinies of his forefathers thousands of years ago" (4). With its "precise and inflexible" rituals (11), convention rules old New York despotically, and the dictates of taste and form are followed without question or even reflection. Even the rather silly custom of translating the German libretto of a French opera into Italian in order to enhance the English-speaking audience's comprehension was "as natural to Newland Archer as all the other conventions on which his life was moulded" (4).

The "inexorable conventions" (31) which shape New York life and which bind its members are not merely unwritten; they are also unspoken. Wharton emphasizes this aspect with her language of silence, subtle symbolism, and muteness. Archer lives in an "atmosphere of faint implications and pale delicacies" (12). In this world, the individual who speaks her mind is pitied ("poor darling!") or shunned, for it was "against all the rules of their code" that people "should even allude to what was uppermost in their thoughts," much less express those thoughts openly and directly (27). Their code relies on subtle hints, with security in the knowledge—rather than the mere hope—that such hints will be correctly interpreted by other, similarly trained members of their class. Silence is the dominant motif, but all silences are fraught with meanings. As Wharton writes, "In reality, they all lived in a kind of hieroglyphic world, where the real thing was never said or done or even thought, but only represented by a set of arbitrary signs" (32). Newland's son, Dallas, puts it less elegantly—but equally eloquently—near the novel's close, when he says to his father, "No, I forgot. You never did ask each other anything, did you? And you never told each other anything. You just sat and watched each other, and guessed at what was going on underneath. A deaf-and-dumb asylum, in fact!" (250).

In some, perhaps many, instances, the silences of their code are benign and the impulse to protect family is both laudable and generous.

Newland's wordless gesture of support (correctly understood by all) in coming to May's family's box at the opera in solidarity with their having championed their cousin Ellen as the novel opens is but one example. Yet Wharton's treatment of custom seems particularly to emphasize its ability to stifle individual freedom and desires in the name of society's survival and social cohesion.[6] As Archer notes, "The individual . . . is nearly always sacrificed to what is supposed to be the collective interest: people cling to any convention that keeps the family together" (79). Nonconformity is not tolerated, for as Newland's mother observes, "if we don't all stand together, there'll be no such thing as Society left" (36).

Nowhere, however, is the force of society's unwritten code more visible than in the farewell dinner May gives for Ellen. The evening is a "tribal rally around a kinsman about to be eliminated from the tribe" (234) and around May herself. Silence and family are the evening's dominant motifs, thus mirroring the values of the society being defended. As the dinner unfolds, Archer realizes that all of his circle assume that he and Ellen are lovers; their presence at Ellen's send-off is part of a "conspiracy of rehabilitation and obliteration," yet another example of "elaborate mutual dissimulation" within the "silent organization which held his little world together" (236).[7] Wharton's language of confinement escalates as she paints the scene of the dinner, moving from the psychological imprisonments of silence and mutual silence to the language of physical imprisonment. Archer feels "like a prisoner in the centre of an armed camp," whose "captors" show no mercy in indicating—via their discussion of Beaufort's shunning—what would happen to Archer himself, were he to abandon May for Ellen (235). Ironically, the tirade against Beaufort is delivered by Lawrence Lefferts, who is seeking to deflect attention from his own infidelities. The irony of Lefferts acting as moral authority is not lost on the reader, but a comment by Sillerton Jackson provides another window into old New York's code: apparently adultery is tolerated but not with members of one's own caste or not if the affair leads one to abandon one's marriage.[8]

On both counts, Archer and Ellen have violated society's unwritten rules, and the dinner party depicts the swift and effective vengeance of their "tribe." Without a word of accusation, the presumed lovers are sentenced. Having also deviated from cultural norms by expressing her desire to divorce her aristocratic husband, Ellen must be banished from the tribe and returned to Europe, where a divorced woman does not disturb society.[9] Archer's penalty is lighter, for his transgressions have not been explicit and also perhaps because he is a man; nevertheless, through the reminder of Beaufort, Archer is cautioned against following Ellen. Whether or not the punishment meted out at the farewell party fits the crime, it does fit the code of their society, for just as the rules are unwritten, the punishment is unsaid, and a thick veil of politeness and tacitly agreed upon deceit prevails in what Nancy Bentley rightly calls a "climactic scene of ritualized violence."[10] Yet while the scene is one of the novel's dramatic highlights, Wharton's narrative commentary emphasizes its routine—even conventional—character.

> It was the old New York way of taking life 'without effusion of blood': the way of people who dreaded scandal more than disease, who placed decency above courage, and who considered that nothing was more ill-bred than 'scenes,' except the behavior of those who gave rise to them. (235)

The embodiment of New York convention is, of course, May Welland. "The young girl who knew nothing and expected everything," May is the "terrifying product of this elaborate system of mystification" (30). Her innocence and blonde beauty serve as a foil for Ellen, as do her reserve, shyness, and "Diana-like aloofness" (147). Prior to their marriage, May's unworldliness appeals to Archer, who imagines himself as a husbandly tutor, expanding her horizons and initiating her into the world beyond their New York. Yet May proves remarkably—even stubbornly—content with the world exactly as she knows it; her horizons want no expanding. Little touches May in a lasting manner—not emotion, not ideas, not experience. As they settle into the life of young newlyweds, Archer notes with pause that "not a thought seemed to have passed behind her eyes or a feeling through her heart. . . . He marveled afresh at the way in which experience dropped away from her" (147).

May's frankness had also appealed to Archer during their courtship, but he soon realizes that what he had perceived as frankness is far from candor. May's training has instilled in her the ability to communicate only indirectly, to hint rather than to speak, and "to conceal imaginary wounds under a Spartan smile" (206). By several years into his marriage, Archer acknowledges that his wife will never be and does not want to be free from convention's strictures. "He had long given up trying to disengage her real self from the shape into which tradition and training had moulded her" (229). He does, however, assume that May has a real self to be liberated, whereas in a moment in which the hopelessness of his marriage stretches before him as a dim specter, Archer wonders whether May's politeness is the conventional mask for her emotions or whether, more disturbingly, "'niceness' carried to that supreme degree were only a negation, the curtain dropped before an emptiness?" (148). In this same vein but less nihilistically, Archer recognizes that May's apparent artlessness is artifice, for "untrained human nature was not so frank and innocent; it was full of twists and defences of an instinctive guile" (32). Similarly, May's apparent naturalness is deceptive, for she is a construct. Unlike Beaufort or Mrs. Mingott, however, she is not a self-construct. Rather, she is a creation of society, carefully trained and "cunningly manufactured by a conspiracy of mothers and aunts and grandmothers and long-dead ancestresses" (32).[11]

Wharton repeatedly uses the word *childishness* in her descriptions of May,[12] yet while May retains the appearance of girlish innocence and inexperience throughout her life, she is no simpleton. While certainly neither analytic nor deep, May is often given bursts of intuition which allow her understanding to penetrate beyond its natural limits.[13] Before her marriage to Archer, May understands the waning of his affections (though she seems—explicitly, at least—to have misunderstood their redirection); later, she recognizes Archer's attachment to Ellen and the apparent inevitability of their affair. More than having insights, however, May uses her flashes of intuition in order to achieve the outcomes she desires. It is May's intelligent use of her intuitive knowledge that redeems her character from insipidness, making her (and the conventional codes she embodies) both more interesting and more sympathetic to readers.

If May's "triumphant smile" as she looks at Archer through her bridal veil (130) leaves open some doubt as to whether her triumph consists in having fulfilled a young woman's conventional duty of finding a mate within her social circle or whether her triumph consists in having successfully gambled that Archer would not accept her offer to free him from the engagement, another scene provides irrefutable evidence of May's ability to manipulate their social code to her own advantage. Following her farewell dinner for Ellen, May tells Archer she is pregnant, "her blue eyes wet with victory" (241). Having successfully banished the rival for her husband's affections would be reason enough for May to feel triumphant, as would the simple fact of pregnancy, for while Archer might perhaps have abandoned May for Ellen, the codes of both society and basic decency forbid that he would abandon wife *and* child. The scene of May's triumph, however, adds another significant detail: May's pregnancy has only been confirmed that morning, but she had informed Ellen of her pregnancy two weeks *earlier.* Reading backward, the full extent of May's gamble and her "victory" is instantly clear. May's revelation prompted Ellen to change her mind about embarking on a sexual relationship with Archer, and it was a—if not the—key factor in Ellen's decision to return, alone, to Europe.

Learning of May's pregnancy silences Archer, who had been on the verge of announcing his intention to leave her, and learning that Ellen had known brings him to a standstill. Stumbling over his words, he asks May how she could have told Ellen before she was certain herself. May, drawing on the strength of the code which has molded her, responds without hesitation, even admitting the lie. The scene is striking, as Wharton shows us the power of convention: "'But that was a fortnight ago, wasn't it? I thought you weren't sure til today.' Her colour burned deeper but she held his gaze. 'No; I wasn't sure then—but I told her I was. And you see I was right!' she exclaimed, her blue eyes wet with victory" (241).

Her cousin Ellen Olenska is the most obvious foil to May; Ellen and May are one of several sets of opposing female characters who appear in Wharton's fiction. Their obvious physical contrast—Ellen is small and dark, whereas May is fair and athletically built—is complemented at the novel's beginning by the equally obvious moral contrast between May's virginal innocence and the considerable experience of Ellen, who has lived much of her life in Europe and has returned to New York after having left her husband and having spent several months living with a man—according to the gossip surrounding her—in Lausanne. Ellen's distance from old New York's unwritten rules is evident from her appearance at the opera in the opening scene. Sillerton Jackson and Lawrence

Lefferts, respectively society's authorities on family and on form, express shock at the presence of a woman with a scandal hanging over her head in the Mingott opera box. Although the vices of Ellen's husband seem well known ("when he wasn't with women he was collecting china. Paying any price for both, I understand" [11]) and are reprehensible to polite society, Ellen's having fled with his secretary cannot be condoned, under any circumstance. For Ellen to separate quietly from her philandering and degenerate husband and for her to return to her family's protection does not seem too grave a breach of New York's mores, but "this parading her at the Opera's another thing!" (11–12).

Virtually everything about Ellen puts her at odds with her American cousins' conventions. Her opera attire suggests foreignness, its style out of step with American fashions and its headdress evoking imperial France. With Ellen's foreignness is the suggestion of decadence and sensuality; hence, "the way that her dress (which had no tucker) sloped away from her thin shoulders shocked and troubled" Archer, particularly with his virginal fiancée seated next to the Countess (11).[14] When Ellen takes up permanent residence in New York, she settles into a "strange quarter," peopled by writers, dressmakers, and taxidermists (47). Even the sitting room of her rented house has an atmosphere different from any Archer has ever encountered: "something intimate, 'foreign,' subtly suggestive of old romantic scenes and sentiments" which awakens Archer's sense of adventure (50). Beyond the question of having left her husband and taken up with his secretary, Ellen's personal relationships are also deeply unsettling to New York. She is, for example, on friendly terms with her maid, Nastasia; she has no reservations keeping "unfashionable" company, being seen with Julius Beaufort, or inviting a bachelor to her home. Finally—and perhaps most important—Ellen's forthrightness and lack of guile set her at odds with New York's unwritten language of murmured hints and meaning-laden symbols.

Wharton repeatedly associates Ellen with the novel's two other iconoclasts, Mrs. Mason Mingott and Julius Beaufort. Mrs. Mingott, Ellen's grandmother and the matriarch of the Mingott clan, rose through marriage from a humble (even slightly scandalous) beginning to social prominence and respectability. Wharton observes that Mrs. Mingott's own fearlessness and strength of will allowed her to remake her own life and brought her to a position of social prominence. Yet, far from conforming to society's dictates, as one might expect of someone newly stamped respectable, Mrs. Mingott eschews many New York conventions. As Archer explains, "whatever man dared (within Fifth Avenue's limits) that old Mrs. Manson Mingott . . . would dare." To be sure, Mrs. Mingott's daring is of a limited nature, and the fact that she does not break society's sexual taboos seems particularly important in securing her unique freedom among the women in Wharton's New York.[15]

On virtually every other level, however, Mrs. Mingott refuses to conform to the expected and pushes society's envelope to its furthest limits. With her "characteristic independence" (20), she "went her way fearlessly, mingled freely in foreign society," married her daughters to members of European nobility, "associated familiarly with Papists" and "entertained Opera singers" (10). Her tastes favor the new over the old, boldness over reticence. Her New York abode, said to be modeled on French architecture, is built in a "new" area, far away from the fashionable neighborhoods of the 1870s. Because of her immense bulk—itself another breach of form?—and in "flagrant violation of all the New York proprieties," her bedroom is located on the first floor, and we are told that the "foreignness" of this floor plan both "startled and fascinated" her visitors (20).[16]

Mrs. Mingott shows particular affection for Ellen and for Archer himself, championing the former and helping the latter overcome familial resistance to an accelerated engagement to May. She also "had always professed a great admiration for Julius Beaufort, and there was a kind of kinship in their cool domineering way and their short-cuts through the conventions" (22). Beaufort is a parvenu who "passed for an Englishman" but whose origins were shrouded in mystery. Having insinuated himself into society, he amassed a fortune and connected himself through marriage with New York's best families, "but his habits were dissipated, his tongue was bitter, his antecedents were mysterious." Nevertheless, Beaufort had the secret of "carrying things off" with a certain aplomb, stilling New York's moral qualms about his business dealings and his background with his self-assurance, the easy elegance of his home, and the fine fare of his table (14–15).

Though of rather different moral character, both Mrs. Mingott and Julius Beaufort are independent souls who deliberately break New York's conventions, and the paths they blaze set the course for New York's future. Like her grandmother and Beaufort, Ellen also flouts New York's unwritten rules, but her defiance is less deliberate than theirs. Rather, she misunderstands New York, confusing its lack of explicit rules with freedom more generally, and thus overestimating the scope of individual independence. Her decision to return to America seems related to her having viewed it as a place of "peace and freedom" (122). In this same vein, and perhaps operating from the memories of those portions of her childhood spent in New York society, Ellen mistakenly believes everything in America is uncomplicated and "straight up and down—like Fifth Avenue." As she says to Archer, "If you knew how I like it for just *that*—the straight-up-and-downness, and the big honest labels on everything" (54; original emphasis). Ellen gradually learns, however, that the signs and signals of New York society are far from the "big honest labels" she believed she would find. Moreover, some of New York's unwritten conventions run directly counter to the explicitly stated rules.

This is especially true in one area with particular significance for Ellen: divorce. Having fled her husband, she seeks the "honesty" of legally freeing herself from the marriage. She tells Archer, "I want to be free; I want to wipe out all the past" (77). She assumes that a straightforward divorce is the appropriate path in America, best suited to that country's character, which she believes is distinguished by frankness and a lack of pretence.[17] Having misjudged the American (or at least the New York) character, Ellen has also misjudged its attitude toward divorce. When Archer hints that divorce might be problematic, Ellen cannot see the obstacles. Puzzling, she first confirms that her husband's character and behavior are well known, that she has justification for divorce. Next, she confirms that there are neither legal nor ecclesiastical impediments: "Well—then—what more is there? In this country, are such things tolerated? I'm a Protestant—our church does not forbid divorce in such cases" (77). Archer's response explains that while the law has adopted a more progressive stand concerning divorce, mores remain deeply conservative; thus, what is essentially a prohibition against divorce is rooted in mores rather than law. Although the principle of freedom might appear to be America's chief value, Ellen learns that New York's reality is something different, and that preservation of the family is more highly valued that individual liberty. "But my freedom—is it nothing?" she asks, and Archer offers a "rambling" explanation of society's position: "The individual, in such cases, is nearly always sacrificed to what is supposed to be the collective interest: people cling to any convention that keeps the family together" (79).

Although she has misjudged New York's mores, Ellen has no wish to defy them. She repeatedly expresses her desire to conform to society's conventions—"But I suppose I've lived too independently; at any rate, I want to do what you all do—I want to feel cared for and safe" (52)—and she turns to Archer for guidance in negotiating society's complex codes. Witnessing Archer's apparent dedication to the values of family and his honor in keeping his promise to May even in the face of his growing attraction to Ellen, she becomes persuaded of the principles instantiated in New York's conventions. Ellen comes to understand that "right" is an "ugly word"; rather than seek individual freedom, she embraces the "dignity of duty" and the ethos of self-renunciation (123).[18] It is Ellen, no longer a stranger to New York's code, who is able to articulate the value of that code, something that May is unable to articulate herself and that Archer can no longer see when his own desires conflict with society's unwritten rules.

Vis-à-vis his adherence to custom, Archer stands somewhere between the utterly conventional May and the unconventional (albeit often unwittingly so) Ellen. It initially seems that he adheres to convention as closely as May, timing his opera arrival to just the "correct" moment and following "the duty of using two silver-backed brushes with his monogram in blue enamel to part his hair, and of never appearing in society without a flower (preferably a gardenia) in his buttonhole." These, and "all of the other conventions on which his life was moulded," seem completely natural to Archer (4). His choice of a future wife is similarly appropriate, and he "thanked heaven" that he was "about to ally himself with one of his own kind" (23). The idea of rebellion from society's dictates is "deeply distasteful" to Archer, to whom "conformity to the discipline of a small society had become almost . . . second nature" (225). In particular, Archer defers to collective judgment in moral matters, for he "instinctively felt that in this respect it would be troublesome—and also rather bad form—to strike out for himself" (6).

Yet Archer also feels a certain distance from his peers. He prides himself on keeping up with the latest literary, scientific, and artistic developments, and on these fronts at least, he considers himself superior to the majority. Narrating from Archer's point of view, Wharton writes, "He had probably read more, thought more, and even seen a good deal more of the world, than any other man of the number" (6). Archer's self-assessment may be slightly generous, however, insofar as his knowledge of art and literature seems a little superficial. For example, he is unfamiliar with the European prints in Ellen's home, he "hazily" confuses the settings of various literary works, and he has at best a passing acquaintance with his native city's artistic scene. Yet he perceives himself as different from his peers on this front at least, and to a certain extent this is true, for Archer is something of an intellectual who is interested in what lies beyond his narrow world.[19] These interests give him a certain ironic distance from many of the conventions which dictate behavior and from the ideas underlying those conventions.

But Wharton twice describes Archer as a "dilettante" (4, 243), or an amateur rather than a deep intellectual. She also calls him a "contemplative" (243). The idea—or ideal—of a thing draws Archer more strongly than its actual form. Ellen's appearance in Archer's world provides him with a concrete object for many of his vague feelings or yearnings. During Mr. Jackson's attack on Ellen's unorthodox behavior and various breaches of taste, "a spirit of perversity" moves Archer to defend her unconventionality. His defense pushes to the extreme of expressing his support for her possible divorce from Count Olenski and his distaste for society's double standard. In the heat of the moment, Archer declares "Women ought to be free—as free as we are" (30).[20] Yet Archer's rejection of convention seems only possible within its safety, and despite his defense of gender equality in the abstract during a heated moment, reflection returns him to the conventional position, which is that "'Nice' women, however wronged, would never claim the kind of freedom he meant, and generously-minded men like themselves were therefore—in the heat of the argument—the more chivalrously ready to concede it to them" (31). As an abstraction, Ellen offers Archer a channel for many of his hazy ideas and for his inchoate dissatisfactions with his world and the life stretching before him, but the reality of Ellen is something altogether different. Archer repeatedly struggles with his own needs to class her under some heading—Beaufort's mistress, for example—he can easily understand, and he falls back into conventional judgments time after time as he tries to understand her.[21]

To suggest, however, that Archer is wholly conventional would be going too far, and falling in love with Ellen does cause him to question accepted principles. Although some of the principles underlying New York's code may be laudable, the code exists primarily for the sake of society's preservation rather than for the flourishing of individuals within it. From the social standpoint, its mores are just if they preserve the order, though they may do injustice to particular individuals, and it is in this conflict of self and society that Archer begins seriously to question what had always seemed natural to him. Wrestling with the moral dilemma of acting on his love for Ellen while married to May, Archer intuits the conflict.

> But to love Ellen Olenska was not to become a man like Lefferts: for the first time Archer found himself face to face with the dread argument of the individual case. Ellen Olenska was like no other woman, he was like to other man: their situation, therefore, resembled no one else's, and they were answerable to no tribunal but that of their own judgment. (214)

Archer approaches an outright break from convention following the farewell dinner for Ellen. He is on the brink of telling May he plans to leave her—scandal be damned—but the announcement of her pregnancy forestalls his declaration. After May's announcement, Archer cannot bring himself to abandon wife and child, nor does Wharton seem to imply that defying these particular mores would be a good thing. The suggestion is that many of the values represented in New York's unwritten code are good ones: family, fidelity, duty, self-sacrifice. It is part of the novel's tragic irony that it is Archer who teaches Ellen the importance of these principles (of which custom is merely an image) and Ellen who teaches him their limitations. Nevertheless, these very principles keep them apart, for only by remaining apart can they "be themselves"—that is, their best, principled selves, those selves worthy of another principled individual's love (204).[22]

In her autobiography Wharton described the social structure of 1870s New York as dominated by "a blind dread of innovation" (Wharton 1934, 22). *The Age of Innocence* certainly conveys that dread, depicting a New York whose mores seem both rigid and unchanging. Despite their apparent immobility, however, mores can and do shift over time. New laws, new populations, new discoveries, simply the passage of time can act upon mores, slowly modifying them, just as they slowly modify other aspects of a society. Even the mores of New York's aristocracy[23] are not exempt from gradual modification, and while the narrative opens by highlighting the time-bound rituals of the New York opera season, social convention is placed in the context of change from the very outset. The novel's second sentence announces the impending displacement of the Academy of Music by the Metropolitan Opera House—"there was already talk of the erection, in the remote metropolitan distances 'above the Forties,' of a new Opera House" (4)—thus framing the contrast between change and tradition in physical terms.

Daring souls like Beaufort and Mrs. Mingott have already constructed their residences beyond society's conventional boundaries, and other changes accompany their territorial innovations. Customs once considered chic, like holding an evening ball in the drawing room rather than in a separate ballroom, have become outmoded and provincial, and new customs are being inaugurated. The younger generation has begun to find fault with some of the older generation's practices, such as paying after-dinner social calls, and some of its old ideas are also beginning to be considered outmoded. Society's composition has also begun to change, with Mrs. Struthers's soirées beginning to be deemed an acceptable engagement and with Lawrence Lefferts assuming the authority to offer social judgments (much to the horror of Mrs. Archer). That the van der Luydens remain the final authority in society reminds us of convention's general resistance to change; the dominance of English surnames over the older Dutch ones, however, reminds us of change's inevitability.

If, despite its reverence for tradition, the New York of the 1870s is in many ways a new society, it is also in the process of being displaced by an even newer one. As the final part of the novel opens, twenty-six years have passed, and the changes which have taken place in the space of those years are manifest. Some are simple, technological ones, such as the invention of the telephone and of ships able to cross the Atlantic in less than a week. But those changes have brought deeper ones, for they have facilitated openness to the world and mobility of all types. This greater openness can be seen, for example, in the range of professional opportunities available to the new generation. Whereas law was one of only a few respectable professions available to Archer as a young man, the new generation's options have expanded. Wharton's language recalls the confinement imposed by the previous conventions: "The young men nowadays were emancipating themselves from the law and business and taking up all sorts of new things" (242), and their horizons were no longer restricted to New York itself. Archer's son Dallas, who is "restless and curious" and who shares his father's "vague leanings toward 'art'" (242), has chosen architecture as a profession, thus finding a concrete outlet into which he can channel those vague affinities and a professional existence about which he can feel passion, in contrast to Archer's rather tepid feelings for his own profession.[24]

Dallas "belonged body and soul to the new generation" (250), not just in his embrace of technology and of a profession which both suits his tastes and sends him around the globe; in his easy and open manners Dallas speaks to Archer in the informal tones of one equal to another rather than in the more reverential tones which characterized parent-child exchanges in Archer's day. Having asked his father to accompany him on a business trip to Europe, Dallas says directly, "I say, Dad, I want your help: do come." When Archer hesitates, Dallas responds, "Think it over? No, sir: not a minute. You've got to say yes now. Why not, I'd like to know? If you can allege a single reason—No; I knew it. Then it's a go, eh?" (245). Dallas's easy manner with his father includes directness and candor on more important subjects. He speaks freely to his father about the elliptical communication that characterized Archer's generation. It is also Dallas who asks Archer directly about the place Ellen held in his heart and why, at the end, he will not see her.[25] Dallas's manner with his father approaches the one Tocqueville observed in democratic families, in which formality dims and the natural bonds of affection between father and son are able to make themselves more strongly felt. Tocqueville wrote, "There reigns, in contrast, in all the words that a son addresses to his father, among democratic peoples, something free, familiar, and tender" (Tocqueville 2010, 1038).[26]

Not only has time altered the mores governing the relations between parents and children, but it has also effaced many of the social distinctions once so crucial to New York society. When Lawrence Lefferts imagined, almost twenty-six years before the time of the novel's close, that "If things go on at this pace, we shall see our children fighting for invitations to swindlers' houses, and marrying Beaufort's bastards" (237), the vision was one of unimaginable, almost apocalyptic, horror. And yet that is exactly what Dallas is preparing to do, in wedding Fanny Beaufort, the daughter of the disgraced Julius Beaufort and his former mistress, the notorious Fanny Ring. That "nobody wondered or reproved" at the match—and, indeed, when Fanny appeared in New York at age eighteen, "society took her joyfully for granted"—served as "the measure of the distance that the world had travelled." By the new standards of the day, both her father's business history and the details of her own birth are not worth remembering, and New York takes Fanny on her own terms: "She was pretty, amusing, and accomplished: what more did any one want?" (247). Family and history no longer signify in this new world, "the huge kaleidoscope where all the social atoms spun around on the same plane" (248).

By the novel's end, it would seem that the barriers which had separated Ellen and Archer no longer exist. He is a widower, no longer bound by a vow of marital fidelity, and she has been living alone in Paris for over a quarter of a century. Were they to rekindle their romance, the old gossip might spark, but in a world in which "no one was narrow-minded enough" to hold Fanny Beaufort's parentage against her and in which the memory of Julius Beaufort's failure had become a generally forgotten and "obscure" incident (247), any gossip would surely be minimal and fleeting. Yet Archer chooses not to meet Ellen again during his visit there with Dallas. Why?

One reading might suggest that although mores have changed, the old ways continue to exercise power over Archer. This is perhaps the simplest response, and Wharton plays to it by suggesting that Archer's habituation to the older code is so complete that he cannot break with its dictates even when they no longer apply. Having stifled his desires for so long, he has become incapable of seizing the opportunity for their release. Wharton observes, "The worst of doing one's duty was that it apparently unfitted one for doing anything else" (246).

A subtler—and more interesting—explanation for Archer's inaction, however, lies in something which Wharton has portrayed as lying beyond the realm of convention and mores: Archer's own character. At the novel's close, Wharton again draws attention to Archer's character and to the fact that custom did not mold his character, nor has time changed it. "He would always be by nature a contemplative and a dilettante" (243), and "thinking over a pleasure to come often gave him a subtler satisfaction than its realization" (4). The idea of Ellen had always attracted Archer more strongly than the reality, and with the passing of time, an idealized life with Ellen had come to represent all of the unlived possibilities of Archer's life, while his real life—and any shortcomings in that real life—receded into the background. "He had built up within himself a kind of sanctuary in which she throned among his secret thoughts and longings. Little by little it became the scene of his real life, of his only rational activities" (184). Just as the reality of Ellen Olenska had proven difficult for the young Archer to grapple with in New York, that same reality—and the imagined and unrealized possibilities of his own life—proves overwhelming to an older Archer in the Paris twilight. In the end, he prefers the mysterious, idealized Ellen to the real woman, and he remains a spectator to his own life, electing to contemplate rather than to experience. Ellen respects his choice and has her servant close the apartment shutters, while Archer sits alone on the park bench, content simply to watch, contemplate, and imagine, as the last light fades away, and then he is finally free to leave.

NOTES

1. See Ammons (1980) or Updike (1999), who notes that Wharton offers her readers a window on "the passions of the past, imprisoned in the conventions of the past" (170).

2. For example, see Wolff 1977, 1996; Ammons 1980. Psychological biography frequently figures in Wharton scholarship (e.g., Erlich 1995).

3. Although Tocqueville's comments on the superior force of mores to laws are best known, he also recognizes the reverse influence: "Laws, however, work toward producing the spirit, the mores and the character of the people. But in what proportion? There is the great problem that we cannot think about too much" (Tocqueville 2010, 499 note m).

4. Wharton's take on the relationship between laws and mores is a subtle one. In stressing the superior force of mores to laws, however, Wharton may also be following a Tocquevillian vein: given the general and legal flux in democratic society, a special power is conferred upon mores, which stand outside of democratic movement, thus serving to anchor society. Mr. Sillerton Jackson calling society's unwritten rules "our little republican distinctions" (Wharton 2006, 64) hints at a similar point about the distinctive force of mores in America.

5. Wharton, *The Age of Innocence* (2006), 78. All subsequent references to the novel are by page number, corresponding to this edition.

6. Ammons casts the social circumscription of individual liberty in gendered terms, asserting "The American dream of personal liberty does not apply to women" (Ammons 1980, 127). Just as such a reading overlooks the significance of female iconoclasts like Mrs. Mingott, one of Wharton's most sympathetic subversive figures, it underestimates the (admittedly lesser) extent to which male freedom is also curtailed by society's code.

7. Wharton repeats the phrase "tribal rally" twice in fairly close succession, once drawing attention to their expulsion of Ellen from their midst and once drawing attention to their support of May.

8. With those provisos, it seems that while not encouraged, male infidelity is tolerated in this New York. The early exchange between Archer and Jackson concerning Ellen's affair with her husband's secretary (29–30) also supports such a conclusion.

9. Ammons emphasizes the gendered aspect, noting that this is an "ancient" form of punishment for transgressing women, "logical from a patriarchal point of view," since female infidelity is too dangerous to the ties – familial and otherwise – which hold that society together (Ammons 1980, 159).

10. Bentley links this to Wharton's "fascinated obsession with what seemed to be the vital energies of aggression in primitive cultures," also calling it a "romancing of aggression" (Bentley 1995, 60).

11. This raises the question of whether there is any self beyond the socially constructed self. Knights asserts that "the suggestion of the unfolding narrative is, more radically, that without the shape, the social mold, there may be no self at all" (Knights 1995, 21). While provocative, such a suggestion seems to go too far, and it must take into account the question of character among the novel's iconoclasts.

12. Ammons also particularly emphasizes May's childishness, as part of the male desire for a child-woman.

13. Wharton deploys this tactic frequently in the novel, and "flashes" of various types—understanding, insight, even anger—allow the individual to transcend society's artifice and access the real.

14. Interestingly, Wharton associated the same foreignness and sensuality with Mrs. Mingott (20).

15. Indeed, "her haughty effrontery . . . was somehow justified by the extreme decency and dignity of her private life" (10).

16. In contrast to this reading of Mrs. Mingott, Ammons reads her as bound by society's strictures (Ammons 1980, 150), concluding that "The American dream of personal liberty does not apply to women" (127). While Ammons's conclusion does not do justice to a figure like Mrs. Mingott, it also overstates the "personal liberty" of the novel's men. Wharton's overall vision seems darker: individuals are embedded in families and societies which limit their freedom; thus, to some extent, the "American dream of personal liberty" is a chimera for both men and women.

17. In conversation with his mother, Archer confirms this. "Countess Olenska thought she would be conforming to American ideas in asking for her freedom." Mrs. Welland dismisses Ellen's thinking as one of the many "extraordinary things that foreigners invent about us" (102).

18. But Ellen does not become utterly convention-bound. As her visit to the shamed and ostracized Regina Beaufort after Beaufort's collapse suggests, Ellen's sympathy continues to trump her obedience to society's dictates.

19. He is, however, part of the "Archer-Newland-van-der-Luyden tribe, who were devoted to travel, horticulture, and the best fiction, and who looked down on the grosser forms of pleasure" (23). In this sense, even Archer's "difference" conforms to the expected familial pattern.

20. Wharton paints this scene with the ironic narrative framing of Archer "making a comment of which he was too irritated to measure the terrific consequences" (30).

21. On the mystery of Ellen in Archer's mind, see Wolff 1977, 435.

22. See also 168–69. M. Rouvière notices the "post-Archer" change in Ellen, and he suddenly notices that "she's an American. And that if you're an American of *her* kind—of your [Archer's] kind—things that are accepted in certain other societies, or at least put up with as part of a general convenient give-and-take—become unthinkable, simply unthinkable" (178).

23. Viewing old New York as an aristocracy offers interesting possibilities about aristocratic mores in a democratic society, with the former gradually giving way to the irresistible latter. Mrs. Archer, however, asserts that "New York has always been a commercial community" rather than an aristocratic one (35). Her claim seems dubious, both because commerce itself and the personal qualities of the successful entrepreneur seem to be little esteemed by society; moreover, old New York is essentially conservative in its values, in contrast with democracy's preference for change, novelty, and progress.

24. If Dallas is meant to be a young Archer, Mary is just as clearly meant to be a young May, though a May adapted to the new era: "Mary, who was no less

conventional, and no more intelligent, yet led a larger life, and held more tolerant views" (245).

25. Dallas's questions about Ellen suit his generation's freedom, while Archer's minimalist responses befit his "inarticulate lifetime" (250).

26. Dallas and Archer's relationship captures many of the key points Tocqueville raises in his discussion, "Influence of Democracy on the Family" (vol. 4, chap. 8).

REFERENCES

Ammons, Elizabeth. 1980. *Edith Wharton's Argument with America.* Athens: University of Georgia Press.

Bell, Millicent. 1995. "Introduction: A Critical History." In *The Cambridge Companion to Edith Wharton,* ed. Millicent Bell, 1–19. Cambridge: Cambridge University Press.

Bentley, Nancy. 1995. "'Hunting for the Real': Wharton and the Science of Manners." In *The Cambridge Companion to Edith Wharton,* ed. Millicent Bell, 47–67. Cambridge: Cambridge University Press.

Erlich, Gloria C. 1995. "The Female Conscience in Edith Wharton's Shorter Fiction: Domestic Angel or Inner Demon?" In *The Cambridge Companion to Edith Wharton,* ed. Millicent Bell, 98–116. Cambridge: Cambridge University Press.

Knights, Pamela. 1995. "Forms of Disembodiment: The Social Subject in *The Age of Innocence.*" In *The Cambridge Companion to Edith Wharton,* ed. Millicent Bell, 20–46. Cambridge: Cambridge University Press.

Tocqueville, Alexis de. 2010. *Democracy in America.* 4 vols. Ed. Eduardo Nolla, trans. James T. Schleifer. Indianapolis: Liberty Fund.

Updike, John. 1999. *More Matter: Essays and Criticism.* New York: Alfred A. Knopf.

Wharton, Edith. 1934. *A Backward Glance.* New York: Charles Scribner's Sons (reprint, 1964).

———. 2006. *The Age of Innocence.* Ed., with Introd. and Notes, Stephen Orgel. Oxford: Oxford University Press.

Wolff, Cynthia. 1977. *A Feast of Words.* New York: Oxford University Press.

———. 1996. "Introduction." In Edith Wharton, *The Age of Innocence.* New York: Penguin Group, 1996.

Chapter Twenty-One

"What's wrong with this picture?"

On The Coast of Utopia

MICHAEL DAVIS

Catherine Zuckert and Michael Zuckert have always mixed together the enormous respect owed the great thinkers of the past with a healthy curiosity for what is going on in the present (Michael Zuckert once eagerly attended a concert given by an orchestra composed of manual typewriters). Political philosophy is not for the Zuckerts simply an academic exercise, dissecting and embalming a corpse. It is trickier than that, for it must attend to what is alive. As the idiosyncrasies of the life of any age show up powerfully in its arts—how an age talks to itself—the boundary between political philosophy and literature is never as clear-cut as the tradition issuing from the phrase "the ancient quarrel between philosophy and poetry" might make it seem. Tom Stoppard is, of course, one of the preeminent playwrights of our time. He writes playfully but also philosophically about philosophy, political and otherwise. I turn to Stoppard, then, in celebration of the lifelong love affair of the Zuckerts with political philosophy and with literature.

In a utopian world where no imperfection intrudes everything must settle harmoniously into its place. A settled world is at odds with the passionate, restless, and noble spirits who long for it and seek to usher it in, for they must always begin by ruthlessly interrogating the present with the question, "What's wrong with this picture?" Tom Stoppard's *The Coast of Utopia* features a collection of such spirits at work, men like Michael Bakunin, Vissarian Belinsky, Alexander Herzen—the mid-nineteenth-century Russian intelligentsia. The first scene of *Voyage,* the first play of Stoppard's trilogy, begins with a reference to the storming of the Bastille (Stoppard 2002, 1:1),[1] that is, to the founding event of political utopianism—the French Revolution. The last scene of *Salvage,* the last play, anticipates perhaps the last great moment of political utopianism—the Russian Revolution of 1917. In a dream, Herzen has Karl Marx announce:

> Now at last the unity and rationality of history's purpose will be clear to everyone. . . . Everything that seemed vicious, mean, and ugly will be understood as a part of a higher reality, a superior morality against which resistance is irrational—a cosmos where every atom has been striving for the goal of human self-realisation and the culmination of history. (3:118–19)

And in the center is *Shipwreck,* the play depicting the failed revolutions of 1848.

The Coast of Utopia is powerfully antiutopian. Still, while there are no simple heroes in these plays (we will have to pay special attention to Alexander Herzen, perhaps the likeliest candidate for heroism), Stoppard seems to have considerable affection for all his characters, even the serially foolish Bakunin ("Our first task will be to destroy authority" by means of "a dedicated group of revolutionaries under iron discipline, answerable to my absolute authority" 3:115)—Bakunin, whose spate of political-philosophical enthusiasms (Kant, Schelling, Hegel, Fichte, etc.) inadvertently reveals a common thread when he airily remarks, "Whatever

I want, that's what *God* wants" (1:19; original emphasis). Now, if utopia is impossible, why this affection for utopians? Stoppard, perhaps *the* great playwright of our age, is never easy, and *The Coast of Utopia* is perhaps the most difficult of his works. Accordingly, what follows is meant not as a complete picture of the trilogy but rather as a provisional suggestion for how one might begin to understand it as a whole so as to place ourselves in the picture it presents.

In the third scene of *Voyage* (1:17–21) Nicholas Stankevich and Bakunin are studying Kant together. Stankevich is explaining the distinction between the phenomenal and the noumenal. We do not experience things as they are in themselves (noumena) but only things (phenomena) as they have been filtered through the fixed structure of what the one experiencing brings to experience—space and time, cause and effect, and so on. "And thus my existence is necessary to a complete description of reality. Without me there is something wrong with this picture" (1:18). Now, the example Stankevich uses to illustrate his point is revealing: "A young woman in a chair reading a book . . . [who] touches her hair where it's come undone" (18). The young woman who catches his eye is, however, not just any young woman. She is Bakunin's sister Liubov, who is in love with Stankevich and who has positioned herself artfully in the chair only pretending to read and loosening her hair just a little to seem more attractive (1:17). Stankevich, in turn, is in love with her—although he is curiously not altogether aware of it. When Liubov and Stankevich finally talk to each other in this scene, she tries to return a penknife to him; because she is sure it belongs to him, she has kept it close as a love token. Stankevich proceeds to tell her matter-of-factly (and truly) that it is not his.

So a man makes a philosophical claim about the incompleteness of any picture of reality that does not take into account the one experiencing reality. He goes on to give an example of such an account but gets everything wrong. He understands *that* he is in the picture but not really *how* he is in the picture. His view is too neat and abstract—somehow not real. In addition, the woman he loves (albeit in ignorance of her return love) and who loves him (in equal ignorance) worships an object not because of what it is but because of its relatedness to him. Yet her picture of the whole in which this object plays a part is also wrong. The penknife, we learn later, actually belongs to Belinsky. Because neither Liubov nor Stankevich sees the whole picture, neither really understands the part that is seen.

That it is only in fiction that we ever see the whole is powerfully brought home to us by the structure of the first two plays. *Voyage* has two acts. The first is set in the edenic Bakunin family estate, Premukhino, the second primarily in various locations in Moscow. The dramatic order is not straightforward. If plotted temporally, the scenes would have the following sequence: I.1, II.1, II.2, I.2. II.3, I.3, II.4, I.4, II.5, I.5, I.6, II.6, II.7, II.8, I.7, II.9, II.10, II.11, I.8, II.12, II.13, I.9, II.14, II.15. As a consequence of this arrangement we are constantly confronted with events in Act I the full significance of which we cannot appreciate until we reach Act II when we discover their antecedent conditions. So, for example, I.1 opens in a celebration of the engagement of Liubov and Baron Renne. At first, therefore, we think we understand the opening words of I.2, "Where are you all? The newlyweds are here," but to our surprise, it turns out that it is not Liubov who has wed (and is now pregnant) but her sister, Varenka. We don't begin to discover what happened between Renne and Liubov (i.e., that Liubov's brother Michael intervened) until the first scene of Act II. It is also in Act II that we discover the real story of how Belinsky's penknife ended up in Liubov's possession in Act I. In the first play, then, Stoppard artfully arranges things so as to make clear to us how owing to the way they unfold in time, the events of our lives are not and can never be wholly intelligible to us.[2] It would be strange to be confident that we know the causes of things with such indeterminate beginnings and ends. A sequence of events is always someone's sequence of events.

The structure of the second play, *Shipwreck,* brings home a similar point differently. In Act 1, the tenth and last scene reprises the end of the fourth scene, but the stage directions indicate to us that this time "instead of the general babel which ensued, the conversation between Belinski and Turgenev is now 'protected,' with the other conversations virtually mimed" (2:55). Apparently it is not just that what unfolds in time is never whole for us; we are also unable wholly to grasp a present where many things take place at the same time. One thing, though, is added to the very end. As the party passes out of Herzen's house to escort

Belinski to the train, Herzen's deaf son, Kolya, is left in the room. They, and we, think he cannot speak, but here when he is alone, he plays with his top and absentmindedly says, "Ko'ya, Ko'ya."

The last scene of Act II is dated "summer of 1846" (2:105). It continues the action at the end of I.1. Ogarev and Herzen's other son Sasha have joined a search to find Kolya. Ogarev yells the boy's name, and Sasha says, "He can't hear you." It thunders. Ogarev says, "There, you see? He heard that." So Ogarev apparently sees what others miss; later, in *Salvage* I.11, he remarks ironically that Kolya "didn't know that he was deaf" (3:51). And yet the continuation of the action in *Shipwreck* II.11 makes us wonder about Ogarev's perspicacity. Moved to tell Sasha about "the happiest day of his life" (2:106), Ogarev first describes how he, Herzen, and their wives knelt together, holding hands. Then, abruptly changing his mind, he cuts the story short. Now, we have heard this story before in *Shipwreck* II.2, when Herzen's wife, Natalie, meets with Ogarev's estranged wife, Maria, to urge her to grant her husband a divorce. In the course of the conversation, Natalie alludes to the time when the four of them "joined hands and knelt and thanked God for each other." To this Maria replies scornfully that she "didn't want to be the only one standing up" and "found it embarrassing . . . childish" (2:69). The final scene of *Shipwreck* thus not only directs us structurally to the problem of grasping the truth of events in time; it also provides us with a striking example of how the events that unfold in time for one person are not the same as those that unfold for another. We are not only in different pictures; even when we are in the same picture, we are so differently.

One further example of Stoppard's temporal legerdemain: In *Shipwreck* II.4, fourteen years before Manet painted it, Stoppard stages *Déjeuner sur l'herbe* with Natalie as the undressed woman in the painting and Herzen and George Herwegh as the two clothed men. Herwegh's wife, Emma, is the woman in the background. Turgenev is out of the picture, apparently sketching the nude Natalie.[3] The conversation we hear doesn't quite add up until we notice that we are really witnessing two separate scenes. In one, Natalie bares herself and declares her love to Herwegh. In the other, Herzen, Emma, and Turgenev converse while Turgenev sketches Emma. We don't at first see the boundaries correctly and so do not understand that the picture is really two pictures. Stoppard has put them in the same place as a way of indicating that they occur at the same time. Incidentally, this scene marks the climax of Natalie's misunderstanding of her own situation, a misunderstanding once again owing to her miscalculation of the powerful irrationalities of love. She believes that she, Herzen, and Herwegh can live together as a threesome. She should have read her Rousseau better; they could never be anything other than two pairs, two pictures.[4]

Now, let us return to reconsider Stankevich's remark at *Voyage* I.3, "Without me there is something wrong with this picture" (1:18). The phrase is picked up at the very end of Act I in a conversation between Turgenev and another of Bakunin's sisters, Tatiana. Reflecting on the death of Stankevich from tuberculosis, Turgenev says of the celebrated philosophical inner life:

> There's something missing in this picture. Stankevich was coming round to it before the end. He said: "For happiness apparently something of the real world is necessary." (1:51)

The very next scene begins Act II. Its first words are uttered by the young Herzen: "What is wrong with this picture?" (1:53). We have no idea at first what he is talking about, for we cut immediately to a conversation between Bakunin's mother and a woman accompanying her on a stroll, a conversation that alludes to Liubov's refusal to marry Baron Renne. Is this the picture where something is wrong? Perhaps, but it is not what Herzen thinks he means, for he goes on to explain himself:

> You remember those picture puzzles when we were children . . . there'd be a drawing with things wrong in it, a clock with no hands, a shadow going the wrong way, the sun and stars out at the same time . . . and it would say "What's wrong with this picture?" . . . Someone sitting next to you in class disappears overnight, nobody knows anything. In the public gardens ice-creams are eaten in all of the usual flavours. What is wrong with this picture? The Kritski brothers disappear for insulting the Tsar's portrait, Antonovich and his friends for forming a secret society, meaning they met in somebody's room to read a pamphlet you can buy on the street in Paris. Young men and women are pairing off like swans on

> the skating ground. A crocodile of Poles goes clanking by in leg-irons on the Vladimir road. There's something wrong with this picture. Are you listening? You're in the picture. (1:54)

So it is not ordinary life alone that Herzen refers to—not men and women pairing off—but the juxtaposition of ordinary life and the horrors of life under a despotic tyranny. What is apparently wrong with this picture is that no one acts as though there is anything wrong. They do not seem to know that they inhabit this picture puzzle. Herzen puts the question, "What is wrong with this picture?" one more time in this scene, and then answers sadly, "Nothing. It's Russia. A landowner's estate is reckoned not in acres but in adult male serfs" (1:59).[5]

The phrase occurs one more time in the trilogy, but to understand its significance, the ground needs some preparation. In the first play we hear an exchange between Herzen and Belinsky. In *Voyage,* Herzen asks what sort of extravagantly redundant animal Hegel's Dialectical Spirit of History would be, and then answers, "a gigantic ginger cat" (1:104). Two pages later, in response to the news that Stankevich has died, Belinsky asks, "Who is this Moloch that eats his children?" to which Herzen replies, "It's the Ginger Cat [now capitalized]" (1:106). In *Shipwreck* I.9, Herzen asks the same question—"Who is this Moloch who eats his children?"—upon hearing of the death of Belinsky (2:54). Yet another life has been sacrificed in the name of the Revolution. In the penultimate scene of *Shipwreck* (II.10), Herzen imagines a conversation with Bakunin, who after hearing of Kolya's death at sea starts to ask, "Who is this Moloch . . . ?" (2:100)—a clear echo of the earlier scenes—but Herzen cuts him off mid-question and says:

> No, no, not at all! His life was what it was. Because children grow up, we think a child's purpose is to grow up. But a child's purpose is to be a child. Nature doesn't disdain what lives only for a *day.* It pours the whole of itself into each moment. We don't value the lily less for not being made of flint and built to last. Life's bounty is in its flow, later is too late. Where is the song when it's been sung, the dance when it's been danced. It's only we humans who want to own the future too. We persuade ourselves that the universe is modestly employed in unfolding our destination. We note

> the haphazard chaos of history by the day, by the hour, [and here is the last occurrence] but there is something wrong with this picture. Where is the unity, the meaning, of nature's highest creation? Surely those millions of little streams of accident and wilfulness have their correction in the vast underground river which, without a doubt, is carrying us to the place where we're expected! But there is no such place, that's why it's called utopia. (2:101)

In another conversation at the very end of the trilogy (it is worth noting that this too is a dream—in real conversation we seldom get the final word), Herzen argues with Marx.

> But history has no culmination! There is always as much in front as behind. There is no libretto. History knocks at a thousand gates at every moment, and the gatekeeper is chance. . . . We need wit and courage to make our way while our way is making us. But that is our dignity as human beings, and we rob ourselves if we pardon us by the absolution of historical necessity. What kind of beast is it, this Ginger Cat with its insatiable appetite for human sacrifice? This Moloch who promises that everything will be beautiful after we're dead? The distant end is not an end but a trap. (3:119)

Two characters, Herzen and Turgenev, seem especially to understand the danger of this trap—the seductiveness of the Ginger Cat. In *Salvage* II.8, Turgenev tells Herzen:

> To value what is relative to your circumstances and let others value what's relative to theirs—you agree with me. That's why despite everything, we're on the same side.

To which Herzen replies:

> But I fought my way here with loss of blood, because it matters to me and you're in my ditch, reposing with your hat over your face, because nothing matters to you very much—which is why despite everything we'll never be on the same side. (3:104)

They agree that the notion that the spirit of history moves ineluctably toward an intelligible end dehumanizes us. They disagree because Turgenev seems content to be a passive onlooker wryly commenting on events.[6] His purpose is to write novels, not to be "society's keeper," "hold attitudes," or take a stand (2:22). Herzen, however, refuses to abandon the life of action and the hope of making things better. Or, perhaps more accurately, he cannot abandon it. He is like Bakunin in that for him the question, "What is wrong with this picture?" is inseparable from the question to be made famous first by Chernyshevsky and then by Lenin, "What is to be done?"[7]

Accordingly, to wage war on the spirit of history that seduces his contemporaries, Herzen must personify it. It becomes the Ginger Cat that "has no plan, no favourites or resentments, no memory, no mind, no rhyme or reason. It kills without purpose, and spares without purpose too" (1:105). It smokes cigars and, after its first appearance, gets capital letters; no longer simply generic, it receives a proper name. Herzen, who knows the dangers of idealizing, nevertheless repeatedly falls into the trap of idealizing. Having observed the self-destruction of the Second Republic in France, he sees that one can neither trust free men to preserve their freedom nor force them to be free without risking their freedom. Herzen then redirects his idealism to the private life, apparently thinking the problem is solely one of scale, but his idealism threatens to destroy his family. Later, in *Shipwreck,* in his imaginary conversation with Bakunin, he renounces utopian idealism—"there is no such place, that's why it's called utopia"—only to launch two pages later into an animated celebration of a new non-European model for the future, what he calls "Russian socialism" (2:101–3). In *Salvage* I.1, Herzen tells the Polish expatriot Worcell that he's "stopped quarrelling with the world" and that "the world will hear no more of [him]." But when one line later Worcell asks him to help start a Polish press, Herzen jumps at the chance. He is suddenly filled with enthusiasm for "A free Russian press!—and Polish" (3:15–16). This is Herzen's leitmotiv in the trilogy: a devastating critique of idealism followed quickly by an idealistic outburst. For example, in *Salvage,* when Herzen gives over the raising of his children to Malwida von Meysenbug (3:21–23), he endorses the "happy, well-ordered childhood" she proposes to provide for them. But this is really utopianism brought down to the family level. Her project gets displaced, when Malwida, not a little jealous, leaves as a result of the chaos accompanying the arrival of Ogarev's new wife, Natalie. But here once more one utopian scheme gives way to another as we witness first the sanctification of the first Natalie and then the very sort of ménage à trois that had proved so catastrophic in *Shipwreck.* Even as he rejects political utopianism, Herzen does not notice the failure all around him of the utopianism of his own household. Act I, scene 7, ends with another rejection of utopianism; scene 8 begins with the death of Tsar Nicholas and a rebirth of Herzen's optimism (3:35–38).

Tom Stoppard has written three plays embodying a scathing critique specifically of utopian politics and tacitly of the utopian impulses displayed in the eroticism of private life. His critique is grounded in an understanding of what limits us owing to our natures as temporal creatures. We cannot know what we would have to know to justify the reign of a beneficent Ginger Cat. At the same time, Stoppard recognizes that the grandest attempt to articulate this sort of knowledge of the whole began with Kant and extended through the tradition of German Idealism and especially Hegel, all of whom see that any account of the whole must put us in the picture. But this is self-knowledge curiously blind to the self. In noticing the girl reading in the chair and touching her hair but neglecting to notice her flirtatious motive and so failing as well to notice the fact that picking this example out is a sign of having unselfconsciously responded to her flirtation, it looks past the incalculability at the core both of us and of the reality we inhabit. It does not see that it is the nature of pictures that there is always something wrong with the picture. The real is not altogether rational; we treat it as though it were at our peril, for we leave the most important thing out. Perhaps the best we can do is to own up to the necessity of our contingency—that is, acknowledge our ignorance.

Stoppard seems to have begun with a simple question: How could the Soviet Union ever have happened? His question leads him, predictably enough, to the great political intellectual figures of nineteenth-century Russia and less predictably to what one might call our erotic indeterminacy. And yet the two prove not easily separable, for even Stoppard's political answer is not so straightforward as it at first seems. The men who prepared the way for the Soviet experiment were a rather noble group and all idealists—even the materialists. To get at the heart of what it means to be an idealist, Stoppard gradually focuses in on Alexander Herzen, whom, of all the nineteenth-century Russian intellectuals, Stoppard finds perhaps least susceptible to utopian politics. By displaying the inconsistencies of Herzen's life, public to be sure but also private, Tom Stoppard means to show that even when we know the folly of projects to "own the future," we cannot resist the temptation of the attempt, for we are most alive in the moment when we anticipate a noble future. Stoppard's affection for his utopians is nothing less than his affection for humanity, for a certain dreaming—idealizing—is at the core of us and places us forever just off the coast of utopia.

NOTES

1. As all three volumes of the trilogy were published in the same year (2002), subsequent citations are to volume and page numbers.

2. It is no accident that Stoppard so often locates the indeterminacy of human life in relations of love. Love structures our lives in ways that are in general quite intelligible but in particular quite random. The illogic of erotic pairing is a recurring theme in the trilogy. In *Arcadia* Stoppard likens this combination of macrocosmic intelligibility with microcosmic unpredictability to fractals.

3. Stoppard's scene is all the more evocative because it contains Rousseau's cottage at Montmorency.

4. Rousseau's own disappointment in sharing Mme de Warrens is the subject of Books 5 and 6 of his *Confessions.*

5. Just prior to this Stankevich, who is part of Herzen's group, admits there is indeed "something wrong" but identifies it with a weather anomaly—the coincidence of summer sunshine and a frozen skating ground—relegating political things to the status of "changing forms in the world of appearances" (1:59).

6. For example, in *Shipwreck* I.5, Turgenev playfully seeks to help Marx find an appropriate translation for the beginning of the *Communist Manifesto*—Ein Gespenst geht um in Europa; for *Gespenst* he tries out "ghost," "phantom," "spook," "spectre," and "spirit" but finally settles on "hobgoblin" (2:39–42).

7. See *Voyage* I.9 and II.1 (1:49–64).

REFERENCE

Stoppard, Tom. *The Coast of Utopia* in 3 volumes. New York: Grove Press, 2002.

Selected Publications by Catherine Zuckert and Michael Zuckert

CATHERINE ZUCKERT

Books

Natural Right and the American Imagination: Political Philosophy in Novel Form. Savage, MD: Rowman and Littlefield, 1990.

Postmodern Platos: Nietzsche, Heidegger, Gadamer, Strauss, and Derrida. Chicago: University of Chicago Press, 1996.

The Truth about Leo Strauss: Political Philosophy and American Democracy (with Michael P. Zuckert). Chicago: University of Chicago Press, 2006.

Plato's Philosophers: The Coherence of the Dialogues. Chicago: University of Chicago Press, 2009.

Edited Volumes

Understanding the Political Spirit: Philosophical Reflections from Socrates to Nietzsche (edited with Introduction). New Haven: Yale University Press, 1988.

Political Philosophy in the Twentieth Century: Authors and Arguments. New York: Cambridge University Press, 2011.

Coedited Journal Special Issue

Politics and Literature (coeditor Michael Zuckert). *Legal Studies Forum* 22, no. 4 (1998).

Articles

"' . . . and in its wake we followed': The Political Thought of Mark Twain" (with Michael Zuckert). *Interpretation* 3, no. 1 (Autumn 1972): 49–66.

"The Political Thought of Nathaniel Hawthorne." *Polity* 13, no. 2 (Winter 1980): 163–83.

"On Reading Classic American Novelists as Political Thinkers." *Journal of Politics* 43, no. 3 (August 1981): 683–706.

"Aristotle on the Limits and Satisfactions of Political Life." *Interpretation* 11, no. 2 (May 1983): 185–206.

"Reagan and That Unnamed Frenchman (de Tocqueville): On the Rationale for the New (Old) Federalism." *Review of Politics* 43, no. 3 (July 1983): 421–42.

"Nietzsche on the Origin and Development of the Distinctively Human." *Polity* 16, no. 1 (Fall 1983): 48–71.

"Law and Nature in the *Adventures of Huckleberry Finn.*" *Proteus* 1 (Fall 1984): 27–35. Reprinted in *Huck Finn among the Critics: A Centennial Selection,* ed. M. Thomas Inge, 231–46. Frederick, MD: University Press of America, 1985.

"Nietzsche's Rereading of Plato." *Political Theory* 13, no. 2 (May 1985): 213–38. Reprinted in *Critical Assessments: Friedrich Nietzsche,* ed. David W. Conway, 4:382–404. New York: Routledge, 1998.

"Martin Heidegger: His Politics and His Philosophy." *Political Theory* 18, no. 1 (February 1990): 51–79.

"The Politics of Derridean Deconstruction." *Polity* 22, no. 3 (Spring 1991): 335–57.

"On the 'Rationality' of Rational Choice." *Political Psychology* 16, no. 1 (1995): 179–98.

"Plato's *Parmenides*—A Dramatic Reading." *Review of Metaphysics* 51 (June 1998): 840–71.

"Leadership—Natural and Conventional—in Melville's *Benito Cereno.*" *Interpretation* 26, no. 2 (Winter 1999): 239–55.

"Who's a Philosopher? Who's a Sophist? The Stranger v. Socrates." *Review of Metaphysics* 54 (September 2001): 65–97.

"Plato's *Laws:* Postlude or Prelude to Socratic Political Philosophy?" *Journal of Politics* 66 (May 2004): 374–95.

"The Socratic Turn." *History of Political Thought* 25 (Summer 2004): 189–219.

"The Life of Castruccio Castracani: Machiavelli as Literary Artist, Historian, Teacher, and Philosopher." *History of Political Thought* 31, no. 4 (Winter 2010): 577–604.

"Socrates and Timaeus: Two Platonic Paradigms of Philosophy." *Epoché* 15, no. 2 (Spring 2011): 331–60.

MICHAEL ZUCKERT

Books

Natural Rights and the New Republicanism. Princeton: Princeton University Press, 1994.

The Natural Rights Republic. Notre Dame: University of Notre Dame Press, 1996.

Launching Liberalism: On Lockean Political Philosophy. Lawrence: University Press of Kansas, 2002.

The Truth about Leo Strauss: Political Philosophy and American Democracy (with Catherine Zuckert). Chicago: University of Chicago Press, 2006.

Edited Volumes

Protestantism and the American Founding (coeditor Thomas S. Engeman). Notre Dame: University of Notre Dame Press, 2004.

The Anti-Federal Writings of the Melancton Smith Circle (coeditor Derek Webb). Indianapolis: Liberty Fund Press, 2009.

Articles

"Fools and Knaves: Reflections on Locke's Theory of Philosophic Discourse." *Review of Politics* 36, no. 2 (October 1974): 544–64.

"Of Wary Physicians and Weary Readers: The Debates on Locke's Way of Writing." *Independent Journal of Philosophy* 2 (Fall 1977): 55–66.

"An Introduction to Locke's First Treatise." *Interpretation* 8, no. 1 (January 1979): 58–74.

"Justice Deserted: A Critique of Rawls' *Theory of Justice.*" *Polity* 13, no. 3 (Spring 1981): 466–83.

"Meaning and Appropriation in the History of Political Philosophy: Reflections on Skinner's New History." *Interpretation* 13, no. 3 (September 1985): 403–25.

"Rationalism and Political Responsibility: Just Speech and Just Deed in *The Clouds* and the 'Apology of Socrates.'" *Polity* 17, no. 2 (Winter 1985): 271–97.

"Locke and the Problem of Civil Religion." In *The Moral Foundations of the American Republic,* 3rd ed., ed. Robert Horwitz, 181–203. Charlottesville: University of Virginia Press, 1986.

"Self-Evident Truths and the Declaration of Independence." *Review of Politics* 49, no. 3 (Summer 1987): 319–39.

"'Bringing Philosophy Down from the Heavens': Natural Right in the Roman Law." *Review of Politics* 51, no. 1 (Winter 1989): 70–85.

"Completing the Constitution: The Fourteenth Amendment." *Publius* 22, no. 2 (Spring 1992): 69–91.

"The New Medea: Portia's Comic Triumph in *The Merchant of Venice.*" In *Shakespeare's Political Pageant,* ed. J. Alulis and V. Sullivan, 3–34. Savage, MD: Rowman & Littlefield, 1996.

"Do Natural Rights Derive from Natural Law?" *Harvard Journal of Law and Public Policy* 20, no. 3 (June 1997): 695–724.

"Founder of the Natural Rights Republic." In *Thomas Jefferson and the Politics of Nature: Essays in Response to Michael Zuckert's "Natural Rights Republic,"* ed. Thomas Engeman, 11–58. Notre Dame: University of Notre Dame Press, 2000.

"Locke's Project of a Natural Law Theory." *Interpretation* 29, no. 1 (Fall 2001): 75–90.

"James Madison's Political Science." In *History of American Political Thought,* ed. Jeffrey Sikkenga and Bryan-Paul Frost, 149–66. Lanham, MD: Lexington Books, 2003.

"Locke—Religion—Equality." *Review of Politics* 67, no. 3 (Summer 2005): 419–31.

"Reconsidering Lockean Rights Theory." *Interpretation* 32, no. 3 (Fall 2005): 257–68.

"The Fullness of Being: Thomas Aquinas and the Modern Critique of Natural Law." *Review of Politics* 69, no. 1 (2007): 28–47.

"The Locke Essay: Achievement and Promise." *Perspectives in Political Science* 39, no. 2 (2010): 92–96.

Contributors

DAVID ALVIS (PhD, Fordham University) teaches American politics and political theory at Wofford College. His publications include essays on a variety of subjects, including Progressivism and American political thought, the films of John Ford, and the origins of the presidency in the Constitutional Convention. He is currently completing a book for the University Press of Kansas on political development and the executive removal power. In 2009 he received the Distinguished Teaching Award from the University of West Florida.

KEVIN M. CHERRY is Assistant Professor in the Department of Political Science at the University of Richmond, in Virginia. He earned an MA and a PhD in political science from the University of Notre Dame, where he wrote his dissertation, under the direction of Catherine Zuckert, on Aristotle's *Politics* as a response to Plato's *Statesman.* Cherry holds an MA from the School of Philosophy at the Catholic University of America. His research on classical political thought has appeared in *History of Political Thought,* the *American Journal of Political Science,* and the *Journal of Politics.* Prior to joining the faculty at the University of Richmond, he was assistant professor in the Department of Politics at Saint Anselm College.

JEFFREY CHURCH is Assistant Professor of Political Science at the University of Houston. He has published several articles on the history of late modern political philosophy in the *Journal of Politics,* the *American Journal of Political Science,* and *History of Political Thought,* among others. His book, *Infinite Autonomy: The Divided Individual in the Political Thought of G. W. F.*

Hegel and Friedrich Nietzsche, is in production with Pennsylvania State University Press.

MICHAEL DAVIS is Professor of Philosophy at Sarah Lawrence College. He also taught for many years in the Graduate Faculty of the New School University and in the graduate program in political theory at Fordham University. His recent books include a translation (with Seth Benardete) of Aristotle's *On Poetics, Wonderlust: Ruminations on Liberal Education,* and, most recently *The Soul of the Greeks: An Inquiry.*

KIRK EMMERT is Professor Emeritus of Political Science at Kenyon College, where he was the Clor Professor and taught courses on statesmanship and on American politics, political thought, and constitutional law. He is the author of *Winston S. Churchill on Empire* and of numerous essays on Churchill's thought and leadership. Currently the mayor of Gambier, Ohio, he earlier worked in the Ford White House assisting Robert A. Goldwin. Emmert graduated from Williams College and earned his PhD from the University of Chicago.

CHRISTINE DUNN HENDERSON is Senior Fellow at Liberty Fund, Inc., an educational foundation located in Indianapolis, Indiana. Prior to joining Liberty Fund in 2000, she taught political science at Marshall University. She received her BA in government and French studies from Smith College, and she holds a PhD in political science from Boston College. She is the contributing editor of *Seers and Judges: American Literature as Political Philosophy* (Lanham, MD: Rowman & Littlefield, 2002) and coeditor of *Joseph Addison's "Cato" and Selected Essays* (Indianapolis: Liberty Fund, 2004). She is also editor of *Tocqueville's Voyages* and cotranslator of *Encyclopedic Liberty: Political Articles from the Dictionary of Diderot and D'Alembert* (both forthcoming). Her research interests and publications include Addison, Pierre Nicole, Alexis de Tocqueville, Gustave de Beaumont, classical liberalism, and politics and literature.

MARY M. KEYS received her BA from Boston College and her MA and PhD in Political Science from the University of Toronto. She is currently an associate professor in political science at the University of Notre Dame, with teaching and research interests in ethics, Christianity, and the history of political thought. Her publications include articles in the *American Journal of Political Science, History of Political Thought,* and *Perspectives on Political Science,* together with a book titled *Aquinas, Aristotle, and the Promise of the Common Good* (Cambridge University Press, 2006). She has held visiting scholar appointments at Harvard University and the University of Chicago and received a National Endowment for the Humanities Fellowship for an ongoing research project on humility, modernity, and the science of politics.

PETER AUGUSTINE LAWLER is Dana Professor of Government at Berry College. He is the author or editor of fifteen books, including his recently published *Modern and American Dignity,* and over two hundred articles and chapters in a wide variety of venues. He is executive editor of the acclaimed scholarly quarterly *Perspectives on Political Science* and on the editorial boards of seven other journals. Lawler was a member of President Bush's Council on Bioethics and the 2007 recipient of the Weaver Prize for Scholarly Letters.

WALTER NICGORSKI is Professor in the Program of Liberal Studies and Concurrent Professor of Political Science at the University of Notre Dame. Nicgorski's essays on Cicero, liberal and character education, the American founding, Leo Strauss, Yves Simon, and Allan Bloom have appeared in collections and in such journals as *Political Theory, Interpretation, Logos,* and the *Political Science Reviewer.* He has served as chief editor of the *Review of Politics.* He is the editor of and a contributor to *Cicero's Practical Philosophy,* forthcoming from the University of Notre Dame Press. Earlier he was a contributor to and coeditor (with Ronald Weber) of *An Almost Chosen People: The Moral Aspirations of Americans* (1977) and (with Kenneth Deutsch) of *Leo Strauss: Political Philosopher and Jewish Thinker* (1994).

MARY P. NICHOLS is Professor of Political Science at Baylor University. Her fields of interest include the history of political philosophy, especially Greek political thought, and politics, literature, and film. She has published numerous articles in *Political Theory,* the *Journal of Politics, Polity,* the *Review of Politics,* and *Perspectives on Political Science.* Among her books on classical thought are *Citizens and Statesmen: A Commentary on Aristotle's* Politics (Rowman and Littlefield) and *Socrates on Friendship and Community: Reflections on Plato's Symposium, Phaedrus, and Lysis* (Cambridge University Press).

DAVID K. NICHOLS is Associate Professor in the Department of Political Science at Baylor University and a senior fellow of the Alexander Hamilton Institute for the Study of Western Civilization. He is the author of *The Myth of the Modern Presidency,* as well as numerous articles on American politics, constitutional law, and politics and literature. He is currently completing a book on responsible government and the separation of powers.

LORRAINE SMITH PANGLE is Professor of Government and Codirector of the Thomas Jefferson Center for the Study of Core Texts and Ideas at the University of Texas at Austin, where she teaches political philosophy and ethics. Her publications include *The Learning of Liberty: The Educational Ideas of the American Founders* (coauthored with Thomas L. Pangle; University Press of Kansas, 1993); *Aristotle and the Philosophy of Friendship* (Cambridge University Press, 2003); *The Political Philosophy of Benjamin Franklin* (Johns Hopkins University Press, 2007); and *Virtue Is Knowledge: Moral Responsibility and Justice in Socratic Political Thought* (University of Chicago Press, forthcoming), as well as articles on Plato, Aristotle, the American founders, and the philosophy of education. Her current research interests include ancient political philosophy and literature, ethics, and problems of justice and moral responsibility.

THOMAS L. PANGLE holds the Joe R. Long Chair in Democratic Studies in the Department of Government at the University of Texas and is codirector of the Thomas Jefferson Center for the Study of Core Texts and Ideas. He has won a Guggenheim Fellowship and four National Endowment for the Humanities fellowships. In addition, Pangle was awarded the Robert Foster Cherry Great Teacher of the World Prize, Baylor University. At the invitation of the Bavarian Academy of Sciences he delivered the Werner Heisenberg Memorial Prize Lecture in 2007. He is a lifetime Fellow of the Royal Society of Canada and the author of many books, including most recently *The Theological Basis of Liberal Modernity in Montesquieu's Spirit of the Laws* (University of Chicago Press, 2010). His DVD and audiotape lecture course, "The Great Debate: Advocates and Opponents of the American Constitution," is marketed by the Teaching Company.

ARLENE W. SAXONHOUSE is the Caroline Robbins Collegiate Professor of Political Science and Women Studies and Adjunct Professor of Classics at the University of Michigan. She is the author of *Women in the History of Political Thought: Ancient Greece to Machiavelli* (1985); *Fear of Diversity: The Birth of Political Science in Ancient Greek Thought* (1992); (with Noel Reynolds) *Hobbes's Three Discourses: A Modern, Critical Edition of Newly Identified Works by the Young Thomas Hobbes* (1995); *Athenian Democracy: Modern Mythmakers and Ancient Theorists* (1996), and *Free Speech and Democracy in Ancient Athens* (2006), as well as numerous articles on the political thought of Thucydides, Plato, Aristotle, the ancient playwrights, Hobbes, and Machiavelli.

DAVID LEWIS SCHAEFER is Professor of Political Science at College of the Holy Cross in Worcester, Massachusetts, teaching courses on political philosophy and American political thought. Among his books are *Illiberal Justice: John Rawls vs. the American Political Tradition* (2007) and *The Political Philosophy of Montaigne* (1990). In addition to his scholarly writings, Schaefer has contributed opinion journalism to such periodicals as the *Wall Street Journal*, the *New York Sun*, and *National Review Online*.

DIANA J. SCHAUB is Professor of Political Science at Loyola University in Maryland. A graduate of Kenyon College, with an MA and a PhD from the University of Chicago, she has also been a postdoctoral fellow of the Program on Constitutional Government at Harvard University (1994–95). In 2001 she was the recipient of the Richard M. Weaver Prize for Scholarly Letters, and from 2004 to 2009 she was a member of the President's Council on Bioethics. Schaub is the author of *Erotic Liberalism: Women and Revolution in Montesquieu's "Persian Letters"* (1995), along with a number of book chapters and articles in the fields of political philosophy and American political thought. She is also a coeditor (with Amy and Leon Kass) of *What So Proudly We Hail: The American Soul in Story, Speech, and Song* (2011). She is a contributing editor to the *New Atlantis* and a member of the publication committee of *National Affairs*. Her essays and articles have appeared in the *Claremont Review of Books*, the *New Criterion, Public Interest, Commentary, First Things, American Interest, City Journal,* and elsewhere.

TIMOTHY SPIEKERMAN teaches political philosophy at Kenyon College. He graduated with a BA from Carleton College and an MA and a PhD from the Committee on Social Thought at the University of Chicago. He is the author of *Shakespeare's Political Realism* (SUNY Press, 2001).

VICKIE B. SULLIVAN is Professor of Political Science at Tufts University. She is the author of *Machiavelli, Hobbes, and the Formation of a Liberal Republicanism in England* (Cambridge University Press, 2004) and *Machiavelli's Three Romes: Religion, Human Liberty, and Politics Reformed* (Northern Illinois University Press, 1996). She is the editor of *The Comedy and Tragedy of Machiavelli: Essays on the Literary Works* (Yale University Press, 2000) and coeditor of *Shakespeare's Political Pageant: Essays in Politics and Literature* (Rowman and Littlefield, 1996). Her articles have appeared in the *American Political Science Review, History of European Ideas, History of Political Thought, Political Theory,* and *Polity.* She is currently at work on a manuscript devoted to Montesquieu's *The Spirit of the Laws.* Sullivan has served as chair of the Department of Political Science, dean of Academic Affairs for Arts and Sciences, and interim dean of the School of Arts and Sciences at Tufts University.

ANN WARD is Associate Professor of Philosophy and Political Science at Campion College, University of Regina, Regina, Canada. Her BA (Hons.) is from the University of Toronto, her MA is from Brock University, and she received her PhD in Political Science from Fordham University. Her research interests are the ancient historians, ancient political philosophy, late modern and nineteenth-century political thought, and feminist philosophy. She is the author of *Herodotus and the Philosophy of Empire* (Baylor University Press, 2008) and the editor of *Matter and Form: From Natural Science to Political Philosophy* (Lexington Books, 2009) and *Socrates: Reason or Unreason as the Foundation of European Identity* (Cambridge Scholars Publishing, 2007). Her coedited volume, with Lee Ward, *The Ashgate Research Companion to Federalism,* was published in 2009 (Ashgate). She has published articles on Herodotus, Plato, Aristotle, Montesquieu, and Kierkegaard in collections and journals such as *POLIS* and the *European Journal of Political Theory.* She is also an Advisory Board editor for *The European Legacy: Toward New Paradigms.*

LEE WARD is Alpha Sigma Nu Distinguished Associate Professor in Campion College at the University of Regina and teaches in the Department of Political Science at the University of Regina. He received his BA (Hons.) from the University of Toronto, an MA from Brock University, and a PhD in Political Science from Fordham University. He previously taught in the Department of Political Science at Kenyon College in Gambier, Ohio, and was the Bradley Post-doctoral Fellow in the Program in Constitutional Government at Harvard University. His research and teaching interests are the history of political philosophy, early modern and American political thought, and liberal constitutional theory. He is the author of *John Locke and Modern Life* (Cambridge University Press, 2010) and *The Politics of Liberty in England and Revolutionary America* (Cambridge University Press, 2004) and coeditor, with Ann Ward, of *The Ashgate Research Companion to Federalism* (Ashgate, 2009). His articles on John Locke, Aristotle, Montesquieu, Algernon Sidney, Plato, and Spinoza have appeared in the *American Political Science Review,* the *Canadian Journal of Political Science, Publius: The Journal of Federalism,* the *American Journal of Political Science,* and the *International Philosophical Quarterly.*

JEAN M. YARBROUGH is Gary M. Pendy Sr. Professor of Social Sciences and Professor of Government at Bowdoin College. She is the author of *American Virtues: Thomas Jefferson on the Character of a Free People* (1998) and editor of *The Essential Jefferson* (2005). Her articles have appeared in the *Review of Politics,* the *Journal of Politics, Publius: The Journal of Federalism, City Journal,* and the *American Scholar,* among other places. She also serves on the editorial boards of the *Review of Politics* and *Polity* and on the Academic Council of the Jack Miller Center. She has twice received fellowships from the National Endowment for the Humanities and has served as the president of the New England Political Science Association. She is currently completing a study of the political thought of Theodore Roosevelt.

Index